ANONYMOUS NOISE

Ryoko Fukuyama

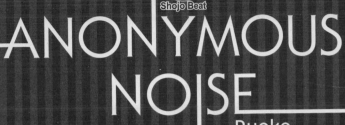

Anonymous
Noise
Volume 7

CONTENTS

SONG 35

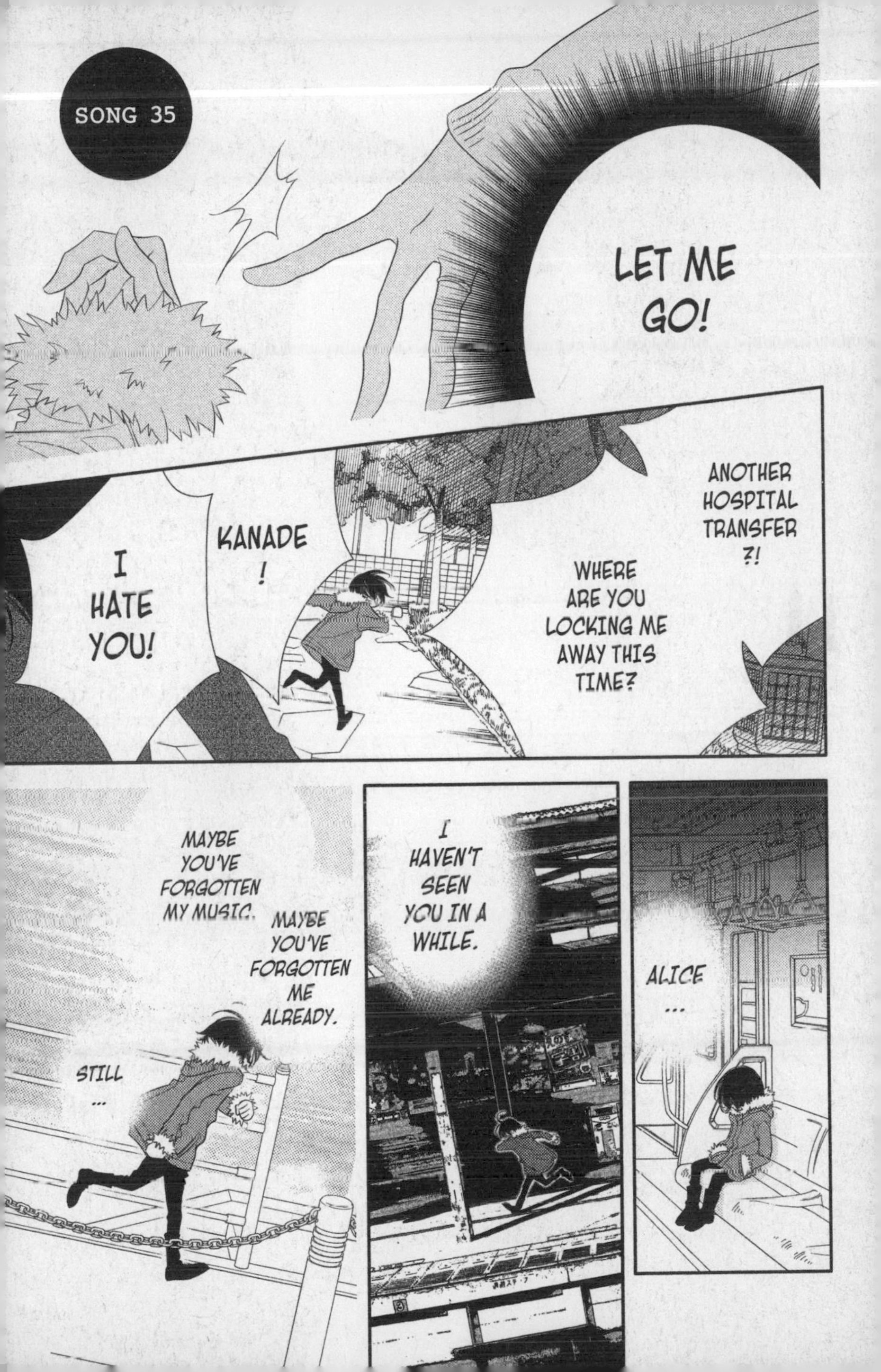
LET ME GO!
ANOTHER HOSPITAL TRANSFER ?!
WHERE ARE YOU LOCKING ME AWAY THIS TIME?
KANADE !
I HATE YOU!
ALICE ...
I HAVEN'T SEEN YOU IN A WHILE.
MAYBE YOU'VE FORGOTTEN MY MUSIC.
MAYBE YOU'VE FORGOTTEN ME ALREADY.
STILL ...

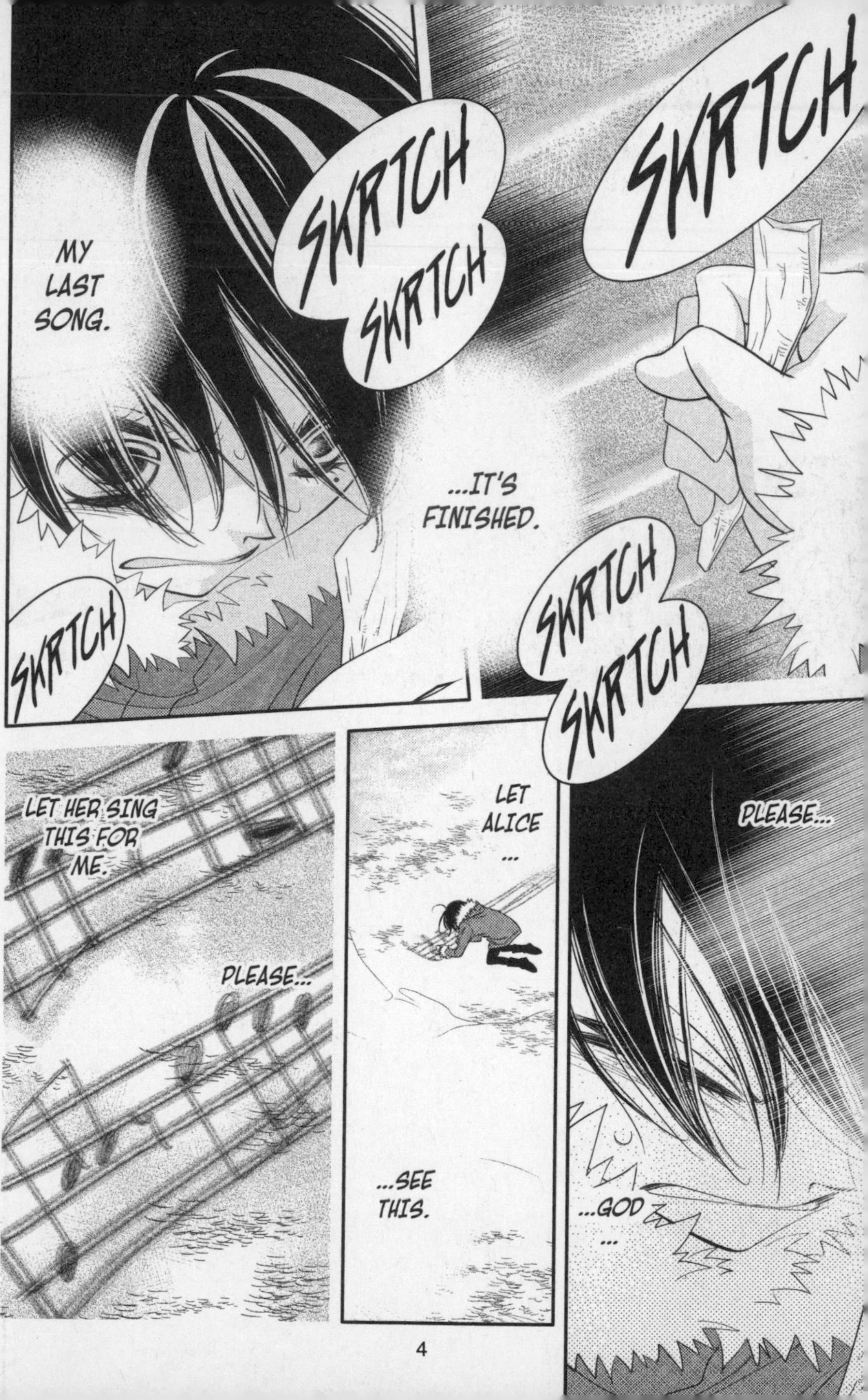
SKRTCH
SKRTCH SKRTCH
SKRTCH SKRTCH
MY LAST SONG.
...IT'S FINISHED.
SKRTCH
PLEASE...
...GOD ...
LET ALICE ...
...SEE THIS.
LET HER SING THIS FOR ME.
PLEASE...

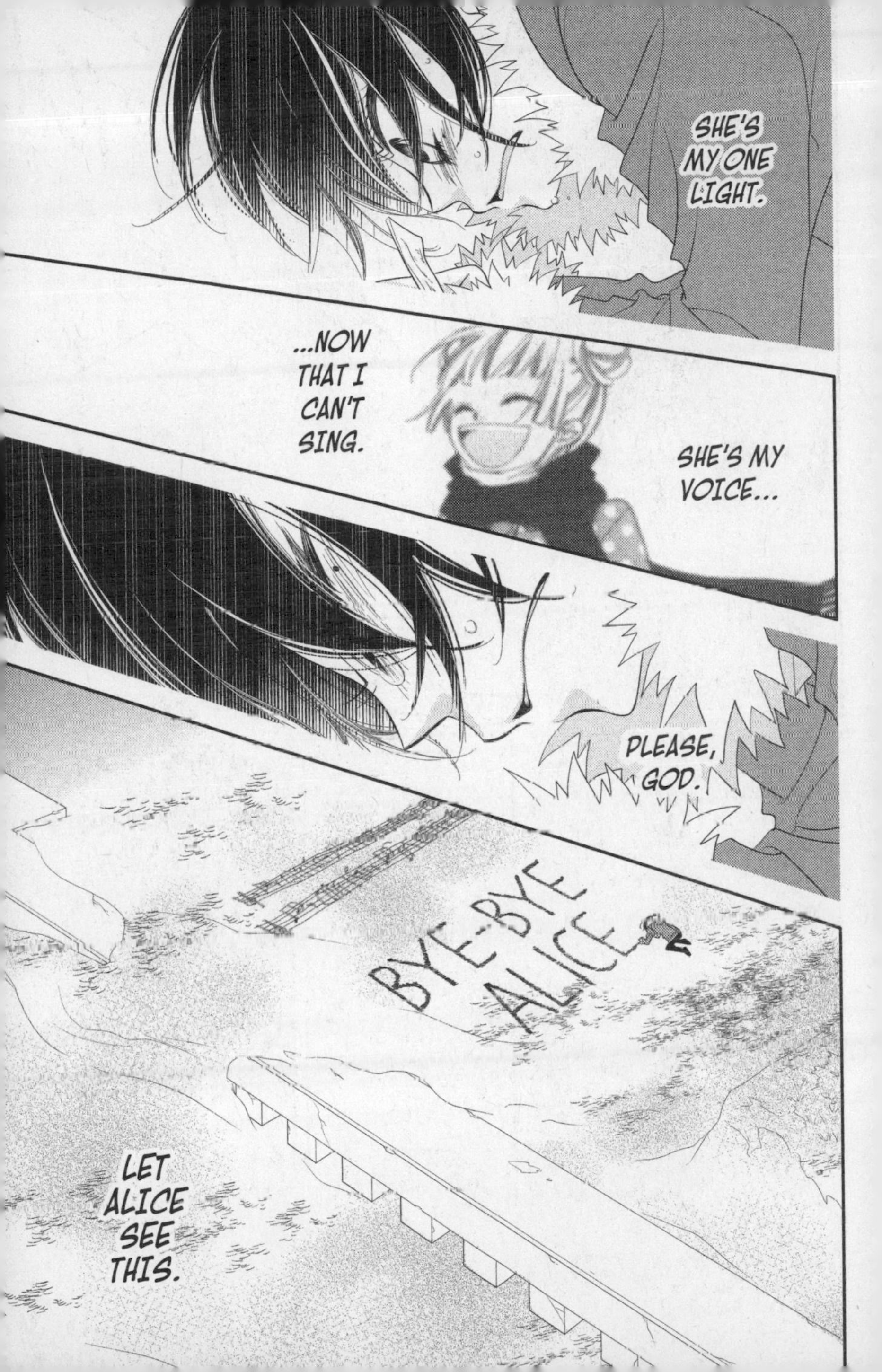
SHE'S MY ONE LIGHT.
SHE'S MY VOICE...
...NOW THAT I CAN'T SING.
PLEASE, GOD.
BYE-BYE ALICE
LET ALICE SEE THIS.

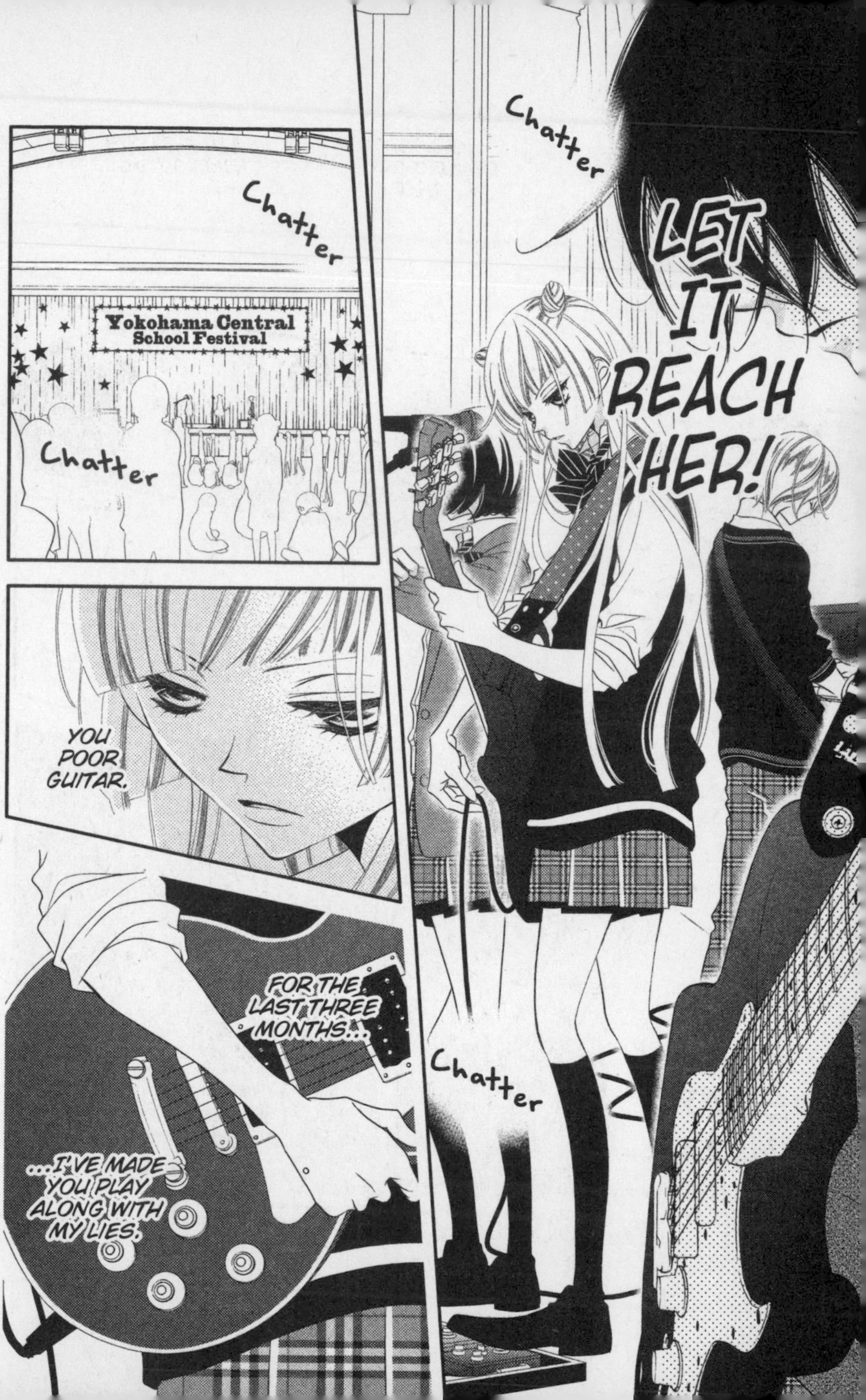
Chatter
LET IT REACH HER!
Chatter
Chatter
Yokohama Central School Festival
Chatter
YOU POOR GUITAR.
FOR THE LAST THREE MONTHS...
...I'VE MADE YOU PLAY ALONG WITH MY LIES.

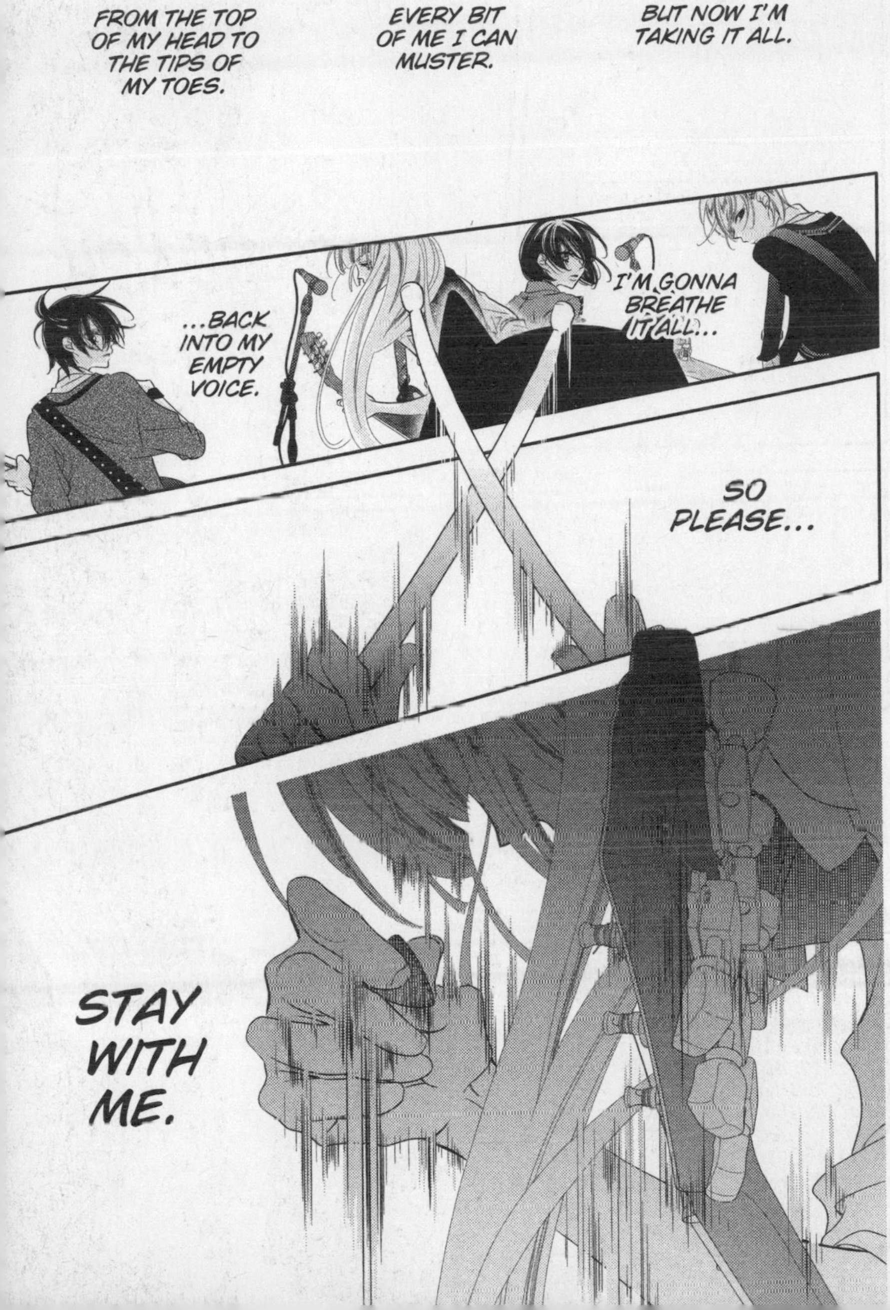
BUT NOW I'M TAKING IT ALL.
EVERY BIT OF ME I CAN MUSTER.
FROM THE TOP OF MY HEAD TO THE TIPS OF MY TOES.
I'M GONNA BREATHE IT ALL...
...BACK INTO MY EMPTY VOICE.
SO PLEASE...
STAY WITH ME.

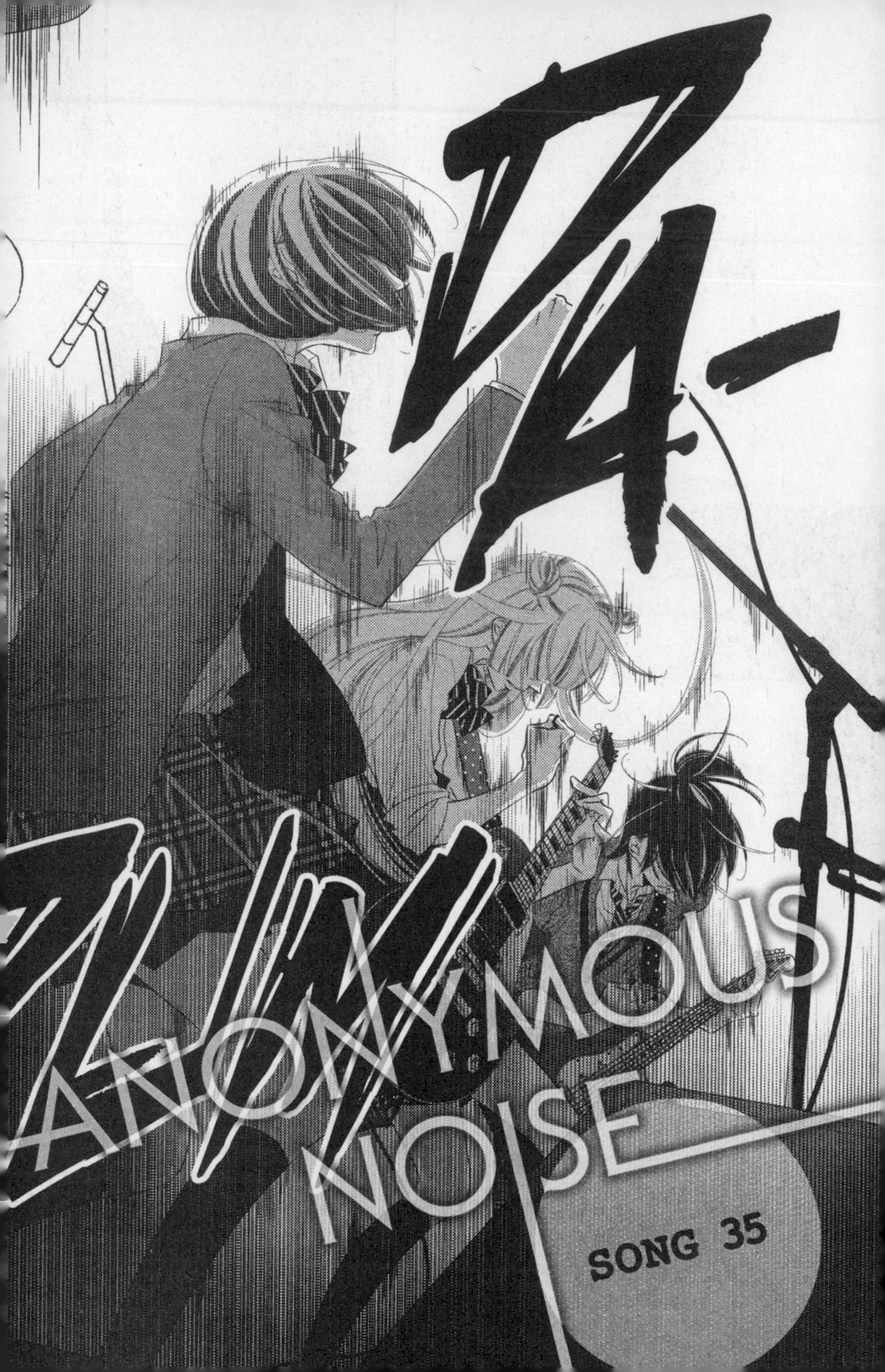
ANONYMOUS NOISE
SONG 35

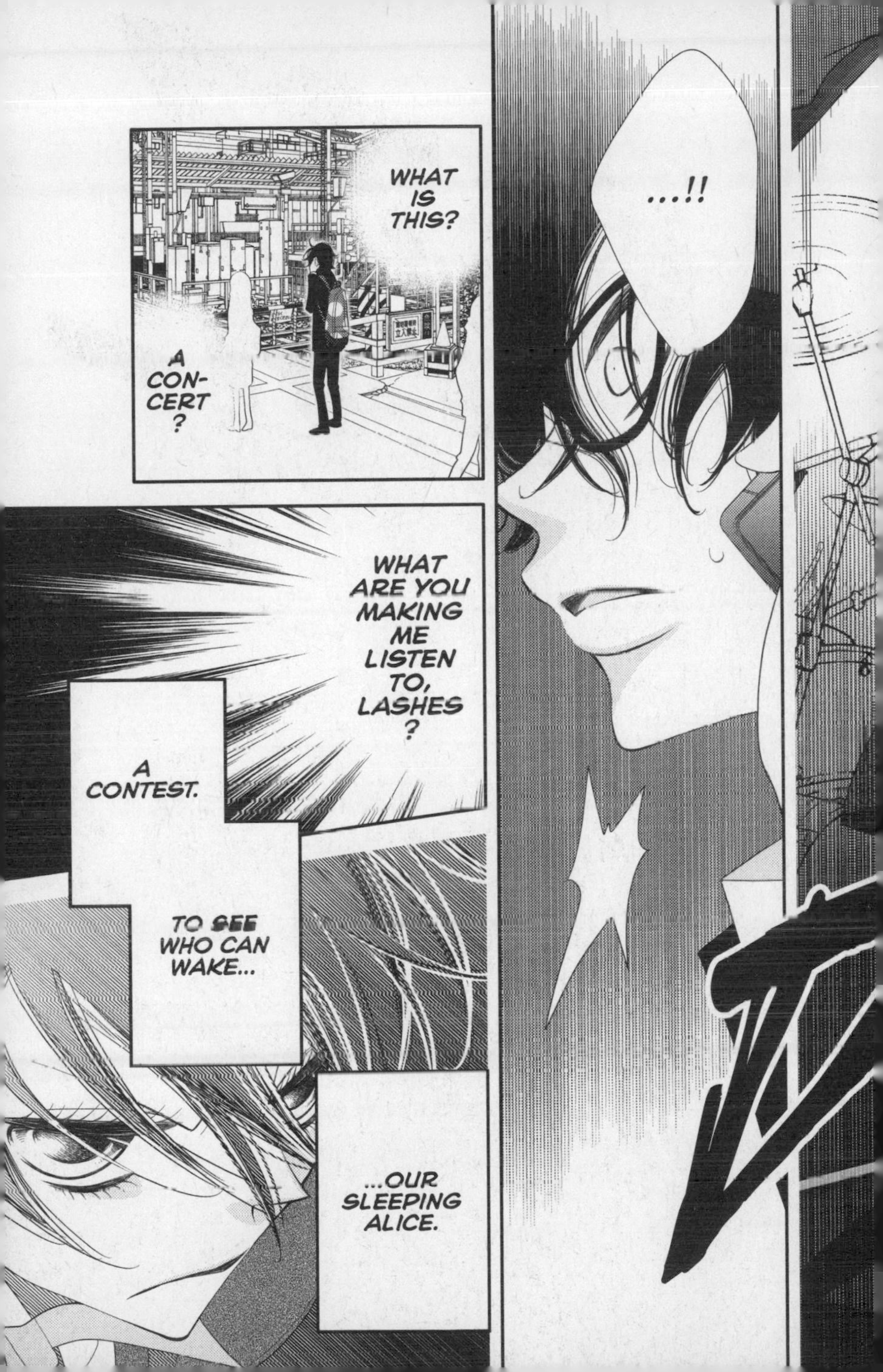
...!!
WHAT IS THIS?
A CON-CERT?
WHAT ARE YOU MAKING ME LISTEN TO, LASHES?
A CONTEST.
TO SEE WHO CAN WAKE...
...OUR SLEEPING ALICE.

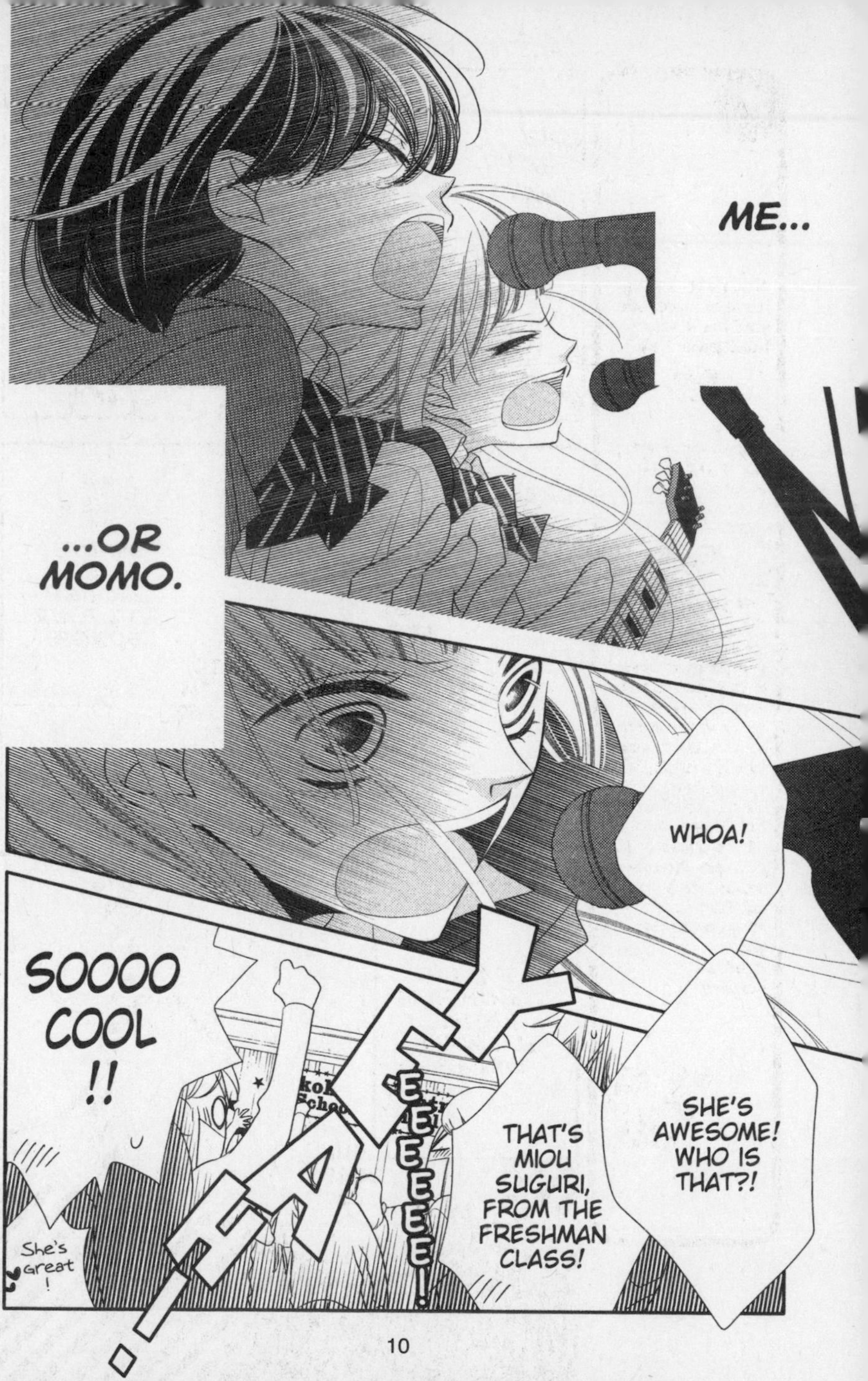
ME...
...OR MOMO.
WHOA!
SHE'S AWESOME! WHO IS THAT?!
THAT'S MIOU SUGURI, FROM THE FRESHMAN CLASS!
EEEEEE!
SOOOO COOL!!
She's Great!

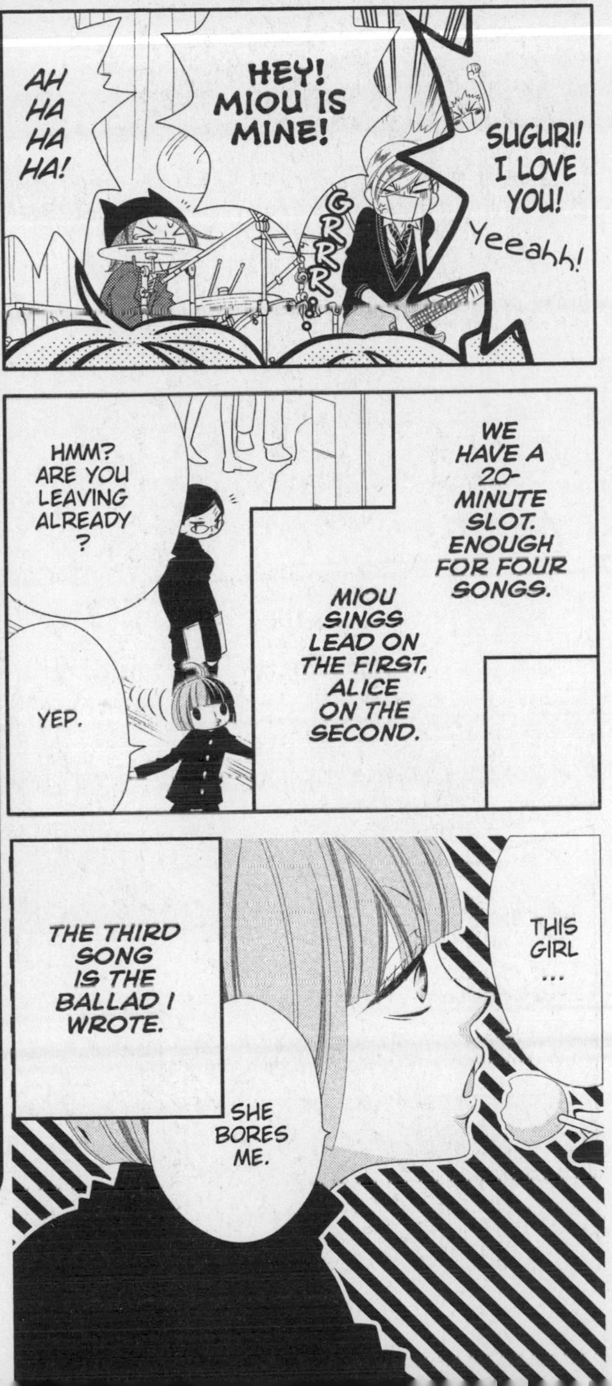
SUGURI! I LOVE YOU!
Yeeahh!
HEY! MIOU IS MINE!
GRRR
AH HA HA HA!
WE HAVE A 20-MINUTE SLOT. ENOUGH FOR FOUR SONGS.
MIOU SINGS LEAD ON THE FIRST, ALICE ON THE SECOND.
HMM? ARE YOU LEAVING ALREADY?
YEP.
THE THIRD SONG IS THE BALLAD I WROTE.
THIS GIRL...
SHE BORES ME.

1

How's it going? It's good to see you! I'm Ryoko Fukuyama! Yay!

Hey, you there—thanks for picking up volume 7 of Anonymous Noise!

I LOVE YOU!

I'm so sorry that my handwriting is only getting worse! After debating over what to do for the cover of this volume, I finally decided on Alice. All the stripes and frills on her costume make her a lot of fun to draw. Anyway, I hope you enjoy reading volume 7!

WOO-HOO!!

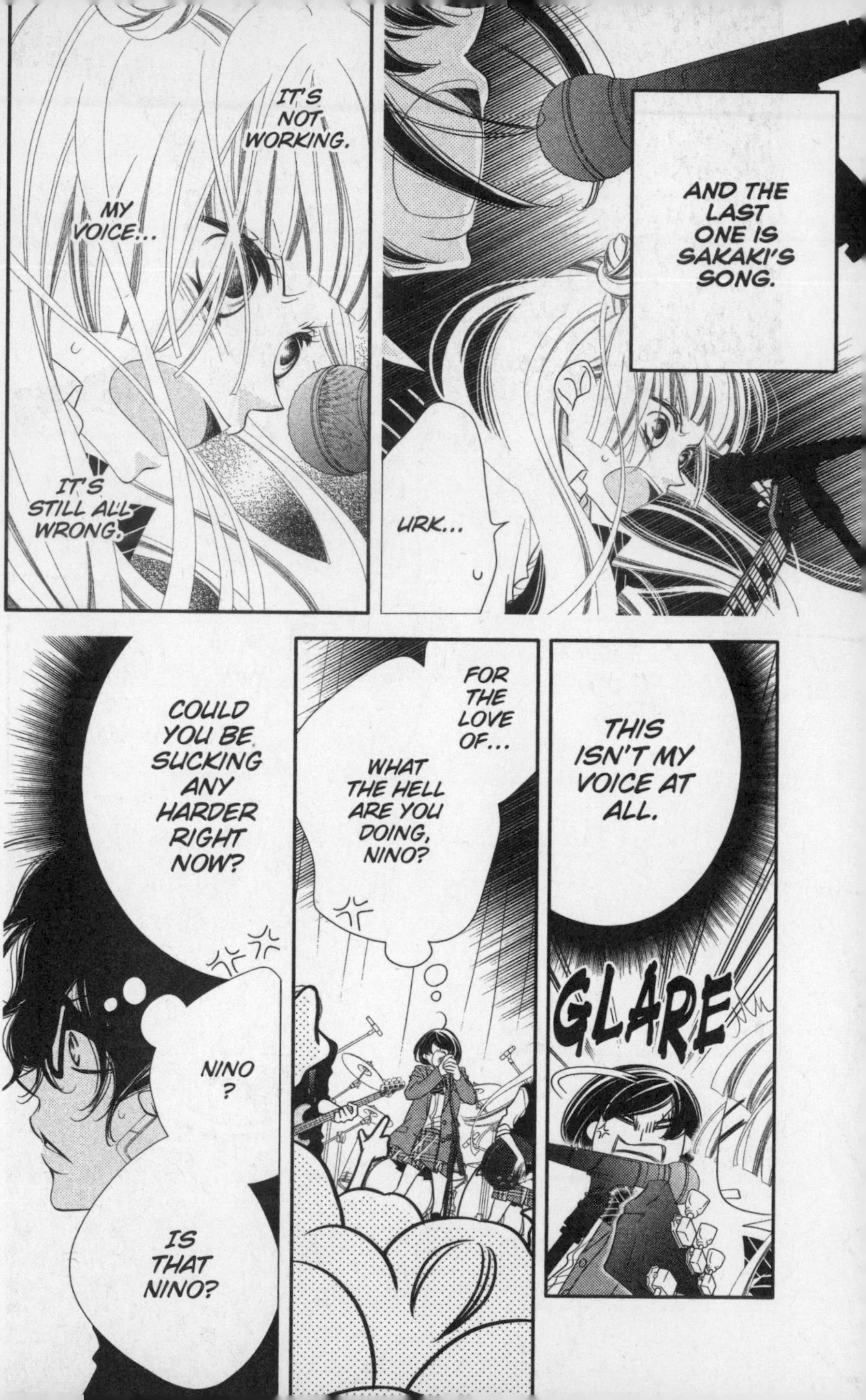
AND THE LAST ONE IS SAKAKI'S SONG.
URK...
IT'S NOT WORKING.
MY VOICE...
IT'S STILL ALL WRONG.
THIS ISN'T MY VOICE AT ALL.
GLARE
FOR THE LOVE OF...
WHAT THE HELL ARE YOU DOING, NINO?
COULD YOU BE SUCKING ANY HARDER RIGHT NOW?
NINO?
IS THAT NINO?

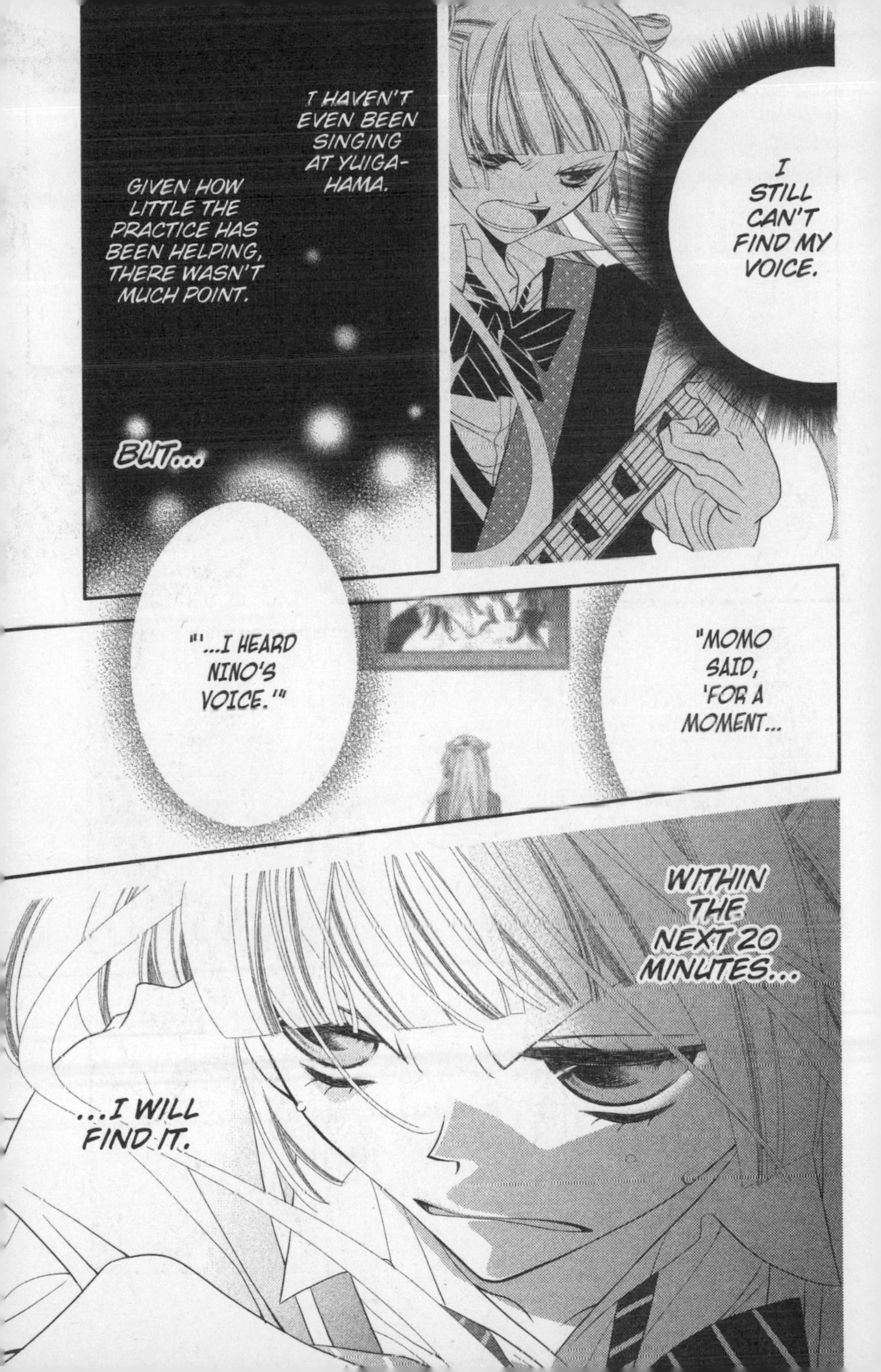
I STILL CAN'T FIND MY VOICE.
I HAVEN'T EVEN BEEN SINGING AT YUIGA-HAMA.
GIVEN HOW LITTLE THE PRACTICE HAS BEEN HELPING, THERE WASN'T MUCH POINT.
BUT...
"MOMO SAID, 'FOR A MOMENT...
"'...I HEARD NINO'S VOICE.'"
WITHIN THE NEXT 20 MINUTES...
...I WILL FIND IT.

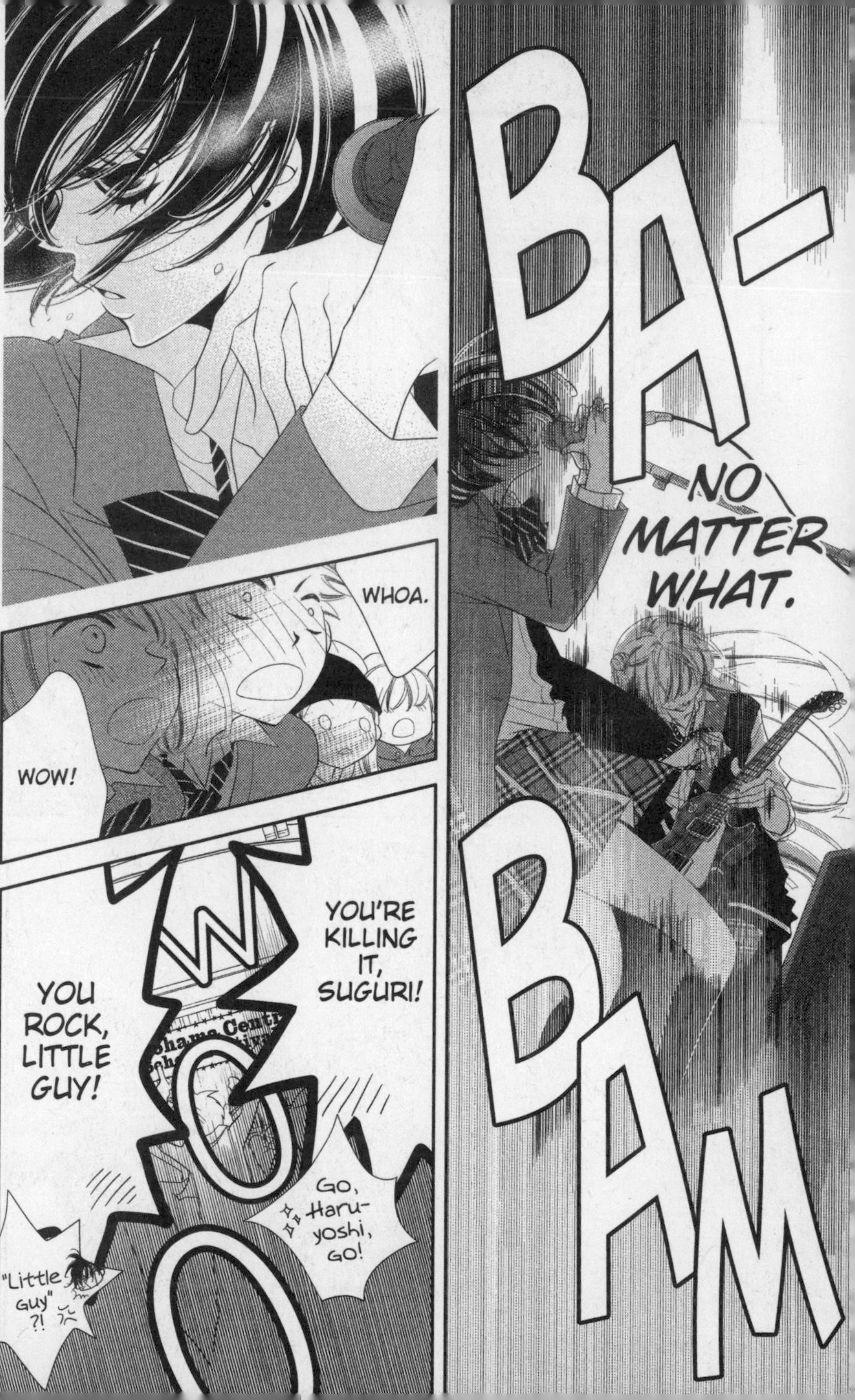
BA-
NO MATTER WHAT.
BAM
WHOA.
WOW!
YOU'RE KILLING IT, SUGURI!
WOO
YOU ROCK, LITTLE GUY!
Go, Haru-yoshi, GO!
"Little Guy" ?!

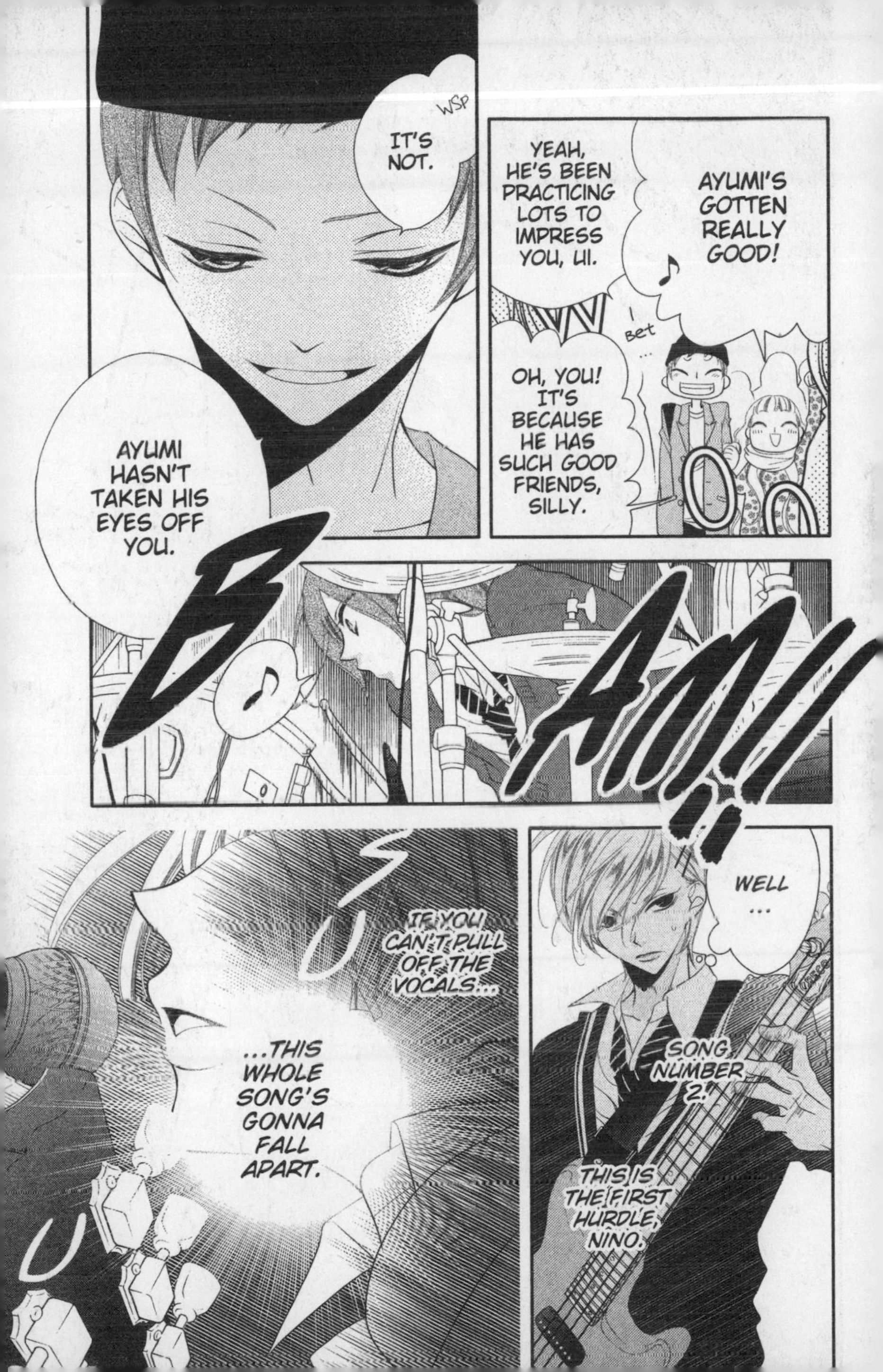
AYUMI'S GOTTEN REALLY GOOD!
YEAH, HE'S BEEN PRACTICING LOTS TO IMPRESS YOU, UI.
I bet...
OH, YOU! IT'S BECAUSE HE HAS SUCH GOOD FRIENDS, SILLY.
WSP
IT'S NOT.
AYUMI HASN'T TAKEN HIS EYES OFF YOU.
BAM!!
WELL...
SONG NUMBER 2.
THIS IS THE FIRST HURDLE, NINO.
IF YOU CAN'T PULL OFF THE VOCALS...
...THIS WHOLE SONG'S GONNA FALL APART.

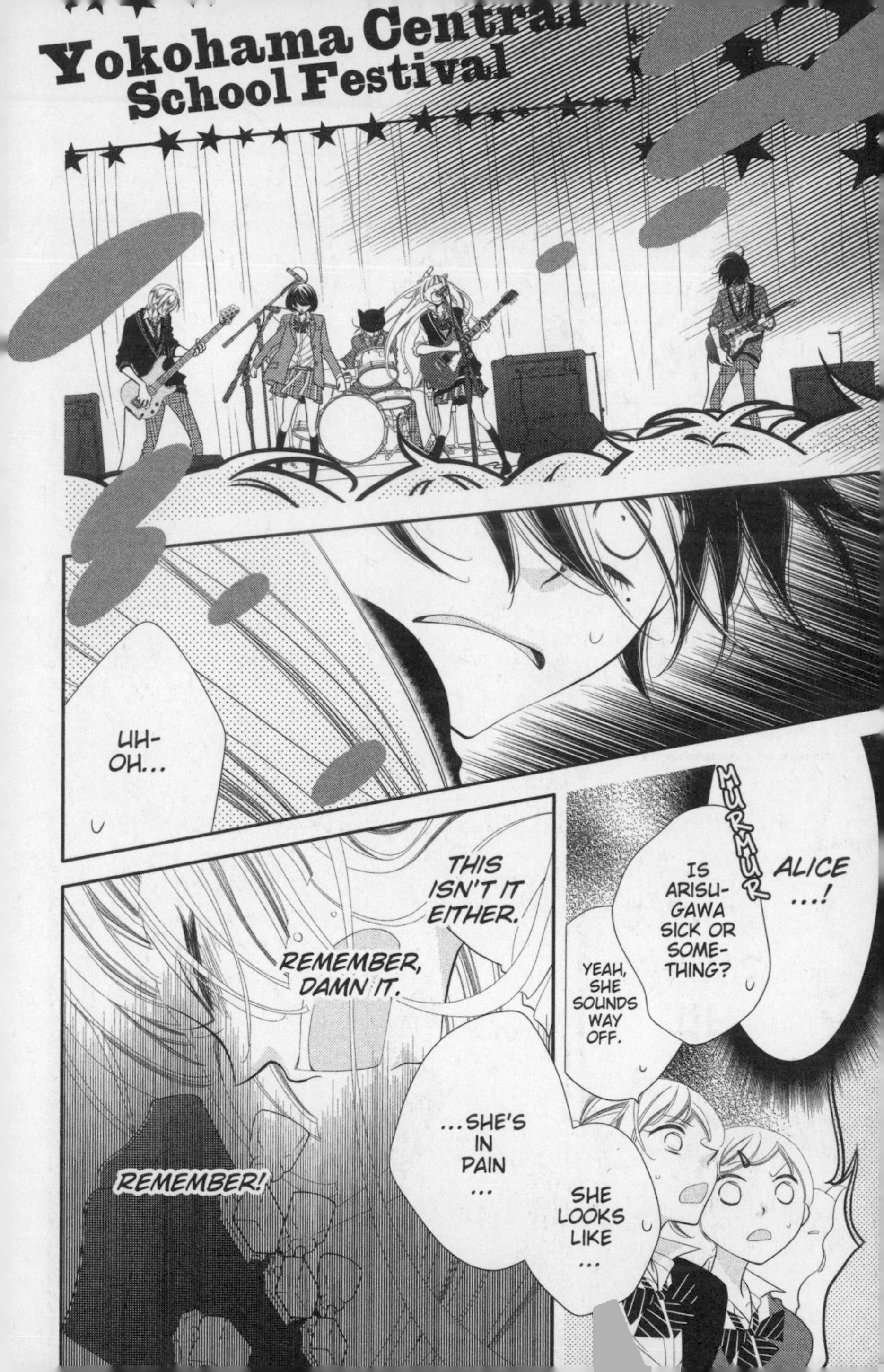

Yokohama Central School Festival
UH-OH...
ALICE ...!
MURMUR
IS ARISUGAWA SICK OR SOMETHING?
YEAH, SHE SOUNDS WAY OFF.
...SHE'S IN PAIN ...
SHE LOOKS LIKE ...
THIS ISN'T IT EITHER.
REMEMBER, DAMN IT.
REMEMBER!

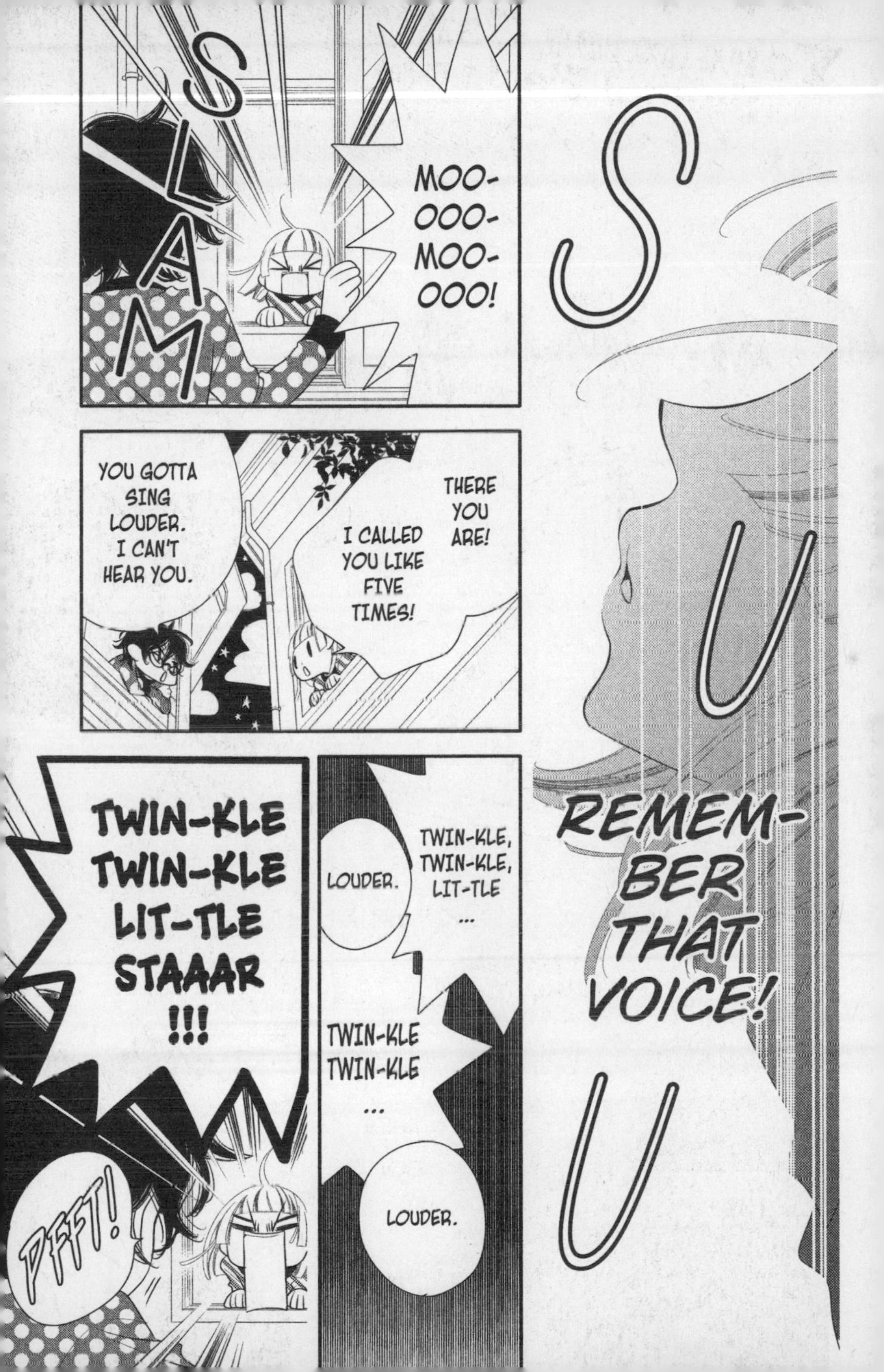
SUU
REMEM-BER THAT VOICE!
MOO-OOO-MOO-OOO!
SLAM
THERE YOU ARE!
I CALLED YOU LIKE FIVE TIMES!
YOU GOTTA SING LOUDER. I CAN'T HEAR YOU.
TWIN-KLE, TWIN-KLE, LIT-TLE ...
LOUDER.
TWIN-KLE TWIN-KLE ...
LOUDER.
TWIN-KLE TWIN-KLE LIT-TLE STAAAR !!!
PFFT!

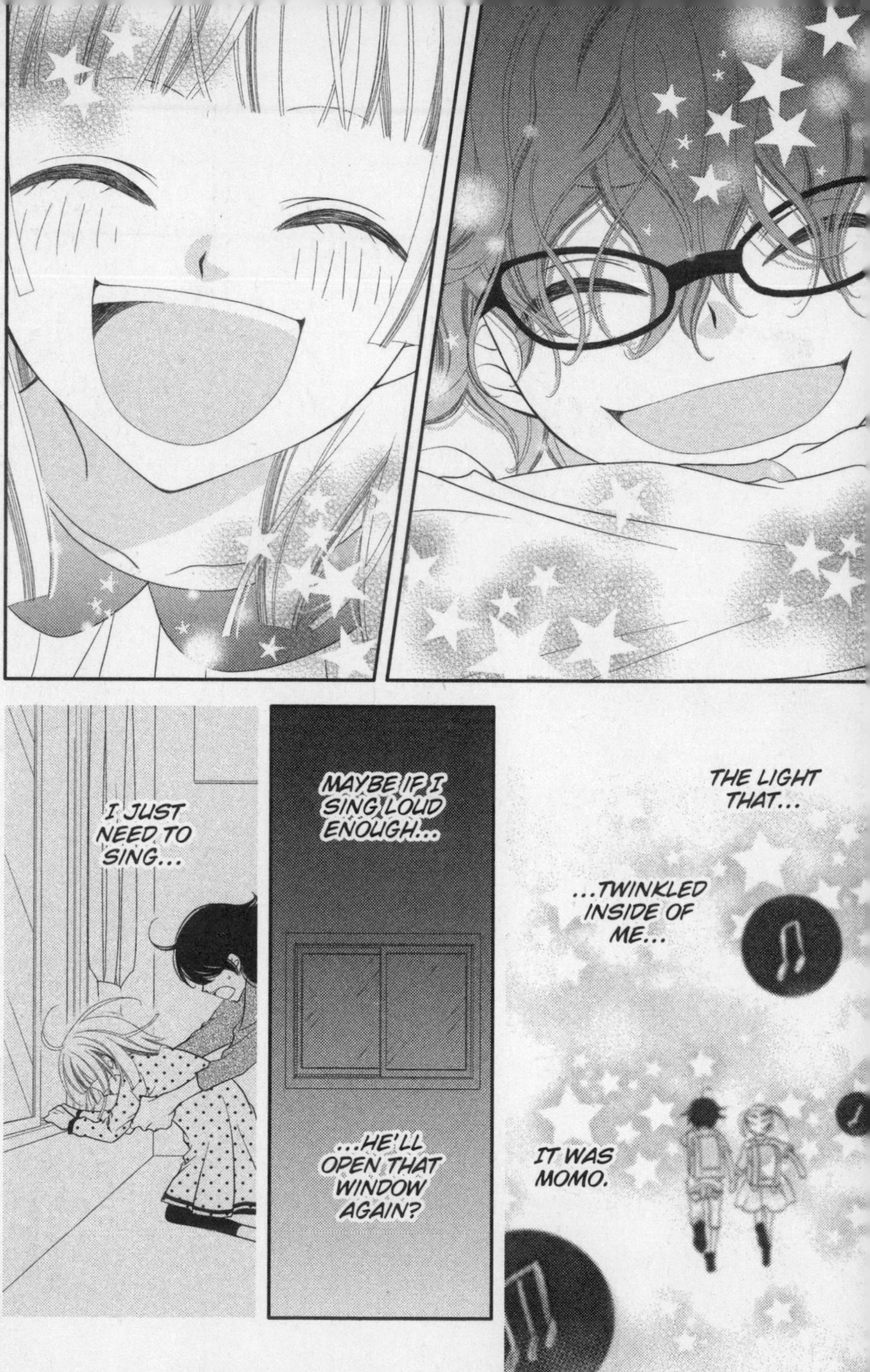
THE LIGHT THAT...
...TWINKLED INSIDE OF ME...
IT WAS MOMO.
MAYBE IF I SING LOUD ENOUGH...
...HE'LL OPEN THAT WINDOW AGAIN?
I JUST NEED TO SING...

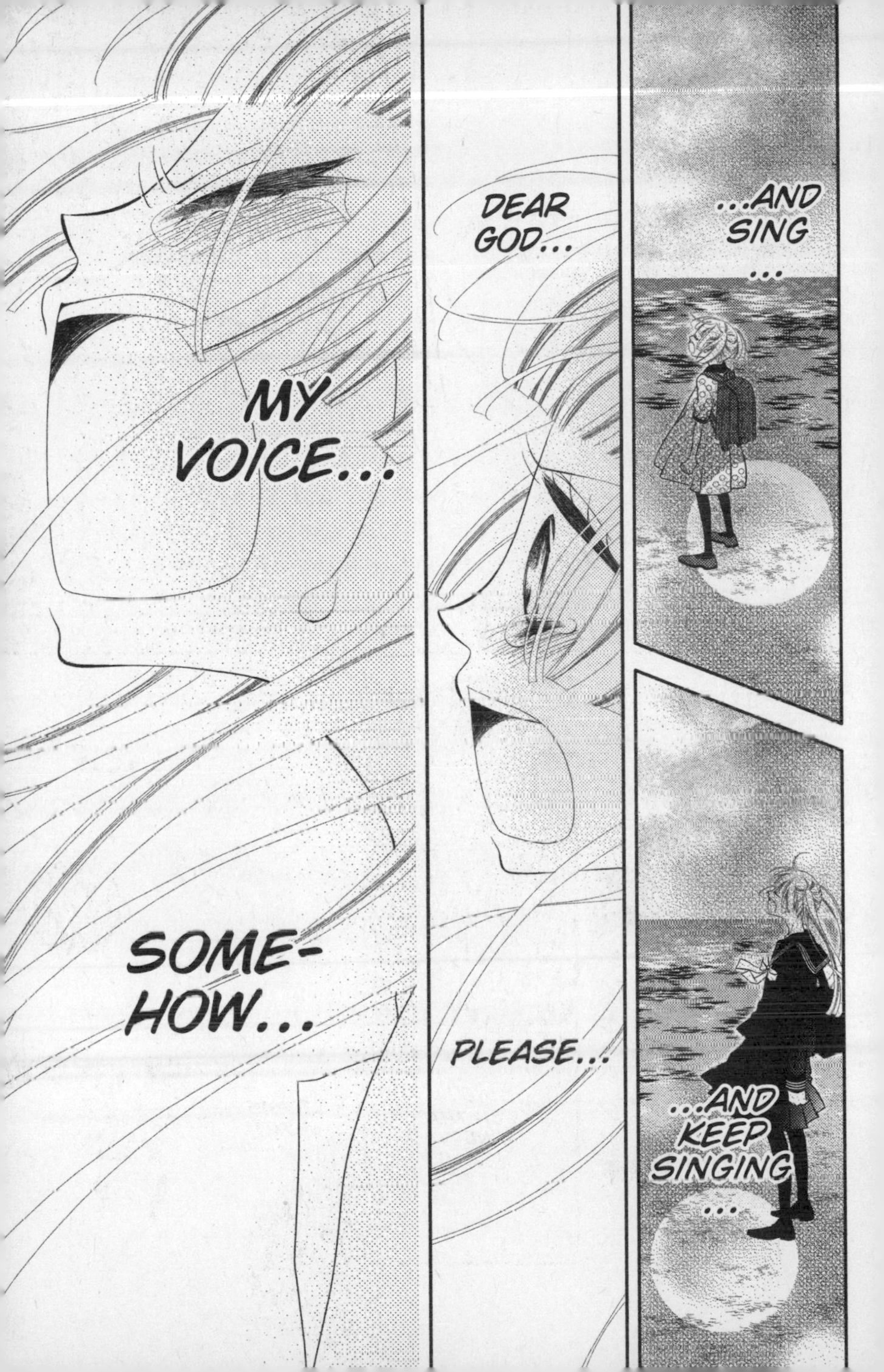
...AND SING ...
...AND KEEP SINGING ...
DEAR GOD...
PLEASE...
MY VOICE...
SOME-HOW...

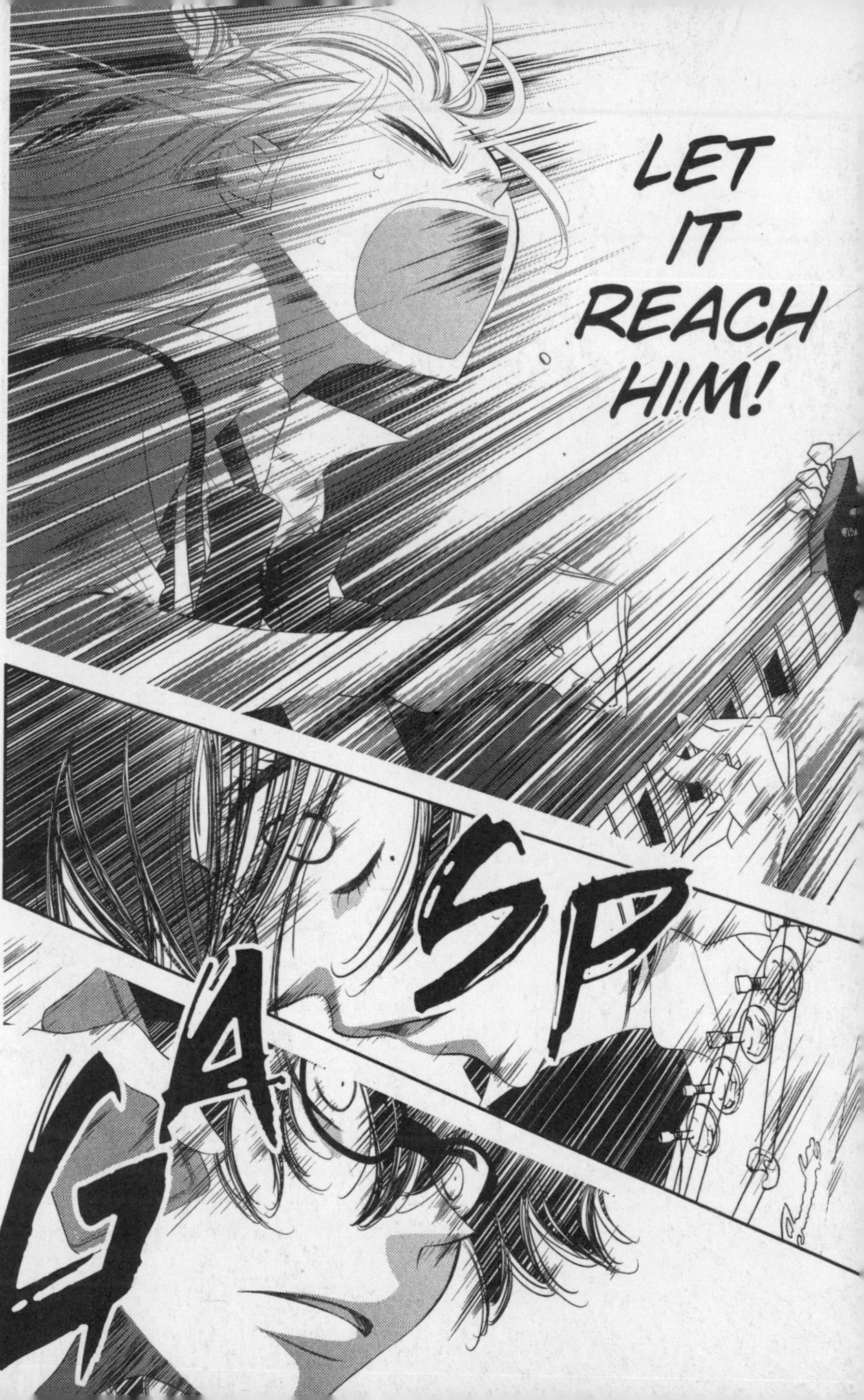
LET IT REACH HIM!
GASP

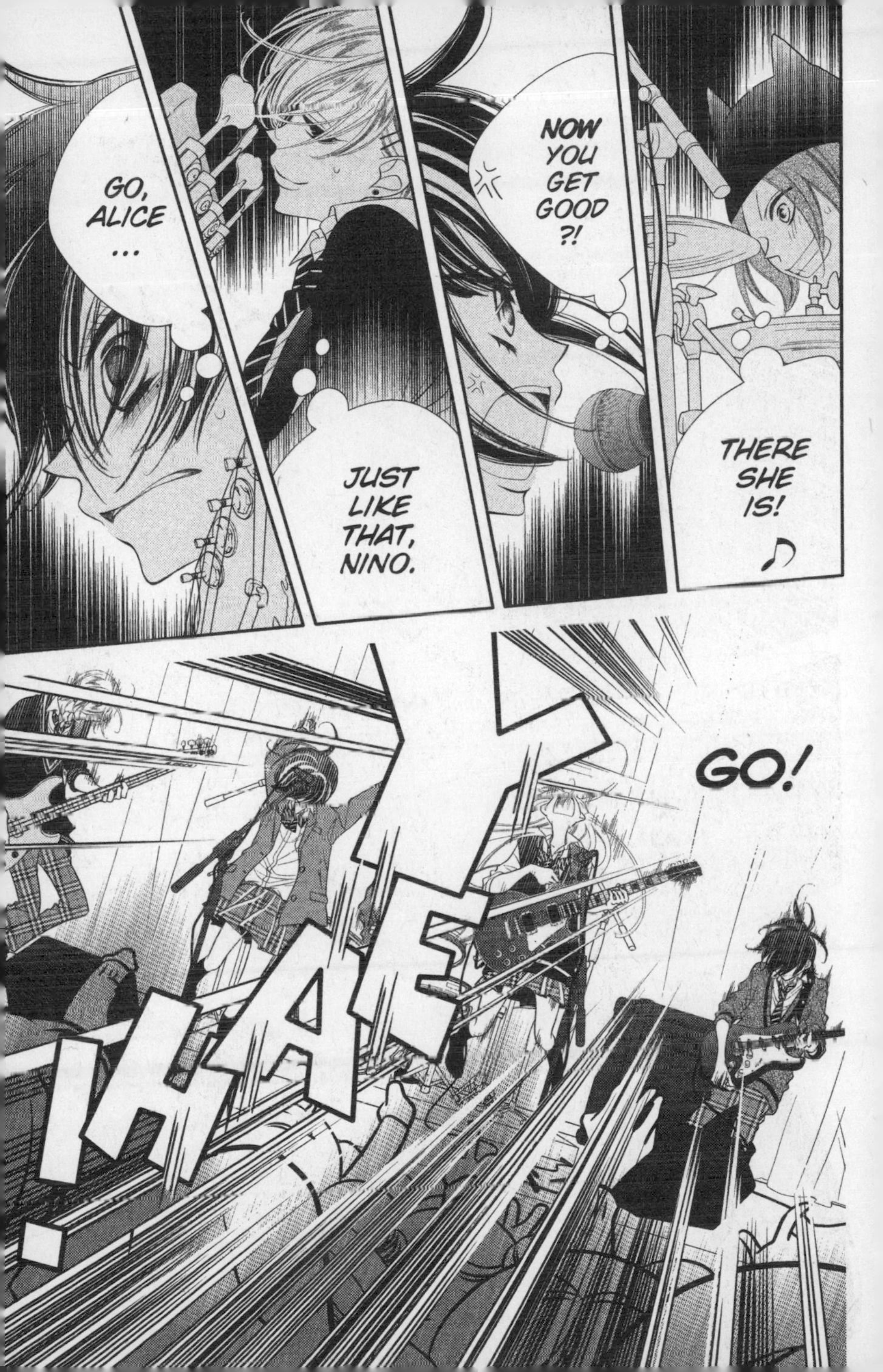
THERE SHE IS! ♪
NOW YOU GET GOOD ?!
JUST LIKE THAT, NINO.
GO, ALICE ...
GO!

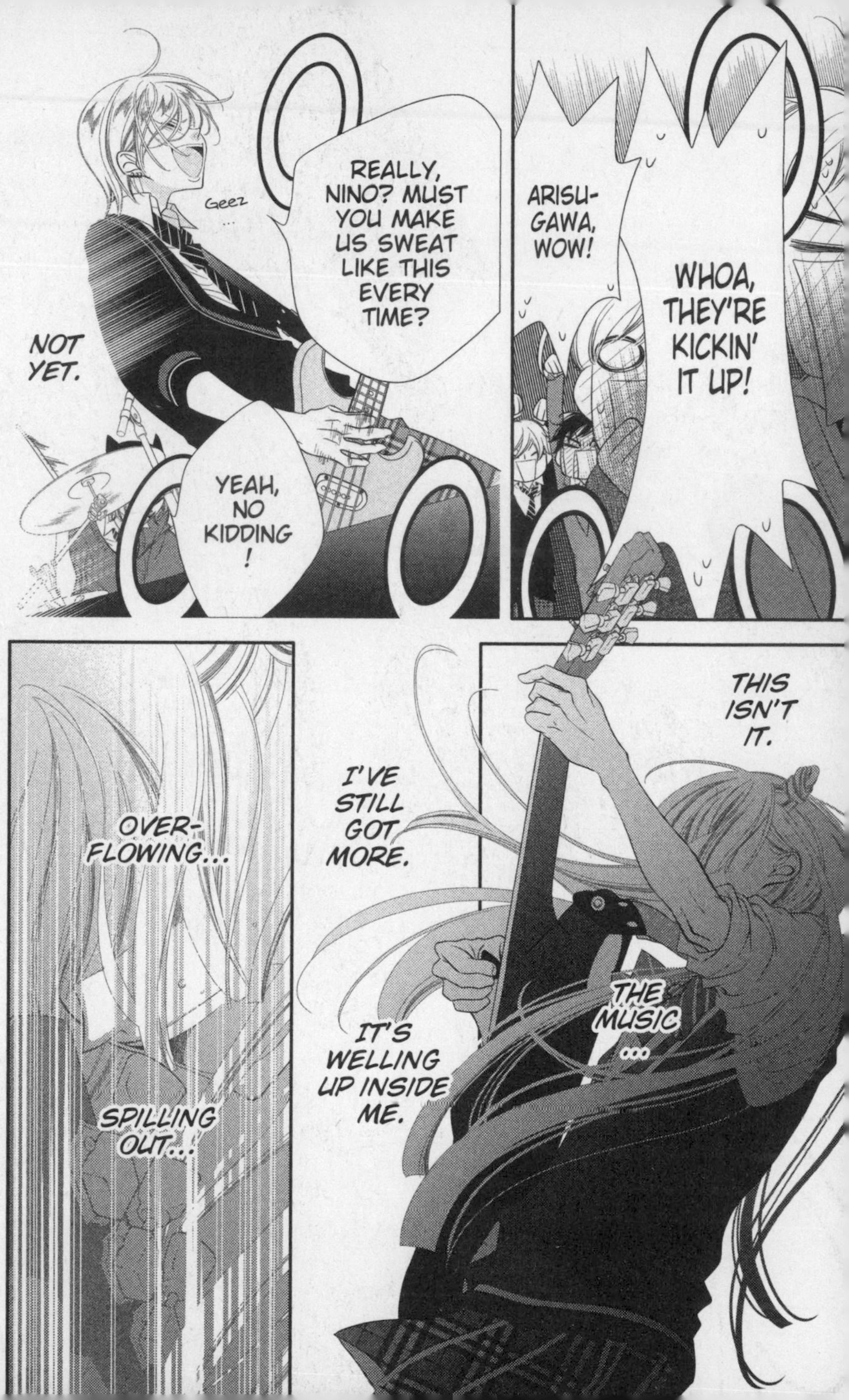
ARISUGAWA, WOW!
WHOA, THEY'RE KICKIN' IT UP!
REALLY, NINO? MUST YOU MAKE US SWEAT LIKE THIS EVERY TIME?
Geez...
YEAH, NO KIDDING!
NOT YET.
THIS ISN'T IT.
I'VE STILL GOT MORE.
THE MUSIC...
IT'S WELLING UP INSIDE ME.
OVER-FLOWING...
SPILLING OUT...

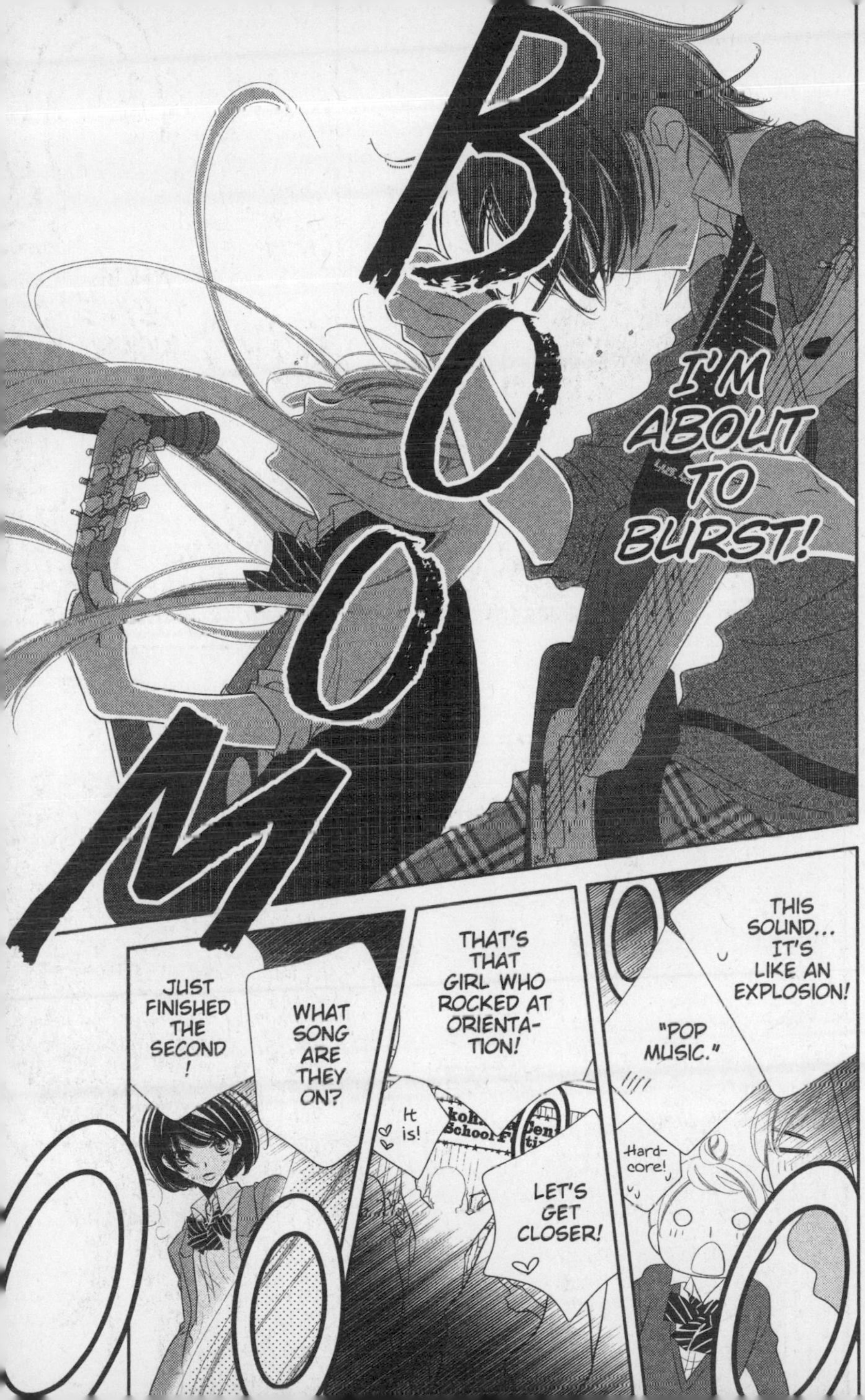
I'M ABOUT TO BURST!
BOOM
THIS SOUND... IT'S LIKE AN EXPLOSION!
"POP MUSIC."
Hard-core!
THAT'S THAT GIRL WHO ROCKED AT ORIENTA-TION!
It is!
LET'S GET CLOSER!
WHAT SONG ARE THEY ON?
JUST FINISHED THE SECOND!

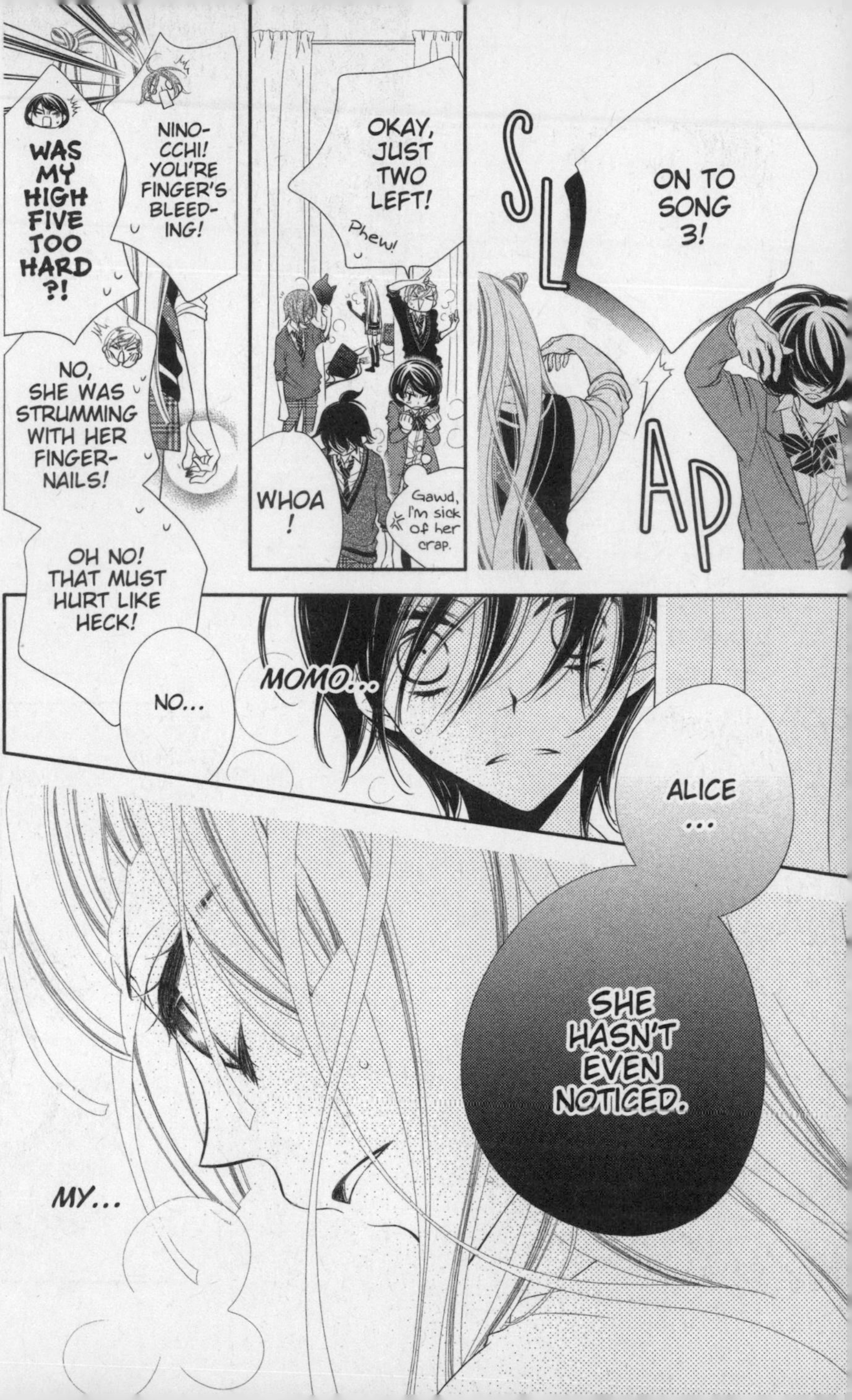
SLAP
ON TO SONG 3!
OKAY, JUST TWO LEFT!
Phew!
WHOA!
Gawd, I'm sick of her crap.
NINO-CCHI! YOU'RE FINGER'S BLEEDING!
WAS MY HIGH FIVE TOO HARD?!
NO, SHE WAS STRUMMING WITH HER FINGERNAILS!
OH NO! THAT MUST HURT LIKE HECK!
MOMO...
NO...
ALICE...
SHE HASN'T EVEN NOTICED.
MY...

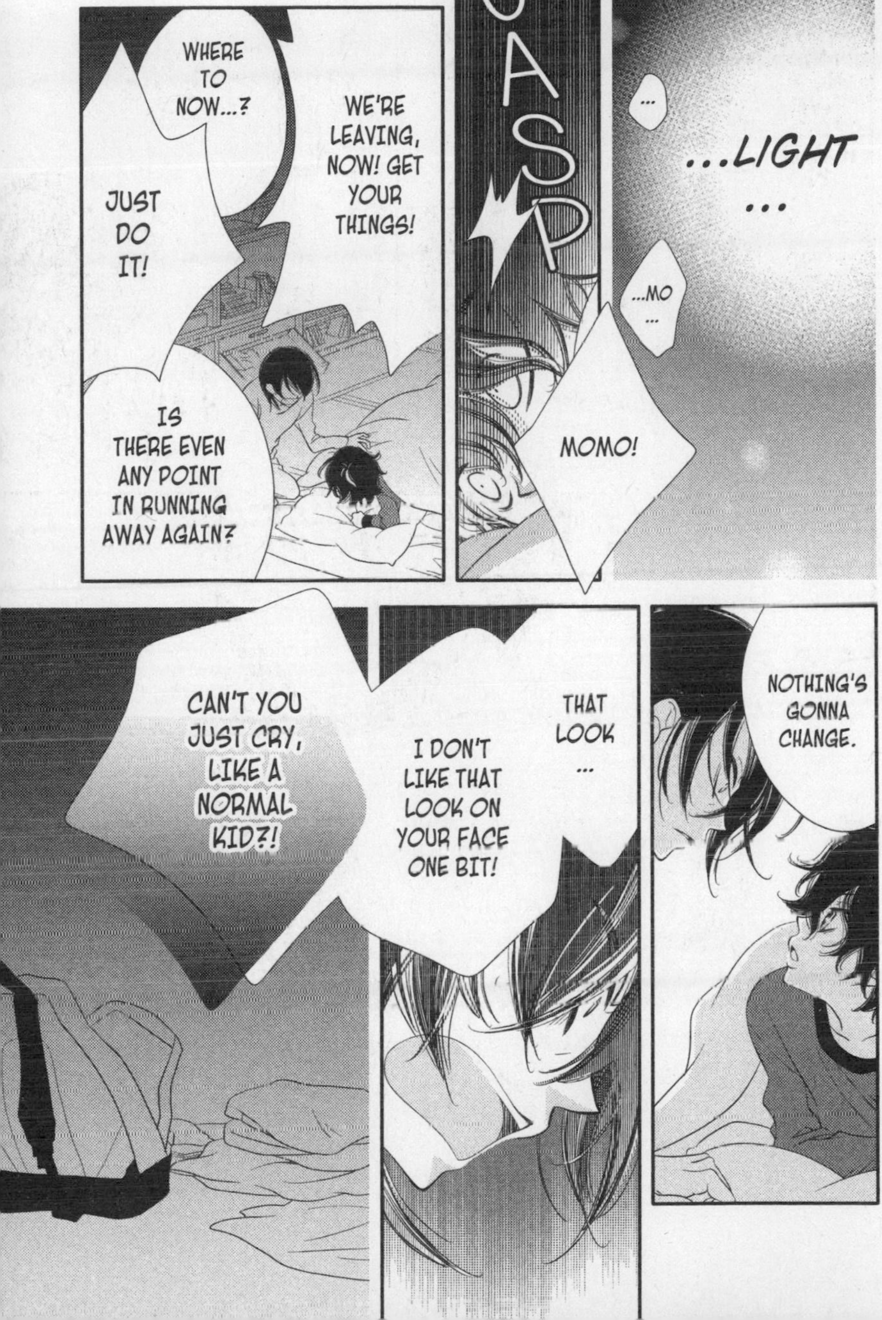
...
...LIGHT ...
...MO ...
GASP
MOMO!
WE'RE LEAVING, NOW! GET YOUR THINGS!
WHERE TO NOW...?
JUST DO IT!
IS THERE EVEN ANY POINT IN RUNNING AWAY AGAIN?
NOTHING'S GONNA CHANGE.
THAT LOOK ...
I DON'T LIKE THAT LOOK ON YOUR FACE ONE BIT!
CAN'T YOU JUST CRY, LIKE A NORMAL KID?!

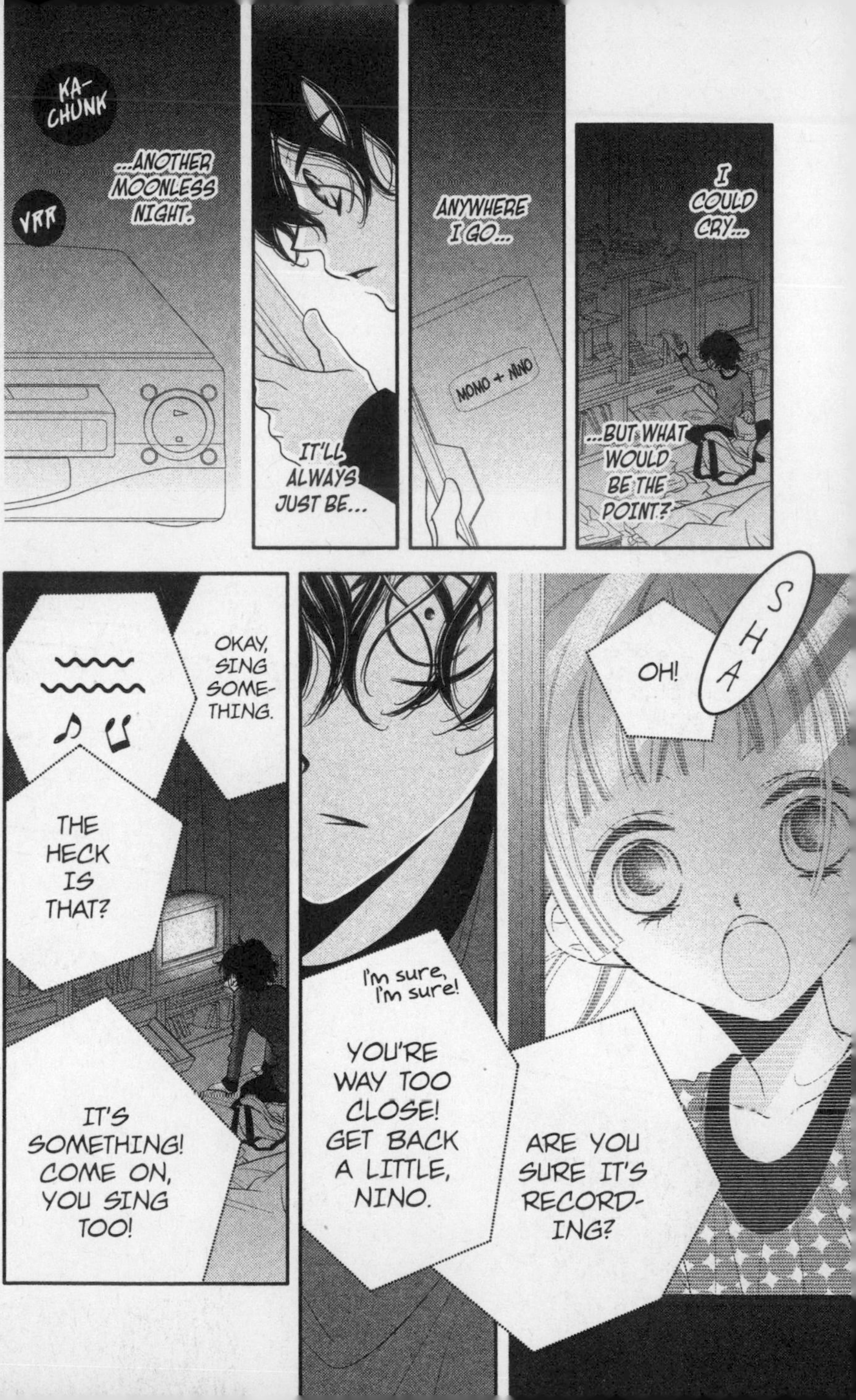
I COULD CRY...
...BUT WHAT WOULD BE THE POINT?
ANYWHERE I GO...
MOMO + NINO
IT'LL ALWAYS JUST BE...
KA-CHUNK
...ANOTHER MOONLESS NIGHT.
VRR
SHA
OH!
ARE YOU SURE IT'S RECORDING?
I'm sure, I'm sure!
YOU'RE WAY TOO CLOSE! GET BACK A LITTLE, NINO.
OKAY, SING SOMETHING.
THE HECK IS THAT?
IT'S SOMETHING! COME ON, YOU SING TOO!

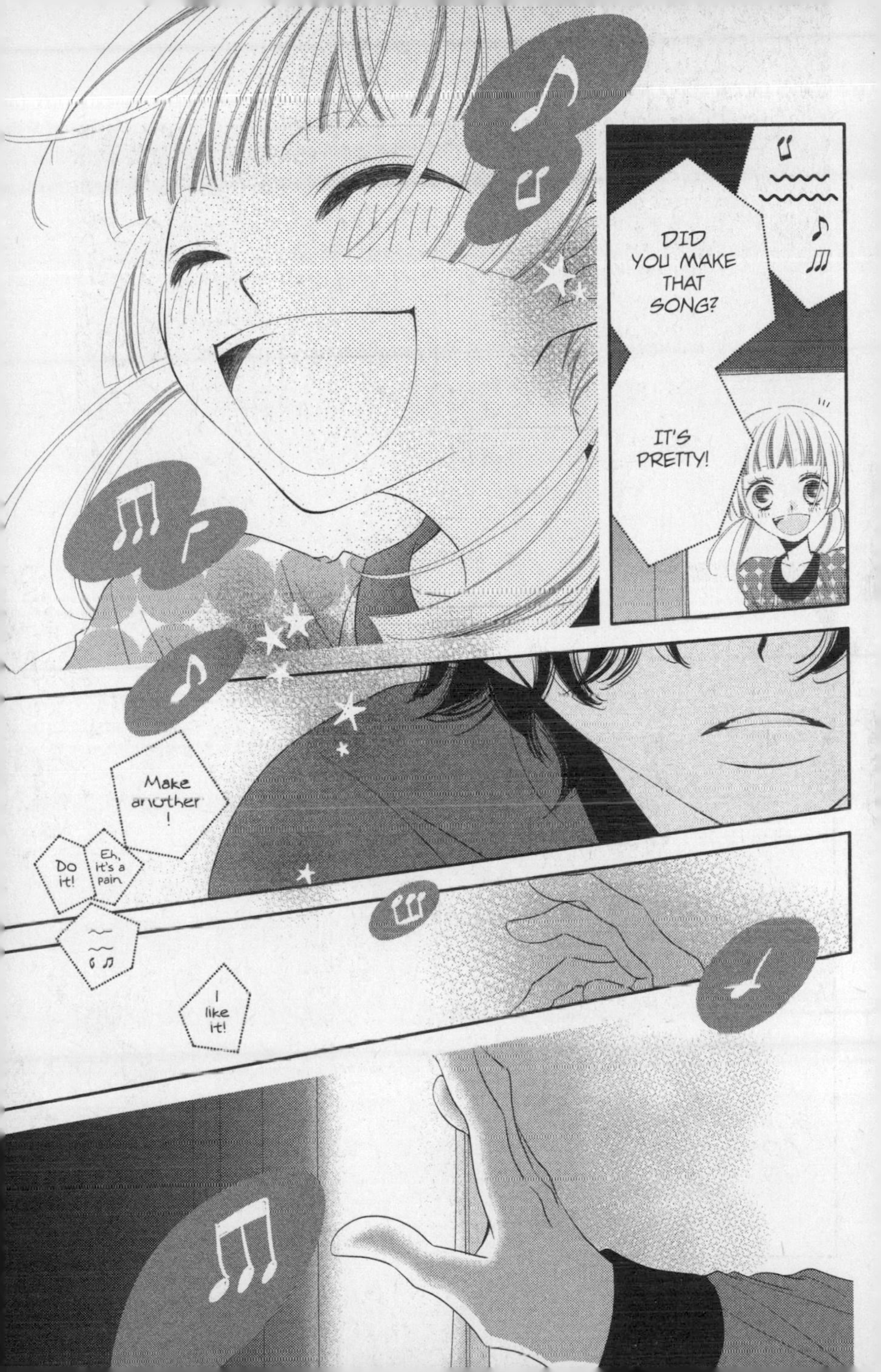
DID YOU MAKE THAT SONG?
IT'S PRETTY!
Make another!
Eh, it's a pain.
Do it!
I like it!

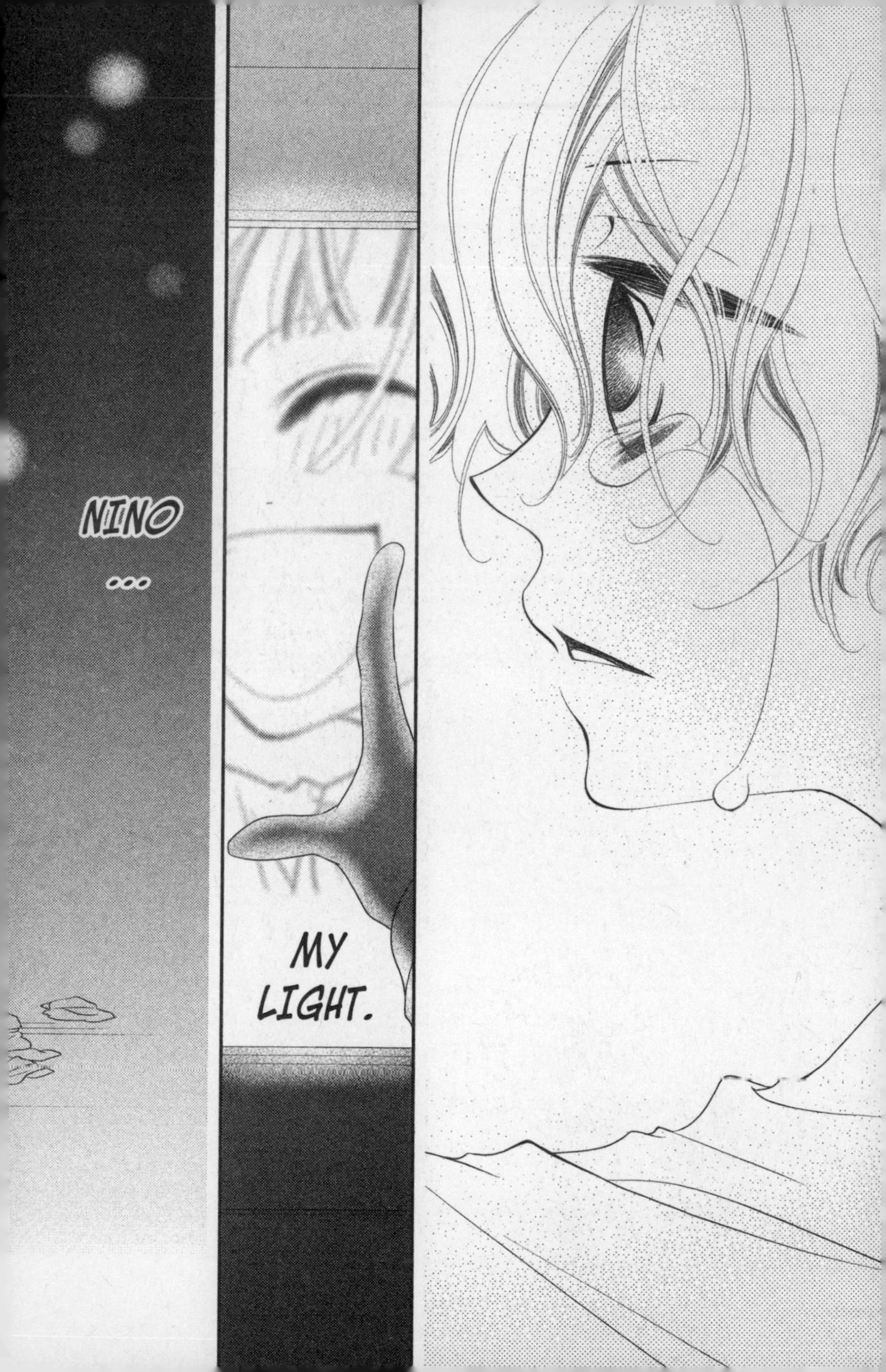
MY LIGHT.
NINO ...

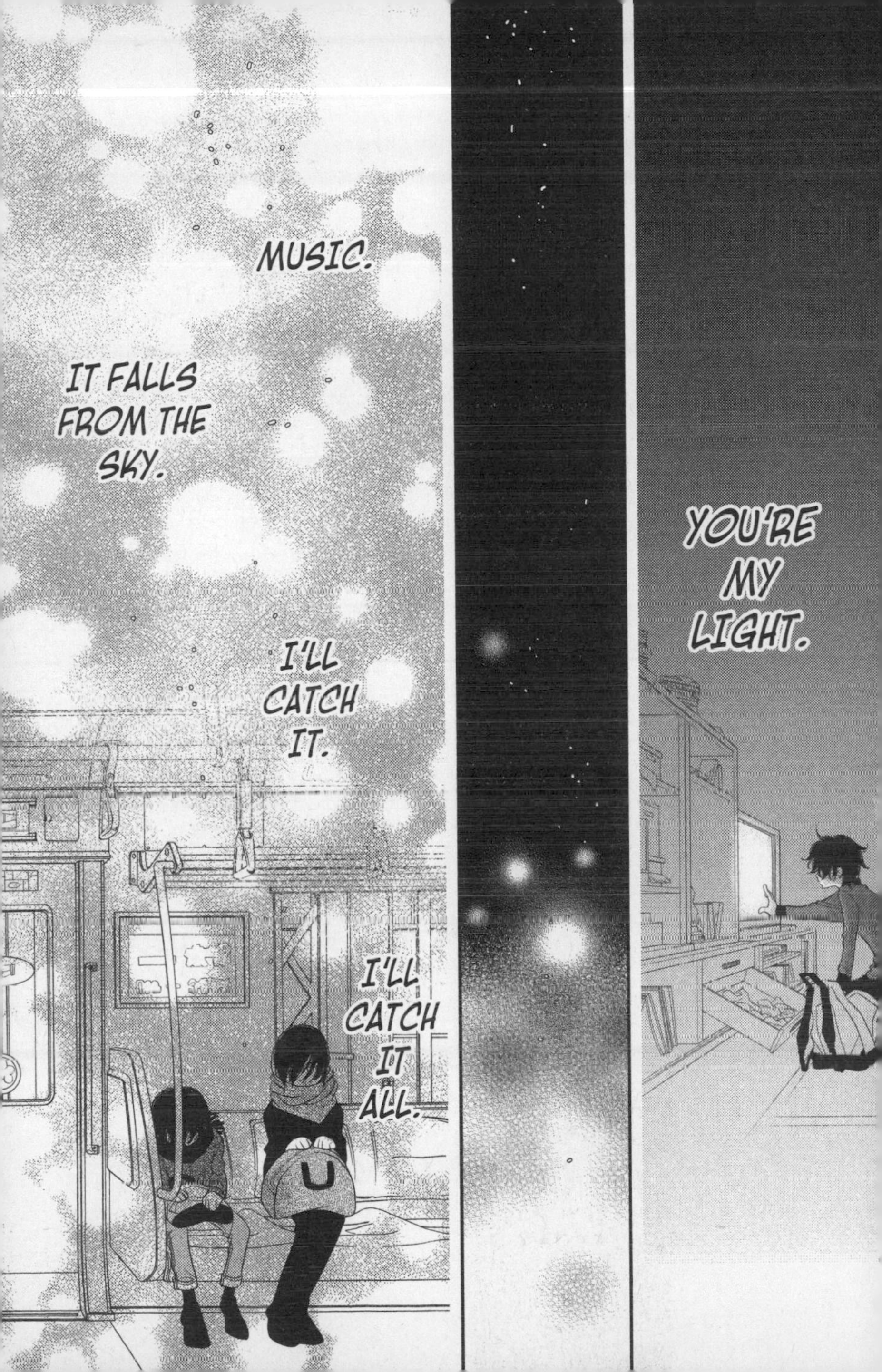
YOU'RE MY LIGHT.
MUSIC.
IT FALLS FROM THE SKY.
I'LL CATCH IT.
I'LL CATCH IT ALL.

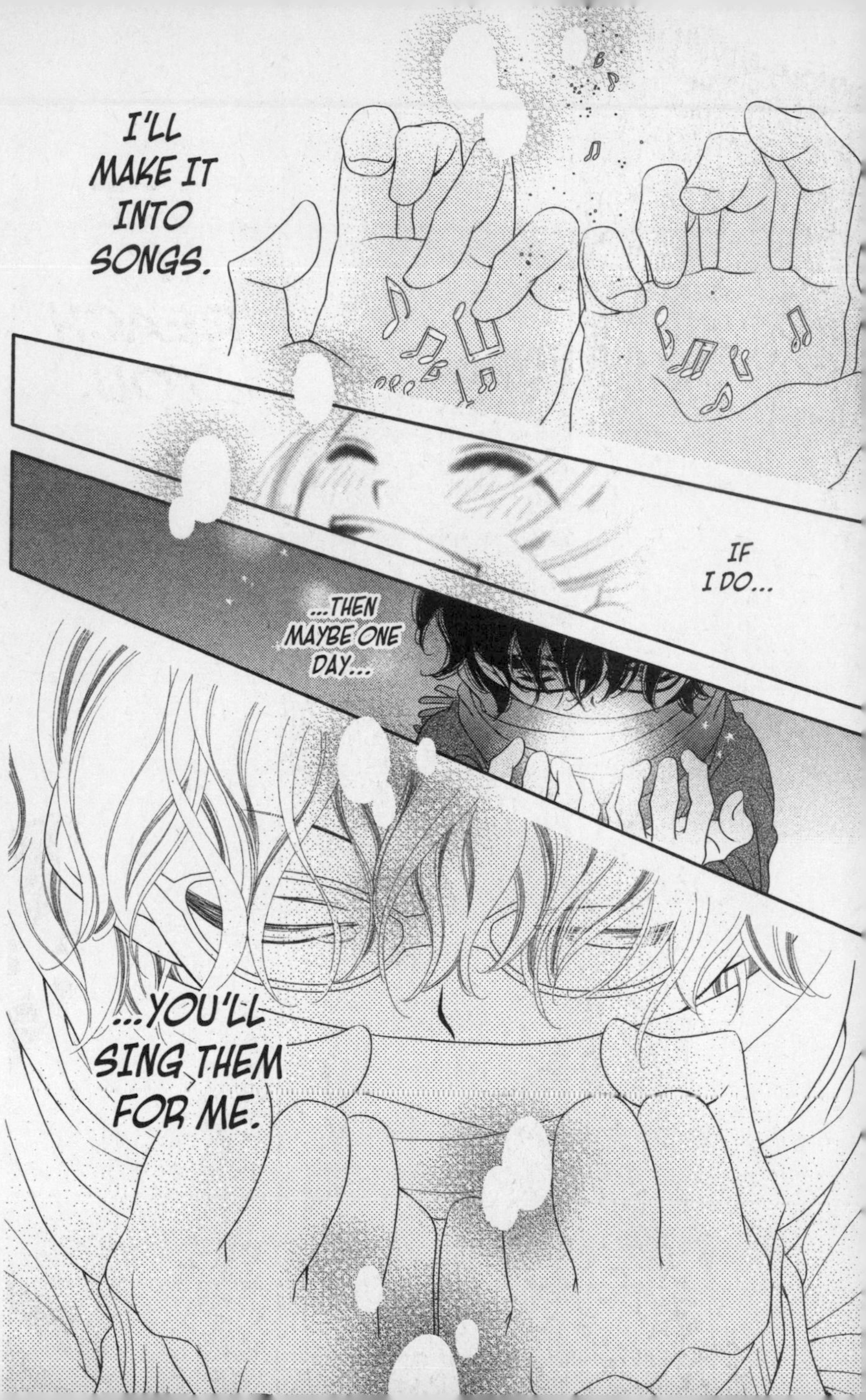
I'LL MAKE IT INTO SONGS.
IF I DO...
...THEN MAYBE ONE DAY...
...YOU'LL SING THEM FOR ME.

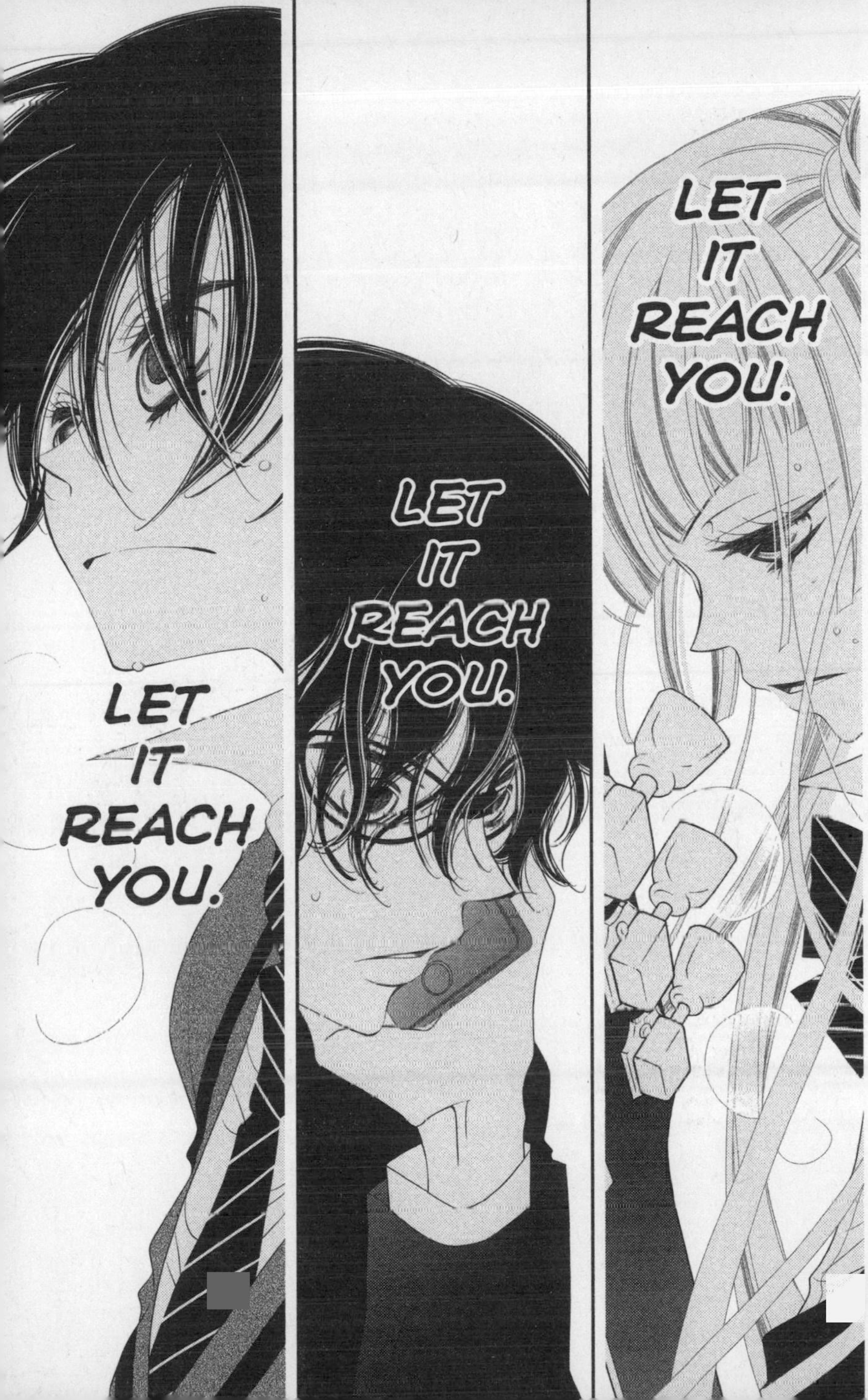
LET IT REACH YOU.
LET IT REACH YOU.
LET IT REACH YOU.

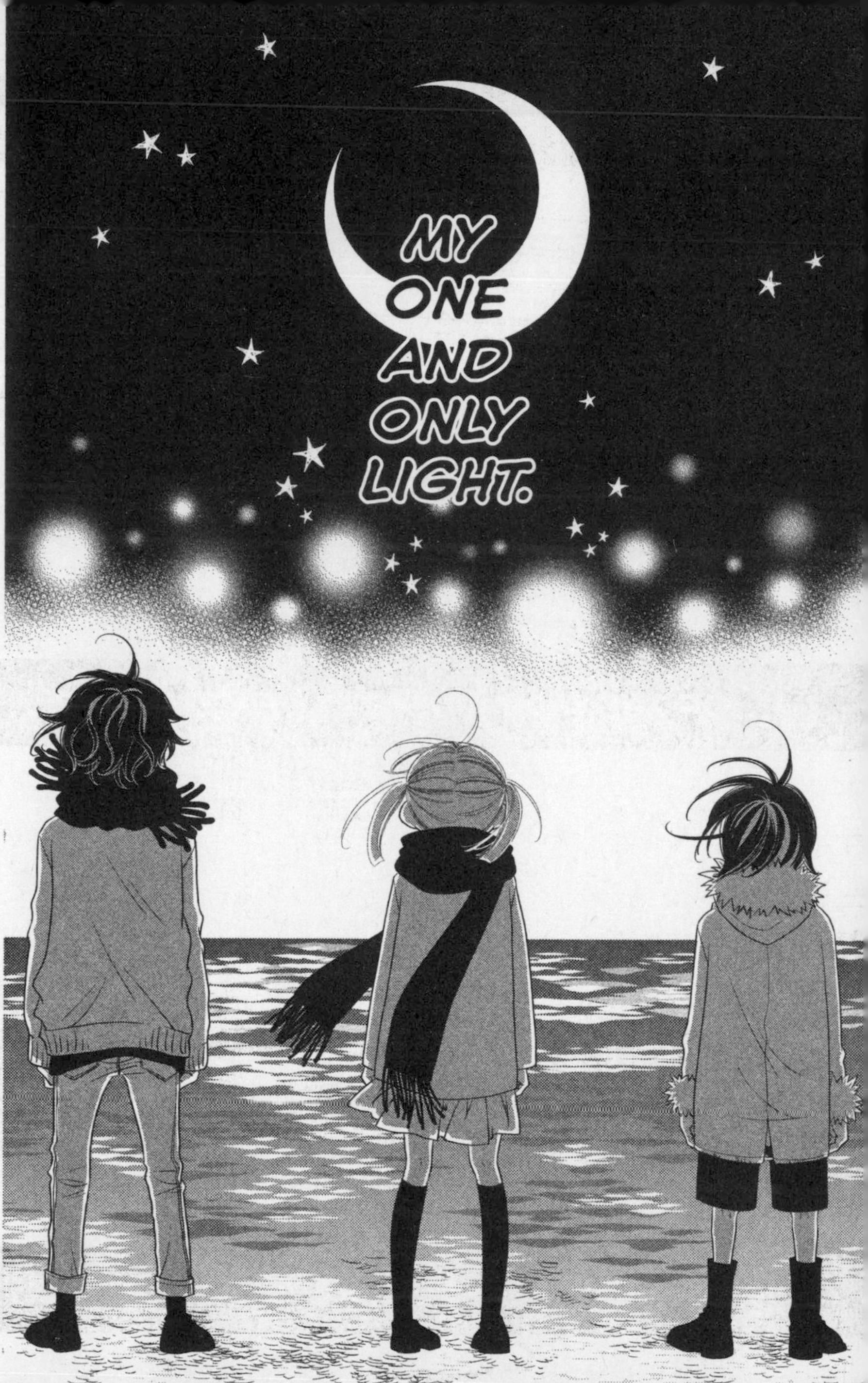
MY ONE AND ONLY LIGHT.

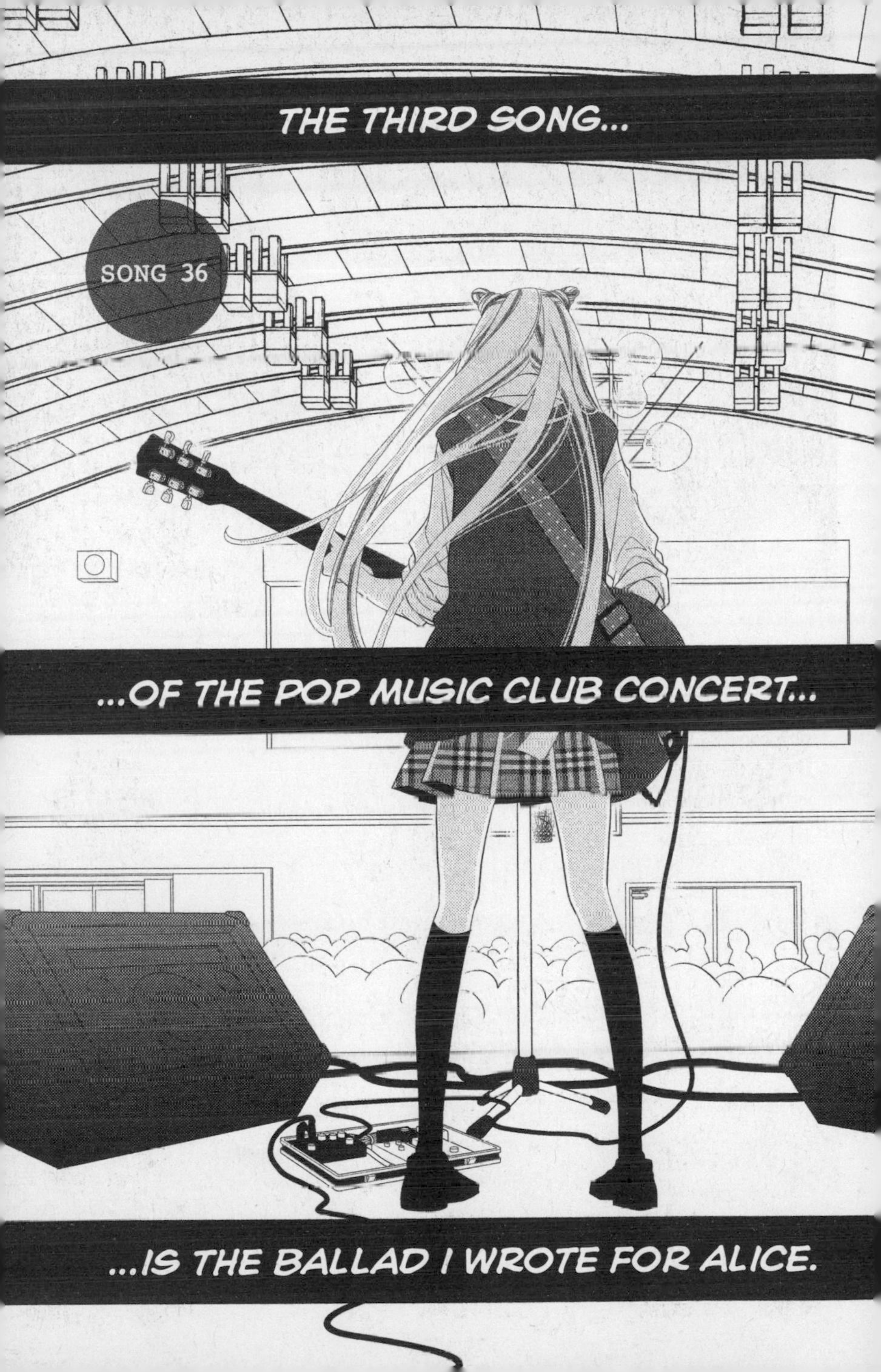
SONG 36
THE THIRD SONG...
...OF THE POP MUSIC CLUB CONCERT...
...IS THE BALLAD I WROTE FOR ALICE.

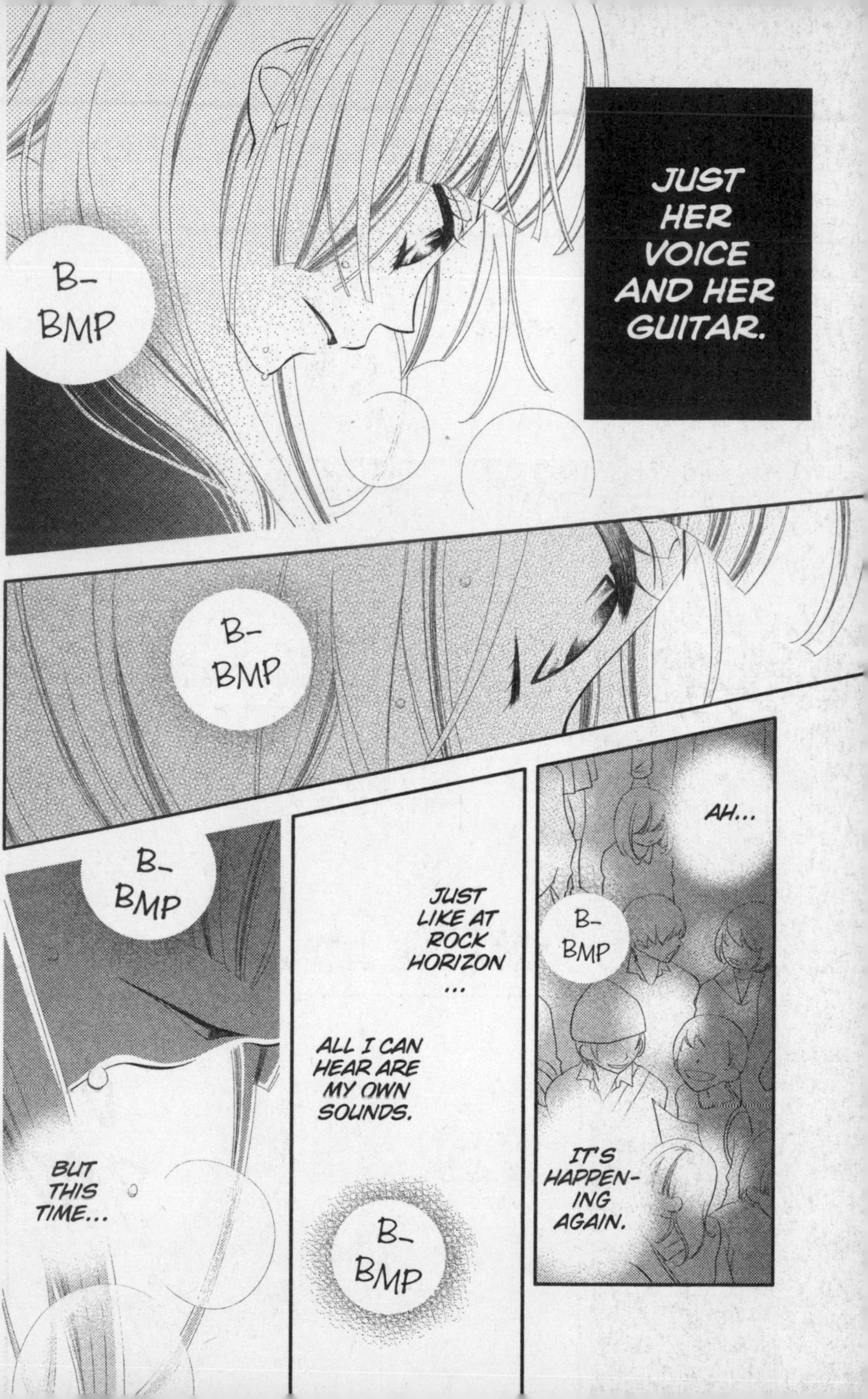
JUST HER VOICE AND HER GUITAR.
B-BMP
B-BMP
AH...
B-BMP
IT'S HAPPEN-ING AGAIN.
JUST LIKE AT ROCK HORIZON...
ALL I CAN HEAR ARE MY OWN SOUNDS.
B-BMP
B-BMP
BUT THIS TIME...

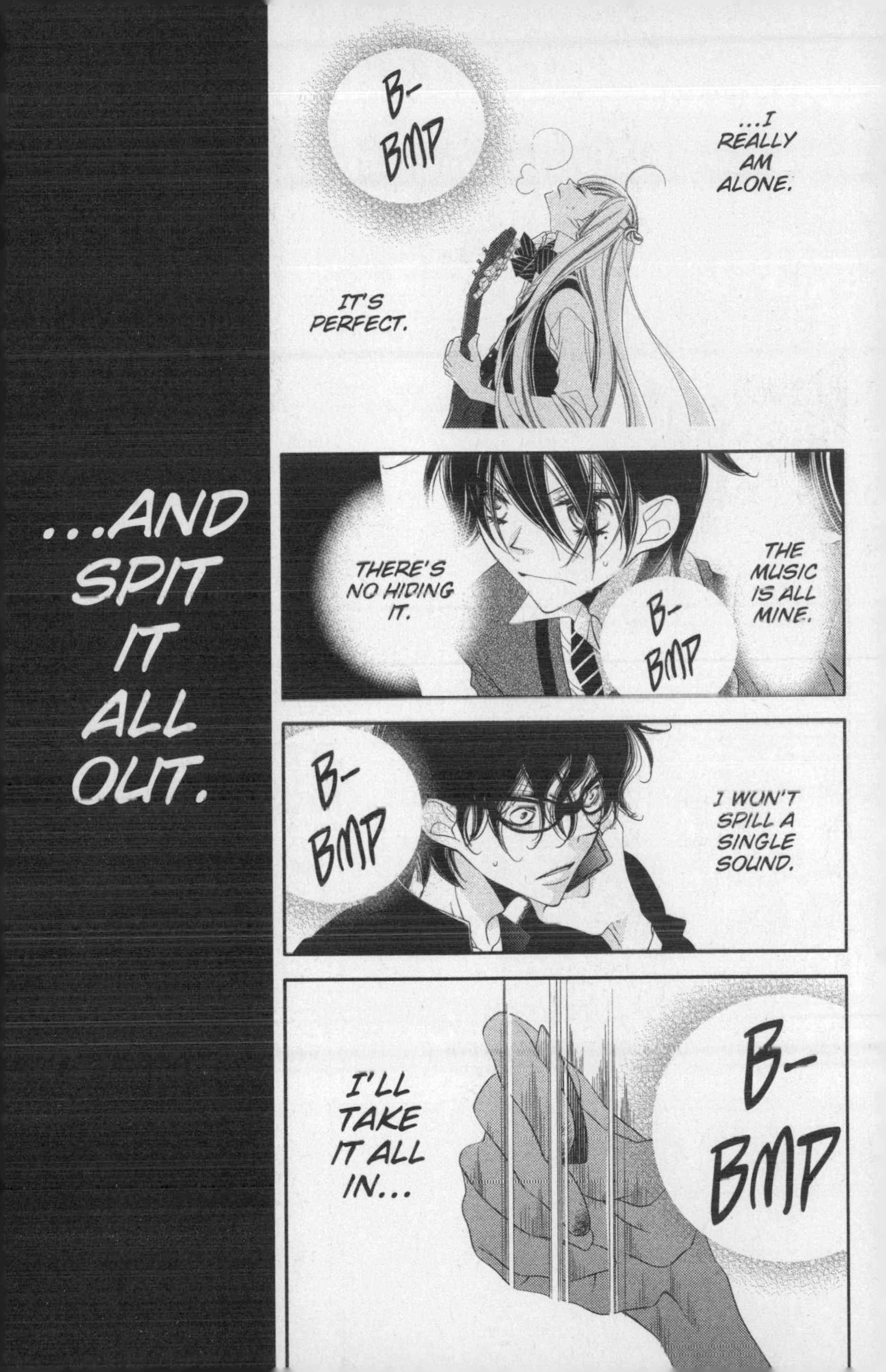
...I REALLY AM ALONE.
B-BMP
IT'S PERFECT.
THE MUSIC IS ALL MINE.
B-BMP
THERE'S NO HIDING IT.
I WON'T SPILL A SINGLE SOUND.
B-BMP
B-BMP
I'LL TAKE IT ALL IN...
...AND SPIT IT ALL OUT.

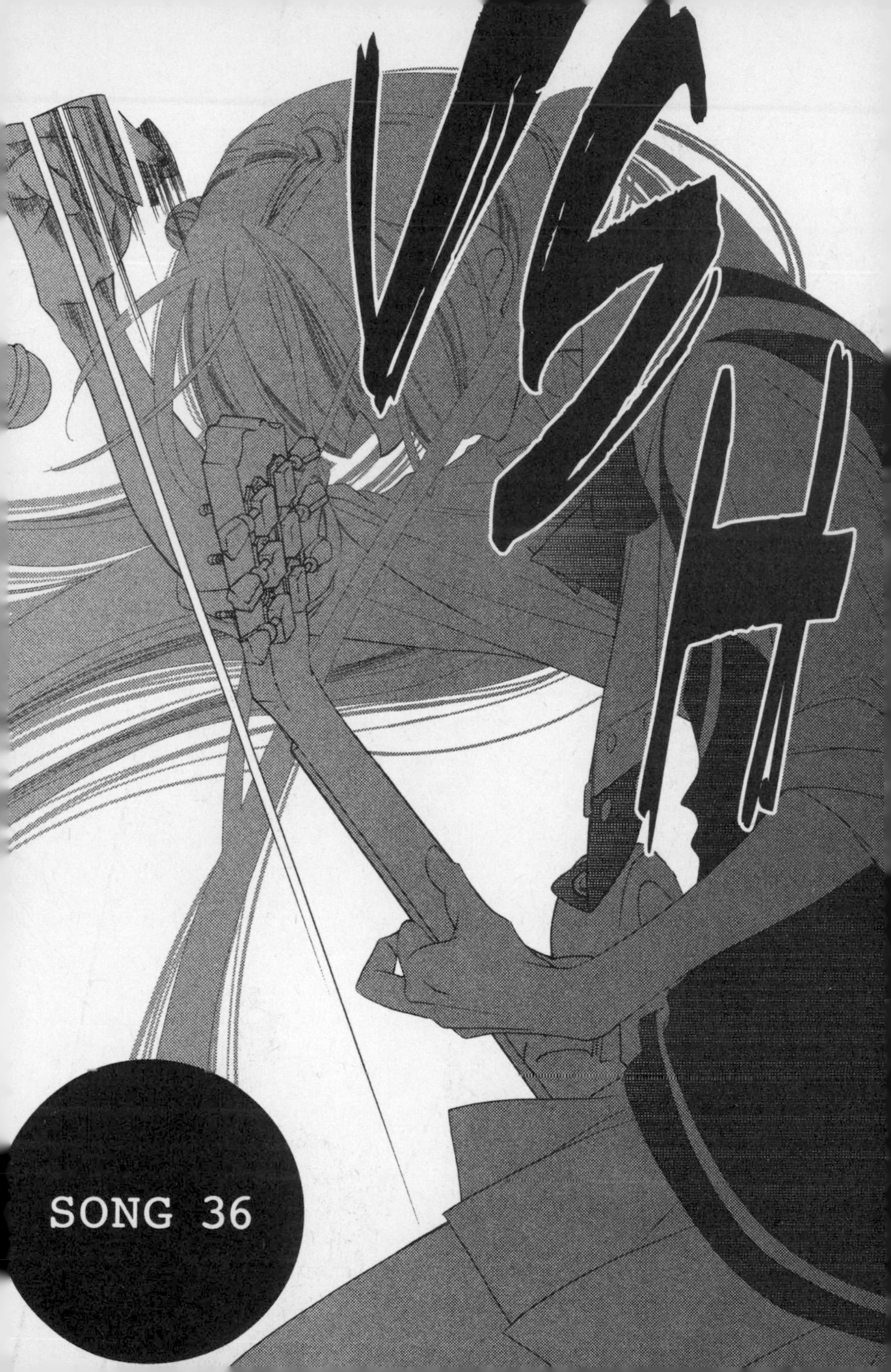
WSH
SONG 36

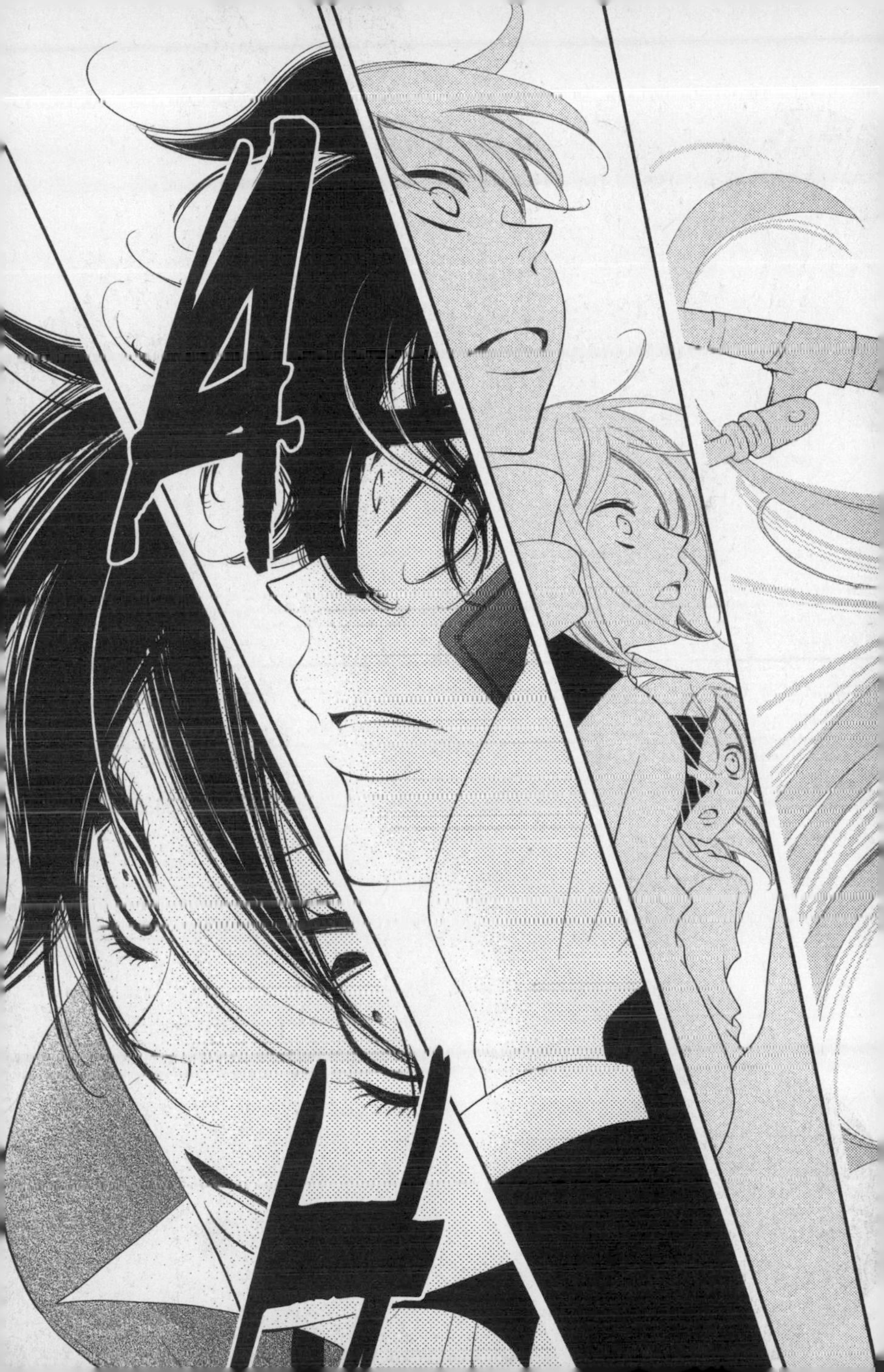

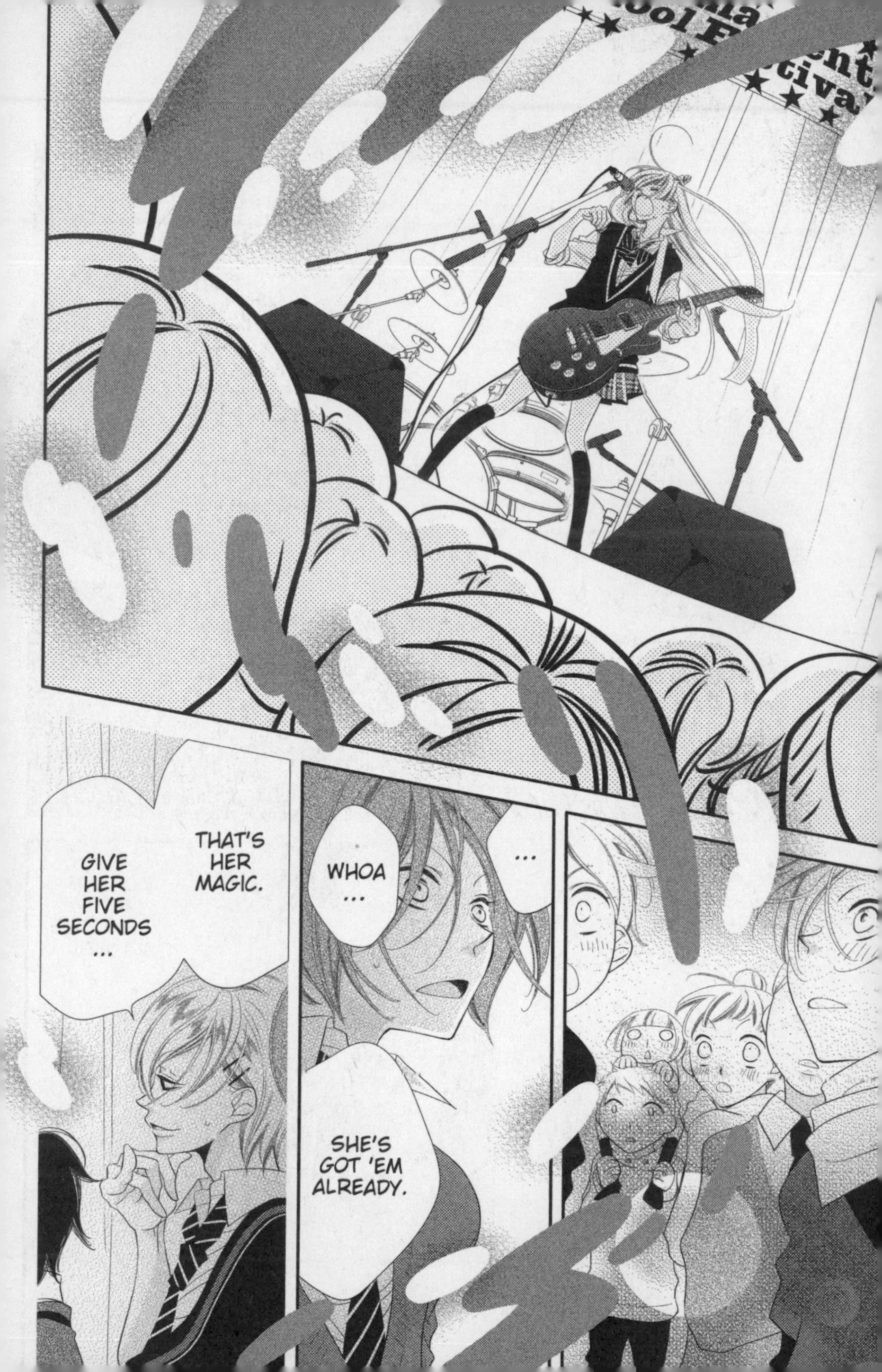
...
WHOA ...
SHE'S GOT 'EM ALREADY.
THAT'S HER MAGIC.
GIVE HER FIVE SECONDS ...

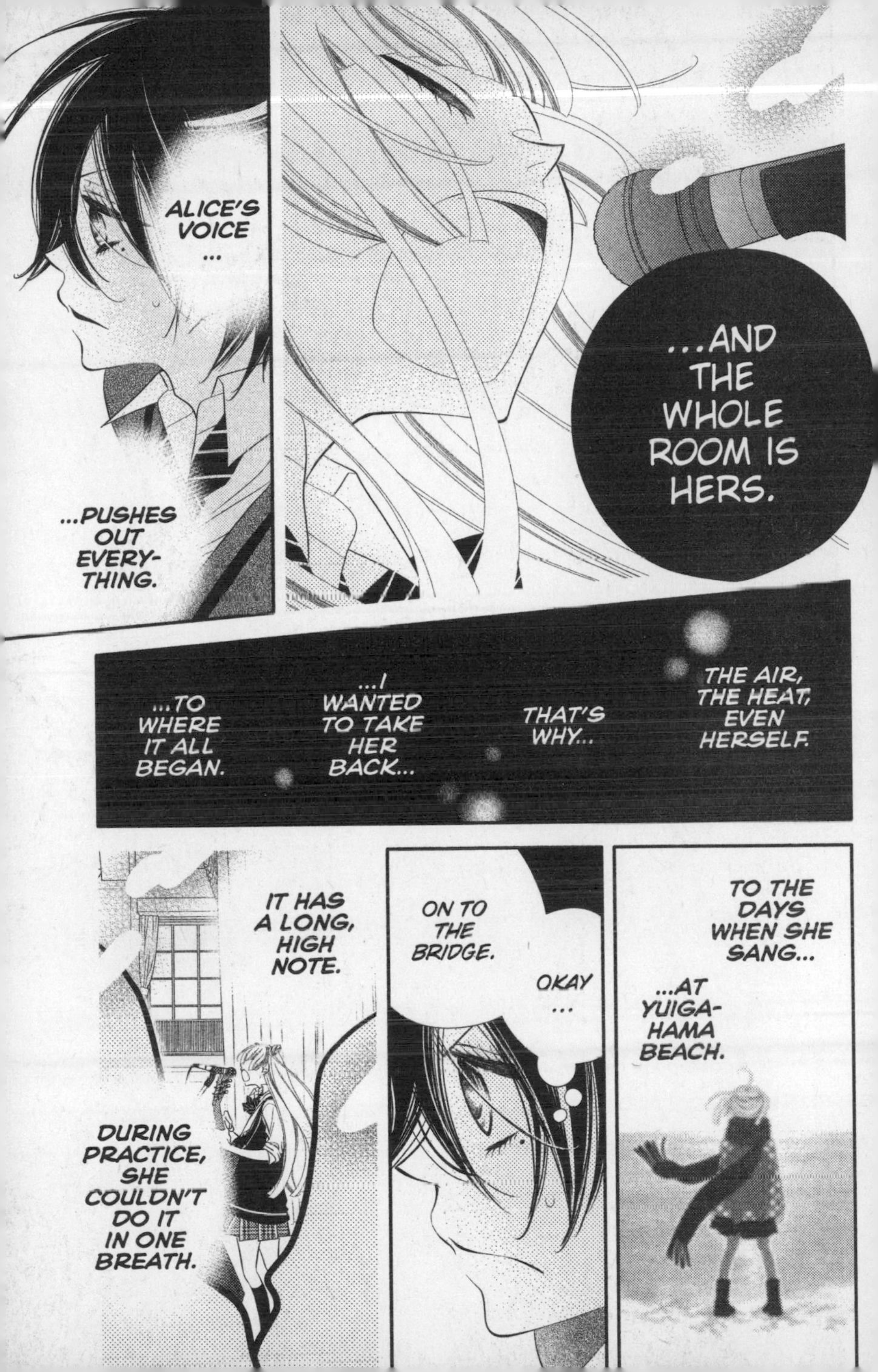
...AND THE WHOLE ROOM IS HERS.
ALICE'S VOICE ...
...PUSHES OUT EVERY-THING.
THE AIR, THE HEAT, EVEN HERSELF.
THAT'S WHY...
...I WANTED TO TAKE HER BACK...
...TO WHERE IT ALL BEGAN.
TO THE DAYS WHEN SHE SANG...
...AT YUIGA-HAMA BEACH.
OKAY ...
ON TO THE BRIDGE.
IT HAS A LONG, HIGH NOTE.
DURING PRACTICE, SHE COULDN'T DO IT IN ONE BREATH.

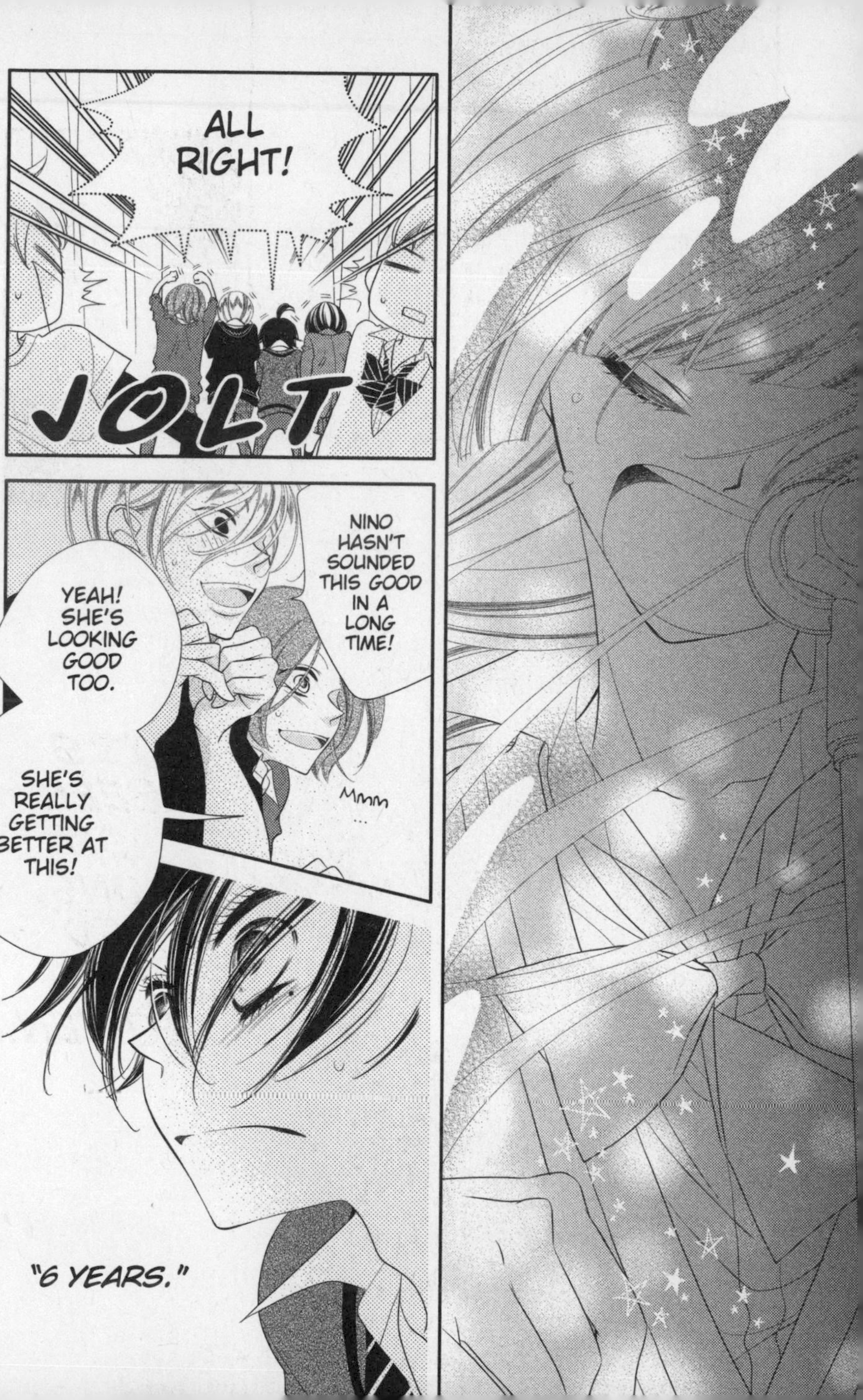
ALL RIGHT!
JOLT
NINO HASN'T SOUNDED THIS GOOD IN A LONG TIME!
YEAH! SHE'S LOOKING GOOD TOO.
Mmm...
SHE'S REALLY GETTING BETTER AT THIS!
"6 YEARS."

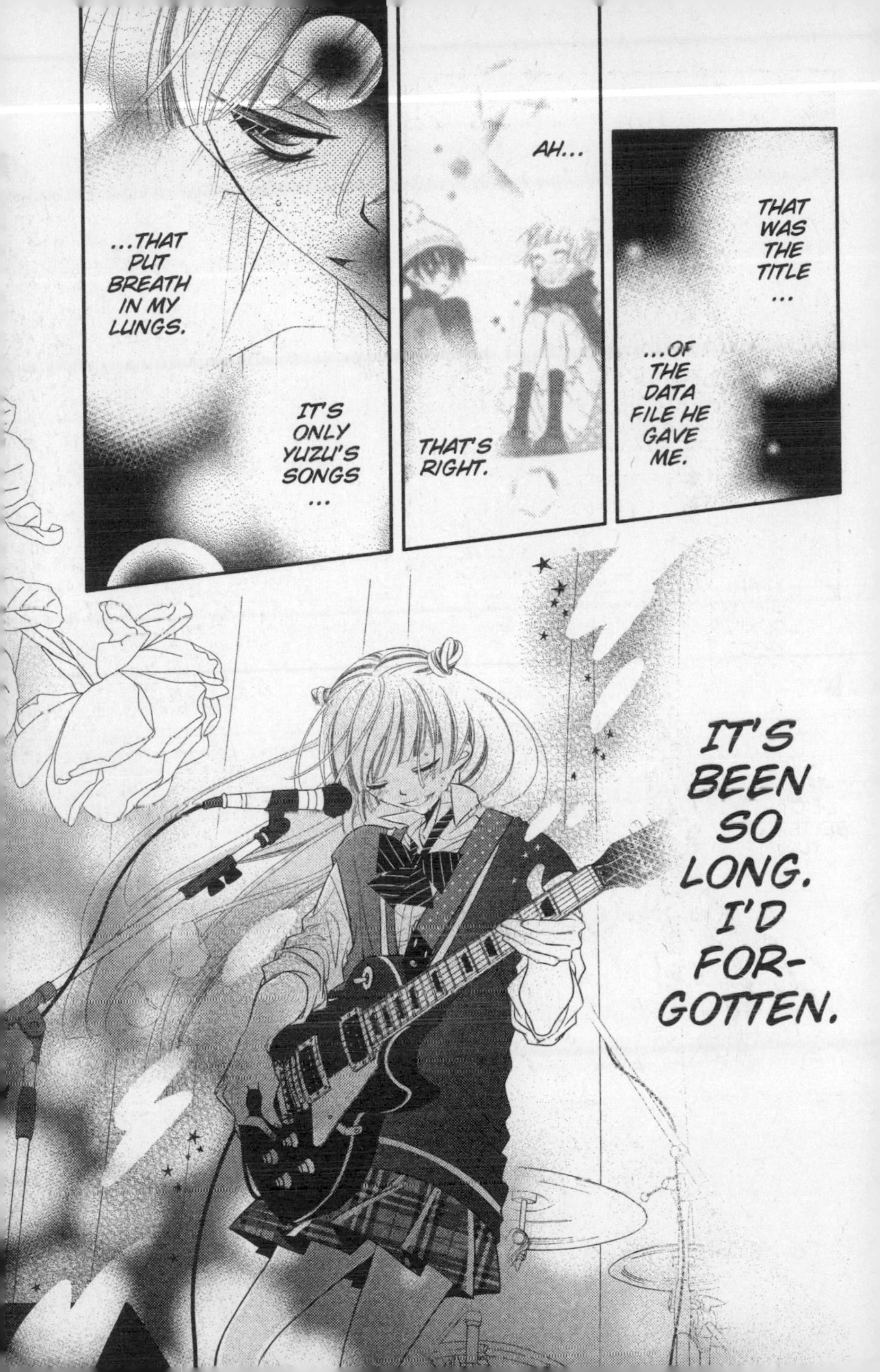
THAT WAS THE TITLE ...
...OF THE DATA FILE HE GAVE ME.
AH...
THAT'S RIGHT.
IT'S ONLY YUZU'S SONGS ...
...THAT PUT BREATH IN MY LUNGS.
IT'S BEEN SO LONG. I'D FOR-GOTTEN.

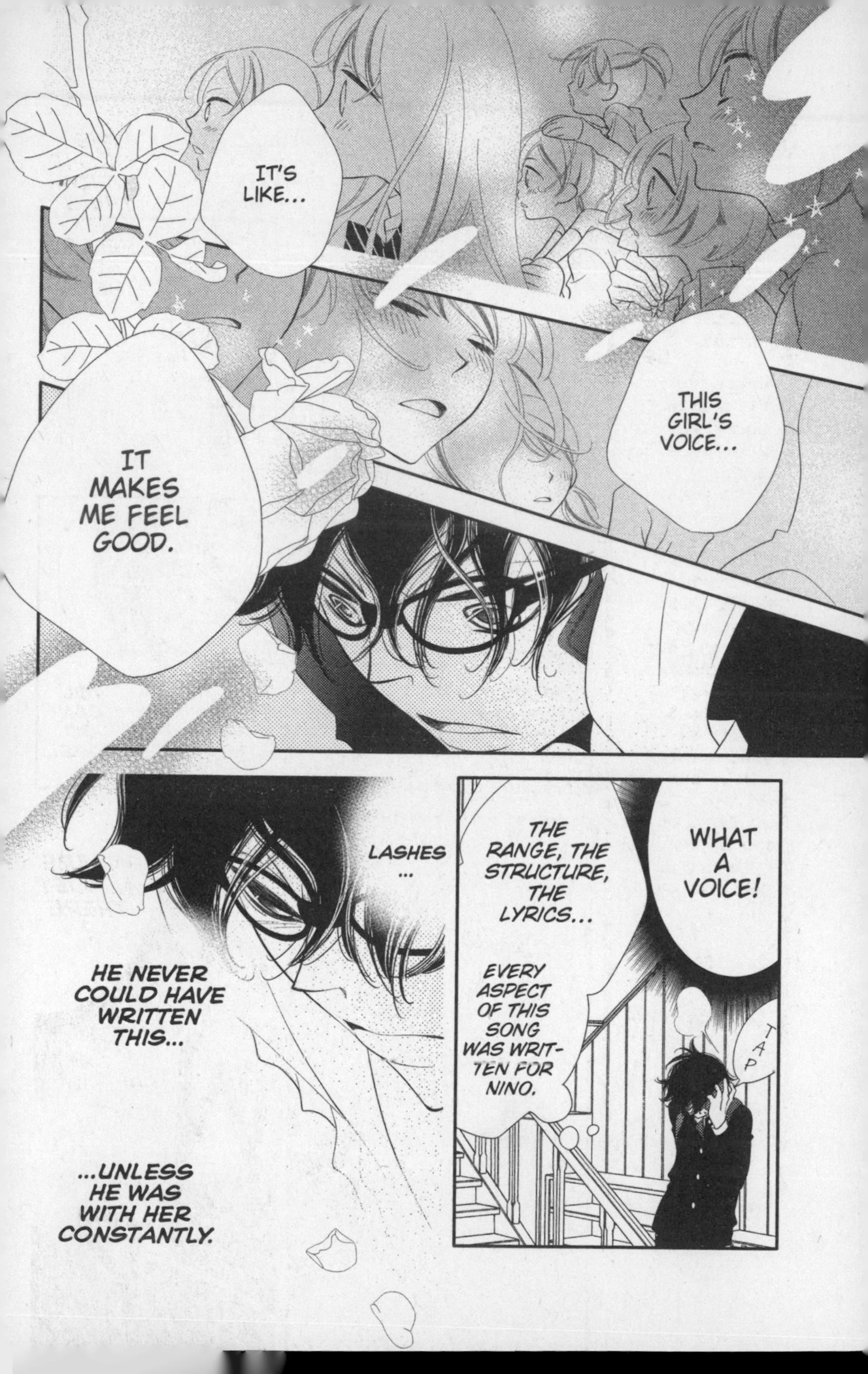
IT'S LIKE...
THIS GIRL'S VOICE...
IT MAKES ME FEEL GOOD.
WHAT A VOICE!
THE RANGE, THE STRUCTURE, THE LYRICS...
EVERY ASPECT OF THIS SONG WAS WRITTEN FOR NINO.
TAP
LASHES ...
HE NEVER COULD HAVE WRITTEN THIS...
...UNLESS HE WAS WITH HER CONSTANTLY.

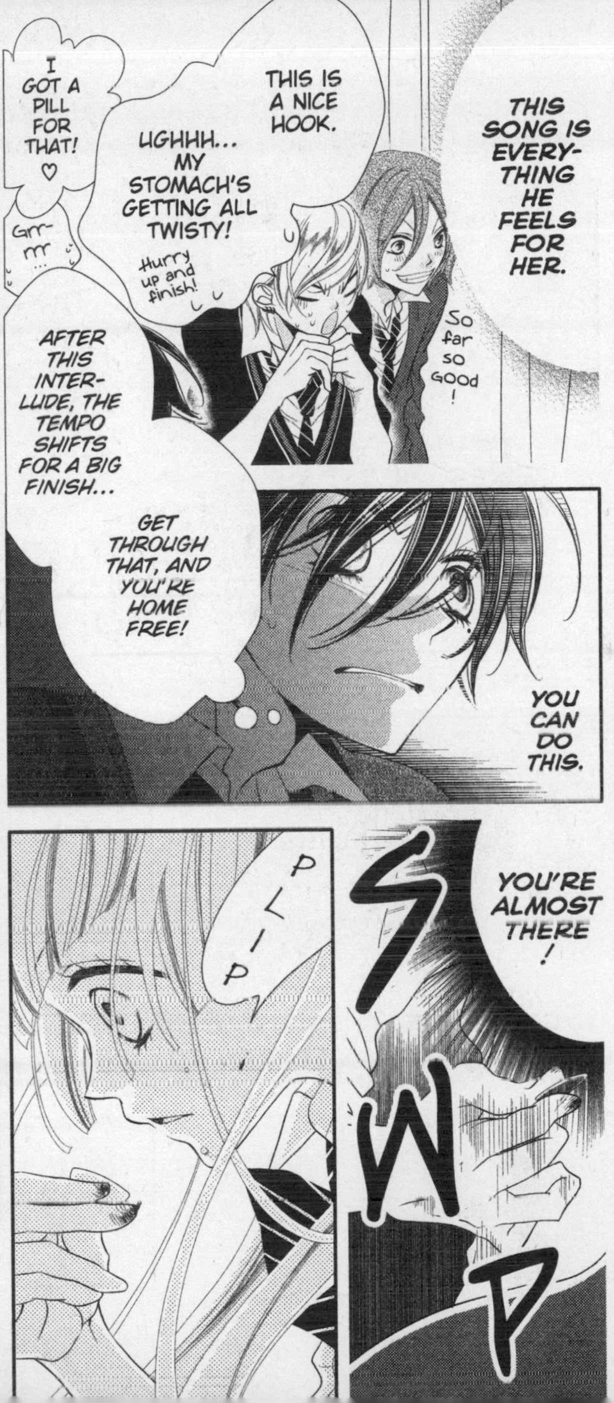
THIS SONG IS EVERYTHING HE FEELS FOR HER.
So far so good!
THIS IS A NICE HOOK.
UGHHH... MY STOMACH'S GETTING ALL TWISTY!
Hurry up and finish!
I GOT A PILL FOR THAT! ♡
Grr-rrr...
AFTER THIS INTERLUDE, THE TEMPO SHIFTS FOR A BIG FINISH...
YOU CAN DO THIS.
GET THROUGH THAT, AND YOU'RE HOME FREE!
YOU'RE ALMOST THERE!
SWP
PLIP

2

Sorry, but my pen was in its death throes, and I had to switch to a marker instead.

Anyway, this summer I went to Rock in Japan again! I brought my digital camera to gather more reference photos, but after what happened last time, this time I knew to bring a 10-24mm wide-angle zoom lens. At the concert, my editor and I ended up splitting up...

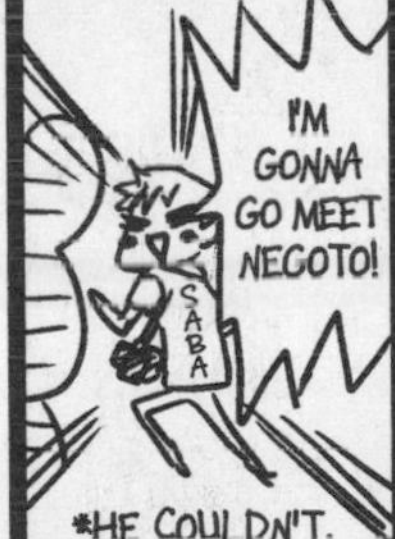
I'M GONNA GO MEET NEGOTO!
SABA

*HE COULDN'T.

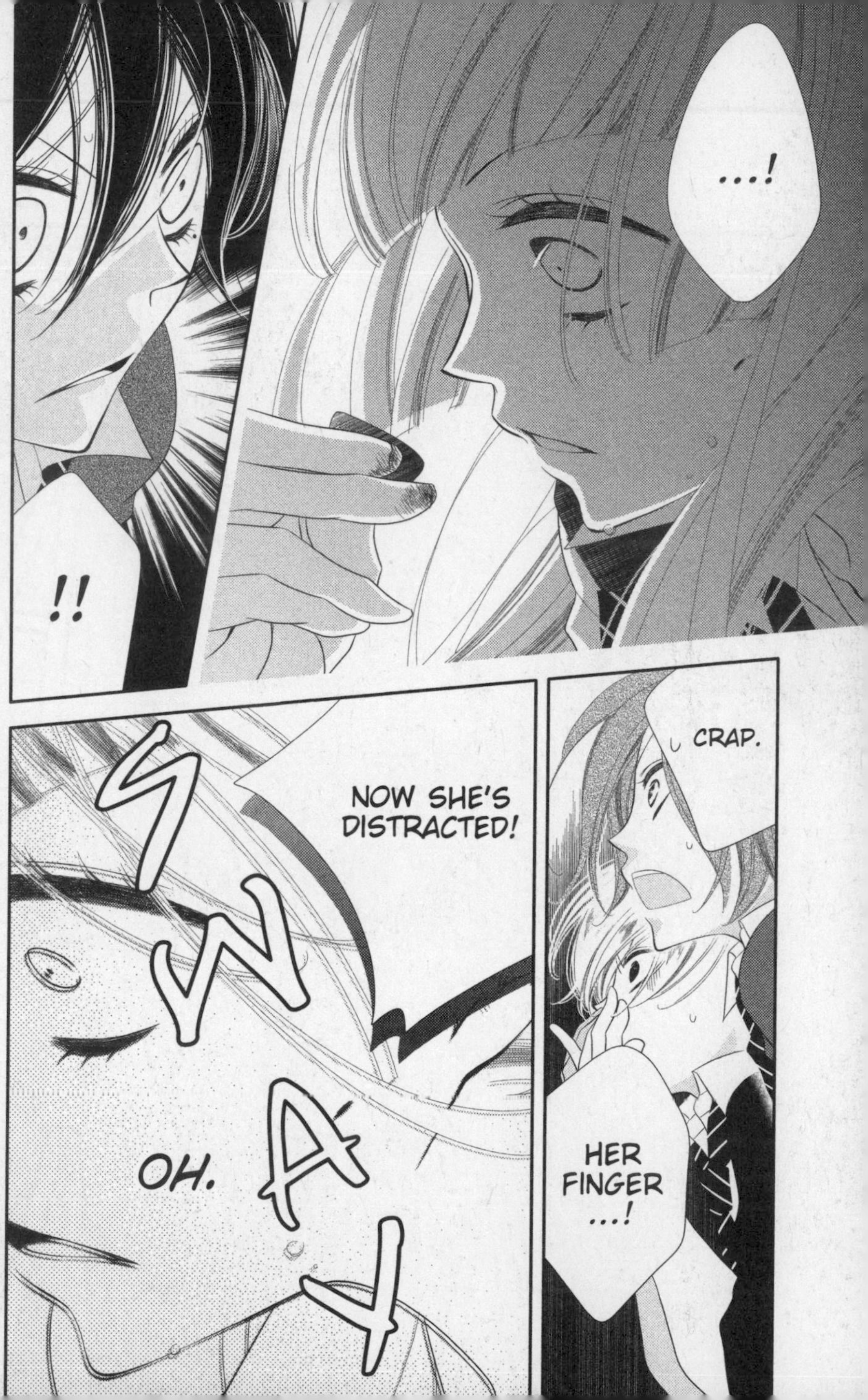

...!
!!
CRAP.
HER FINGER ...!
NOW SHE'S DISTRACTED!
SWAY
OH.

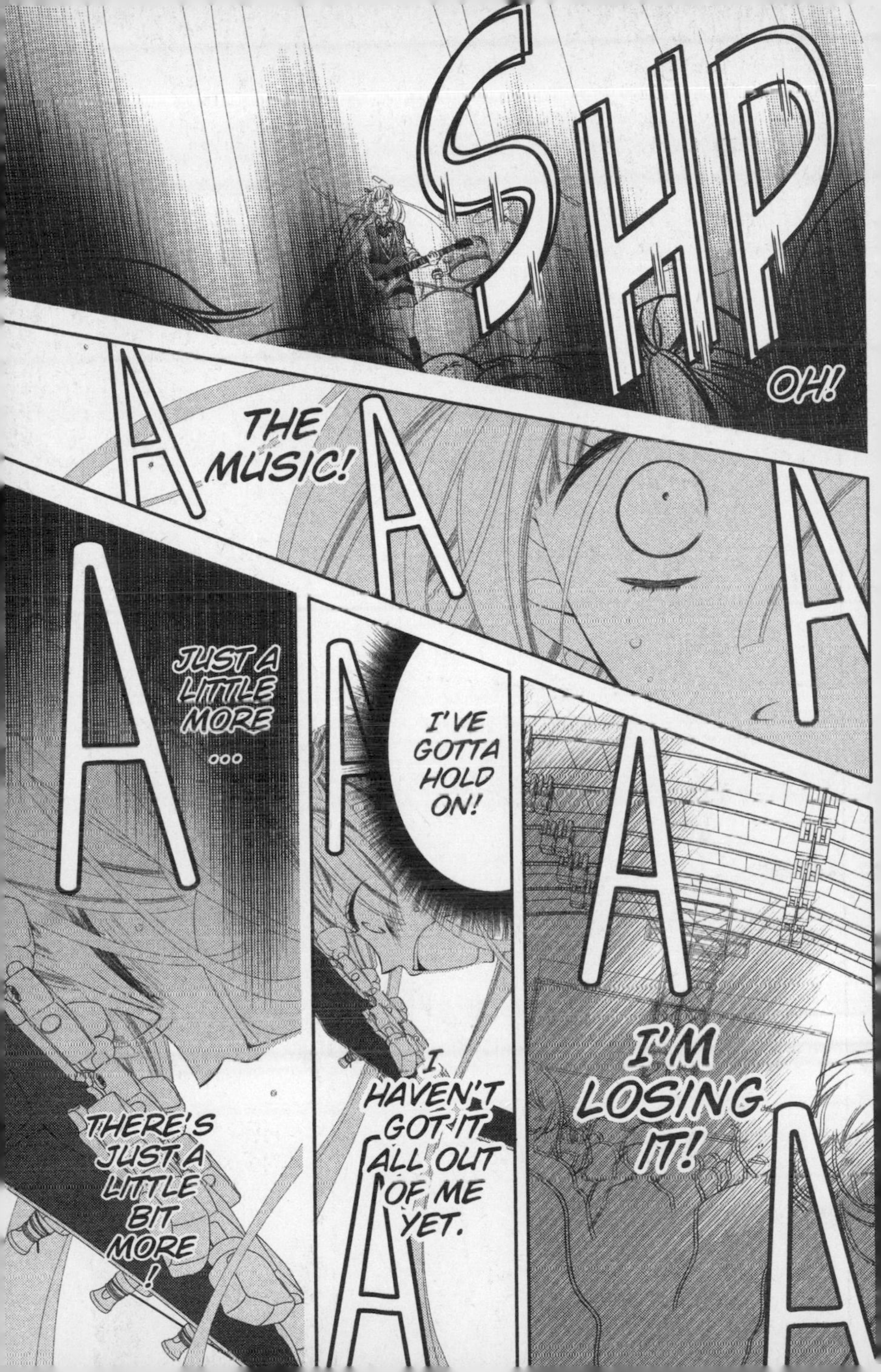
SHP
OH!
THE MUSIC!
AAAAAAAA
I'M LOSING IT!
I'VE GOTTA HOLD ON!
I HAVEN'T GOT IT ALL OUT OF ME YET.
JUST A LITTLE MORE...
THERE'S JUST A LITTLE BIT MORE!

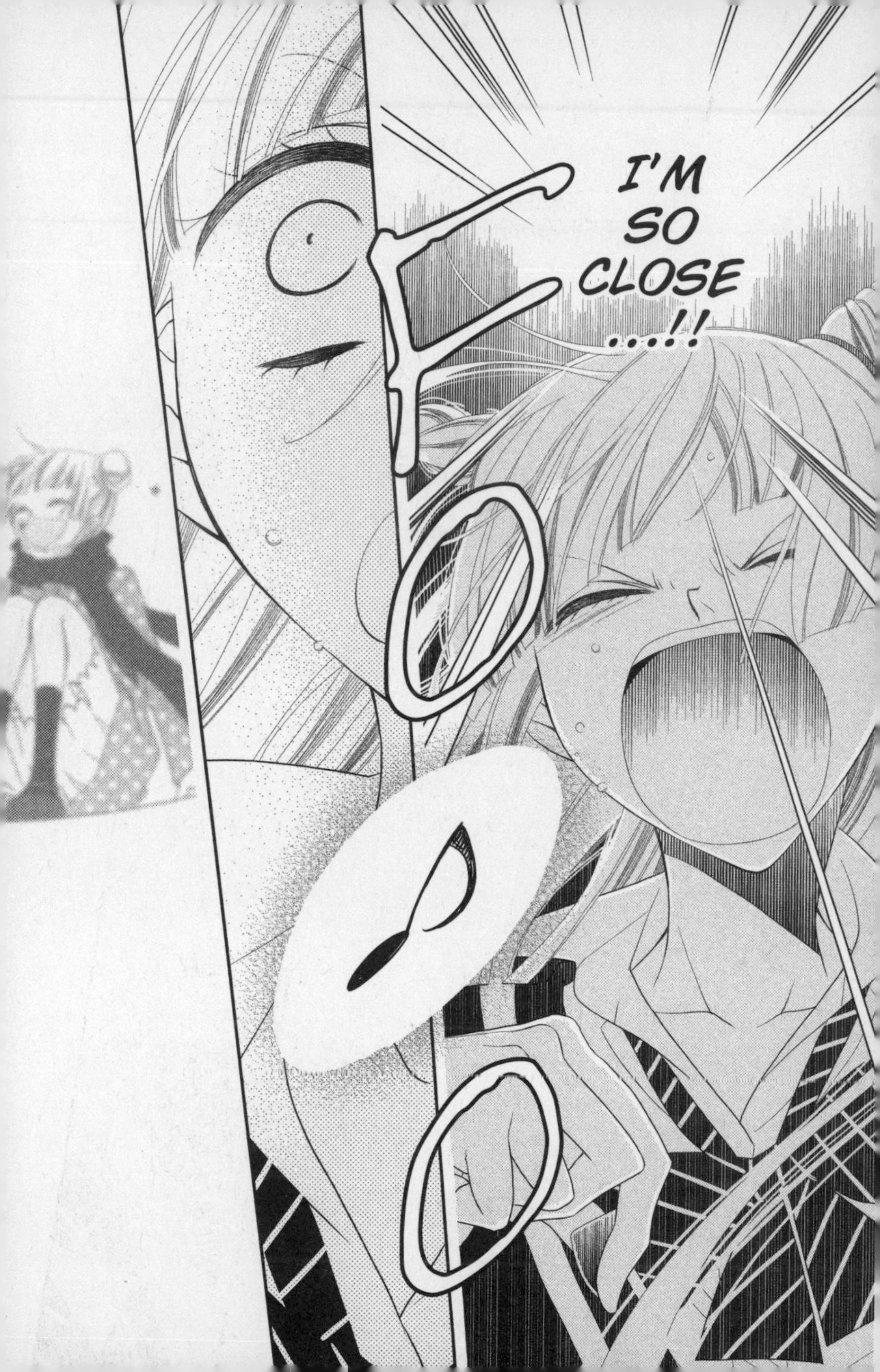
I'M SO CLOSE ...!!

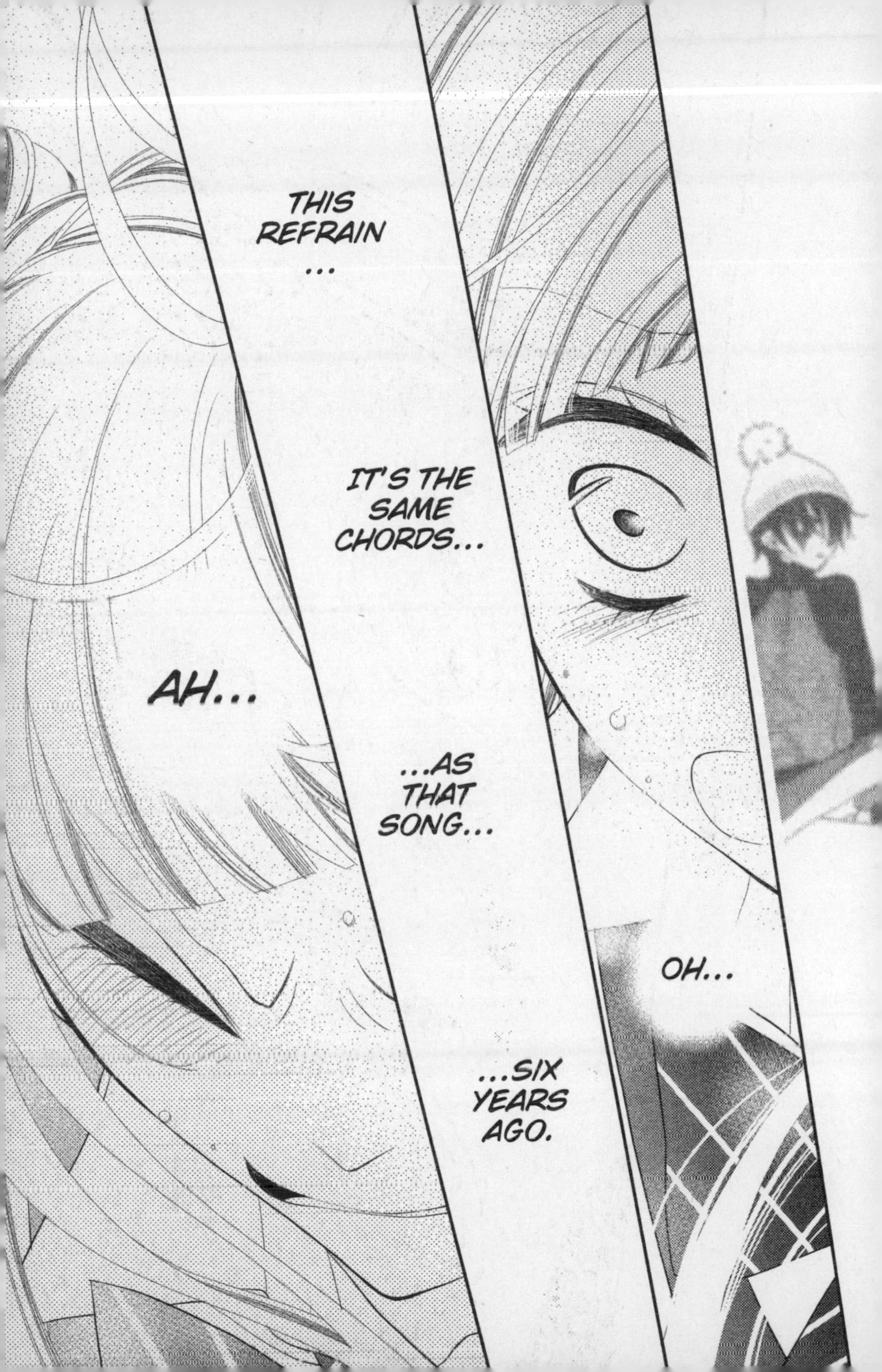
OH...
THIS REFRAIN ...
IT'S THE SAME CHORDS...
...AS THAT SONG...
...SIX YEARS AGO.
AH...

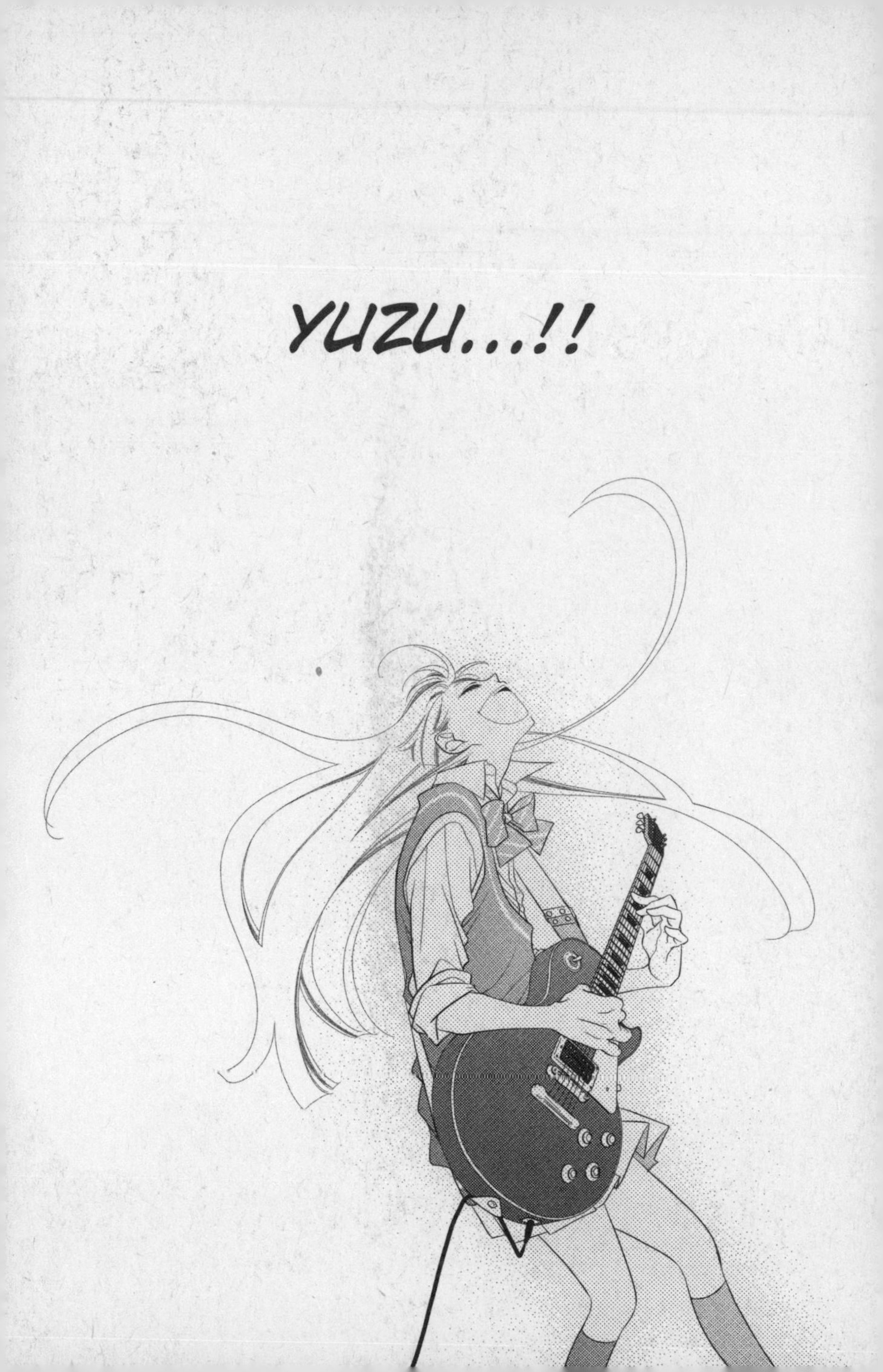
YUZU...!!

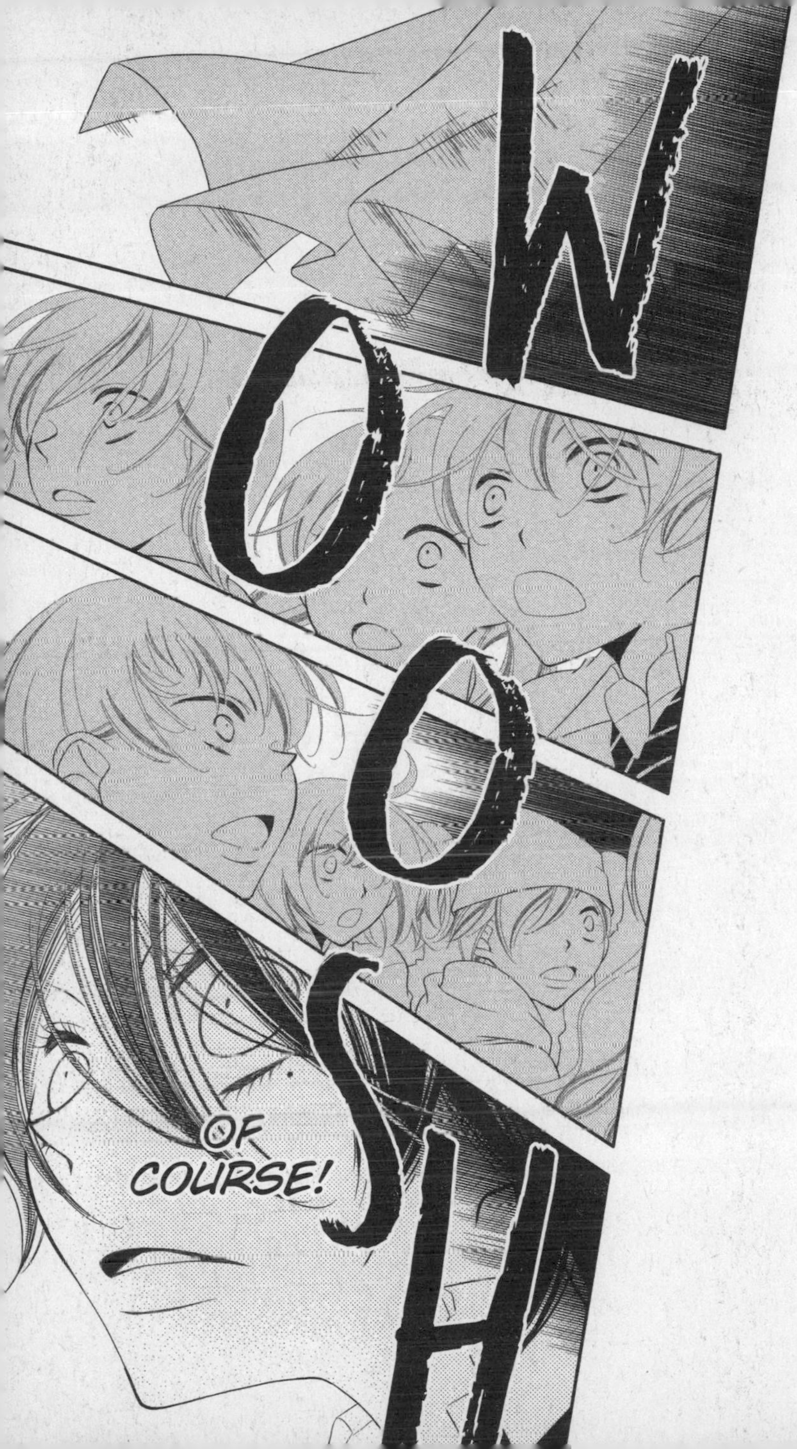
WOOSH
OF COURSE!

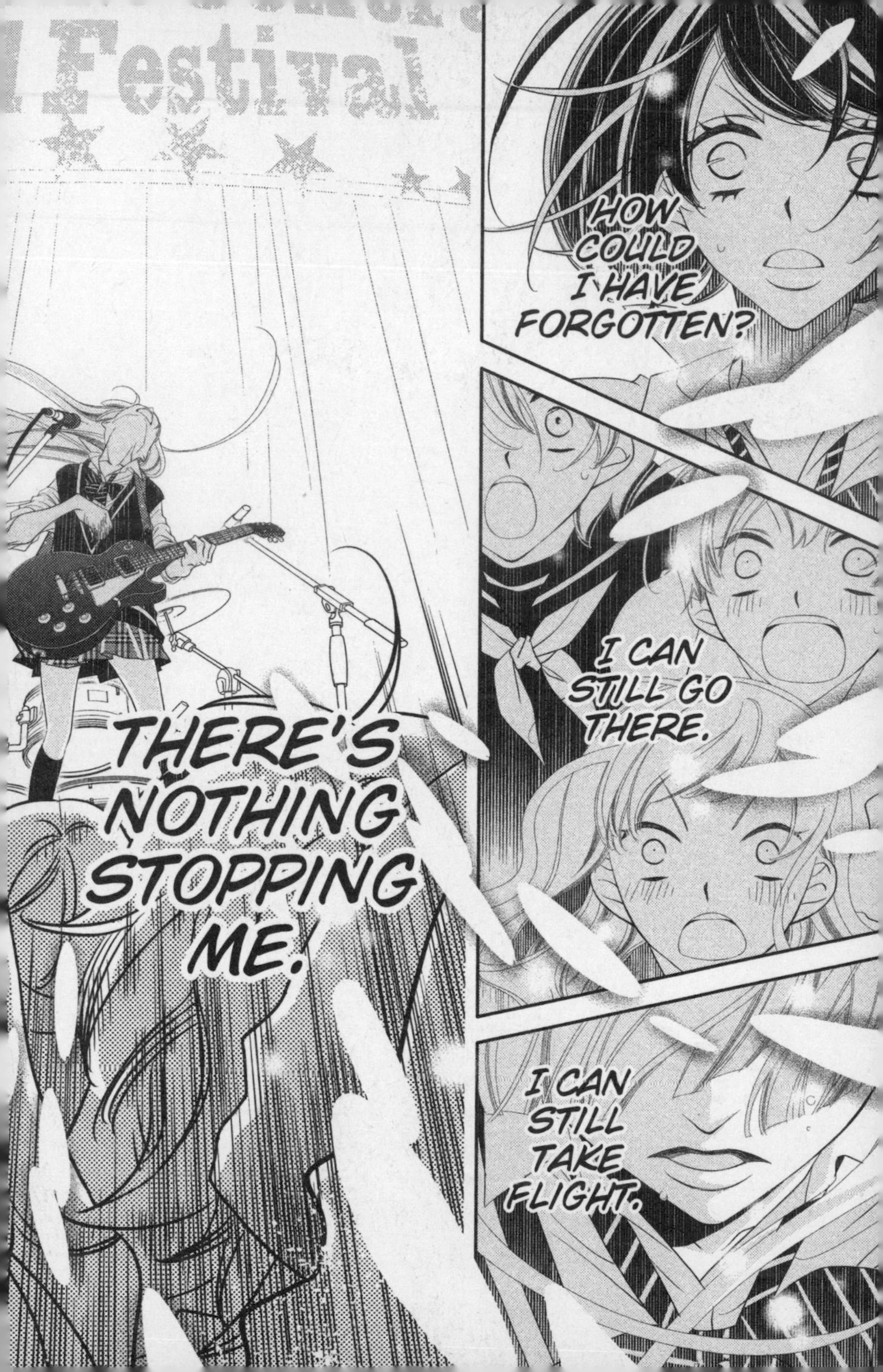
HOW COULD I HAVE FORGOTTEN?
I CAN STILL GO THERE.
I CAN STILL TAKE FLIGHT.
Festival
THERE'S NOTHING STOPPING ME.

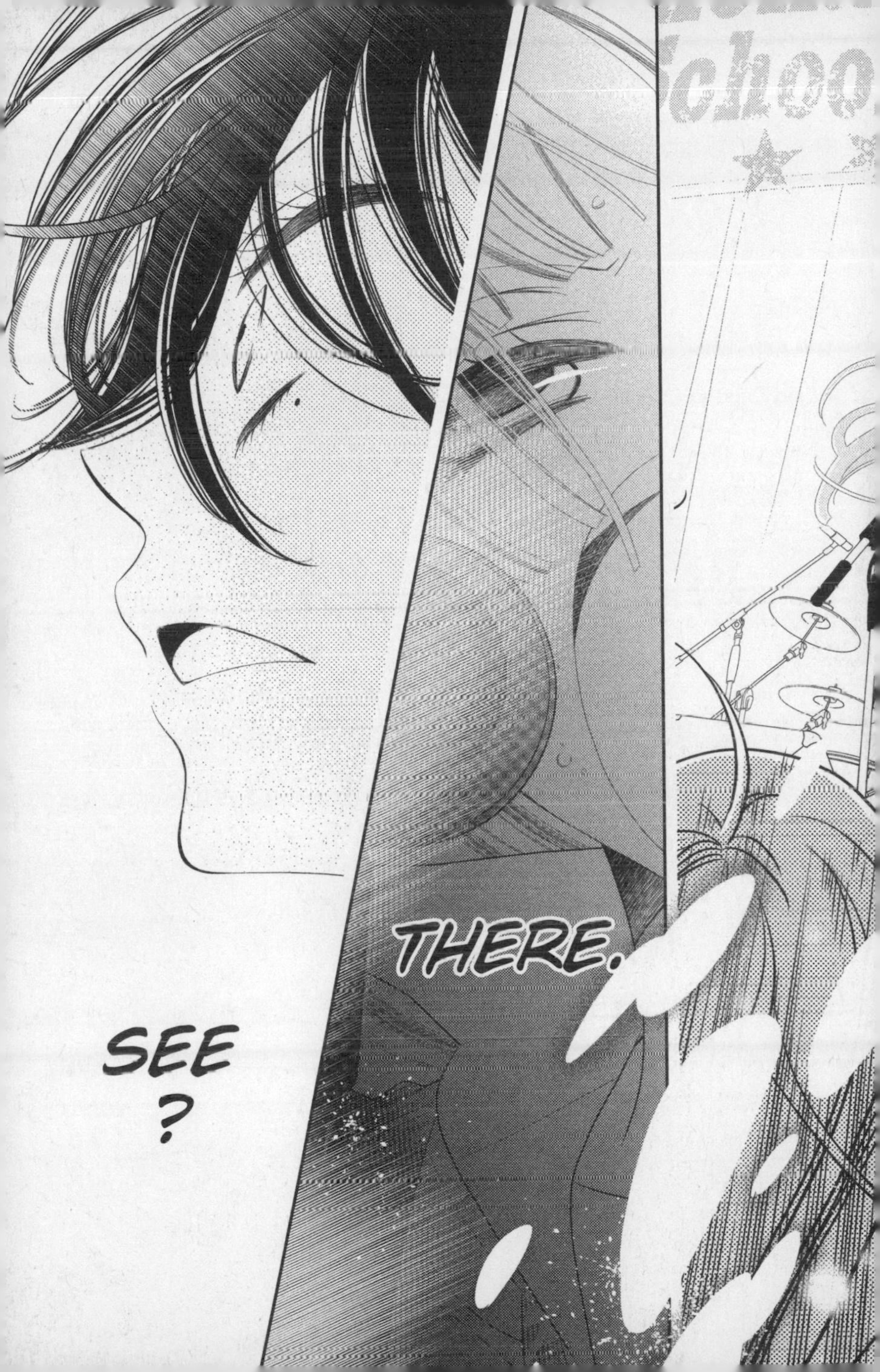
THERE.
SEE ?

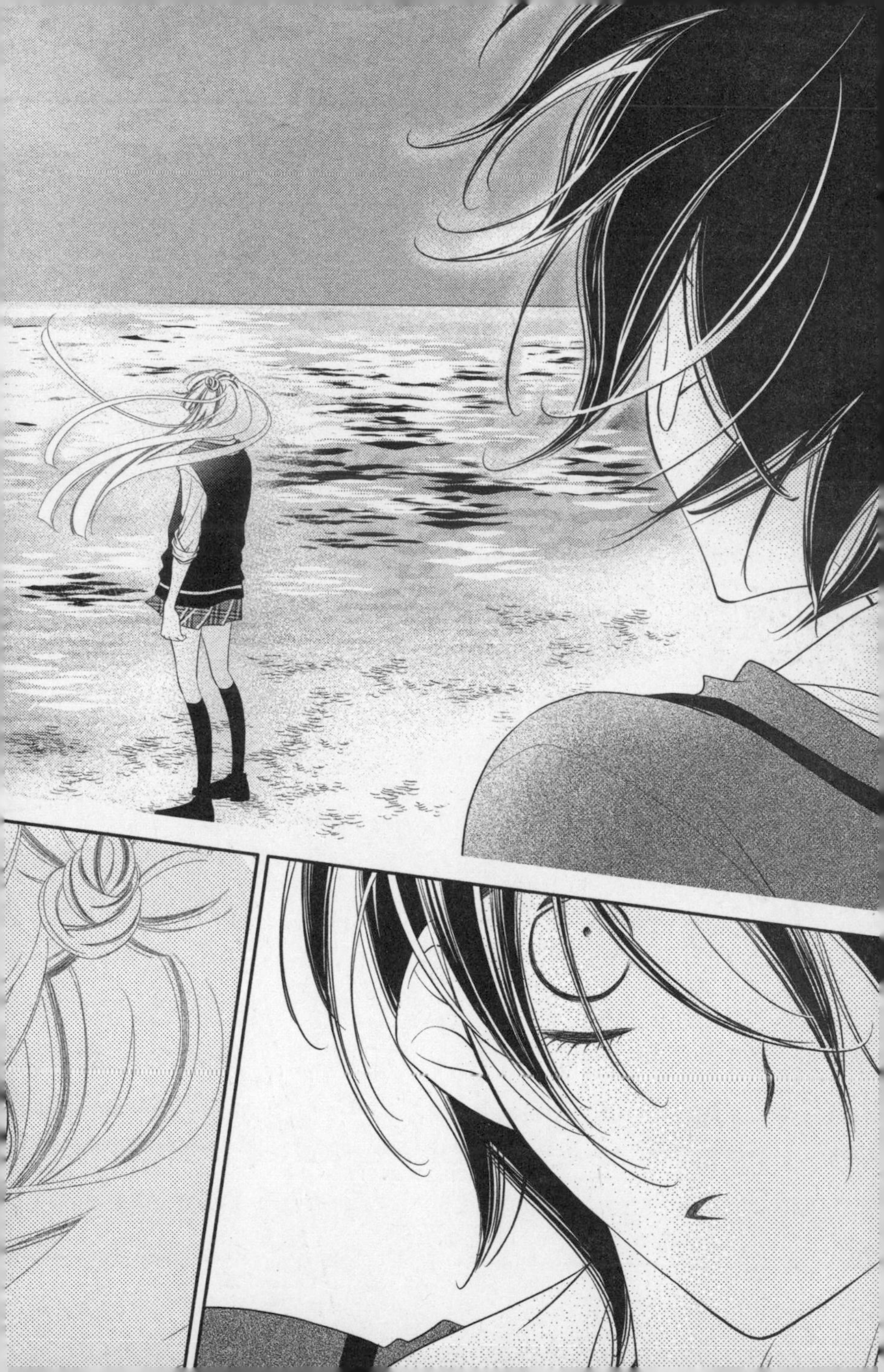

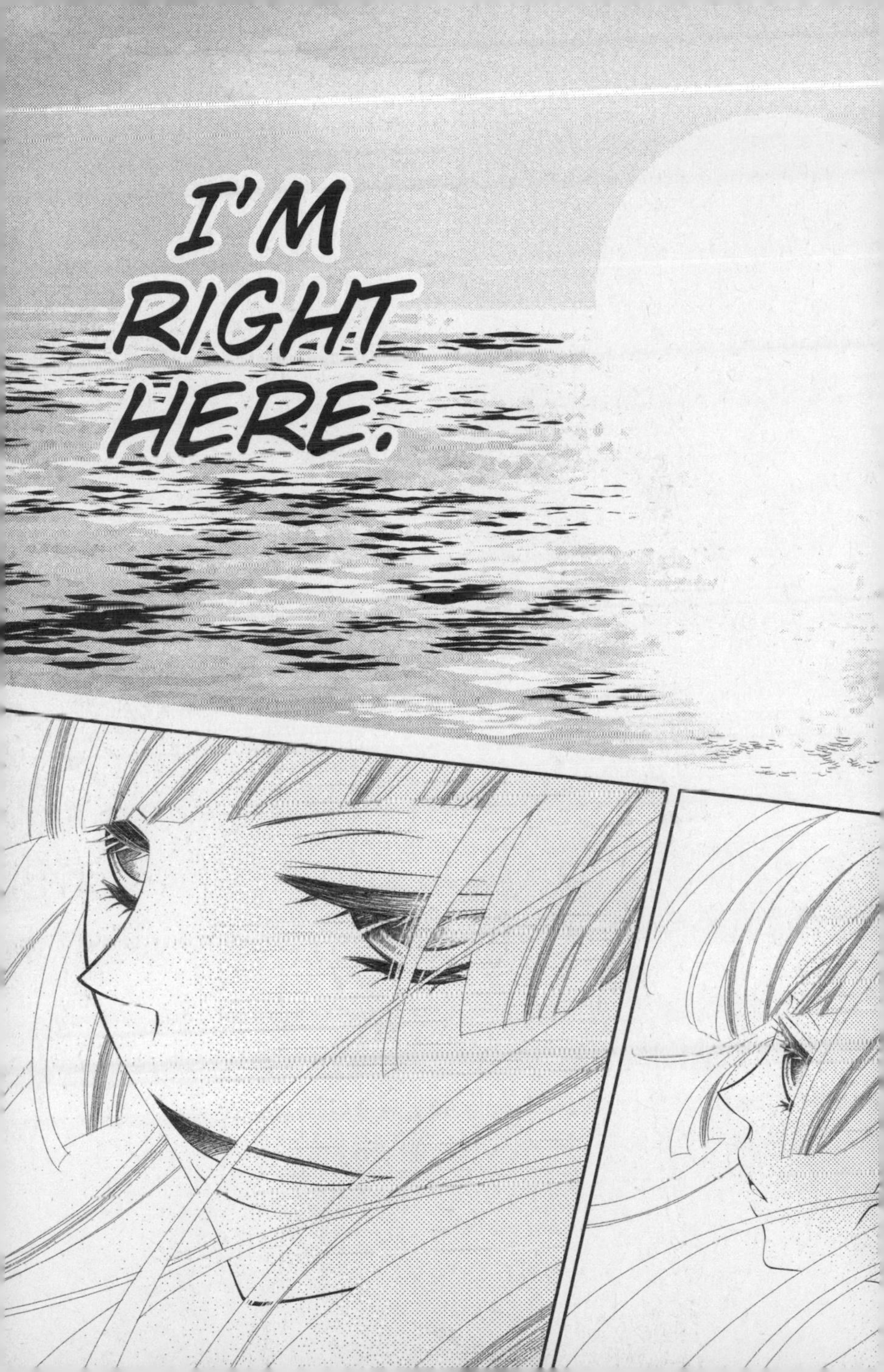
I'M RIGHT HERE.

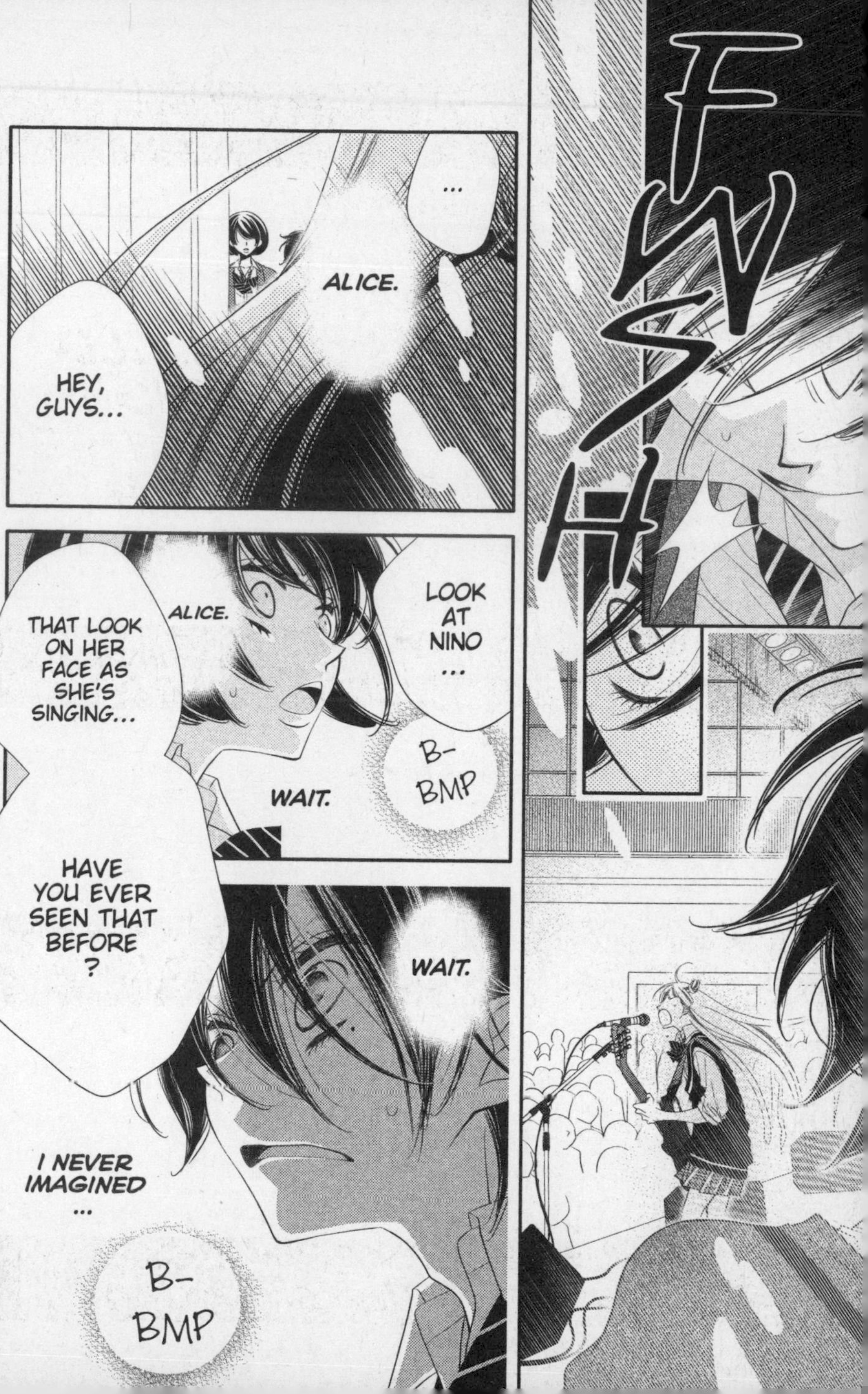
FWSH
...
ALICE.
HEY, GUYS...
LOOK AT NINO...
ALICE.
THAT LOOK ON HER FACE AS SHE'S SINGING...
B-BMP
WAIT.
WAIT.
HAVE YOU EVER SEEN THAT BEFORE?
I NEVER IMAGINED...
B-BMP

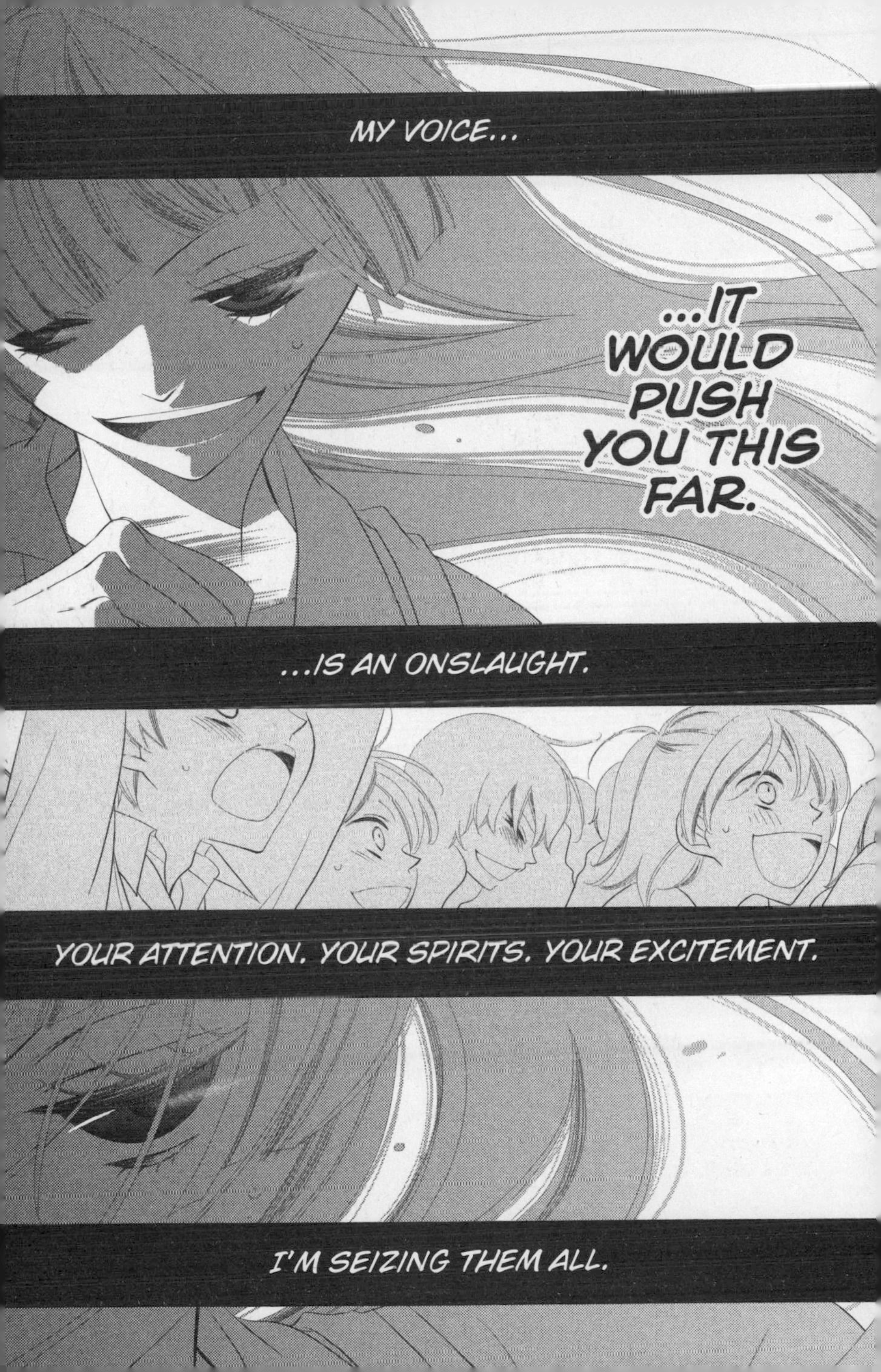
MY VOICE...
...IT WOULD PUSH YOU THIS FAR.
...IS AN ONSLAUGHT.
YOUR ATTENTION. YOUR SPIRITS. YOUR EXCITEMENT.
I'M SEIZING THEM ALL.

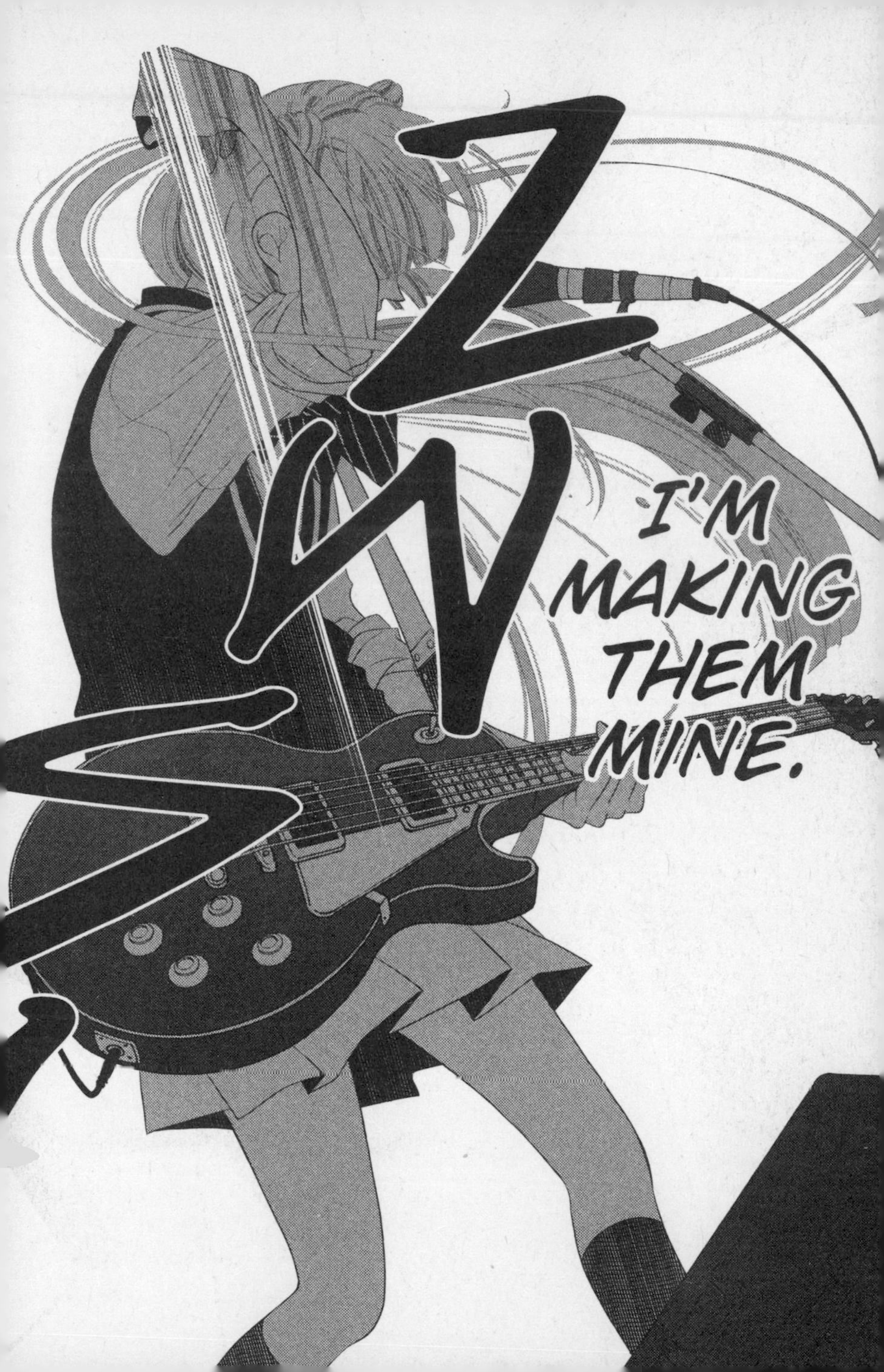
I'M MAKING THEM MINE.

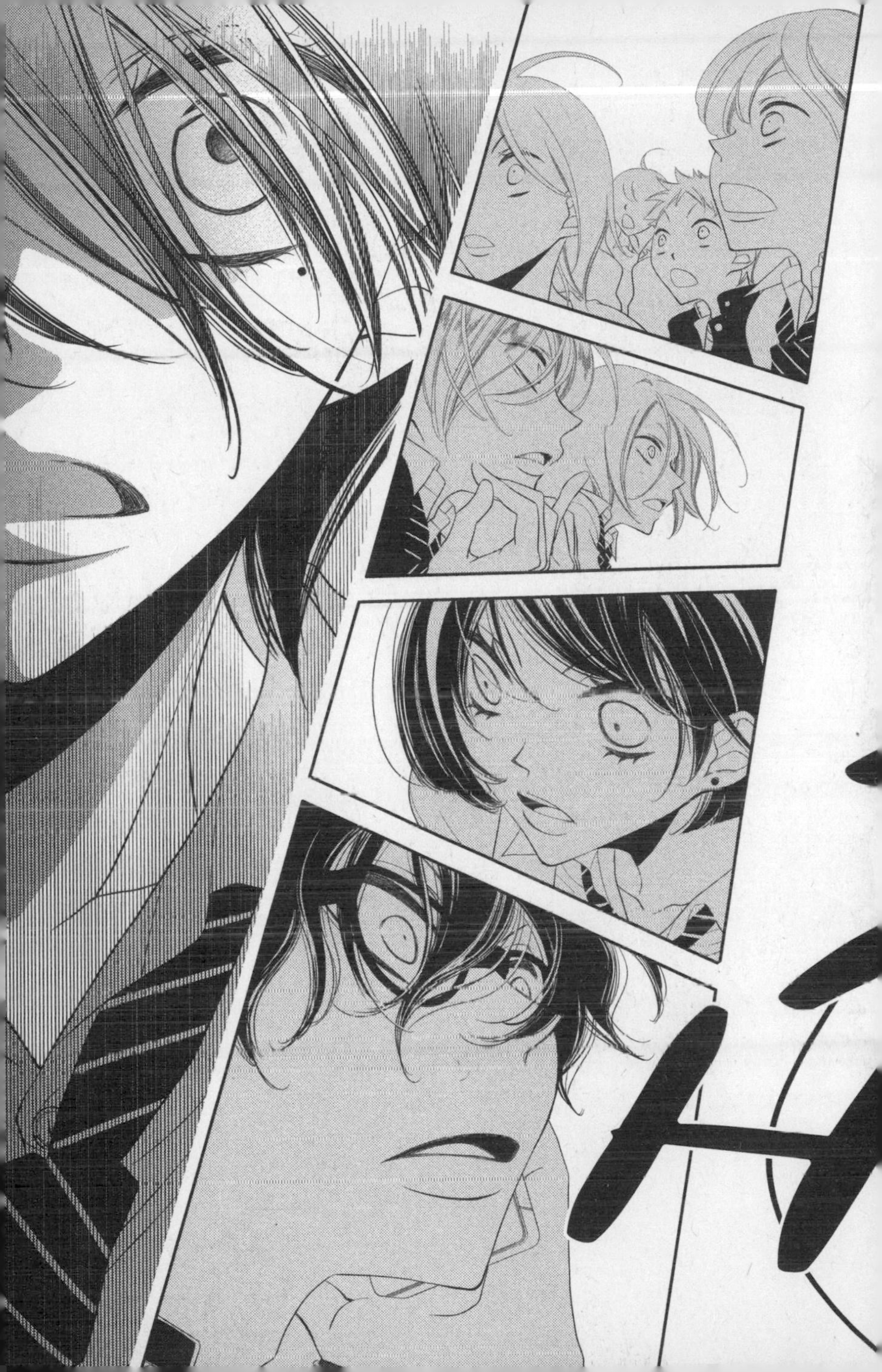

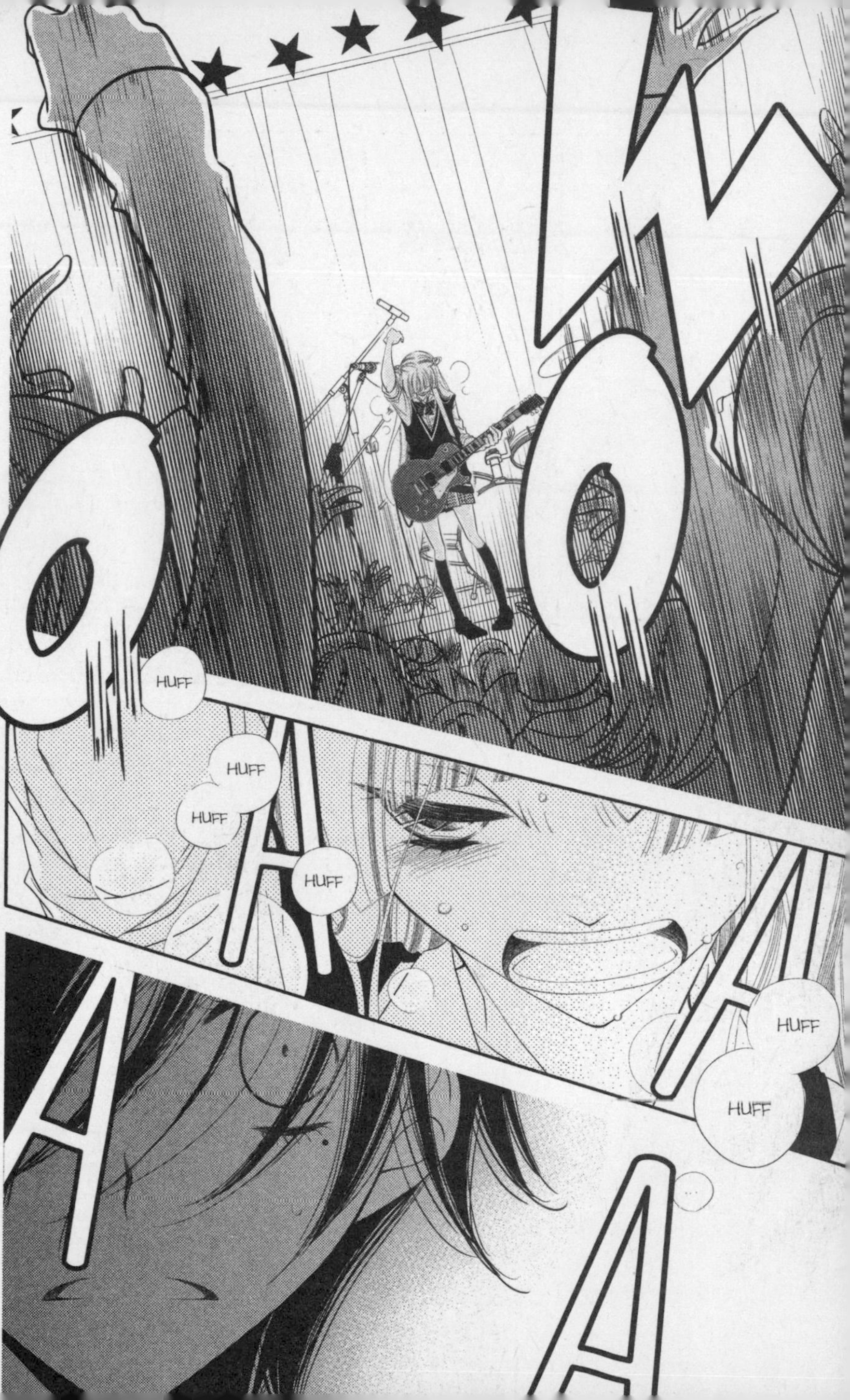
HUFF
HUFF
HUFF
HUFF
HUFF
HUFF
...

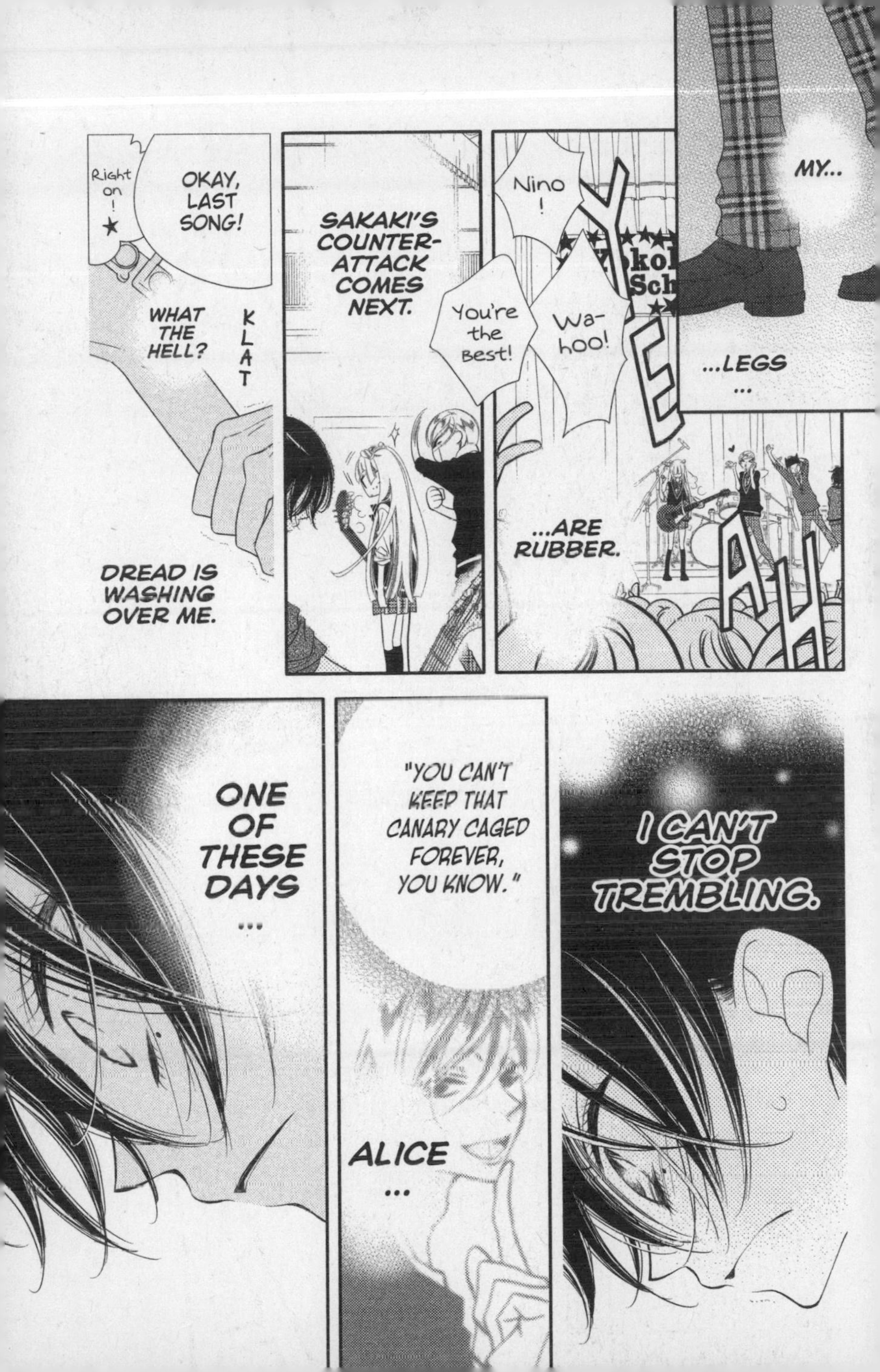
MY...
...LEGS ...
Nino!
Wa-hoo!
You're the Best!
...ARE RUBBER.
SAKAKI'S COUNTER-ATTACK COMES NEXT.
OKAY, LAST SONG!
Right on! ★
WHAT THE HELL?
KLAT
DREAD IS WASHING OVER ME.
I CAN'T STOP TREMBLING.
"YOU CAN'T KEEP THAT CANARY CAGED FOREVER, YOU KNOW."
ALICE ...
ONE OF THESE DAYS ...

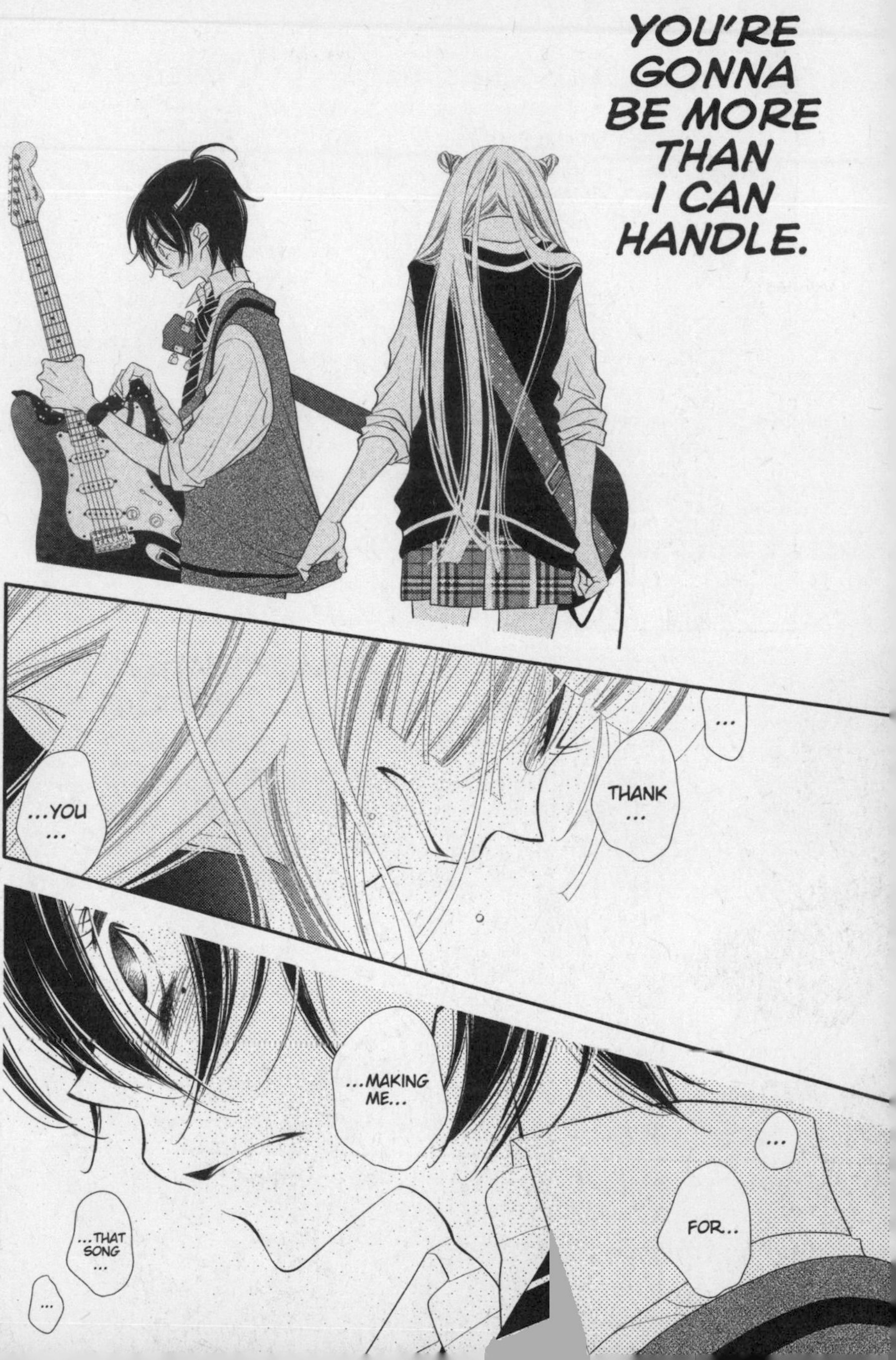
YOU'RE GONNA BE MORE THAN I CAN HANDLE.
...
THANK ...
...YOU ...
...
FOR...
...MAKING ME...
...THAT SONG ...
...

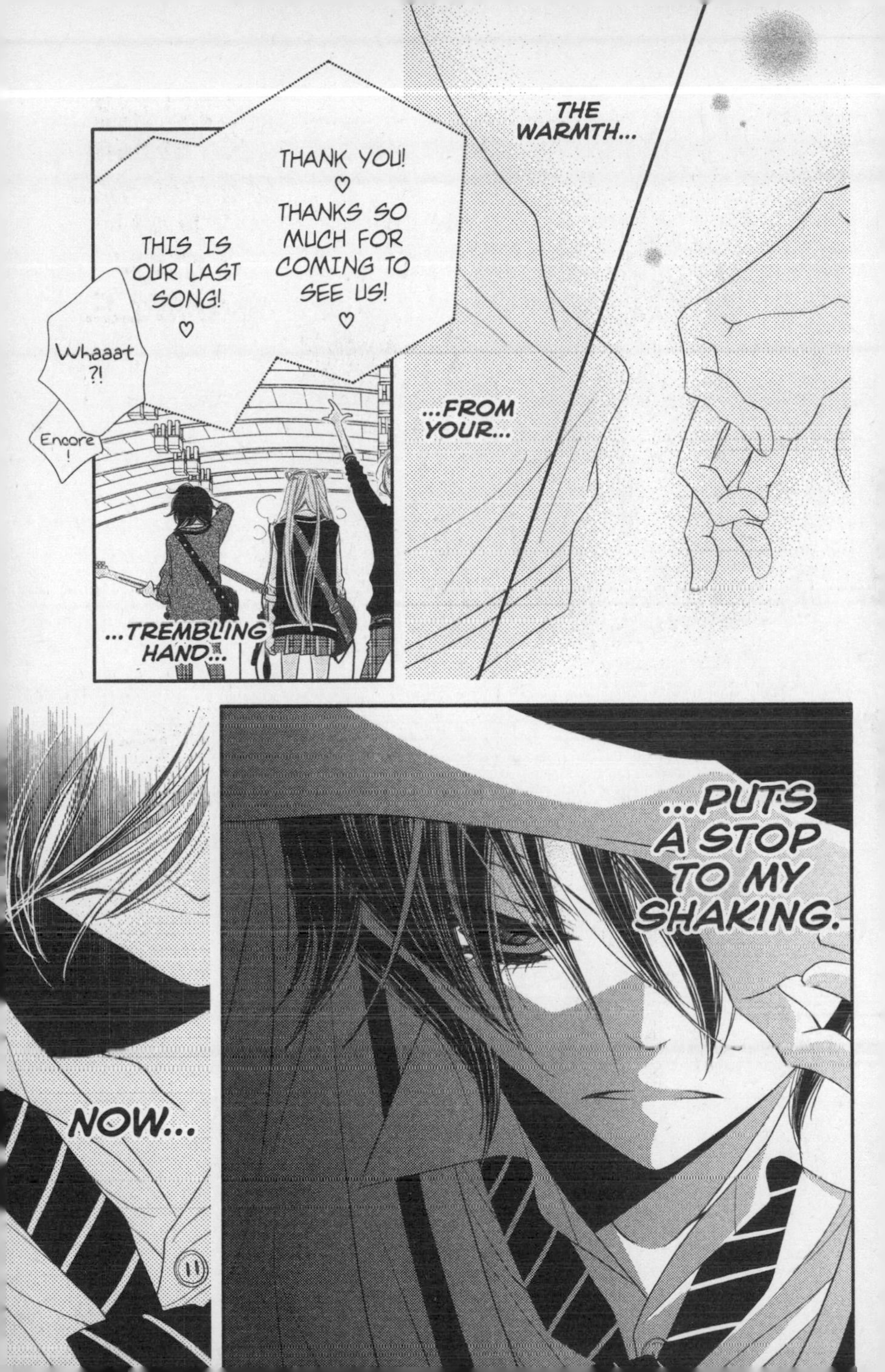
THE WARMTH...
...FROM YOUR...
THANK YOU! ♡ THANKS SO MUCH FOR COMING TO SEE US! ♡
THIS IS OUR LAST SONG! ♡
Whaaat ?!
Encore !
...TREMBLING HAND...
...PUTS A STOP TO MY SHAKING.
NOW...

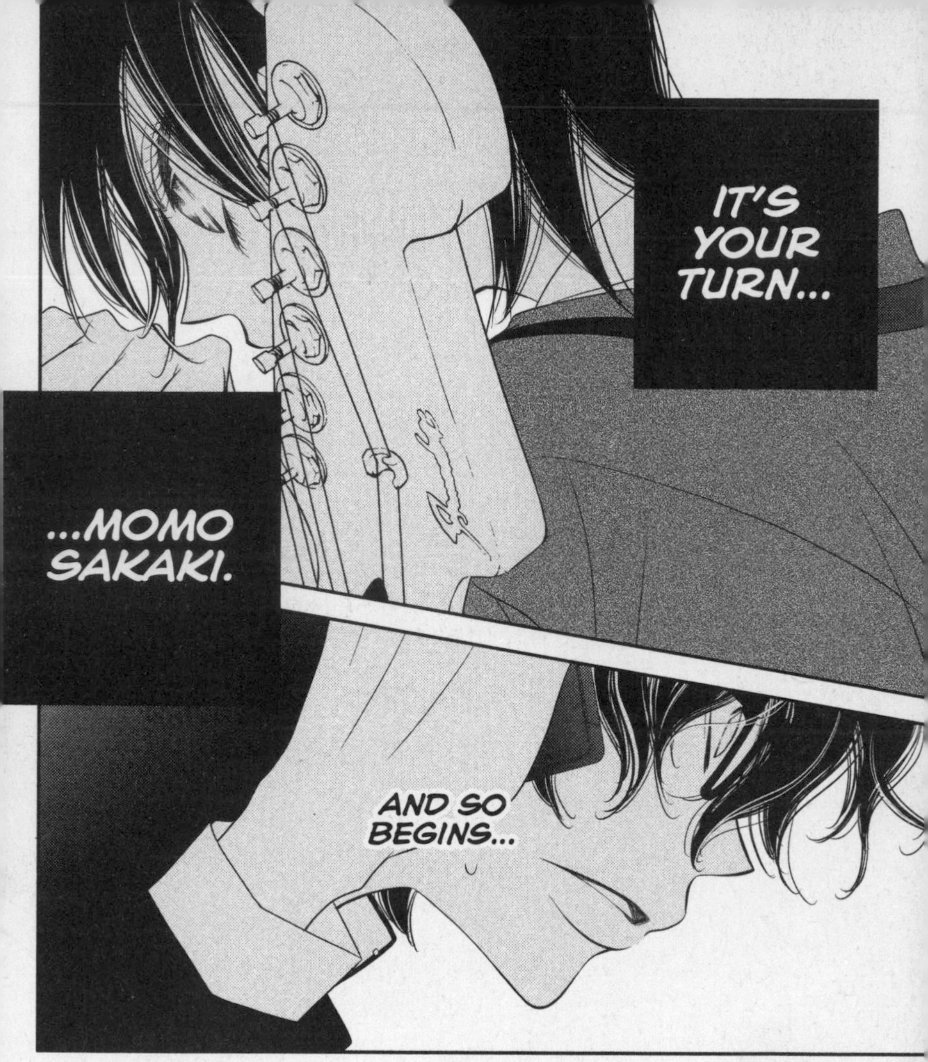
IT'S YOUR TURN...
...MOMO SAKAKI.
AND SO BEGINS...

...OUR THREE MINUTES OF DESTINY.

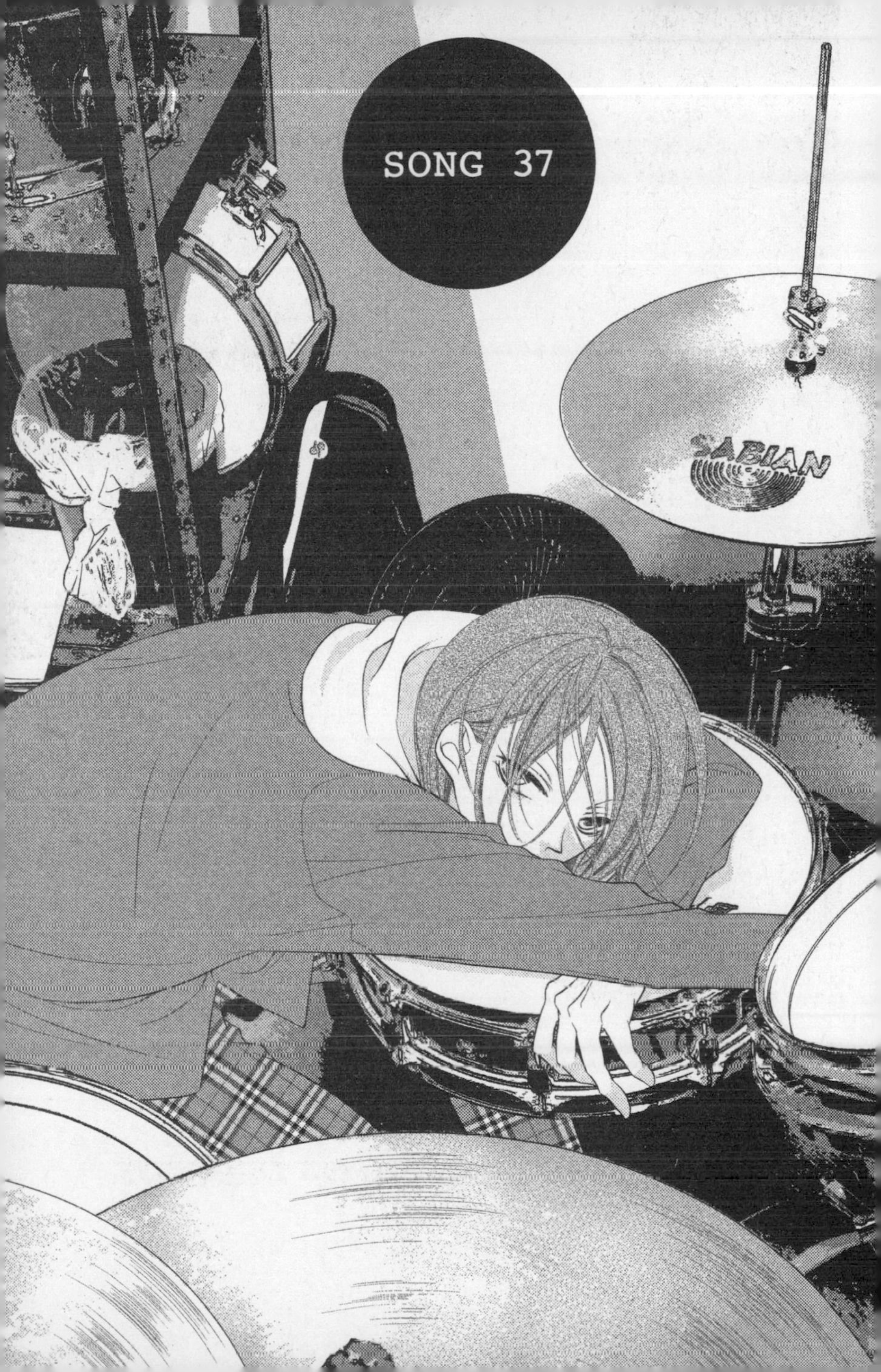
SONG 37
SABIAN

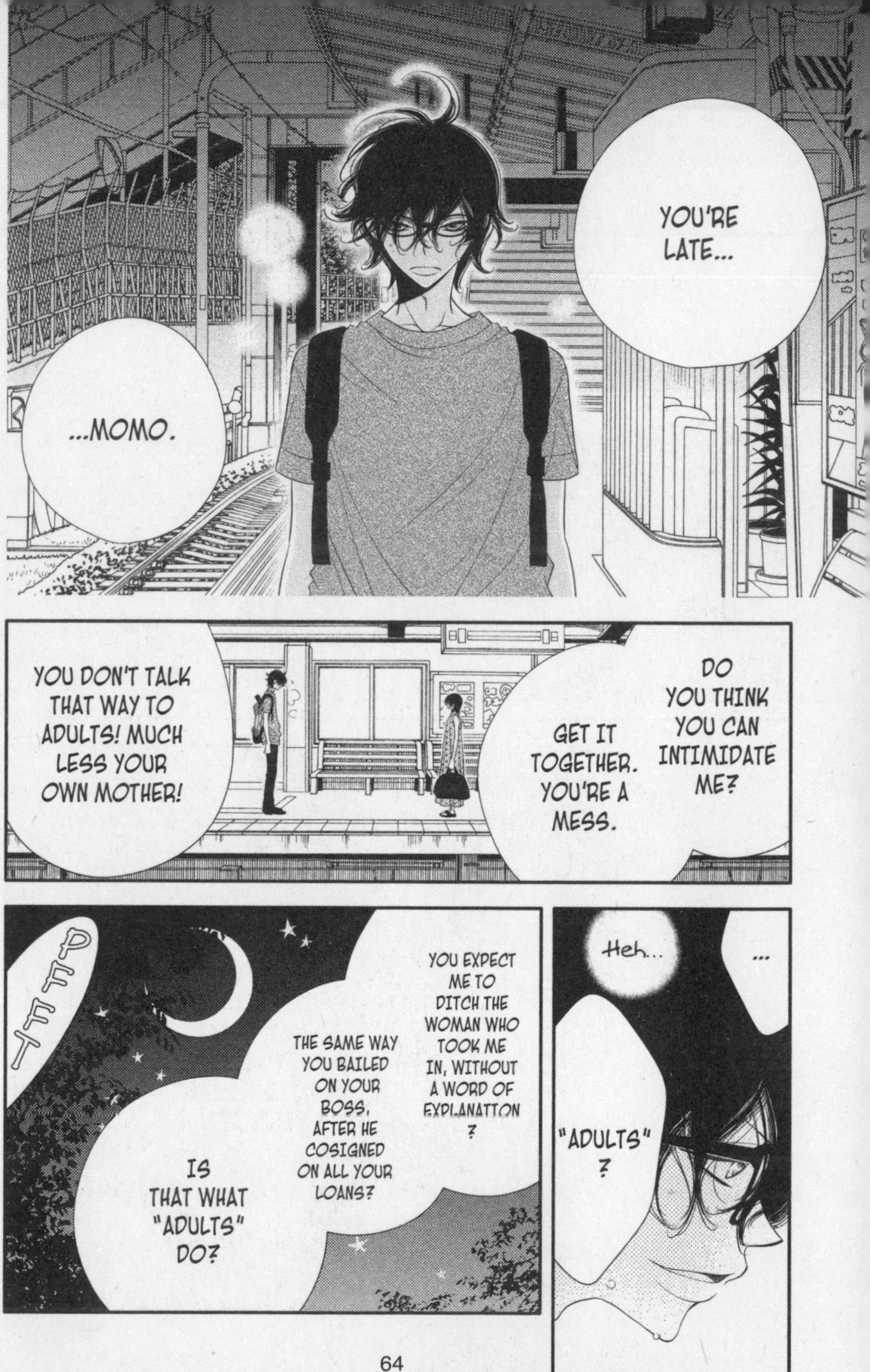
YOU'RE LATE...
...MOMO.
DO YOU THINK YOU CAN INTIMIDATE ME?
GET IT TOGETHER. YOU'RE A MESS.
YOU DON'T TALK THAT WAY TO ADULTS! MUCH LESS YOUR OWN MOTHER!
...
Heh...
"ADULTS"?
PFFFT
YOU EXPECT ME TO DITCH THE WOMAN WHO TOOK ME IN, WITHOUT A WORD OF EXPLANATION?
THE SAME WAY YOU BAILED ON YOUR BOSS, AFTER HE COSIGNED ON ALL YOUR LOANS?
IS THAT WHAT "ADULTS" DO?

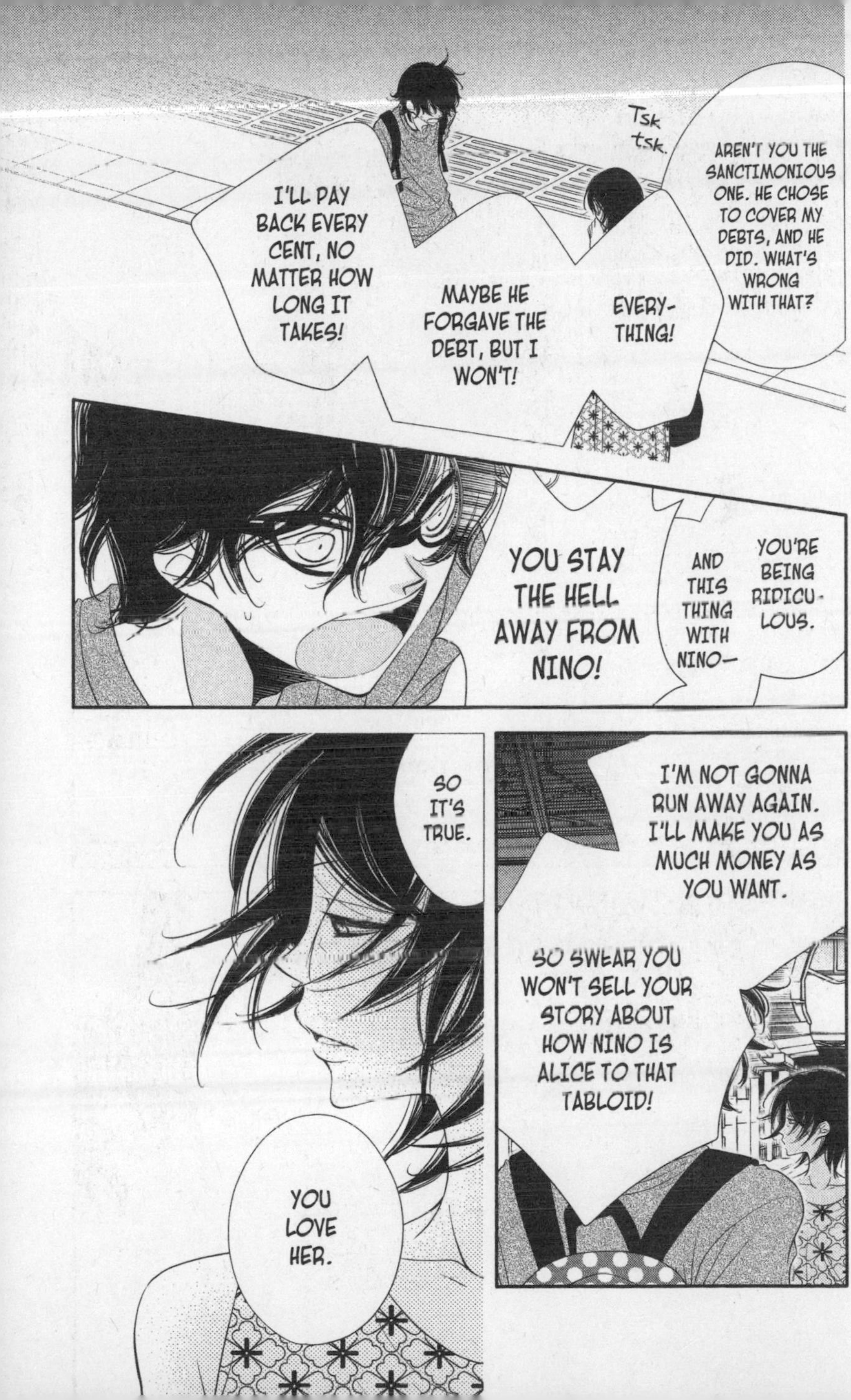

AREN'T YOU THE SANCTIMONIOUS ONE. HE CHOSE TO COVER MY DEBTS, AND HE DID. WHAT'S WRONG WITH THAT?
Tsk tsk.
EVERYTHING!
MAYBE HE FORGAVE THE DEBT, BUT I WON'T!
I'LL PAY BACK EVERY CENT, NO MATTER HOW LONG IT TAKES!
YOU'RE BEING RIDICULOUS.
AND THIS THING WITH NINO—
YOU STAY THE HELL AWAY FROM NINO!
I'M NOT GONNA RUN AWAY AGAIN. I'LL MAKE YOU AS MUCH MONEY AS YOU WANT.
SO SWEAR YOU WON'T SELL YOUR STORY ABOUT HOW NINO IS ALICE TO THAT TABLOID!
SO IT'S TRUE.
YOU LOVE HER.

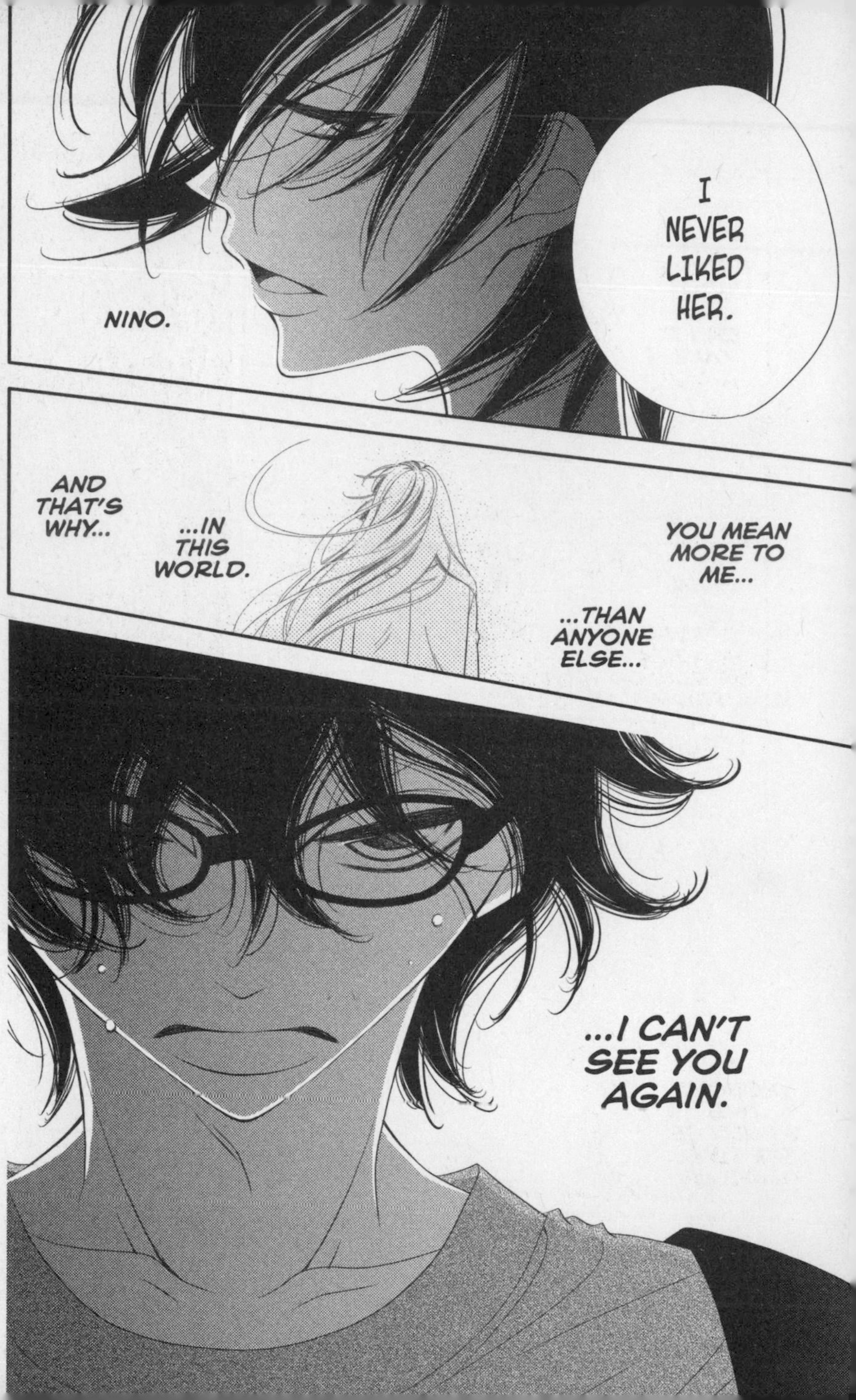
I NEVER LIKED HER.
NINO.
YOU MEAN MORE TO ME...
...THAN ANYONE ELSE...
...IN THIS WORLD.
AND THAT'S WHY...
...I CAN'T SEE YOU AGAIN.

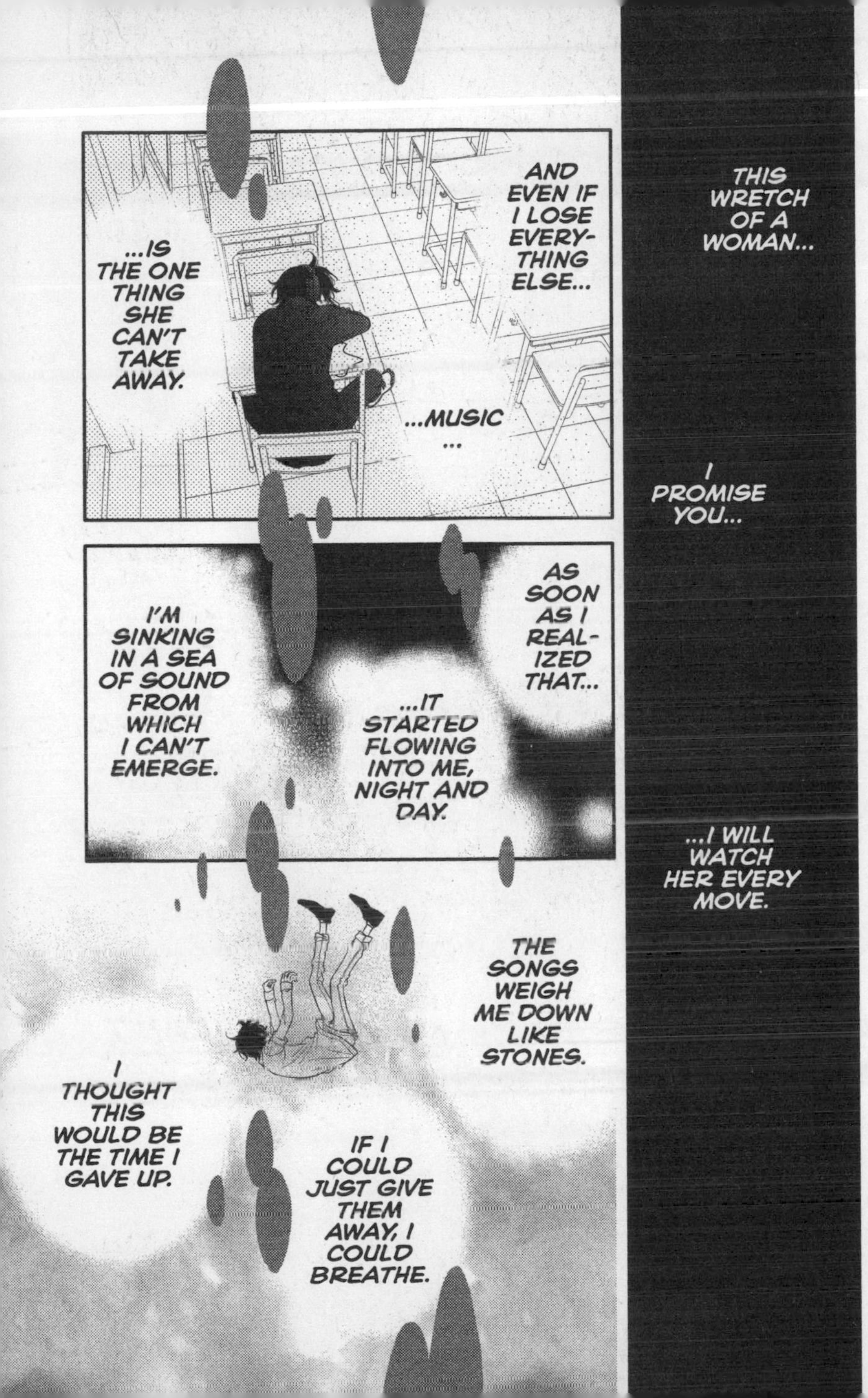
THIS WRETCH OF A WOMAN...
I PROMISE YOU...
...I WILL WATCH HER EVERY MOVE.
AND EVEN IF I LOSE EVERYTHING ELSE...
...MUSIC...
...IS THE ONE THING SHE CAN'T TAKE AWAY.
AS SOON AS I REALIZED THAT...
...IT STARTED FLOWING INTO ME, NIGHT AND DAY.
I'M SINKING IN A SEA OF SOUND FROM WHICH I CAN'T EMERGE.
THE SONGS WEIGH ME DOWN LIKE STONES.
I THOUGHT THIS WOULD BE THE TIME I GAVE UP.
IF I COULD JUST GIVE THEM AWAY, I COULD BREATHE.

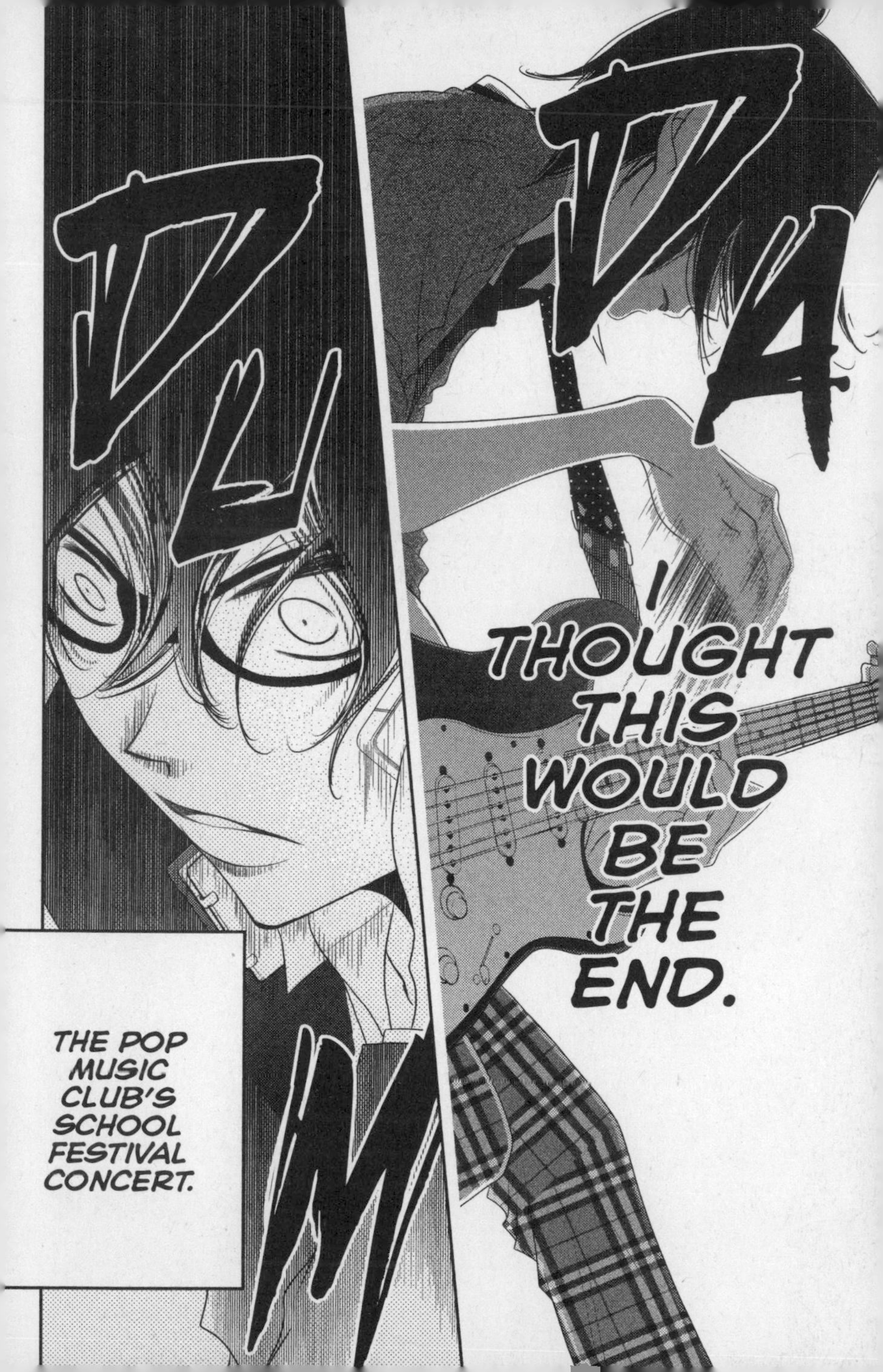
I THOUGHT THIS WOULD BE THE END.
THE POP MUSIC CLUB'S SCHOOL FESTIVAL CONCERT.

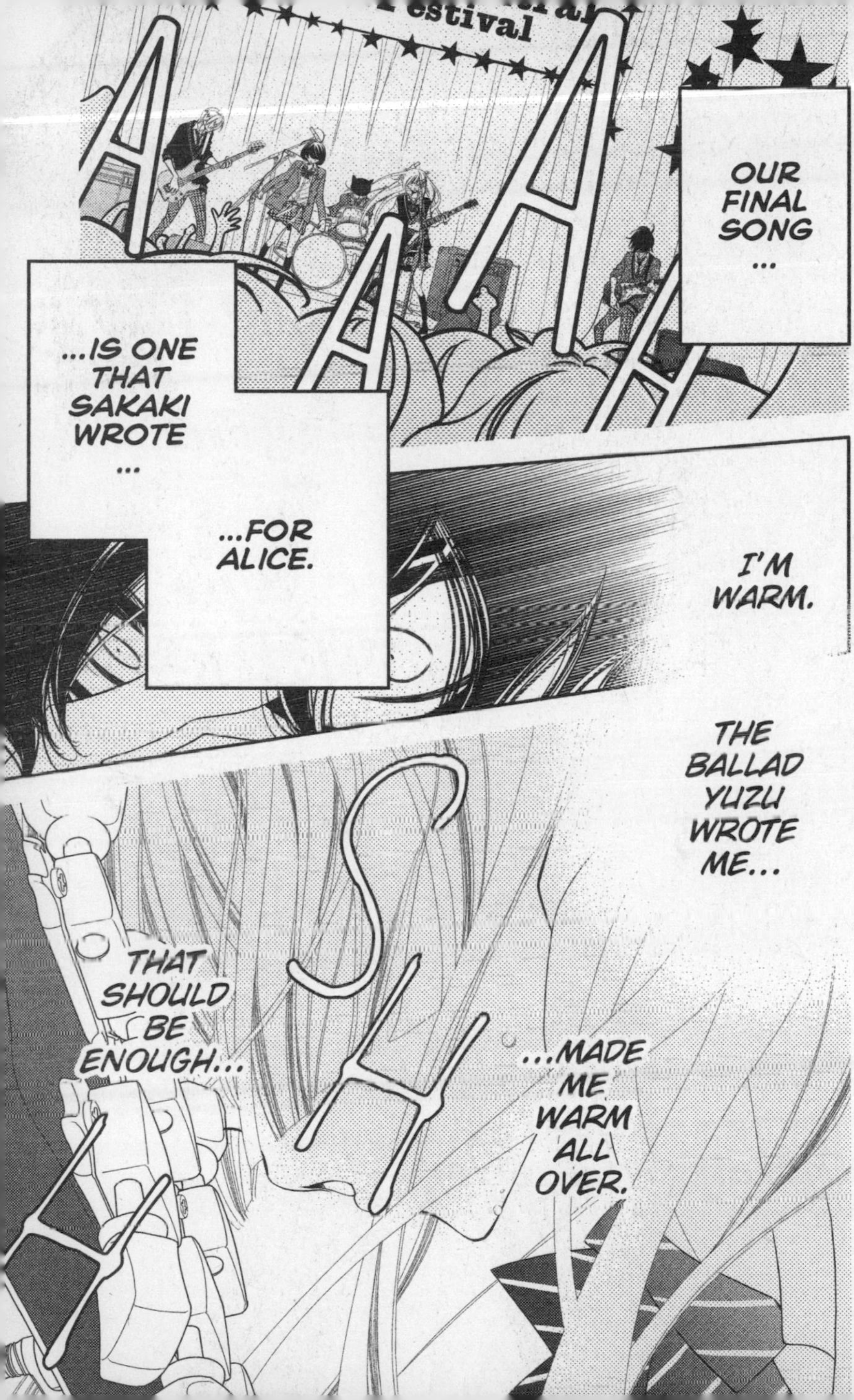
estival
OUR FINAL SONG ...
...IS ONE THAT SAKAKI WROTE ...
...FOR ALICE.
AAAH
I'M WARM.
THE BALLAD YUZU WROTE ME...
...MADE ME WARM ALL OVER.
SH
THAT SHOULD BE ENOUGH...

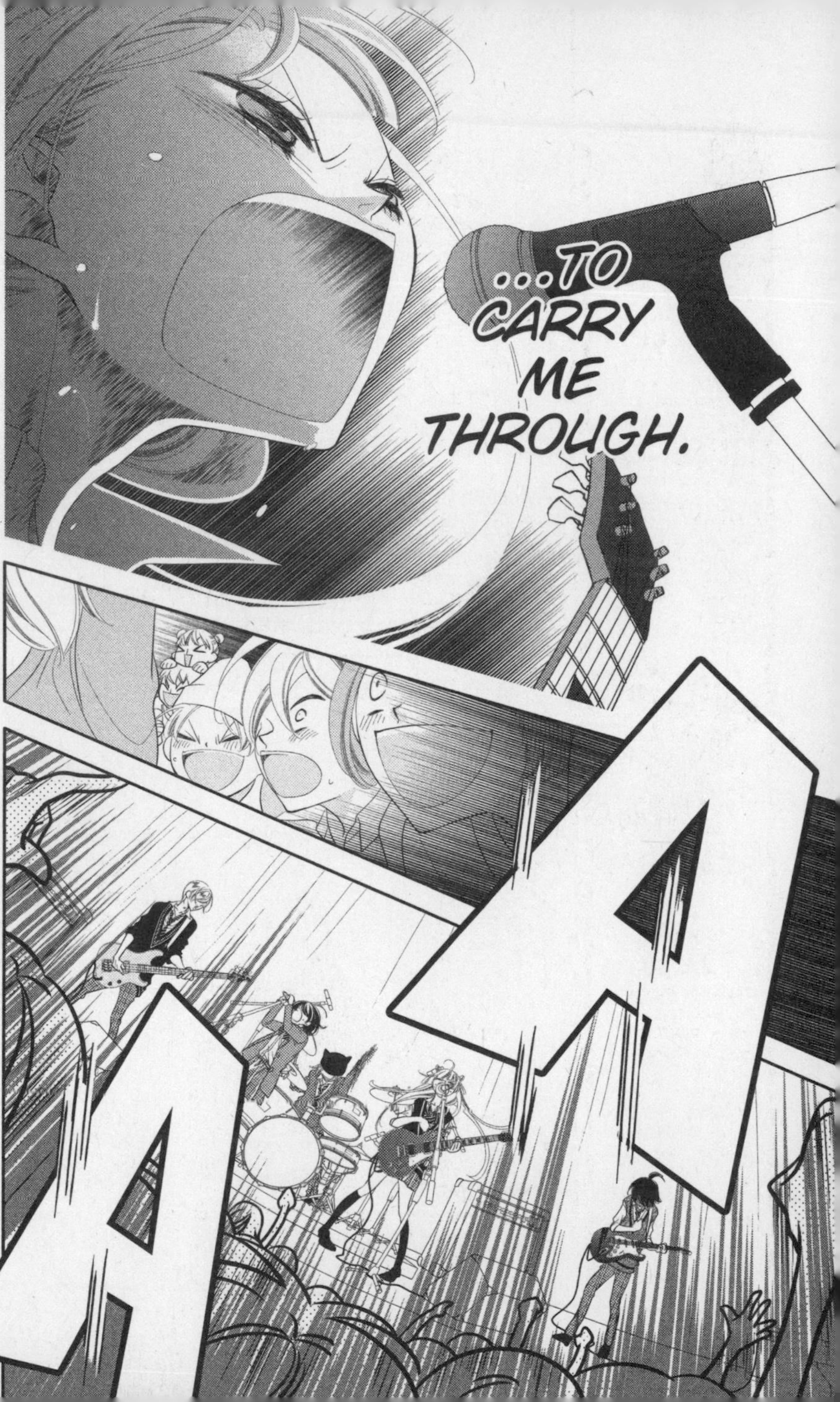
...TO CARRY ME THROUGH.
AAA

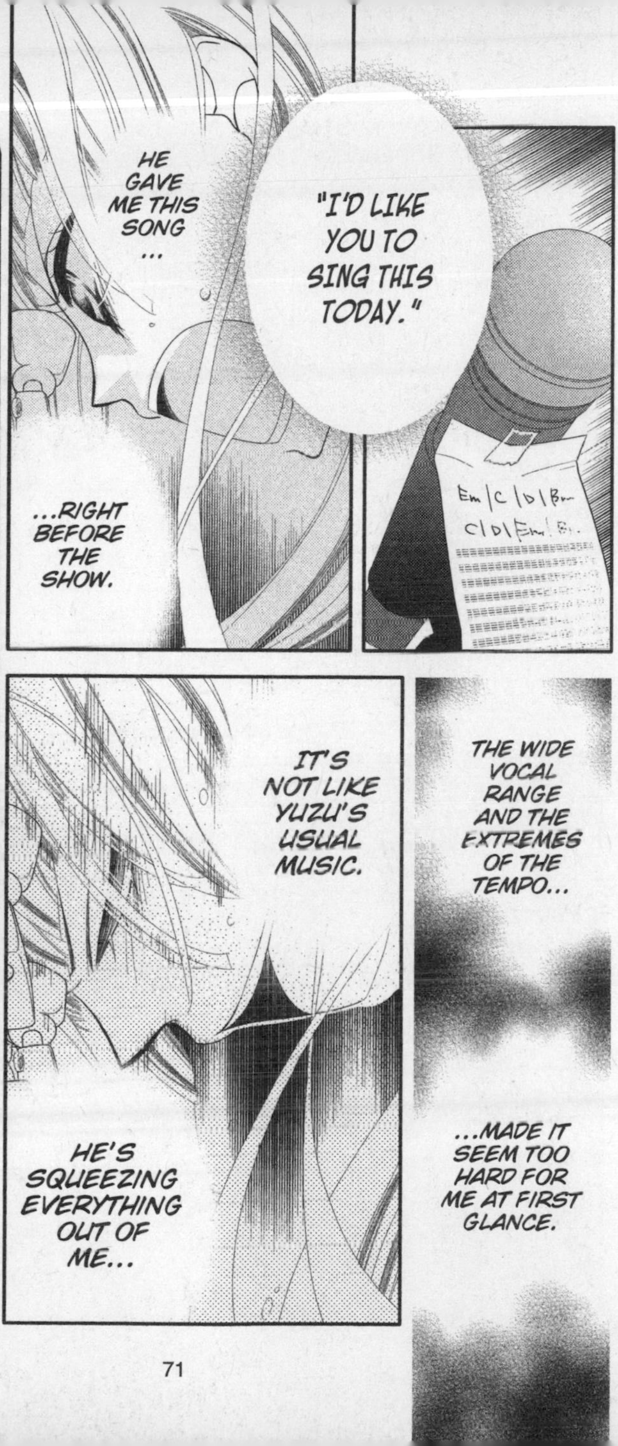
"I'D LIKE YOU TO SING THIS TODAY."
HE GAVE ME THIS SONG ...
...RIGHT BEFORE THE SHOW.
THE WIDE VOCAL RANGE AND THE EXTREMES OF THE TEMPO...
...MADE IT SEEM TOO HARD FOR ME AT FIRST GLANCE.
IT'S NOT LIKE YUZU'S USUAL MUSIC.
HE'S SQUEEZING EVERYTHING OUT OF ME...

3

Yeah, that marker was way too fat. I'll slim it down.

SORRY!

Rock in Japan had the same policy as last year: from the front of the stage, we could only shoot the first two songs. Last year I was too much of a chicken to really get in there and get what I needed, but this year...

...MS. NICE FROG!

NO MORE...

HEEYAH!

...I took 4,000 photographs. I am so very grateful for the opportunity to get so many outdoor photographs of so many different artists! Thank you, Rock in Japan!

GRATE... ...FUL!!

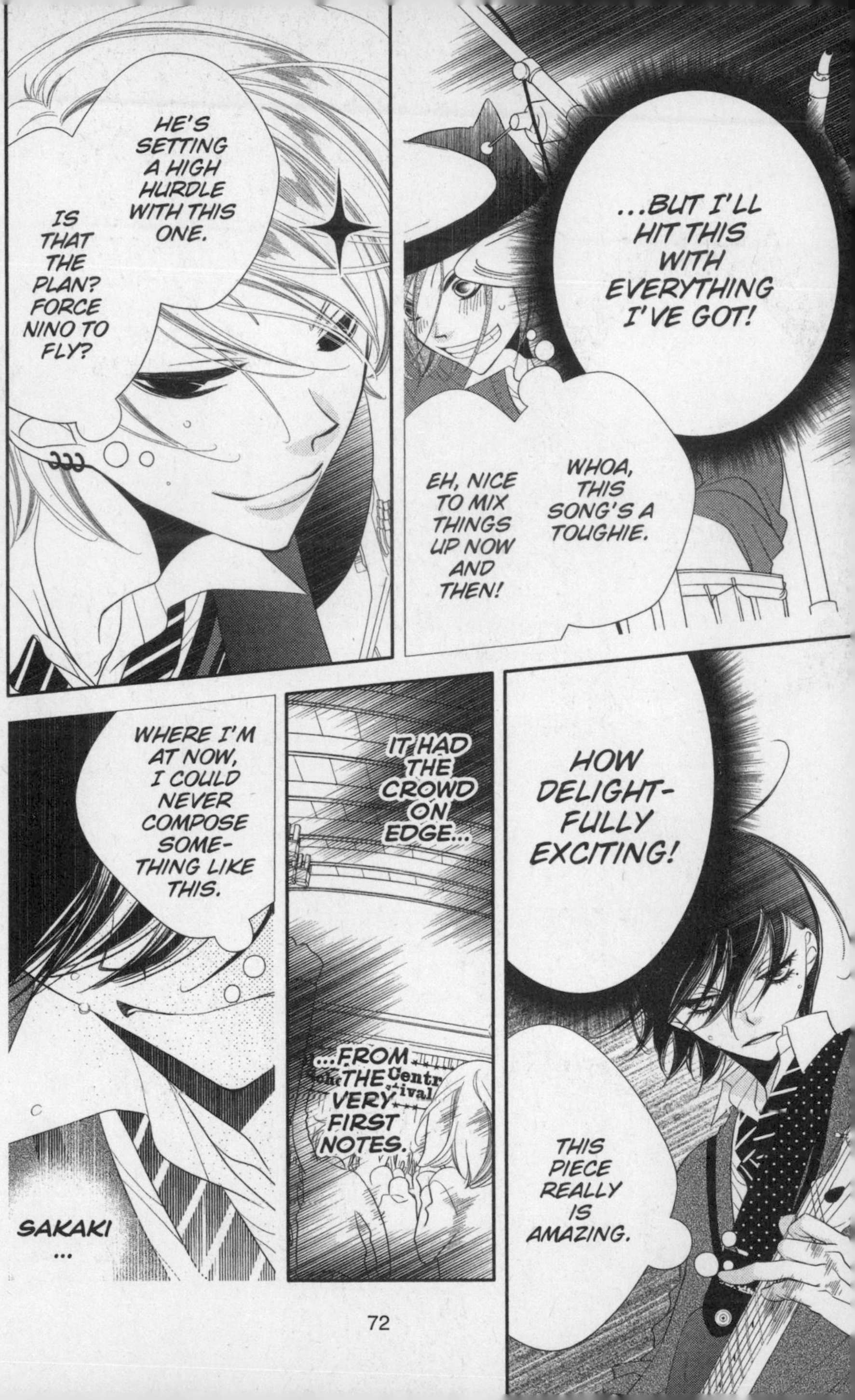
...BUT I'LL HIT THIS WITH EVERYTHING I'VE GOT!
WHOA, THIS SONG'S A TOUGHIE.
EH, NICE TO MIX THINGS UP NOW AND THEN!
HE'S SETTING A HIGH HURDLE WITH THIS ONE.
IS THAT THE PLAN? FORCE NINO TO FLY?
HOW DELIGHTFULLY EXCITING!
THIS PIECE REALLY IS AMAZING.
IT HAD THE CROWD ON EDGE...
...FROM THE VERY FIRST NOTES.
WHERE I'M AT NOW, I COULD NEVER COMPOSE SOMETHING LIKE THIS.
SAKAKI ...

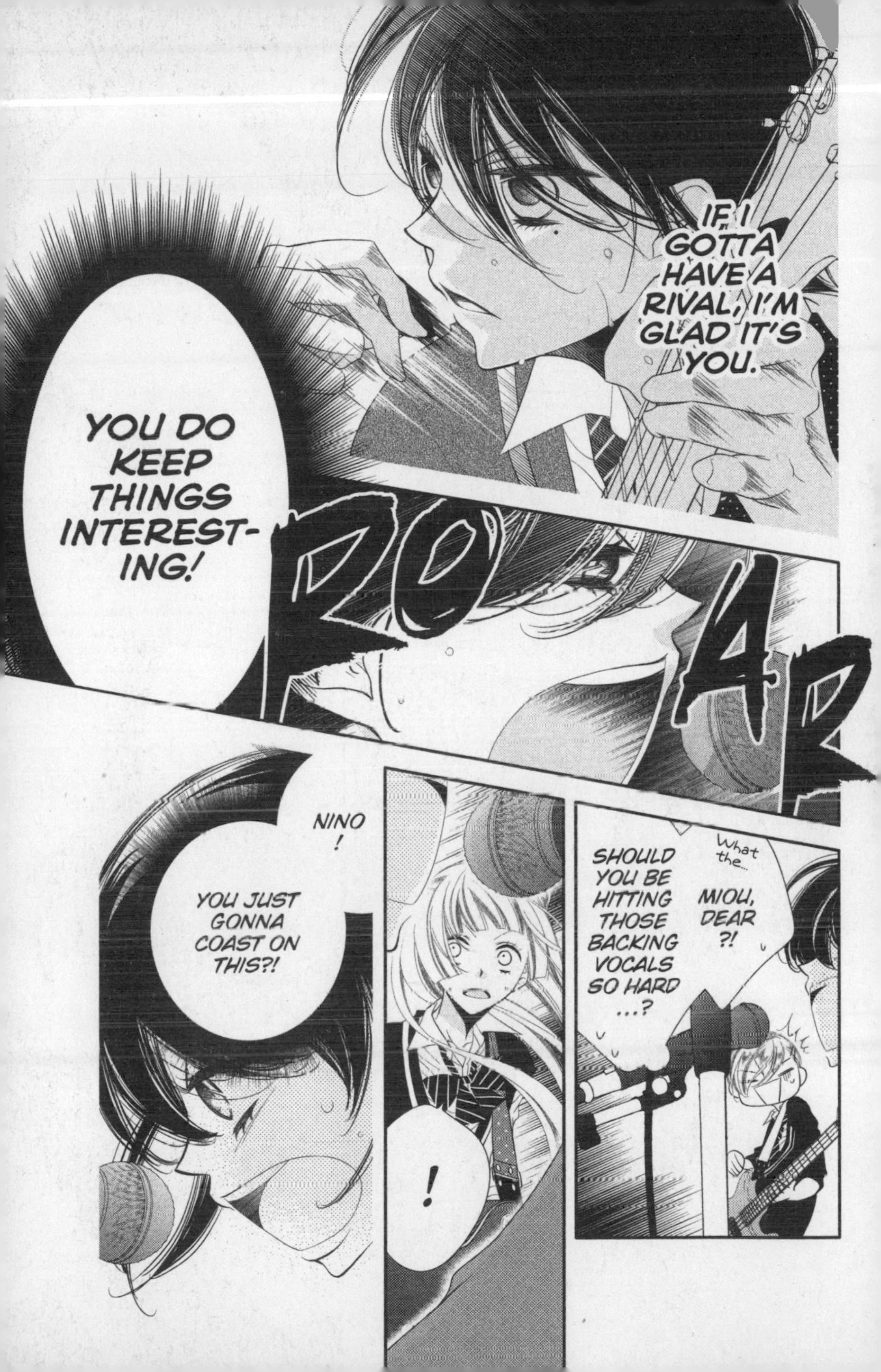
IF I GOTTA HAVE A RIVAL, I'M GLAD IT'S YOU.
YOU DO KEEP THINGS INTERESTING!
What the...
MIOU, DEAR?!
SHOULD YOU BE HITTING THOSE BACKING VOCALS SO HARD...?
!
NINO!
YOU JUST GONNA COAST ON THIS?!

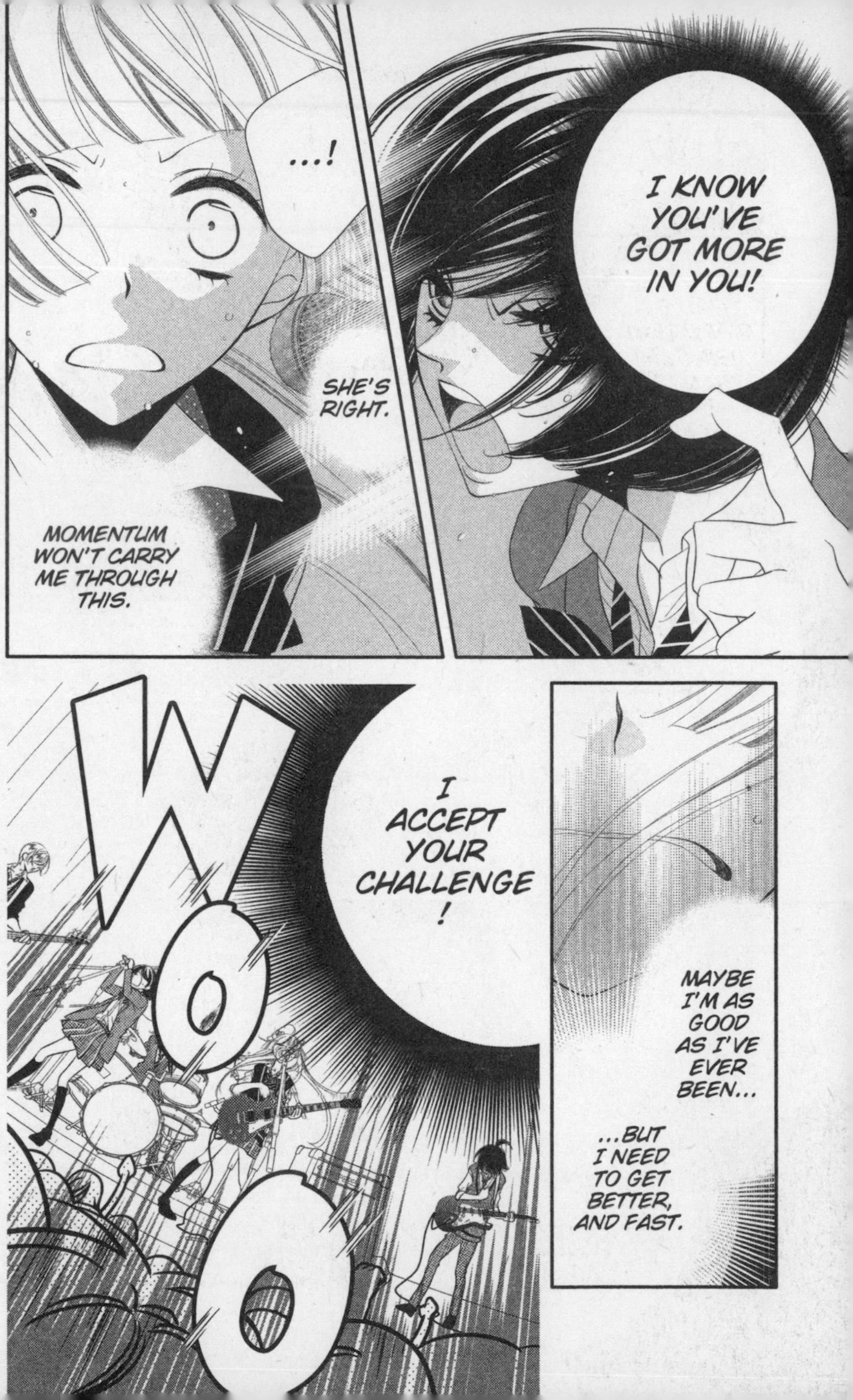
I KNOW YOU'VE GOT MORE IN YOU!
...!
SHE'S RIGHT.
MOMENTUM WON'T CARRY ME THROUGH THIS.
MAYBE I'M AS GOOD AS I'VE EVER BEEN...
...BUT I NEED TO GET BETTER, AND FAST.
I ACCEPT YOUR CHALLENGE!
WOO

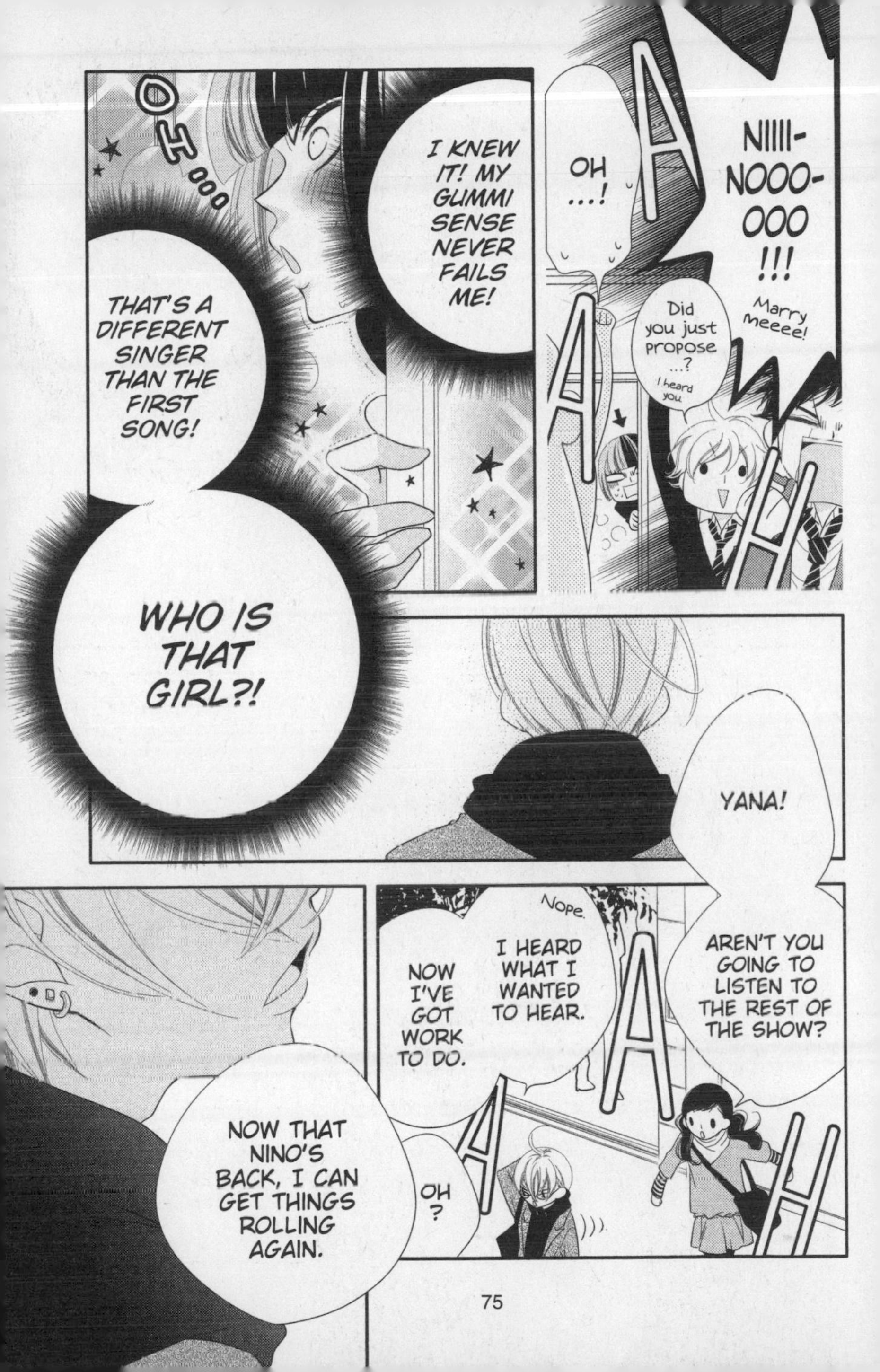
NIIII-NOOO-OOO!!!
Marry meeee!
OH ...!
Did you just propose ...?
I heard you.
I KNEW IT! MY GUMMI SENSE NEVER FAILS ME!
OHooo
THAT'S A DIFFERENT SINGER THAN THE FIRST SONG!
WHO IS THAT GIRL?!
YANA!
AREN'T YOU GOING TO LISTEN TO THE REST OF THE SHOW?
Nope.
I HEARD WHAT I WANTED TO HEAR.
NOW I'VE GOT WORK TO DO.
OH?
NOW THAT NINO'S BACK, I CAN GET THINGS ROLLING AGAIN.

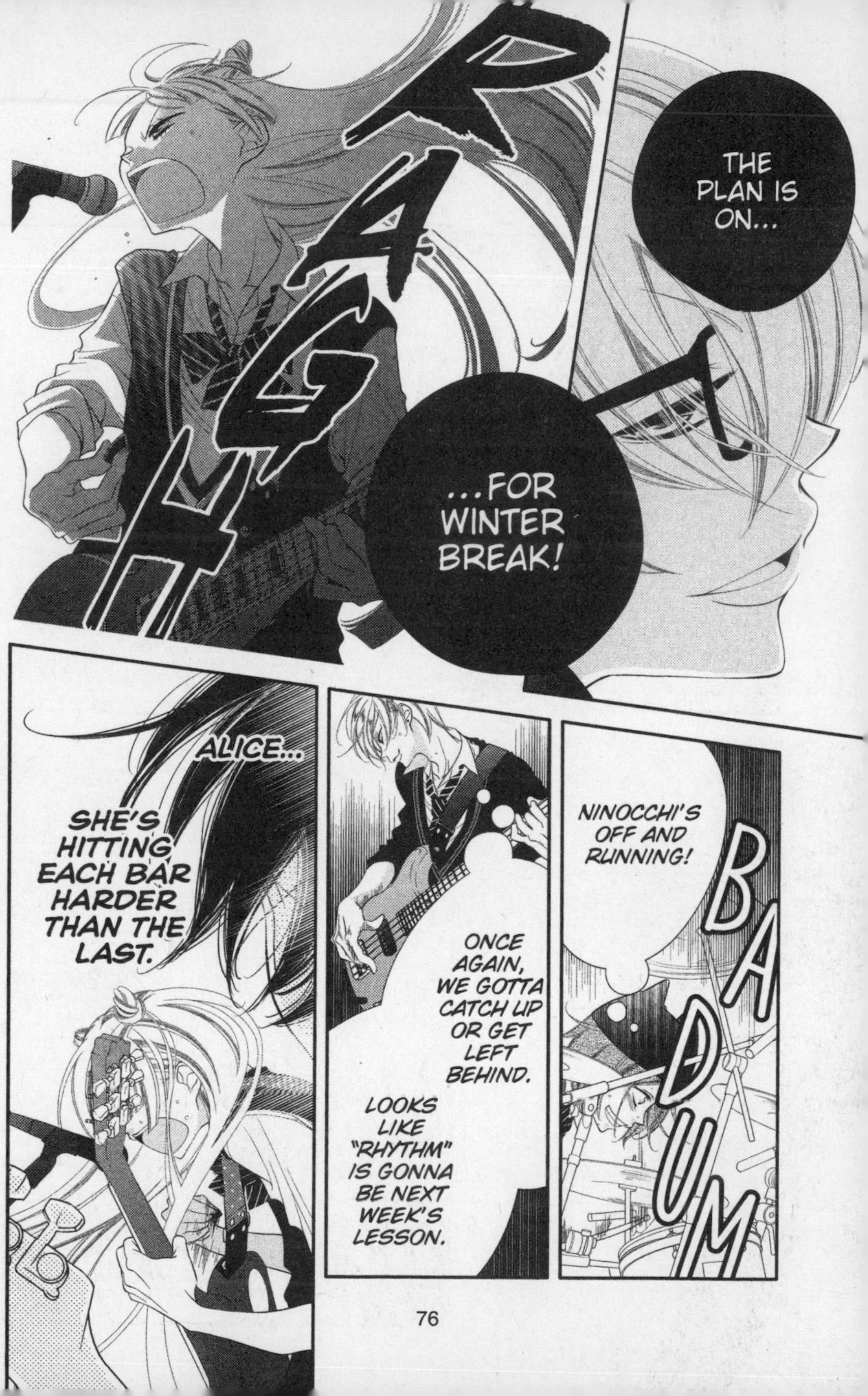
THE PLAN IS ON...
...FOR WINTER BREAK!
RAGGH
NINOCCHI'S OFF AND RUNNING!
BADUM
ONCE AGAIN, WE GOTTA CATCH UP OR GET LEFT BEHIND.
LOOKS LIKE "RHYTHM" IS GONNA BE NEXT WEEK'S LESSON.
ALICE...
SHE'S HITTING EACH BAR HARDER THAN THE LAST.

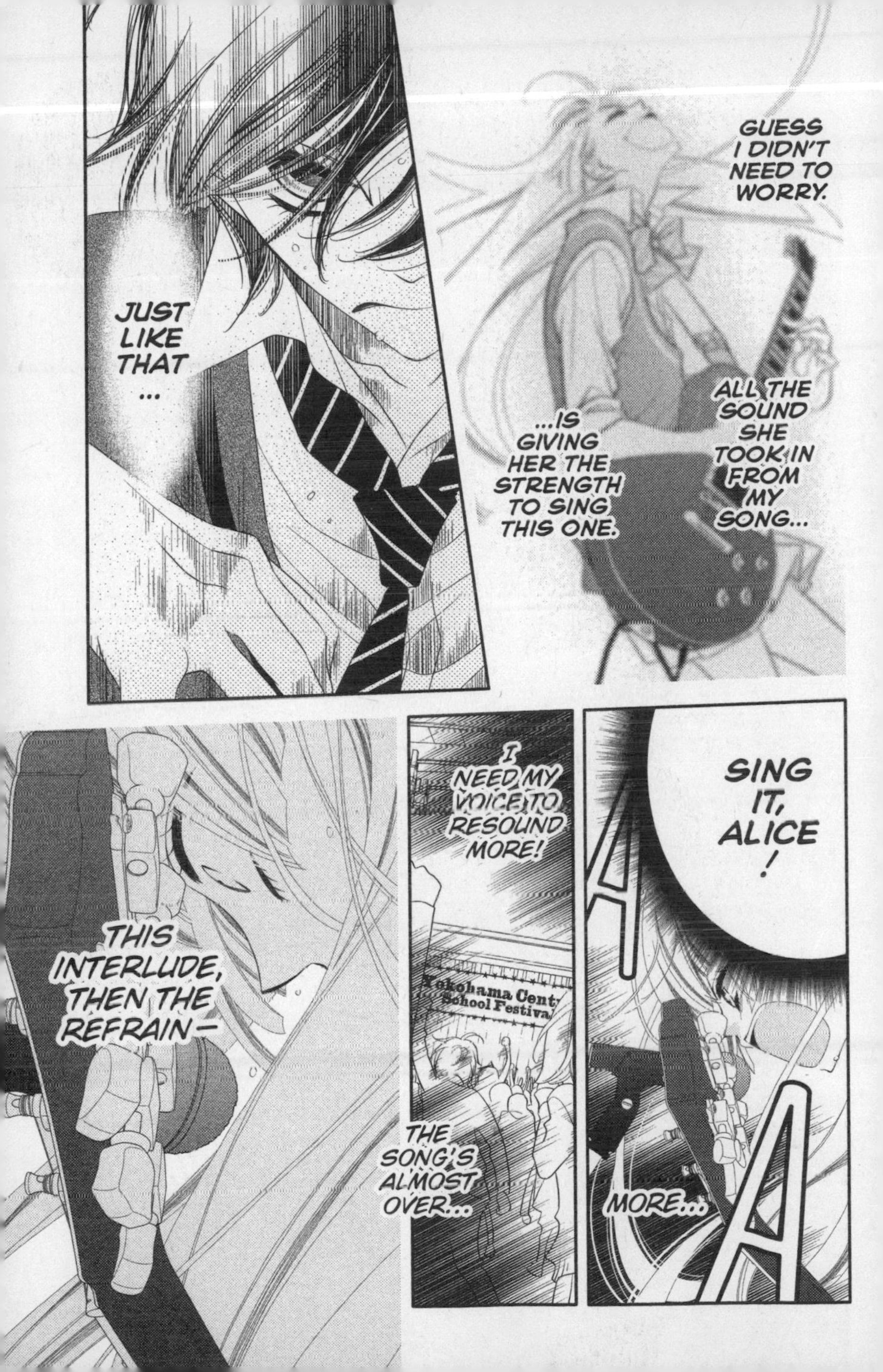
GUESS I DIDN'T NEED TO WORRY.
ALL THE SOUND SHE TOOK IN FROM MY SONG...
...IS GIVING HER THE STRENGTH TO SING THIS ONE.
JUST LIKE THAT...
SING IT, ALICE!
MORE...
I NEED MY VOICE TO RESOUND MORE!
THE SONG'S ALMOST OVER...
THIS INTERLUDE, THEN THE REFRAIN—

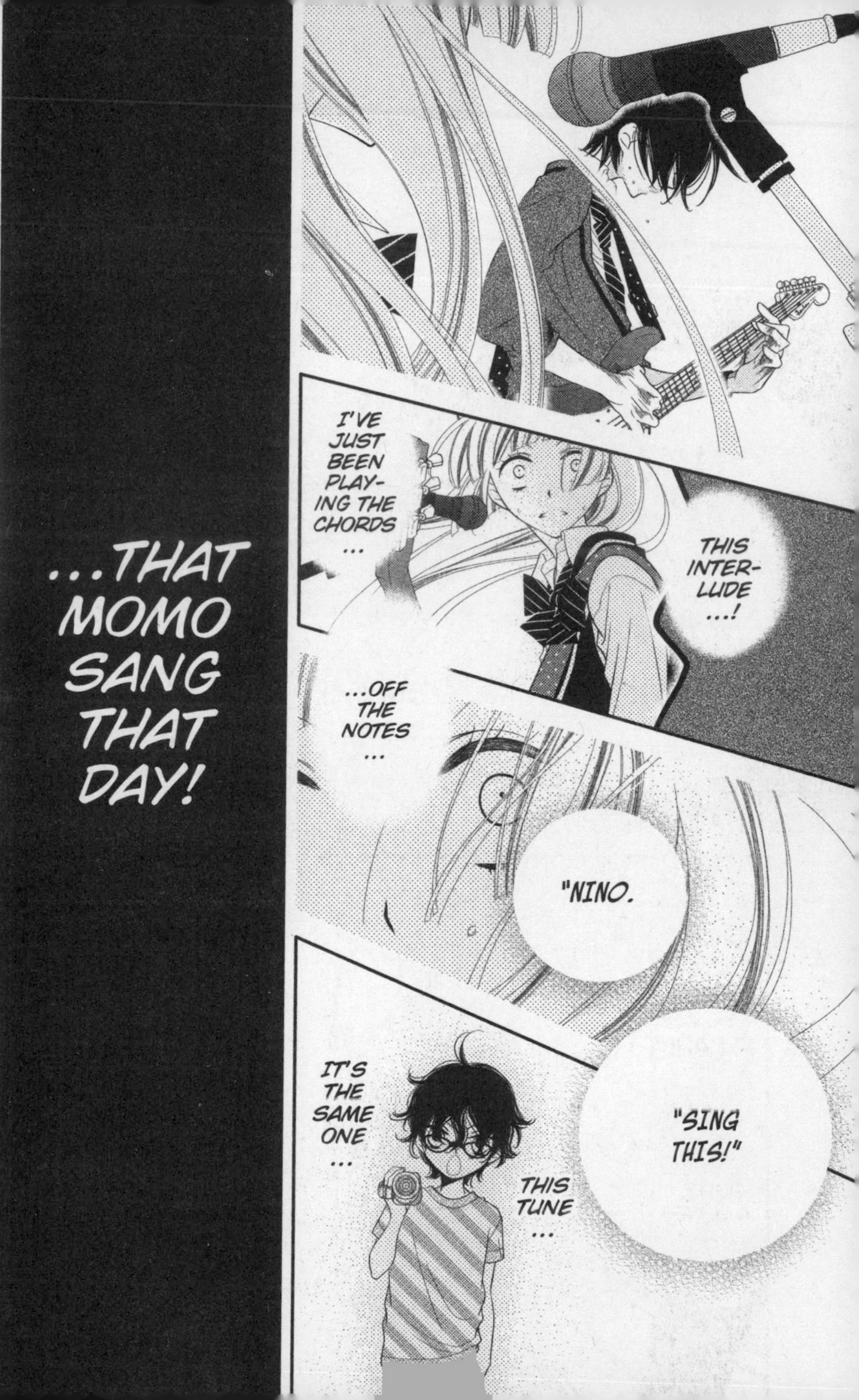
I'VE JUST BEEN PLAYING THE CHORDS ...
THIS INTERLUDE ...!
...OFF THE NOTES ...
"NINO.
"SING THIS!"
THIS TUNE ...
IT'S THE SAME ONE ...
...THAT MOMO SANG THAT DAY!

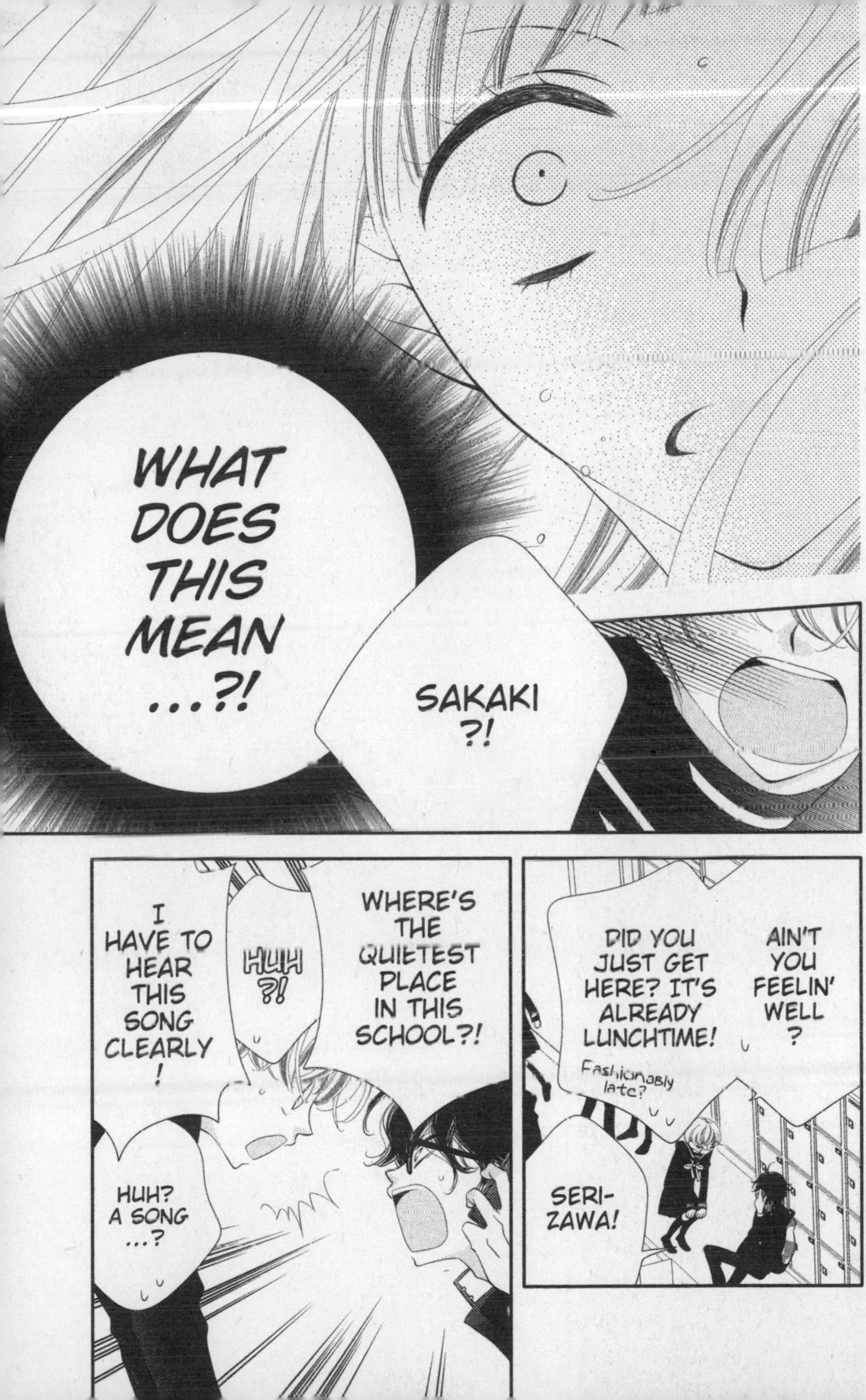
WHAT DOES THIS MEAN ...?!
SAKAKI ?!
AIN'T YOU FEELIN' WELL ?
DID YOU JUST GET HERE? IT'S ALREADY LUNCHTIME!
Fashionably late?
SERI-ZAWA!
WHERE'S THE QUIETEST PLACE IN THIS SCHOOL?!
HUH ?!
I HAVE TO HEAR THIS SONG CLEARLY !
HUH? A SONG ...?

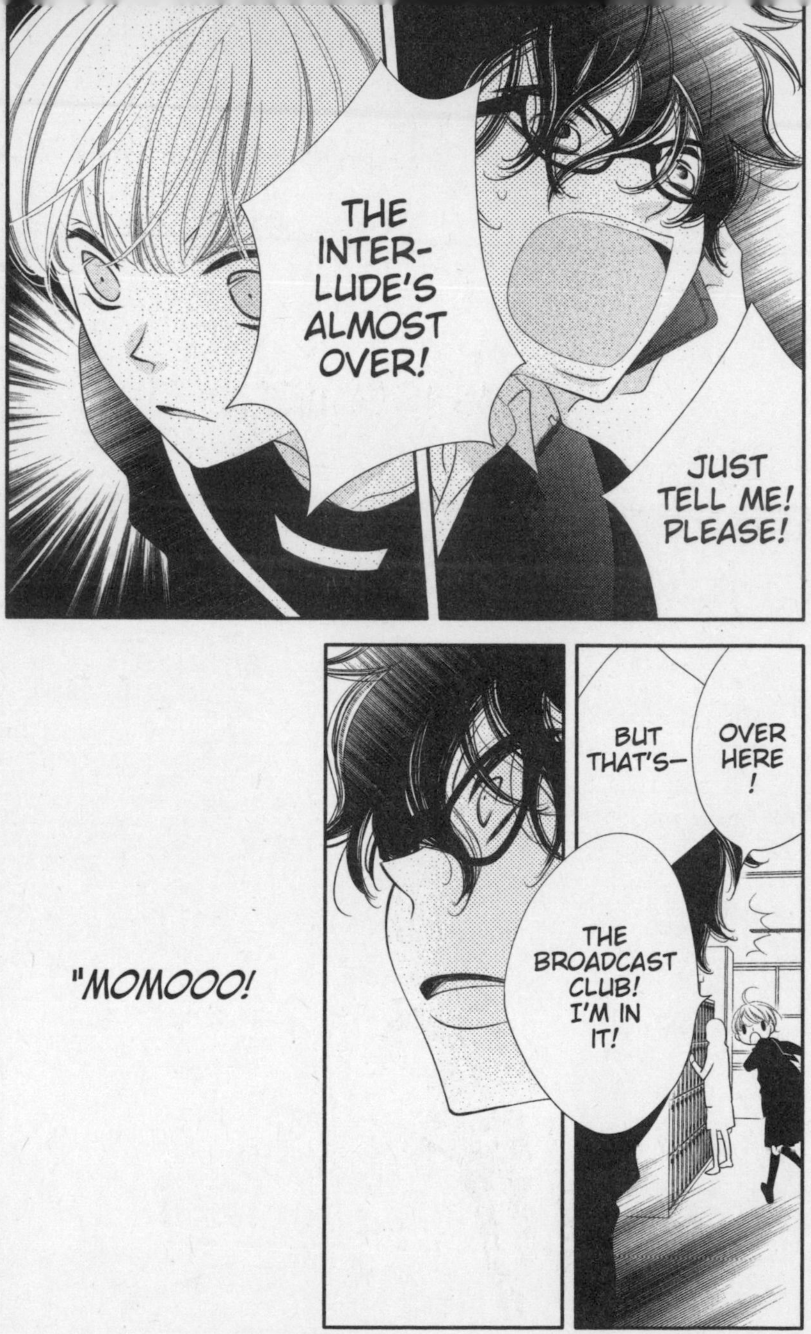
THE INTER-LUDE'S ALMOST OVER!
JUST TELL ME! PLEASE!
OVER HERE!
BUT THAT'S—
THE BROADCAST CLUB! I'M IN IT!
"MOMOOO!

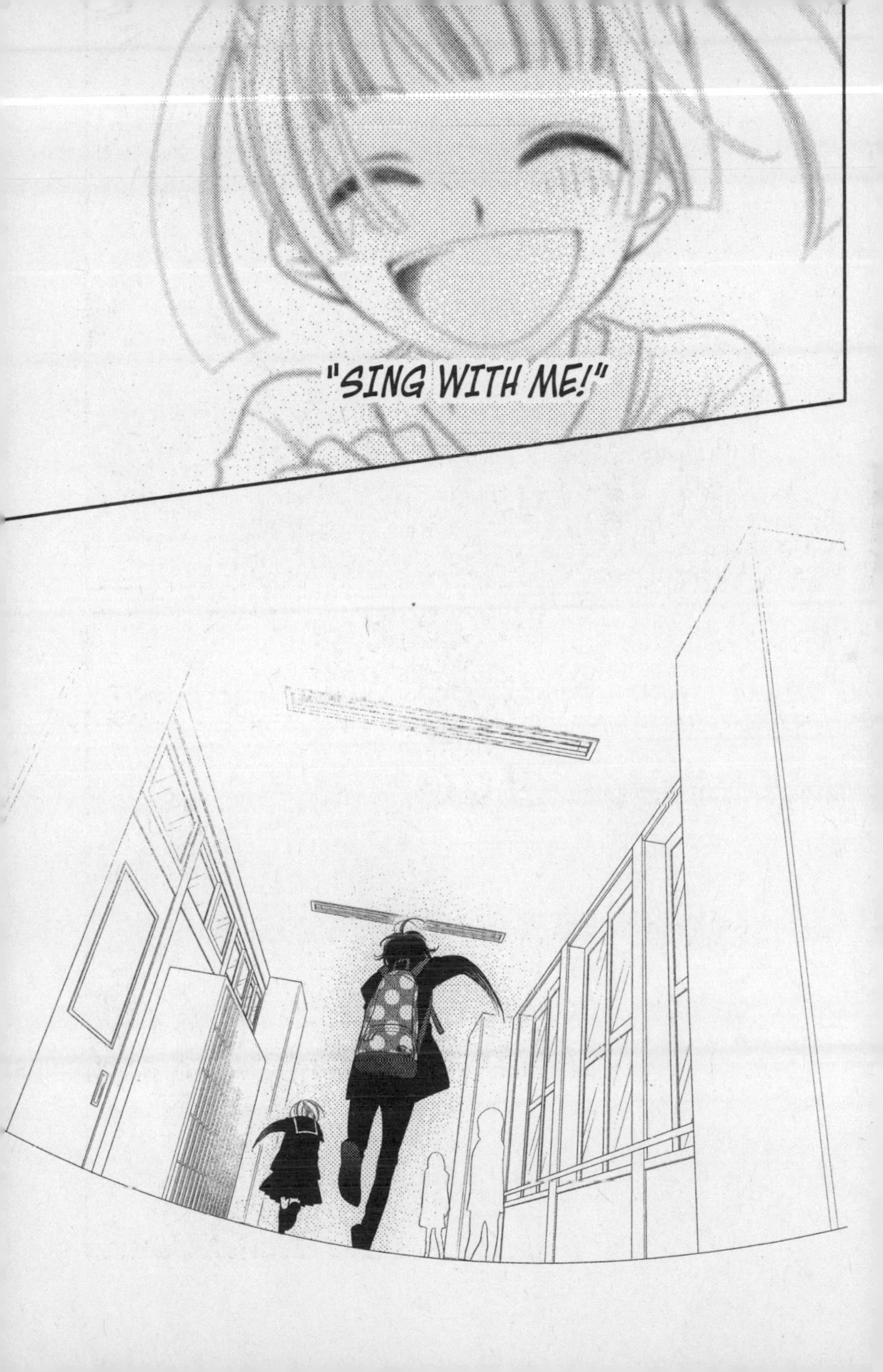
"SING WITH ME!"

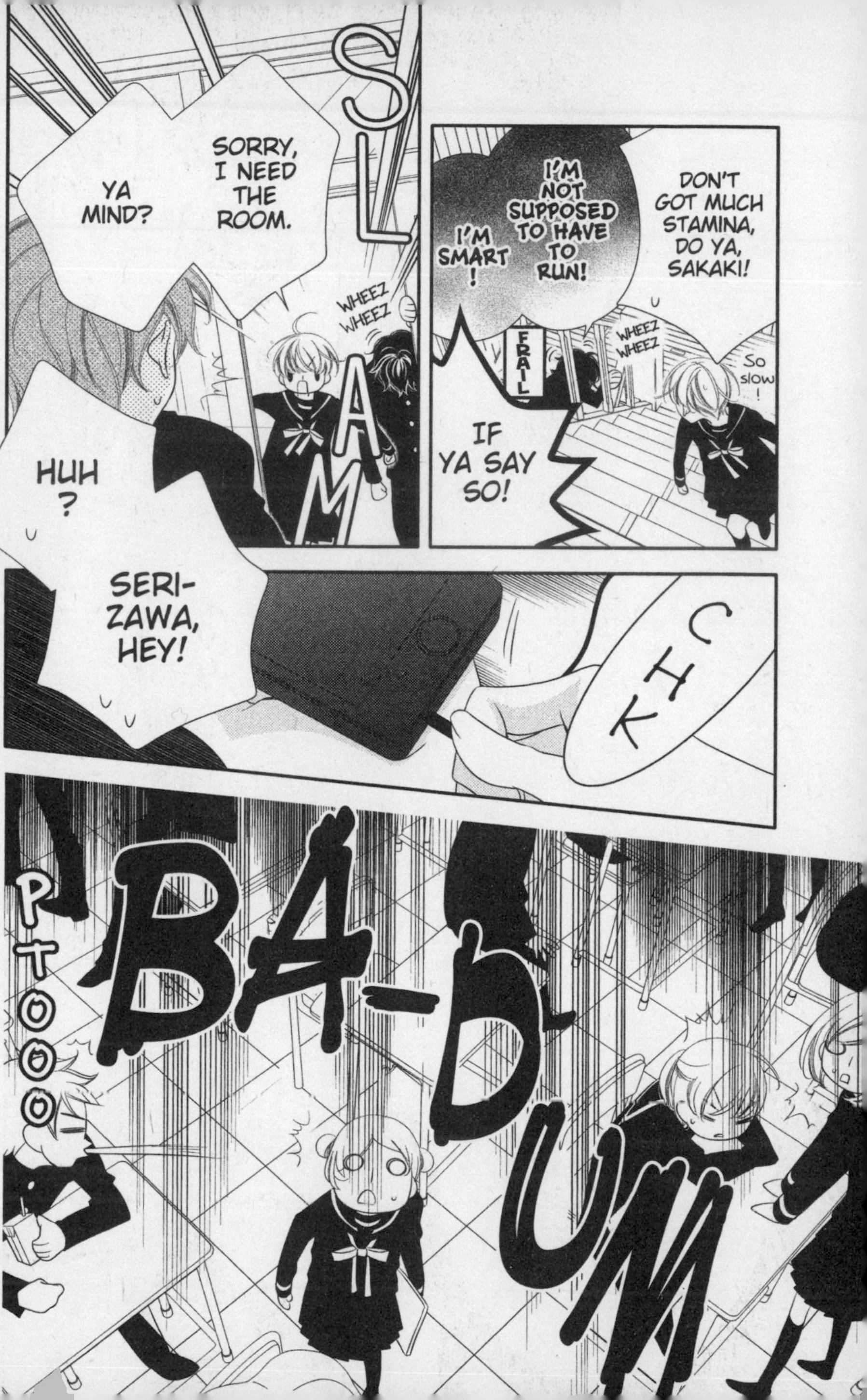
DON'T GOT MUCH STAMINA, DO YA, SAKAKI!
So slow!
WHEEZ WHEEZ
I'M NOT SUPPOSED TO HAVE TO RUN!
I'M SMART!
FRAIL
IF YA SAY SO!
SORRY, I NEED THE ROOM.
YA MIND?
WHEEZ WHEEZ
SLAM
HUH?
CHK
SERI-ZAWA, HEY!
BA-DUM
PTOOOO

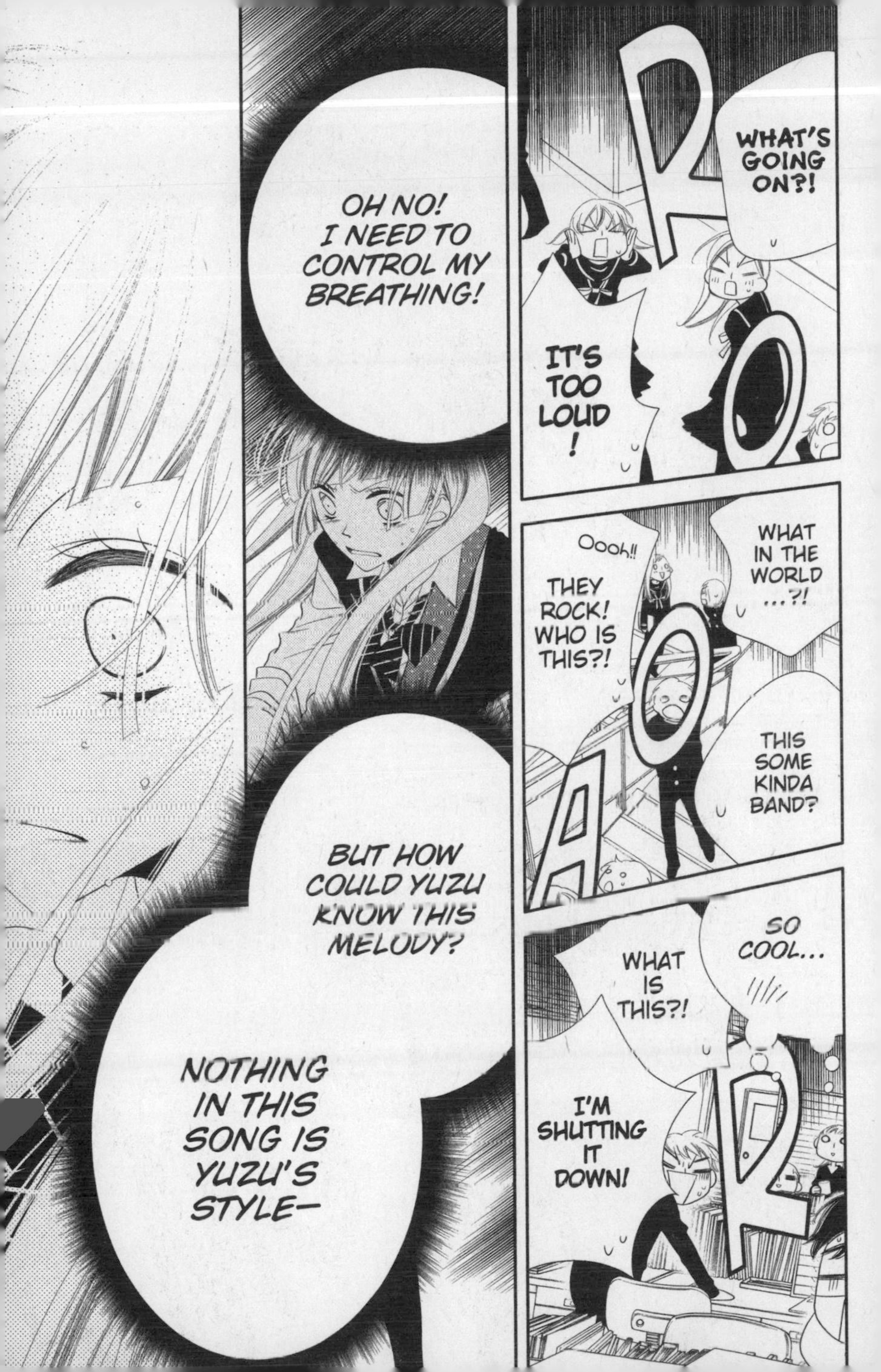
WHAT'S GOING ON?!
IT'S TOO LOUD!
WHAT IN THE WORLD ...?!
Oooh!!
THEY ROCK! WHO IS THIS?!
THIS SOME KINDA BAND?
SO COOL...
WHAT IS THIS?!
I'M SHUTTING IT DOWN!
OH NO! I NEED TO CONTROL MY BREATHING!
BUT HOW COULD YUZU KNOW THIS MELODY?
NOTHING IN THIS SONG IS YUZU'S STYLE—

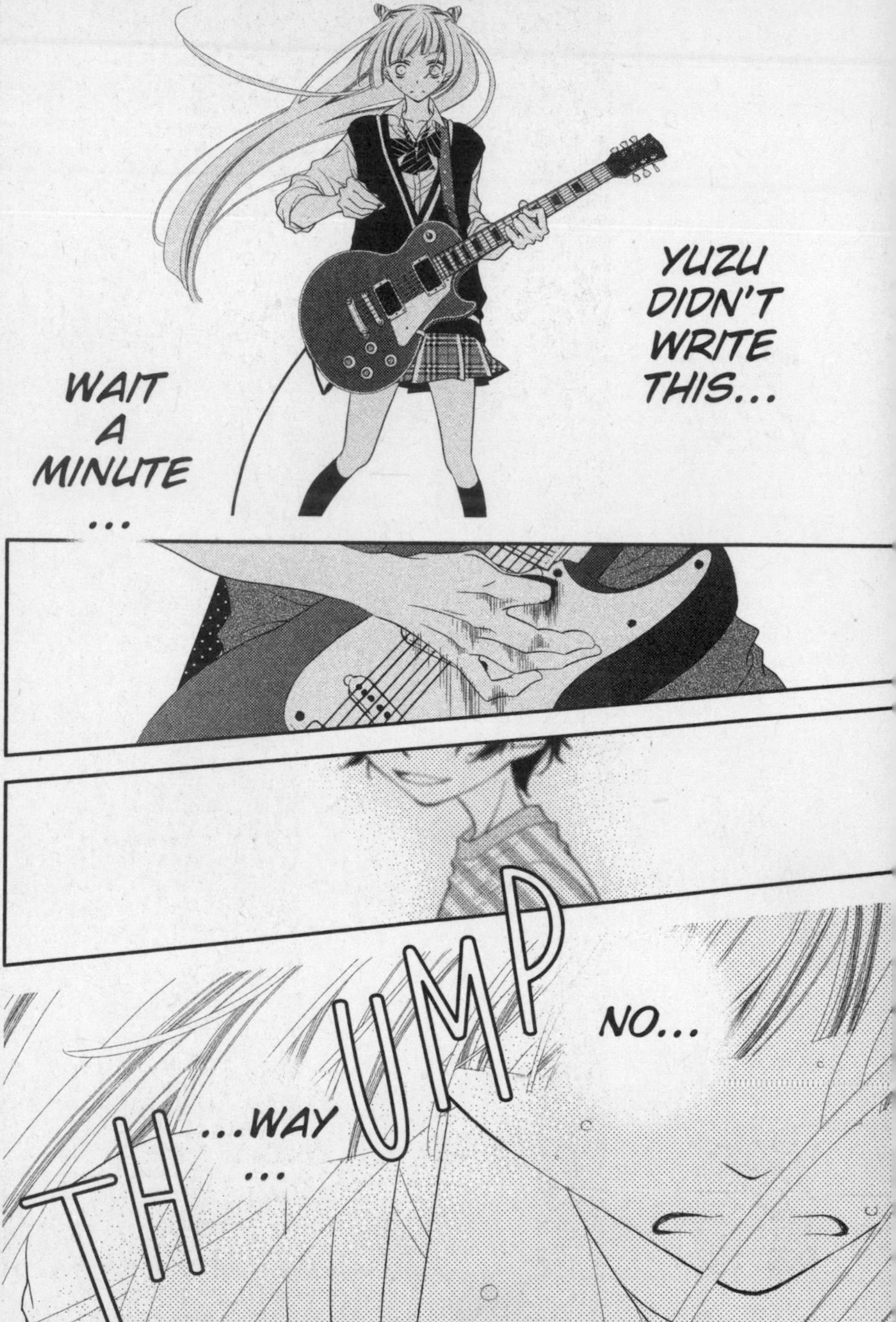
YUZU DIDN'T WRITE THIS...
WAIT A MINUTE ...
NO...
...WAY ...
THUMP

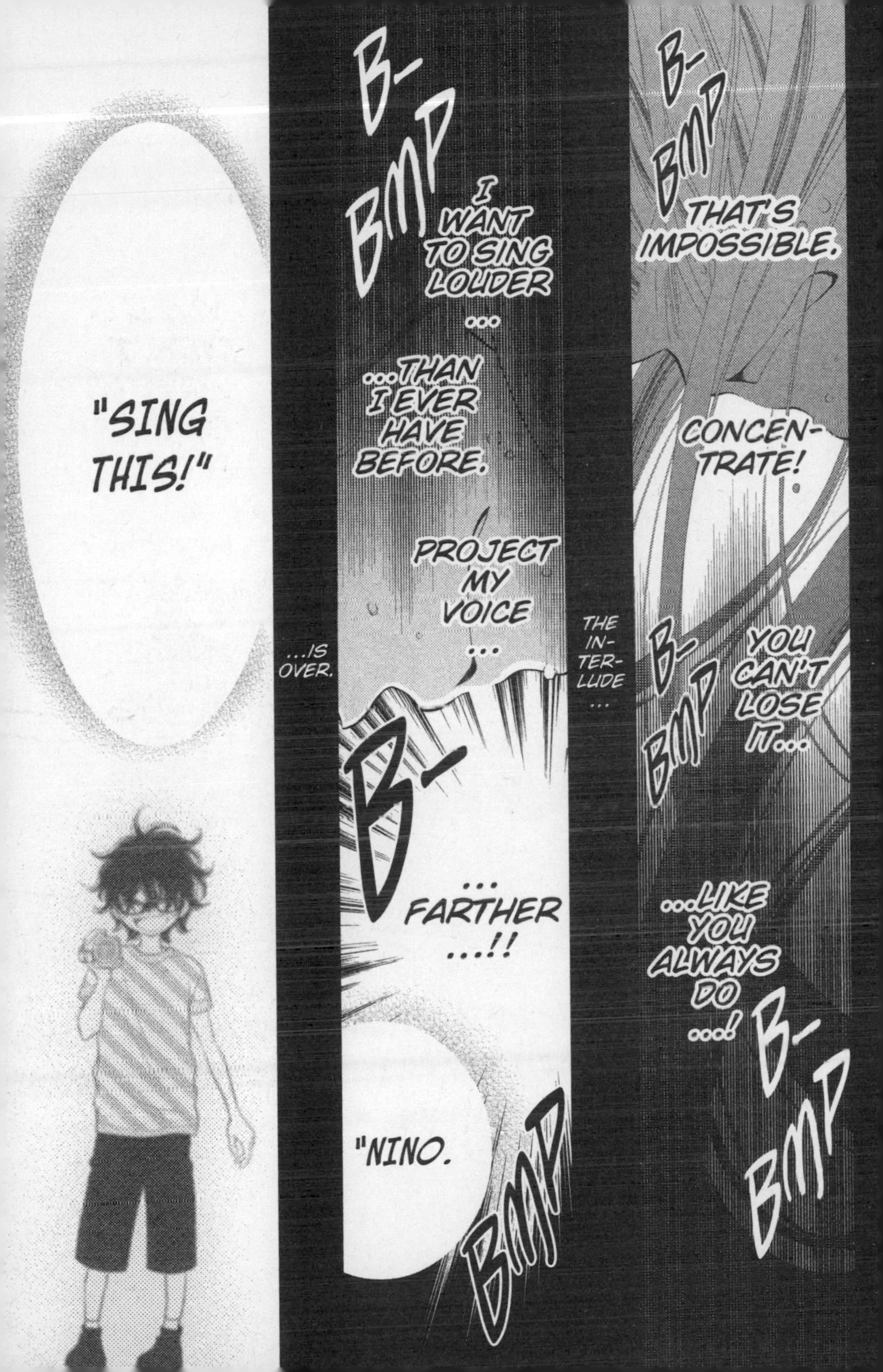
B-BMP
THAT'S IMPOSSIBLE.
CONCENTRATE!
B-BMP
YOU CAN'T LOSE IT...
...LIKE YOU ALWAYS DO ...!
B-BMP
THE INTERLUDE ...
...IS OVER.
B-BMP
I WANT TO SING LOUDER ...
...THAN I EVER HAVE BEFORE.
PROJECT MY VOICE ...
B-BMP
... FARTHER ...!!
"NINO.
"SING THIS!"

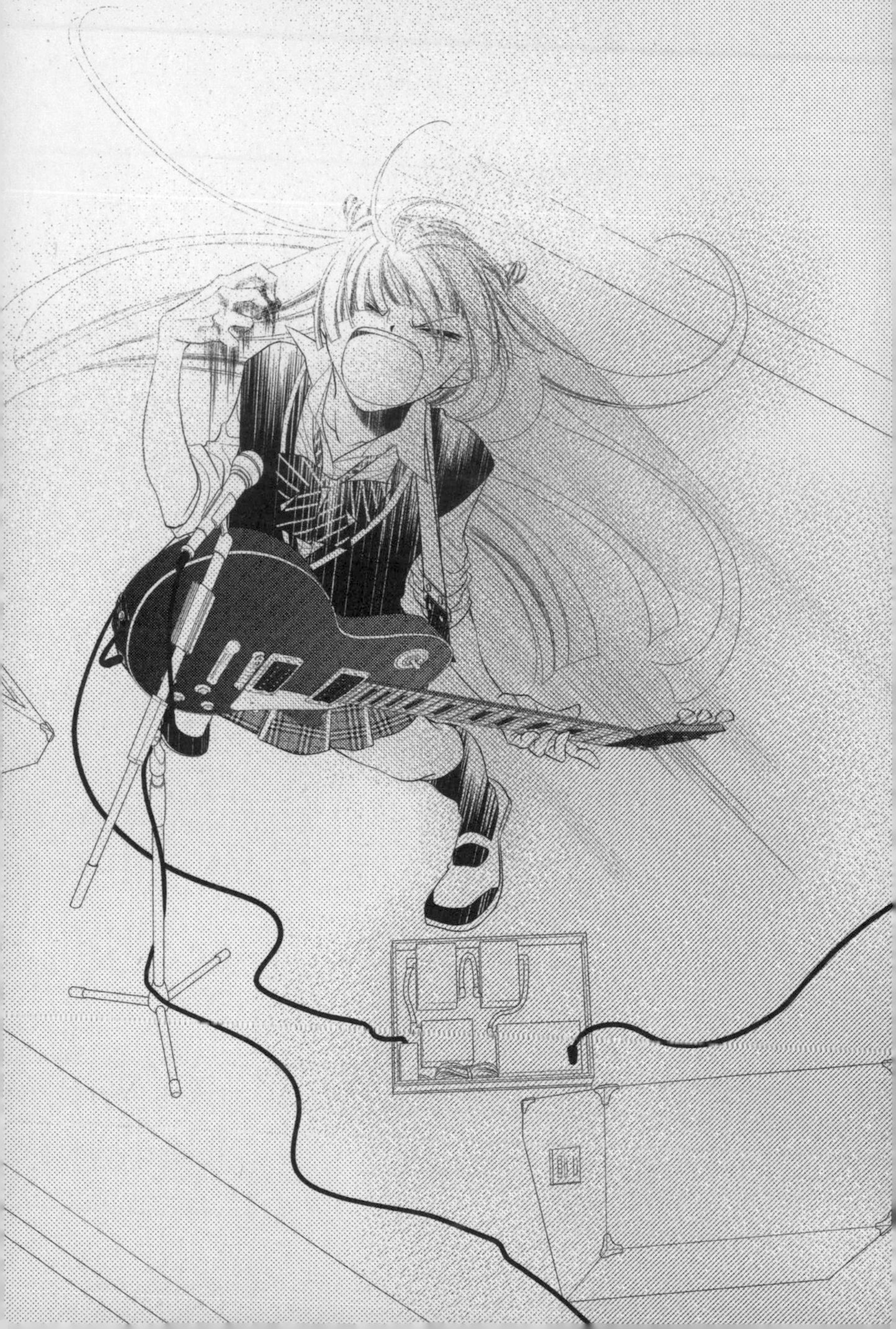

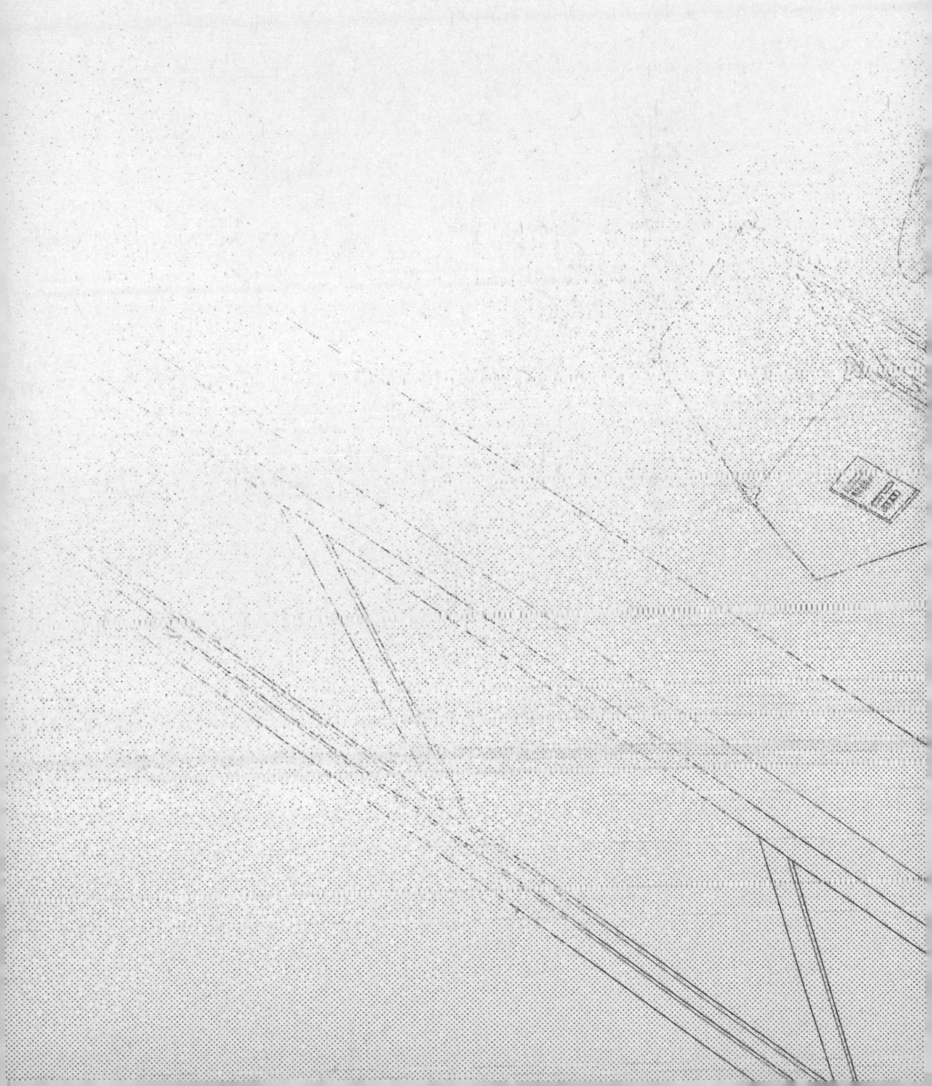

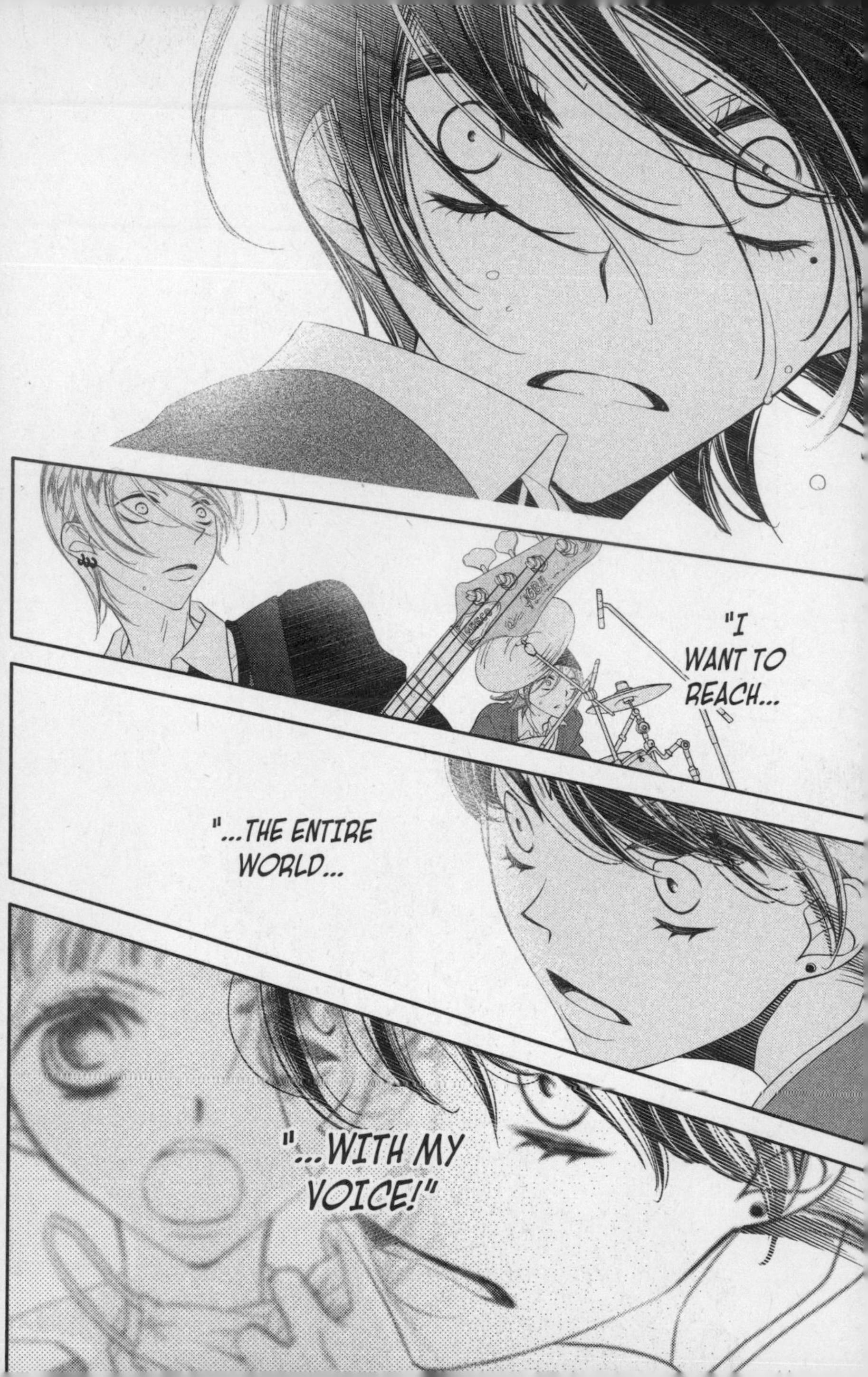
"I WANT TO REACH...
"...THE ENTIRE WORLD...
"...WITH MY VOICE!"

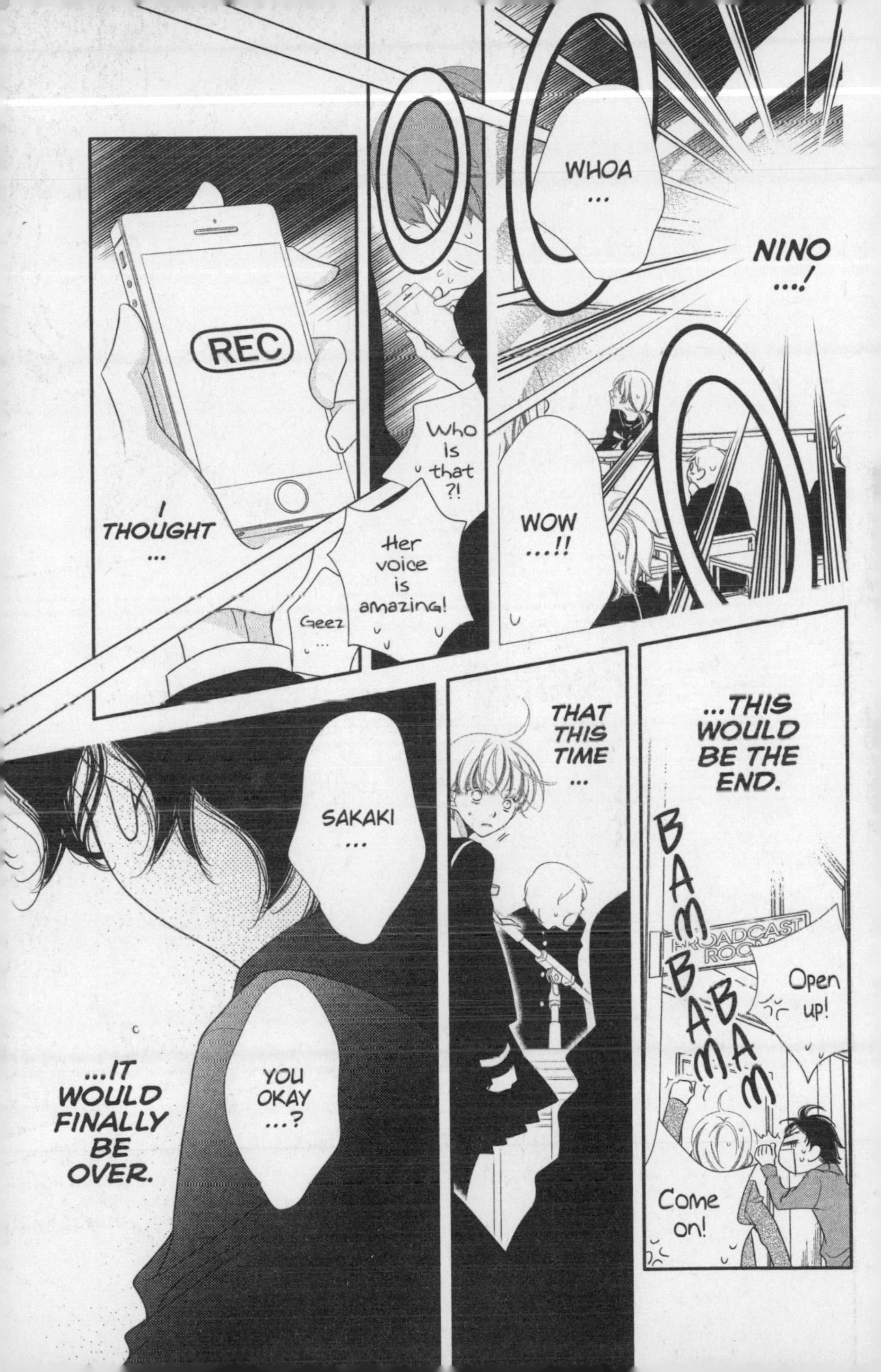
WHOA ...
NINO ...!
WOW ...!!
Who is that ?!
Her voice is amazing!
Geez ...
REC
I THOUGHT ...
...THIS WOULD BE THE END.
BAM BAM BAM BAM
BROADCAST
Open up!
Come on!
THAT THIS TIME ...
SAKAKI ...
YOU OKAY ...?
...IT WOULD FINALLY BE OVER.

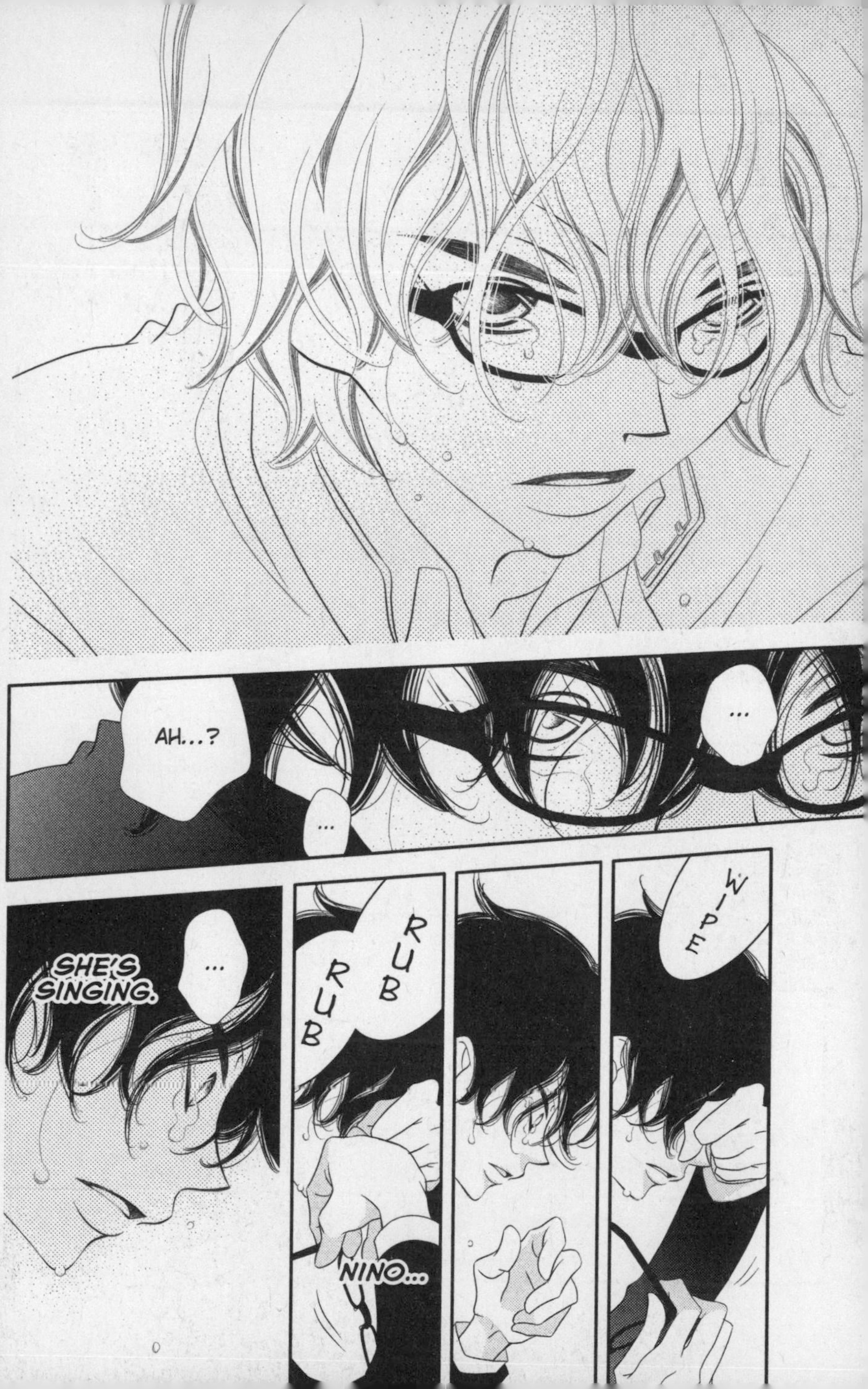
...
AH...?
...
WIPE
RUB RUB
NINO...
...
SHE'S SINGING.

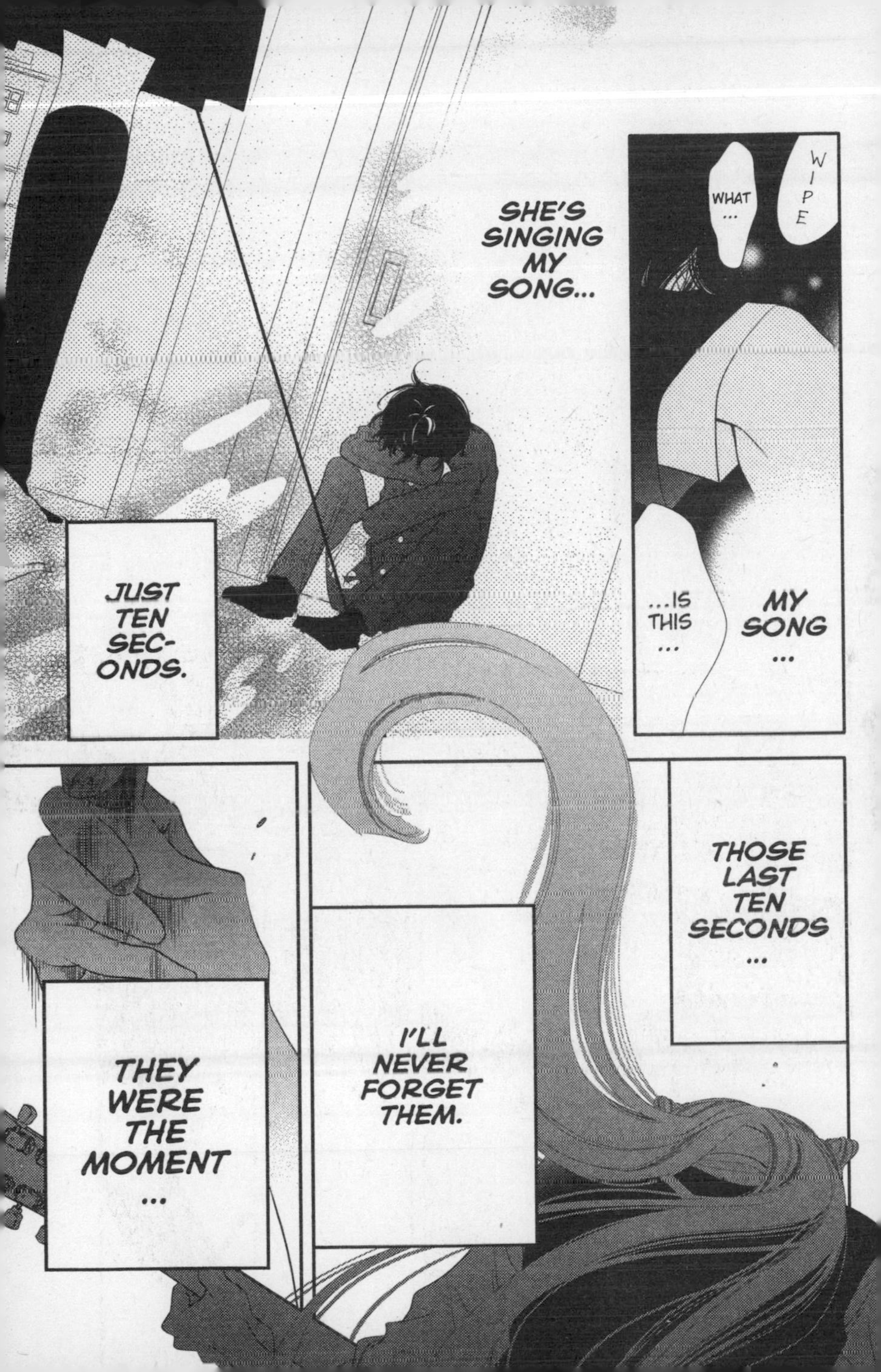
WIPE
WHAT ...
MY SONG ...
...IS THIS ...
SHE'S SINGING MY SONG...
JUST TEN SEC-ONDS.
THOSE LAST TEN SECONDS ...
I'LL NEVER FORGET THEM.
THEY WERE THE MOMENT ...

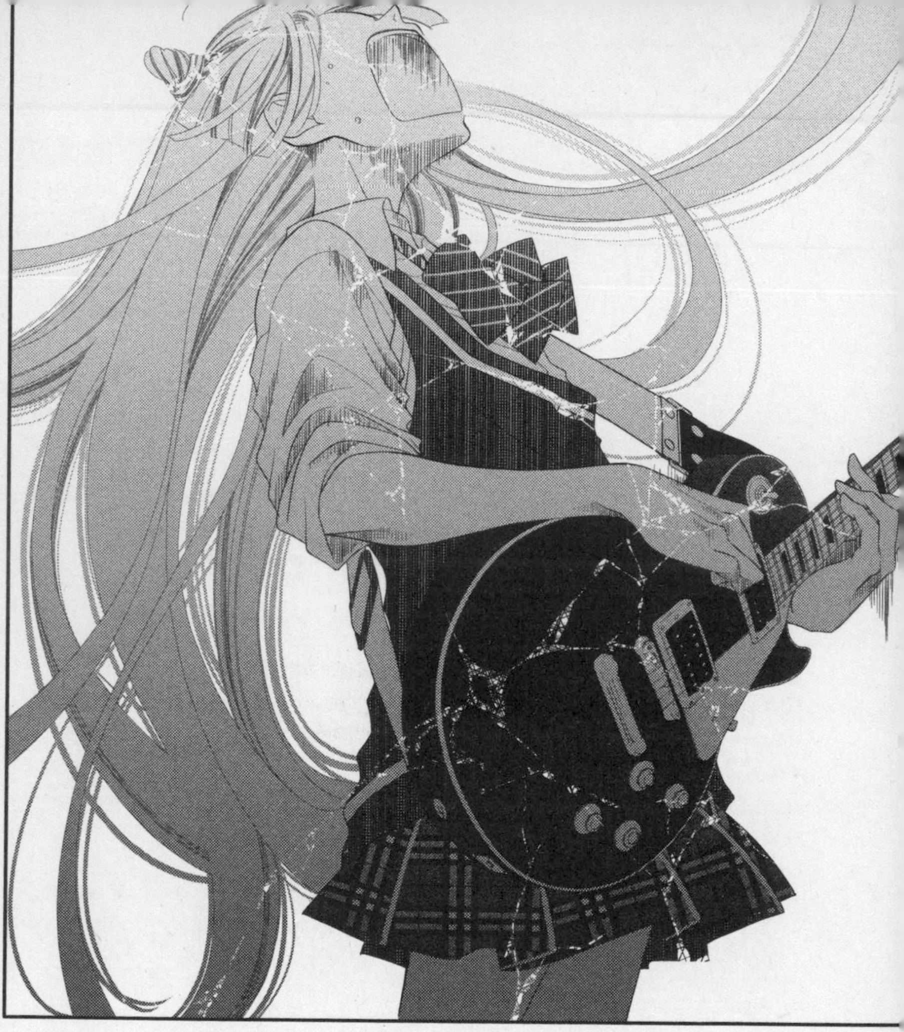

...THAT ALICE'S SHELL WAS TORN AWAY.

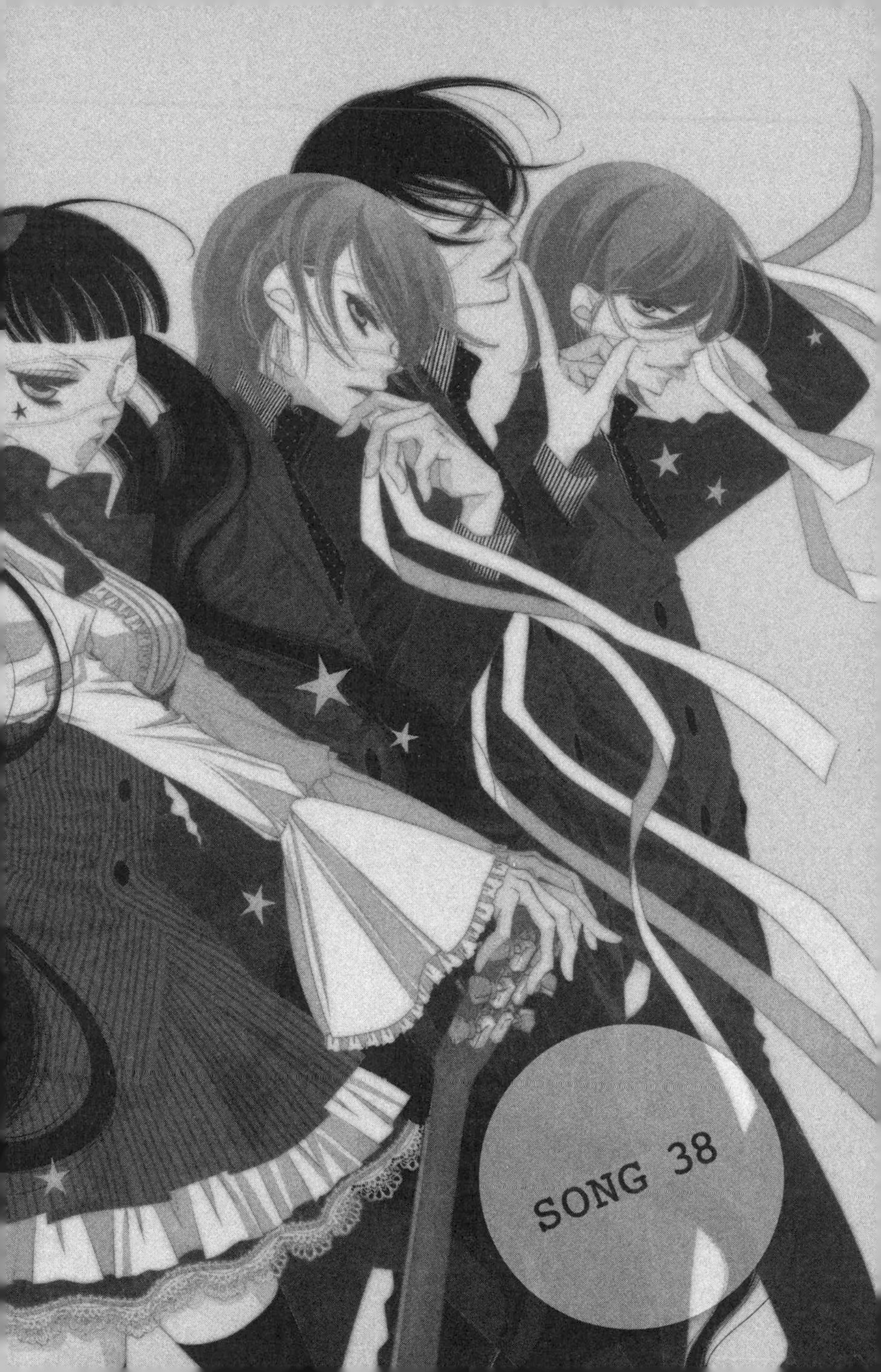
SONG 38

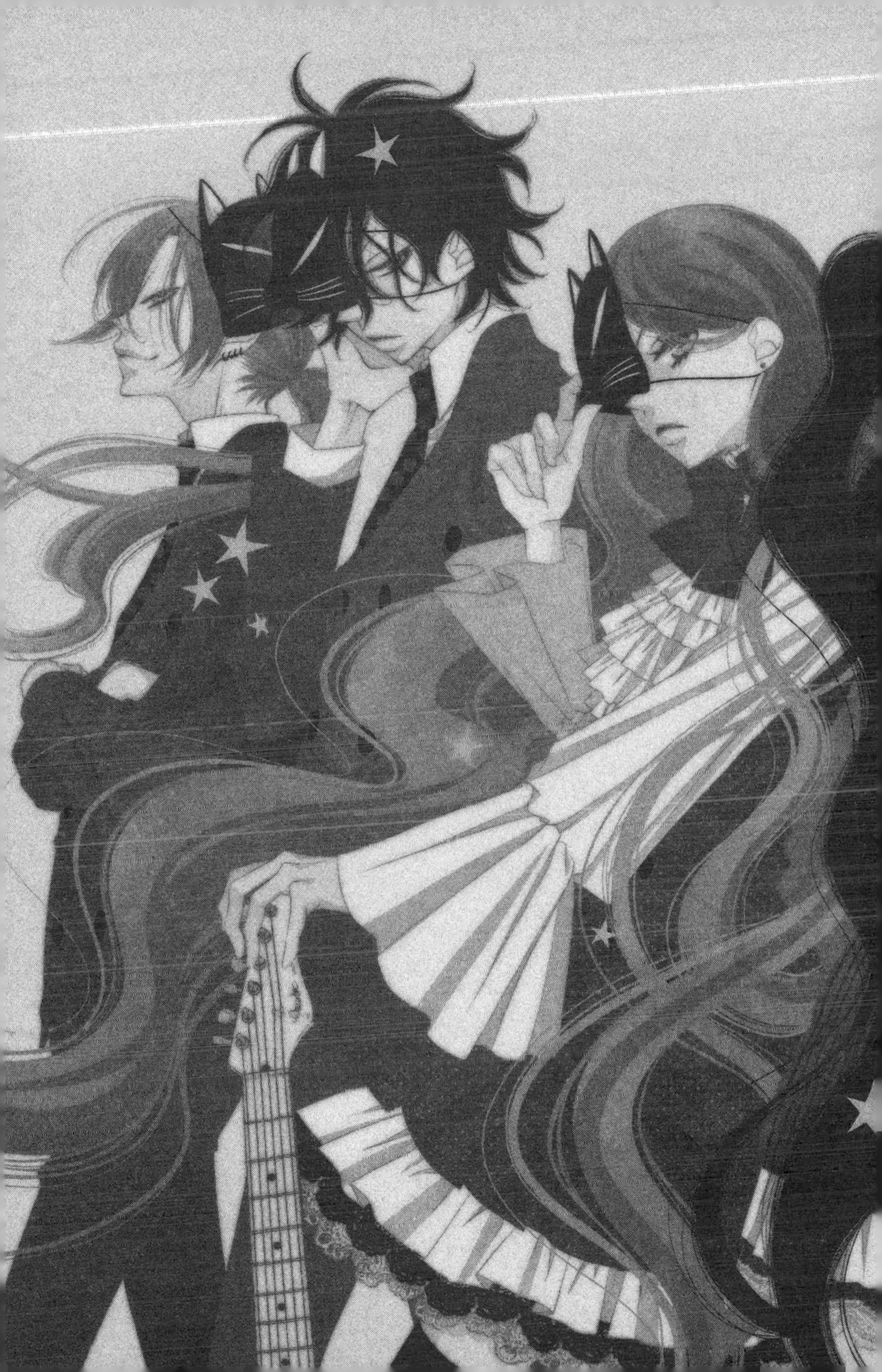

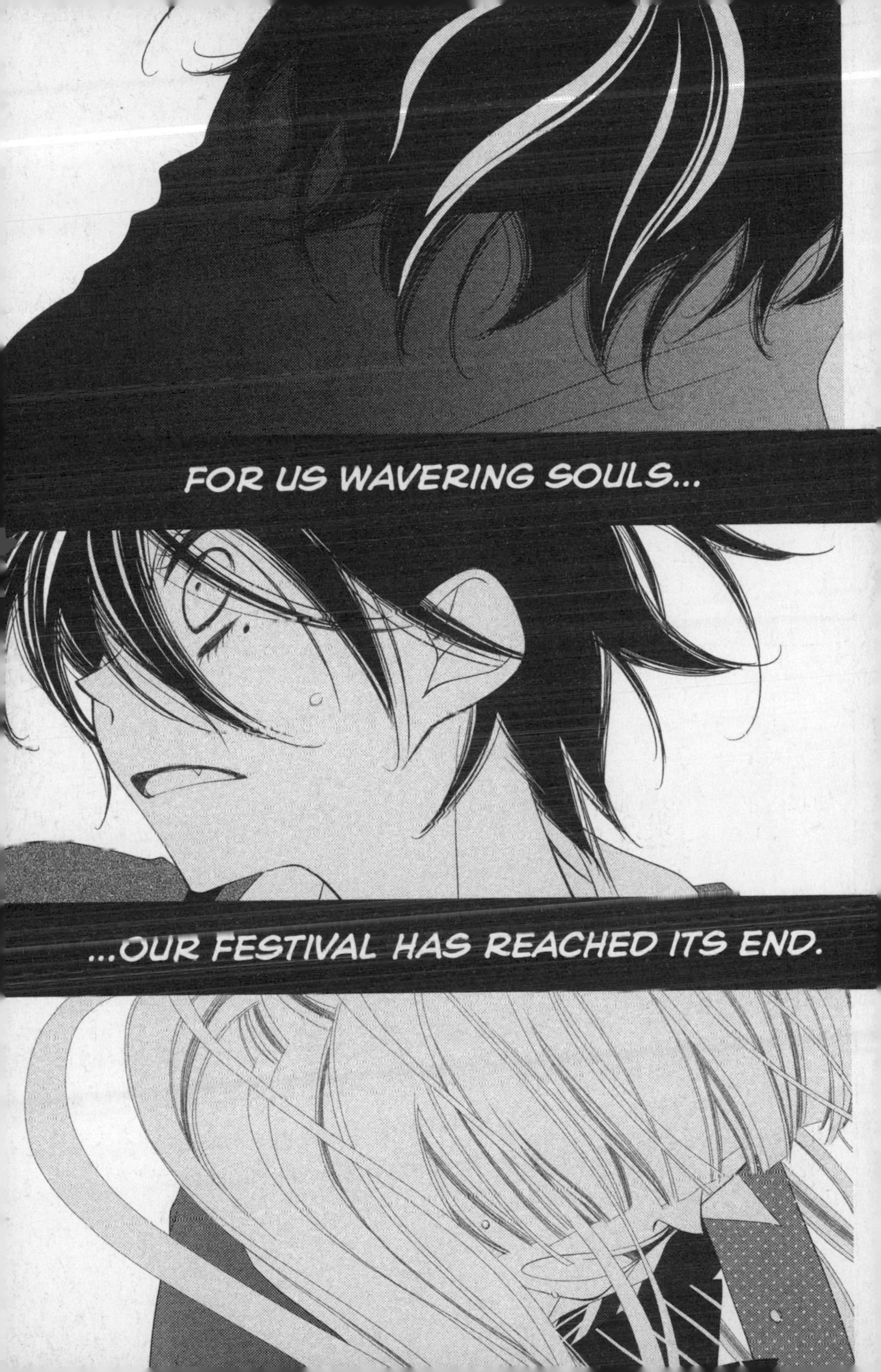
FOR US WAVERING SOULS...
...OUR FESTIVAL HAS REACHED ITS END.

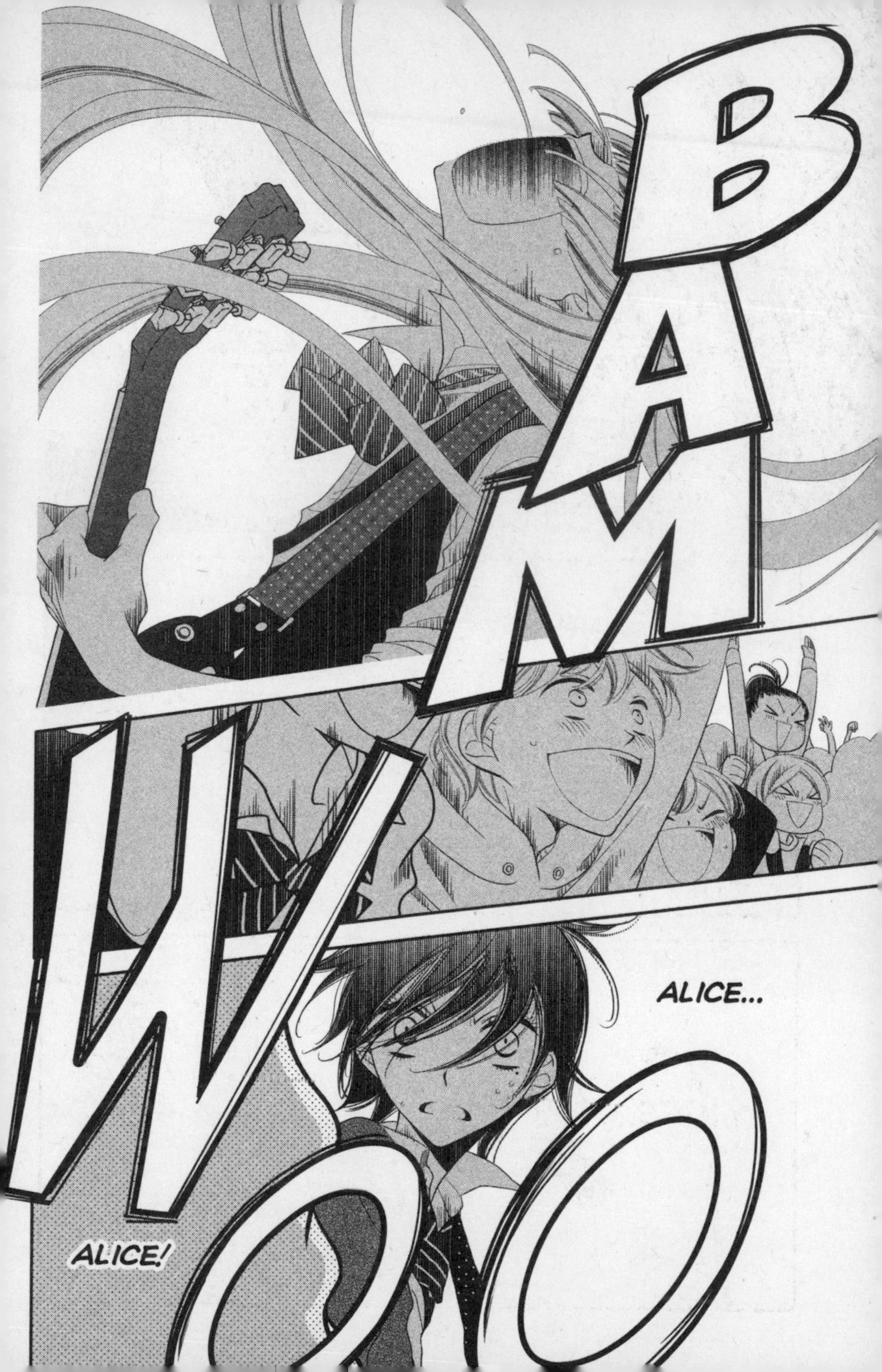
BAM
WOO
ALICE...
ALICE!

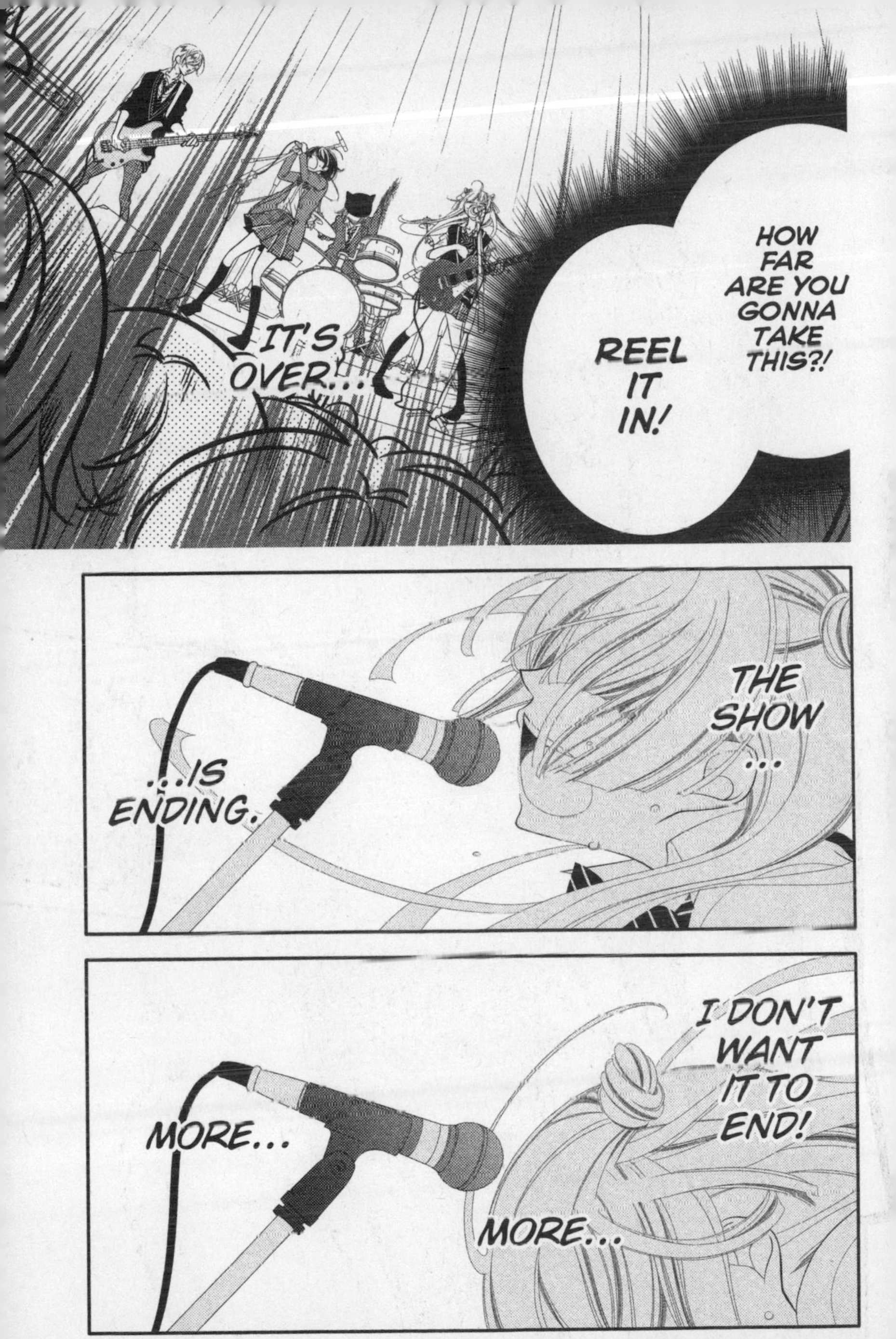
HOW FAR ARE YOU GONNA TAKE THIS?!
REEL IT IN!
IT'S OVER...
THE SHOW...
...IS ENDING.
I DON'T WANT IT TO END!
MORE...
MORE...

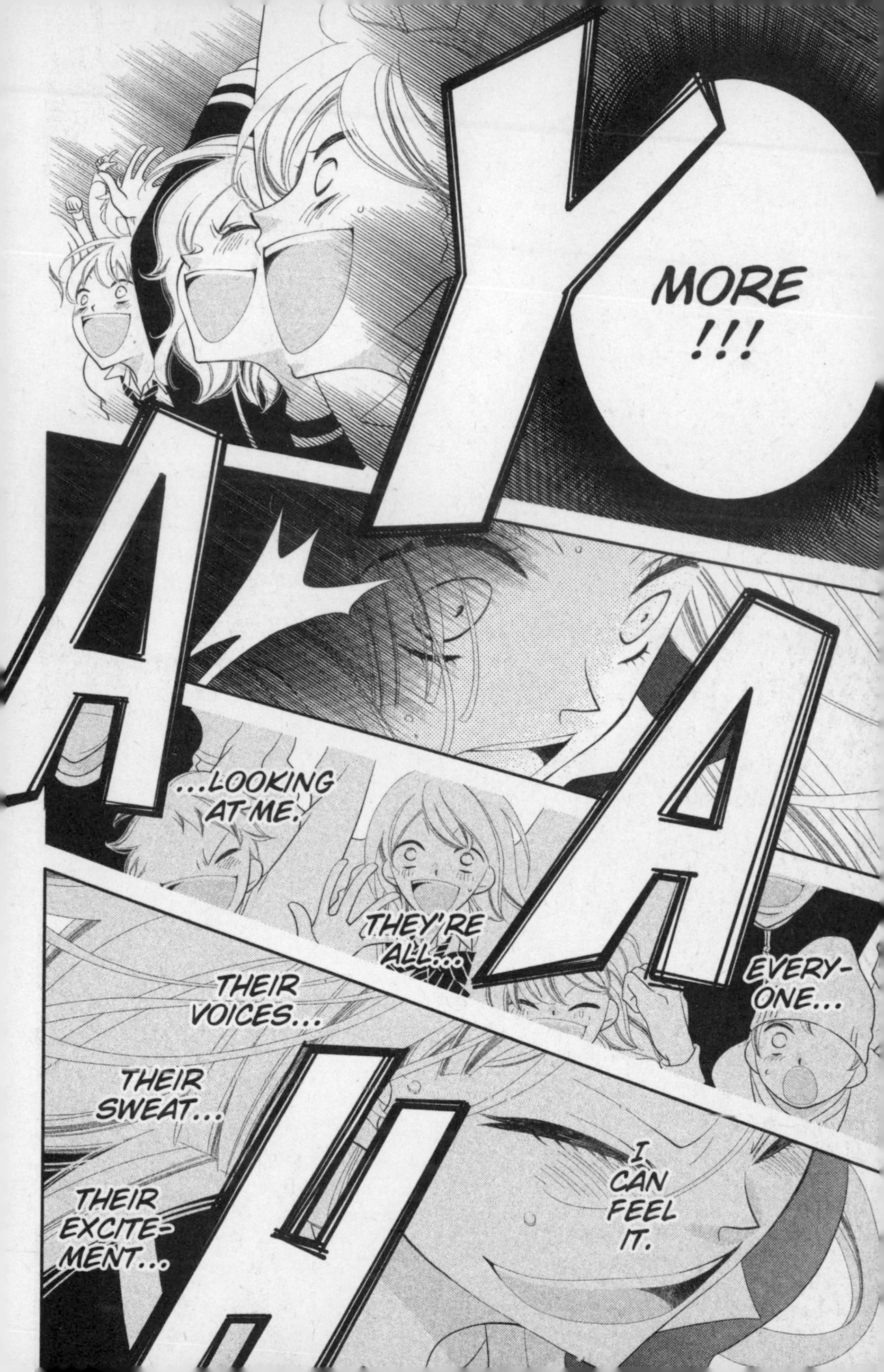
MORE !!!
EVERY-ONE...
THEY'RE ALL...
...LOOKING AT ME.
THEIR VOICES...
THEIR SWEAT...
THEIR EXCITE-MENT...
I CAN FEEL IT.

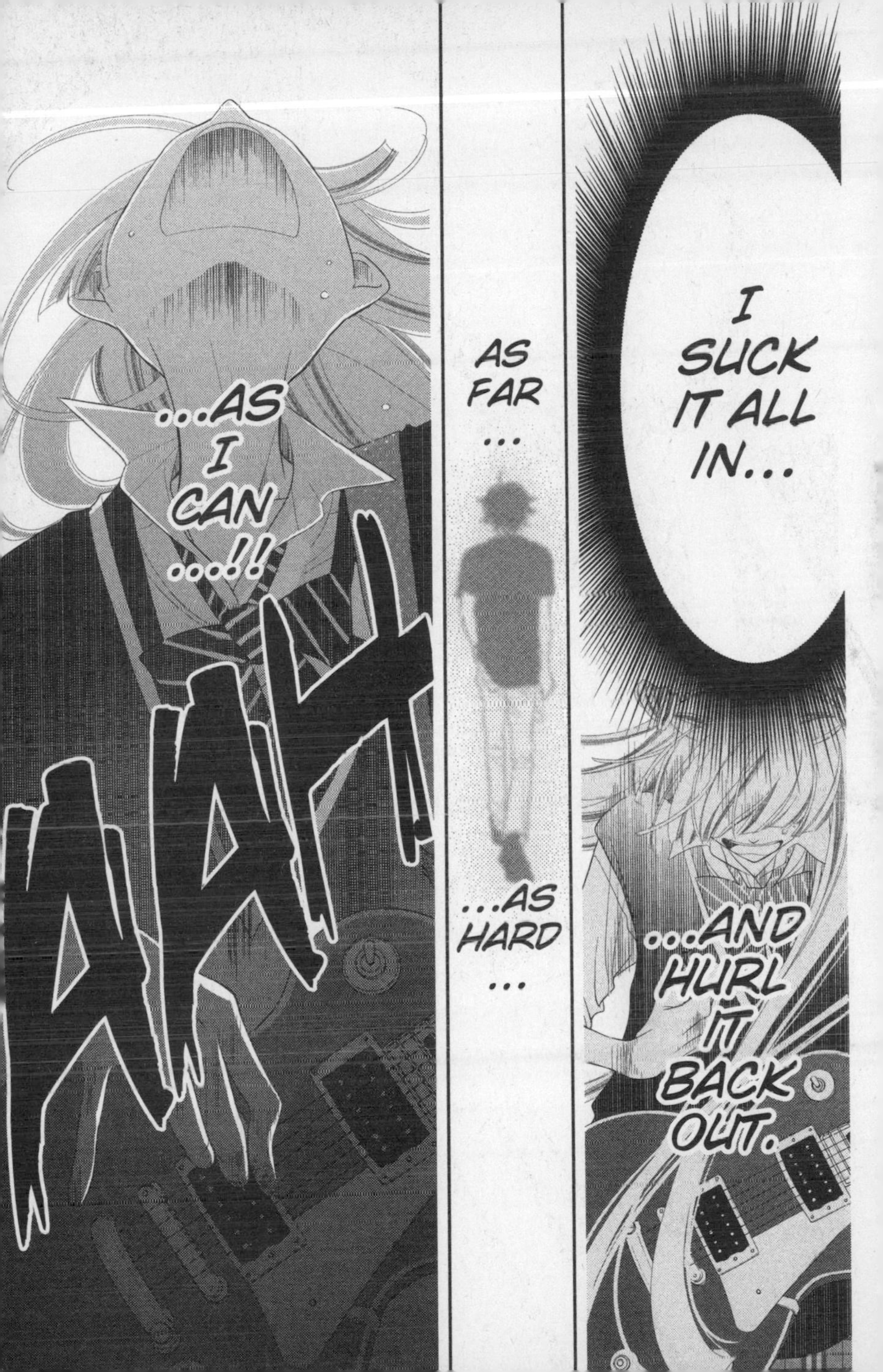
I SUCK IT ALL IN...
...AND HURL IT BACK OUT.
AS FAR ...
...AS HARD ...
...AS I CAN...!!

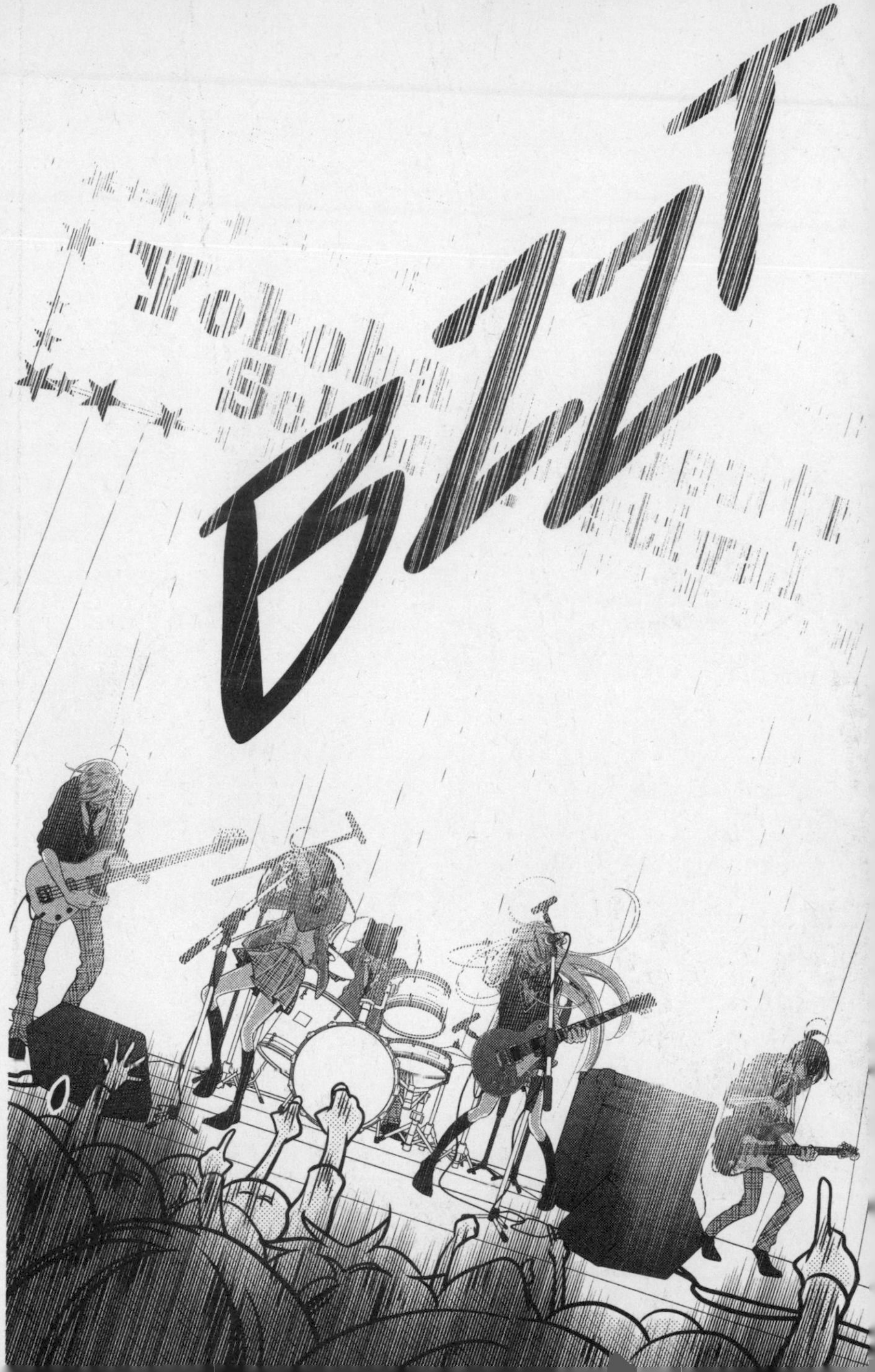
BZZT

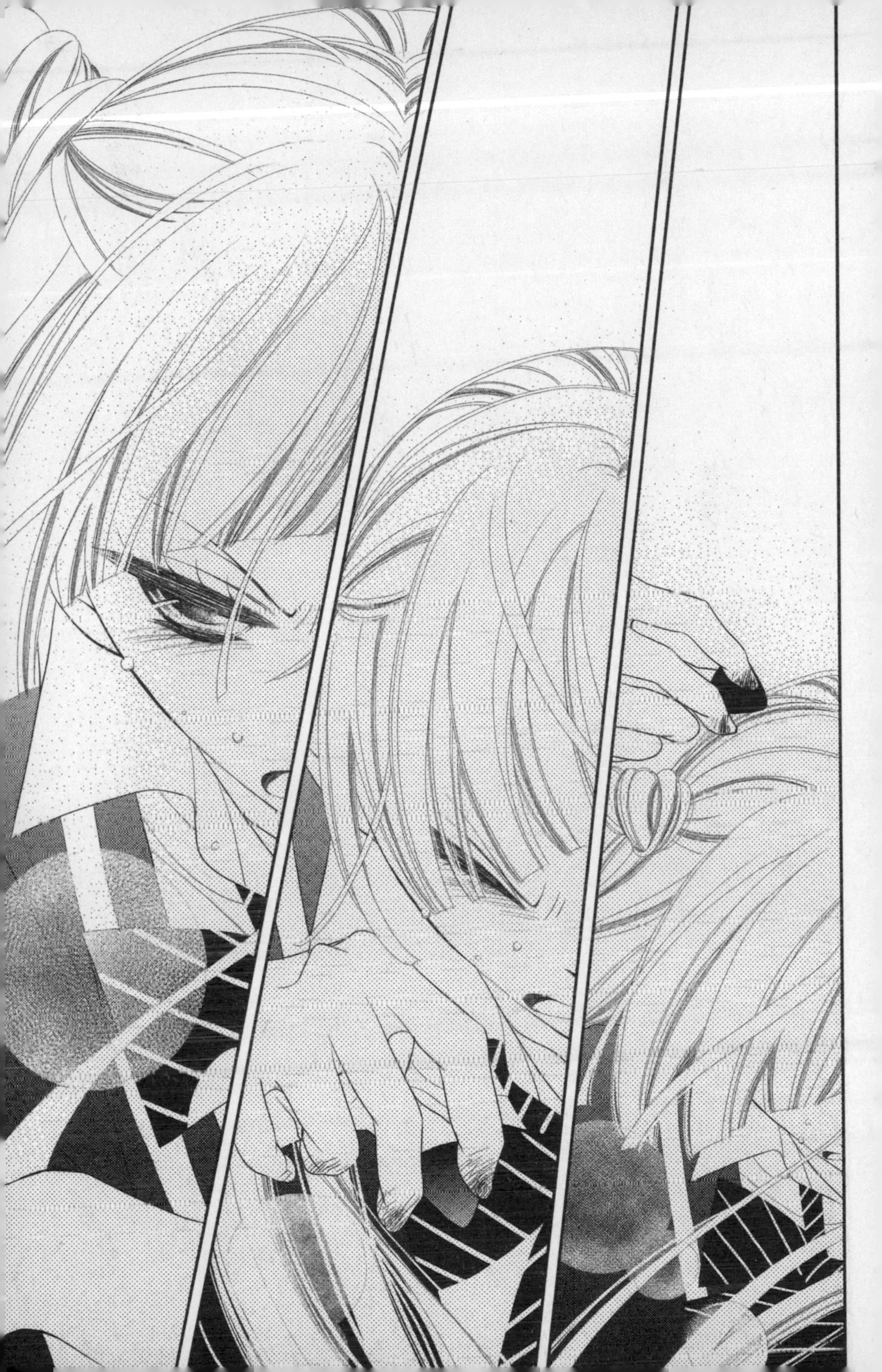

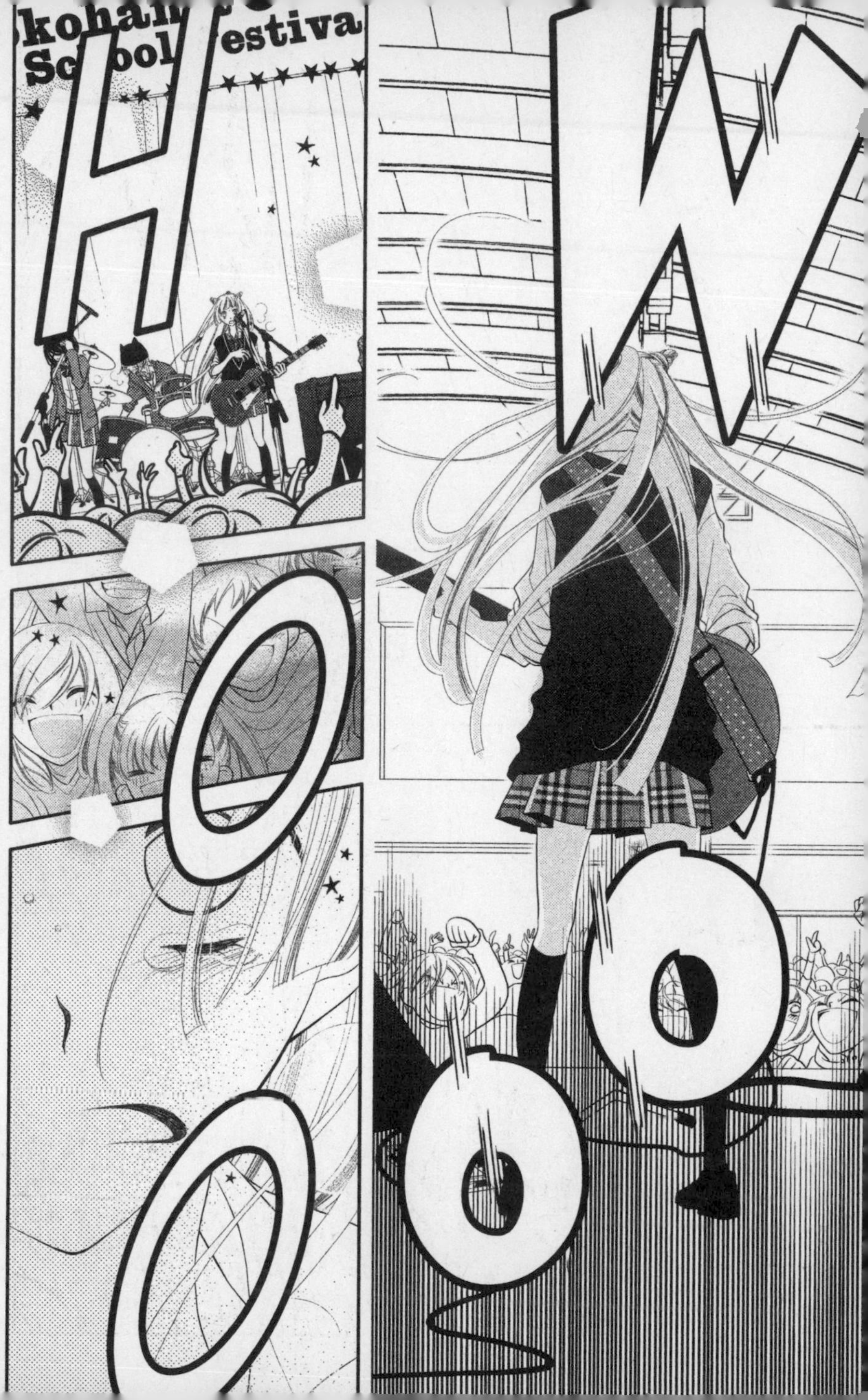
WHOOOO

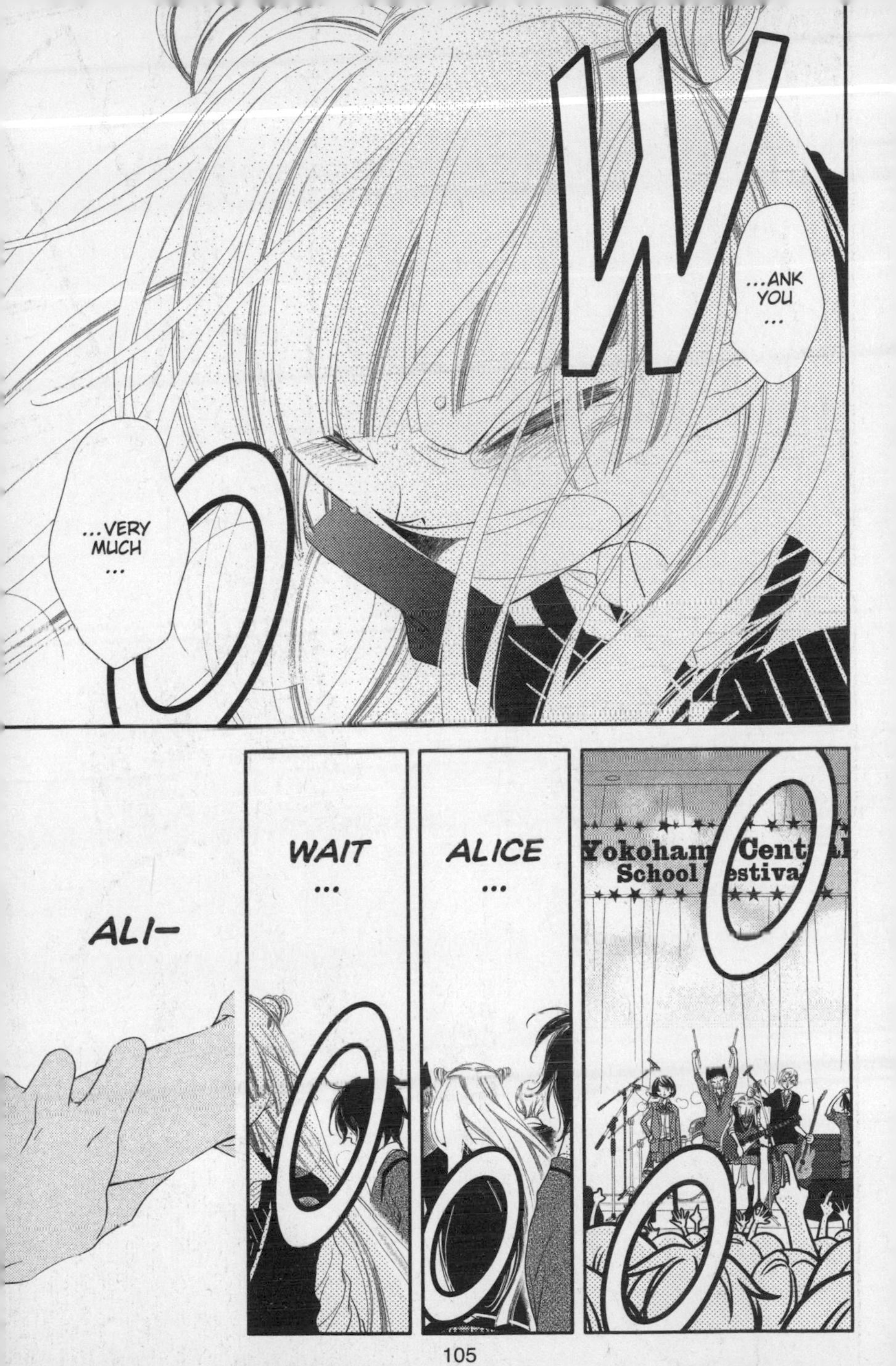
W
...ANK YOU ...
...VERY MUCH ...
ALICE ...
WAIT ...
ALI-

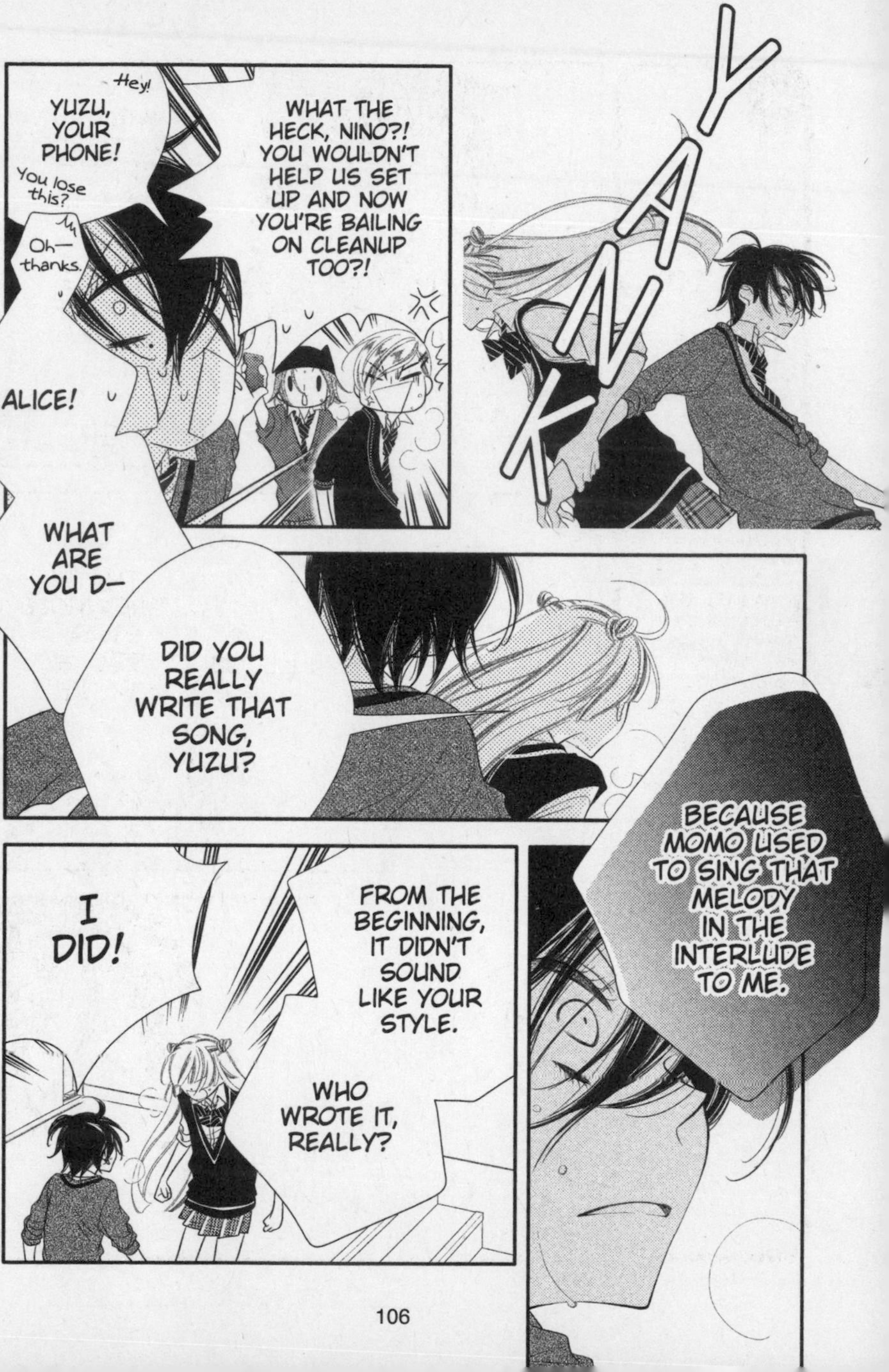
YANK
WHAT THE HECK, NINO?! YOU WOULDN'T HELP US SET UP AND NOW YOU'RE BAILING ON CLEANUP TOO?!
Hey!
YUZU, YOUR PHONE!
You lose this?
Oh— thanks.
ALICE!
WHAT ARE YOU D—
DID YOU REALLY WRITE THAT SONG, YUZU?
BECAUSE MOMO USED TO SING THAT MELODY IN THE INTERLUDE TO ME.
FROM THE BEGINNING, IT DIDN'T SOUND LIKE YOUR STYLE.
WHO WROTE IT, REALLY?
I DID!

4

To all my dear readers holding volume 7 of Anonymous Noise—have you had a chance to see the promotional video for it yet?

Daisuke Ono, who played Haruyoshi in the drama CD, was kind enough to step into the shoes of our favorite effeminate bassist one more time. At the recording session, the dedication he brought to the role left me deeply moved, and once again, his high-energy performance left me in stitches.

You're amazing, Mr. Ono!

YOU REALLY ARE!

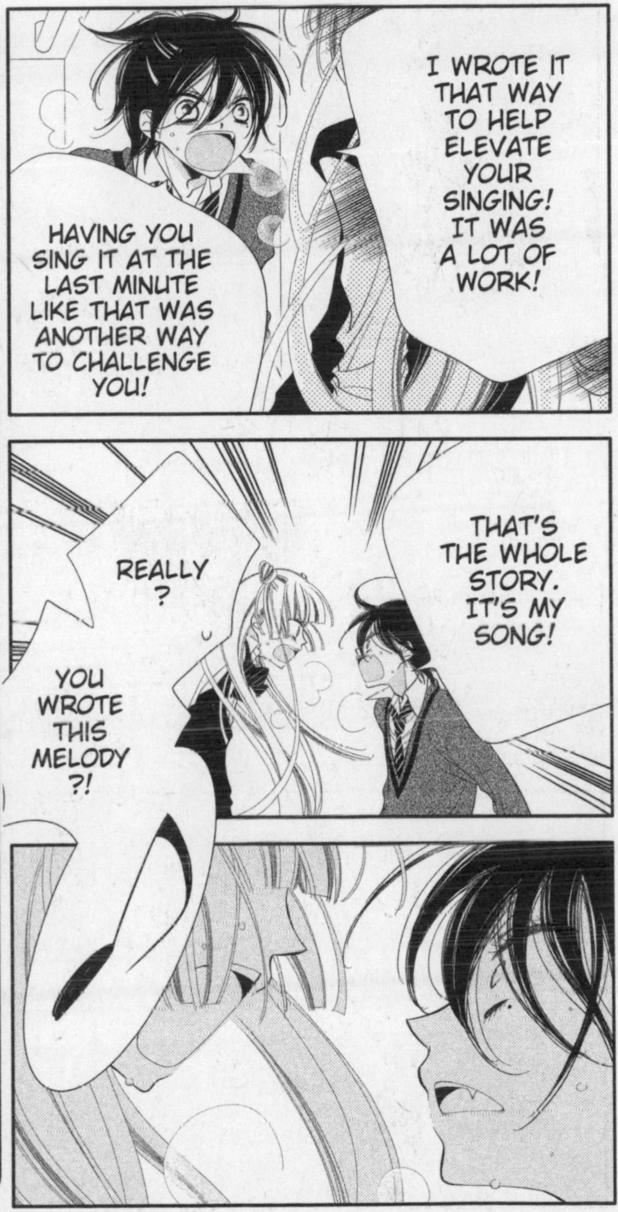
I WROTE IT THAT WAY TO HELP ELEVATE YOUR SINGING! IT WAS A LOT OF WORK!
HAVING YOU SING IT AT THE LAST MINUTE LIKE THAT WAS ANOTHER WAY TO CHALLENGE YOU!
THAT'S THE WHOLE STORY. IT'S MY SONG!
REALLY ?
YOU WROTE THIS MELODY ?!

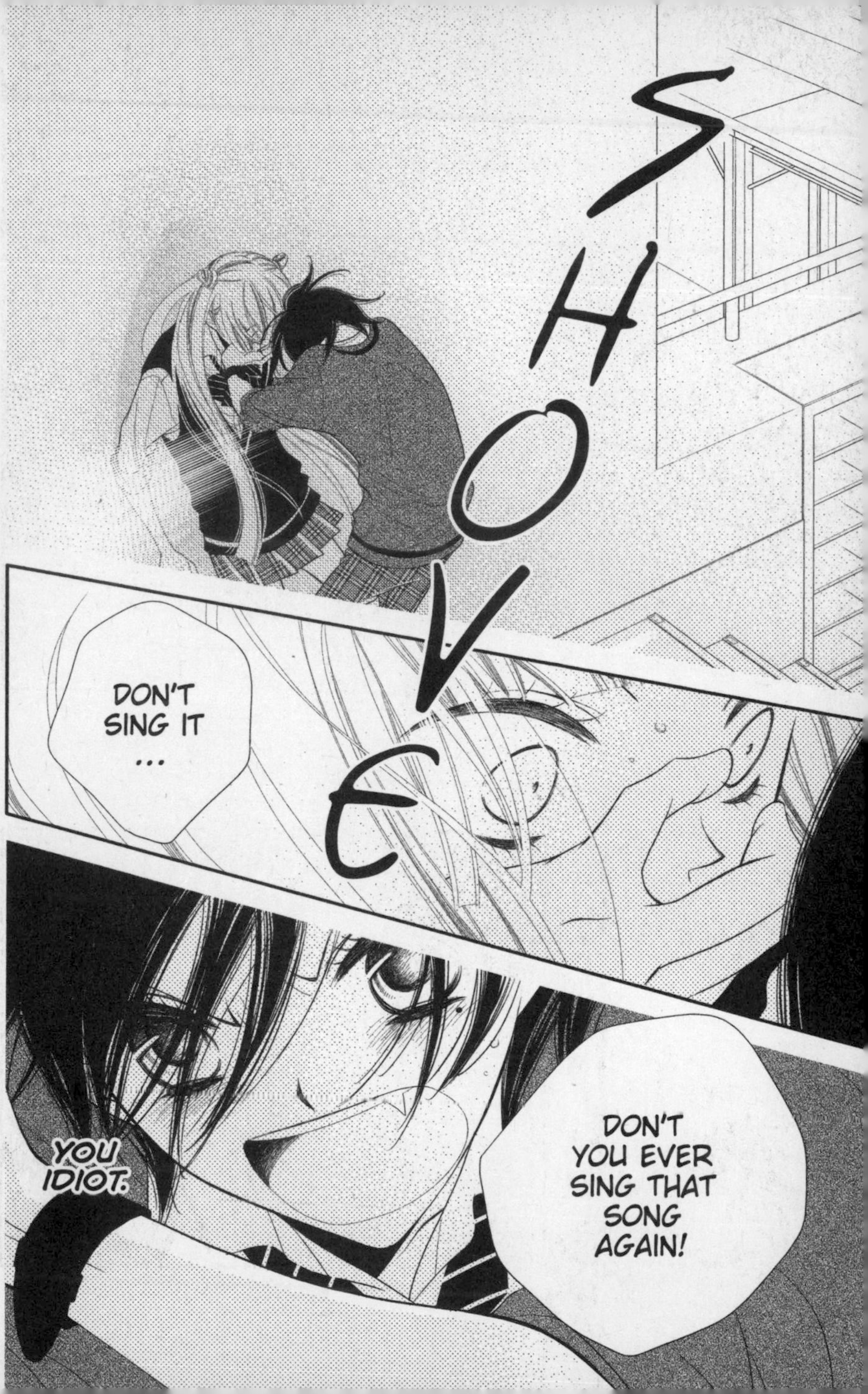
SHOVE
DON'T SING IT ...
DON'T YOU EVER SING THAT SONG AGAIN!
YOU IDIOT.

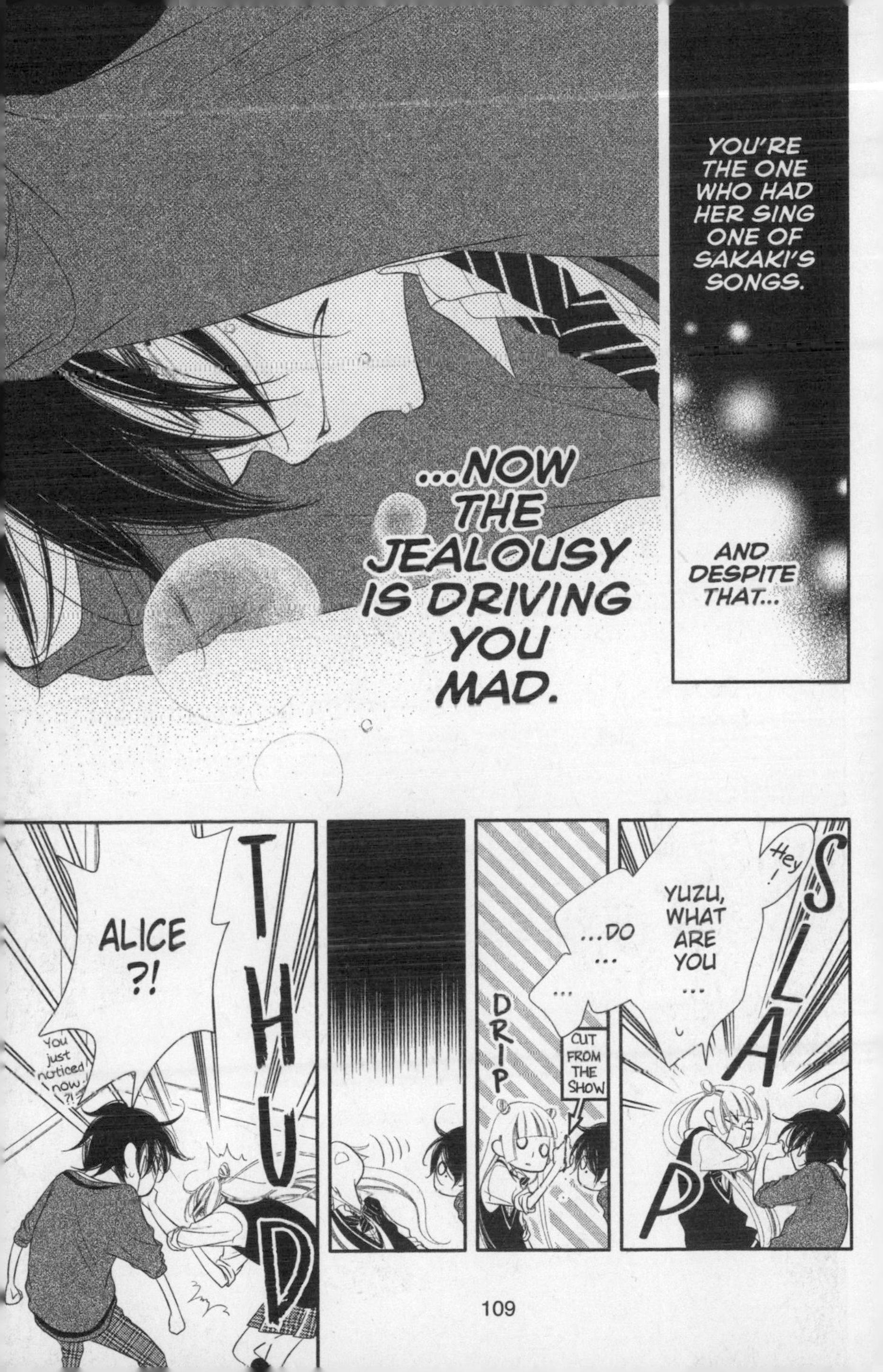
YOU'RE THE ONE WHO HAD HER SING ONE OF SAKAKI'S SONGS.
AND DESPITE THAT...
...NOW THE JEALOUSY IS DRIVING YOU MAD.
Hey!
YUZU, WHAT ARE YOU ...
SLAP
...DO ... ...
DRIP
CUT FROM THE SHOW
THUD
ALICE ?!
You just noticed now ?!

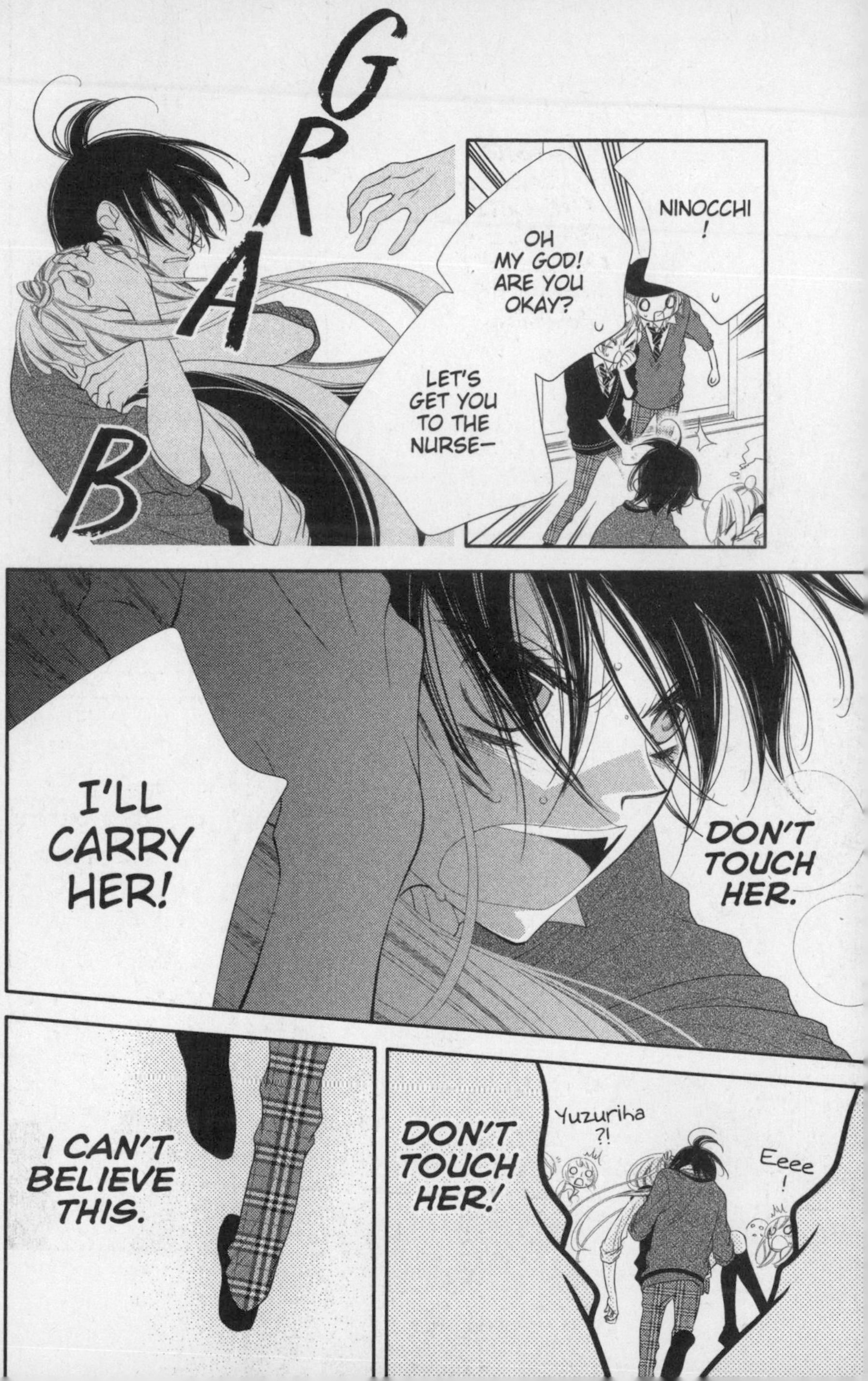
NINOCCHI!
OH MY GOD! ARE YOU OKAY?
LET'S GET YOU TO THE NURSE—
GRAB
DON'T TOUCH HER.
I'LL CARRY HER!
Eeee!
Yuzuriha?!
DON'T TOUCH HER!
I CAN'T BELIEVE THIS.

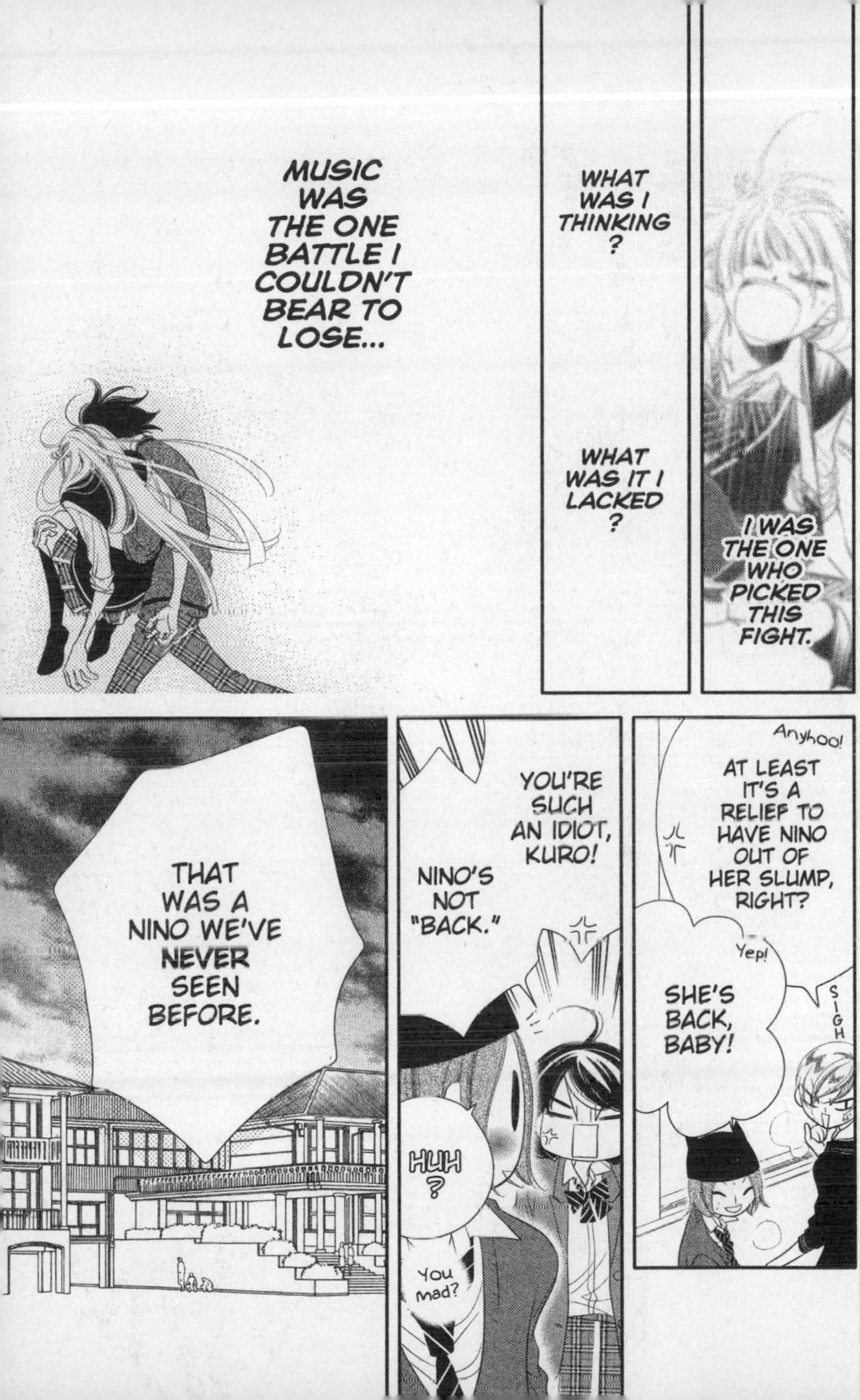
I WAS THE ONE WHO PICKED THIS FIGHT.
WHAT WAS I THINKING?
WHAT WAS IT I LACKED?
MUSIC WAS THE ONE BATTLE I COULDN'T BEAR TO LOSE...
Anyhoo!
AT LEAST IT'S A RELIEF TO HAVE NINO OUT OF HER SLUMP, RIGHT?
SHE'S BACK, BABY!
Yep!
SIGH
YOU'RE SUCH AN IDIOT, KURO!
NINO'S NOT "BACK."
HUH?
You mad?
THAT WAS A NINO WE'VE NEVER SEEN BEFORE.

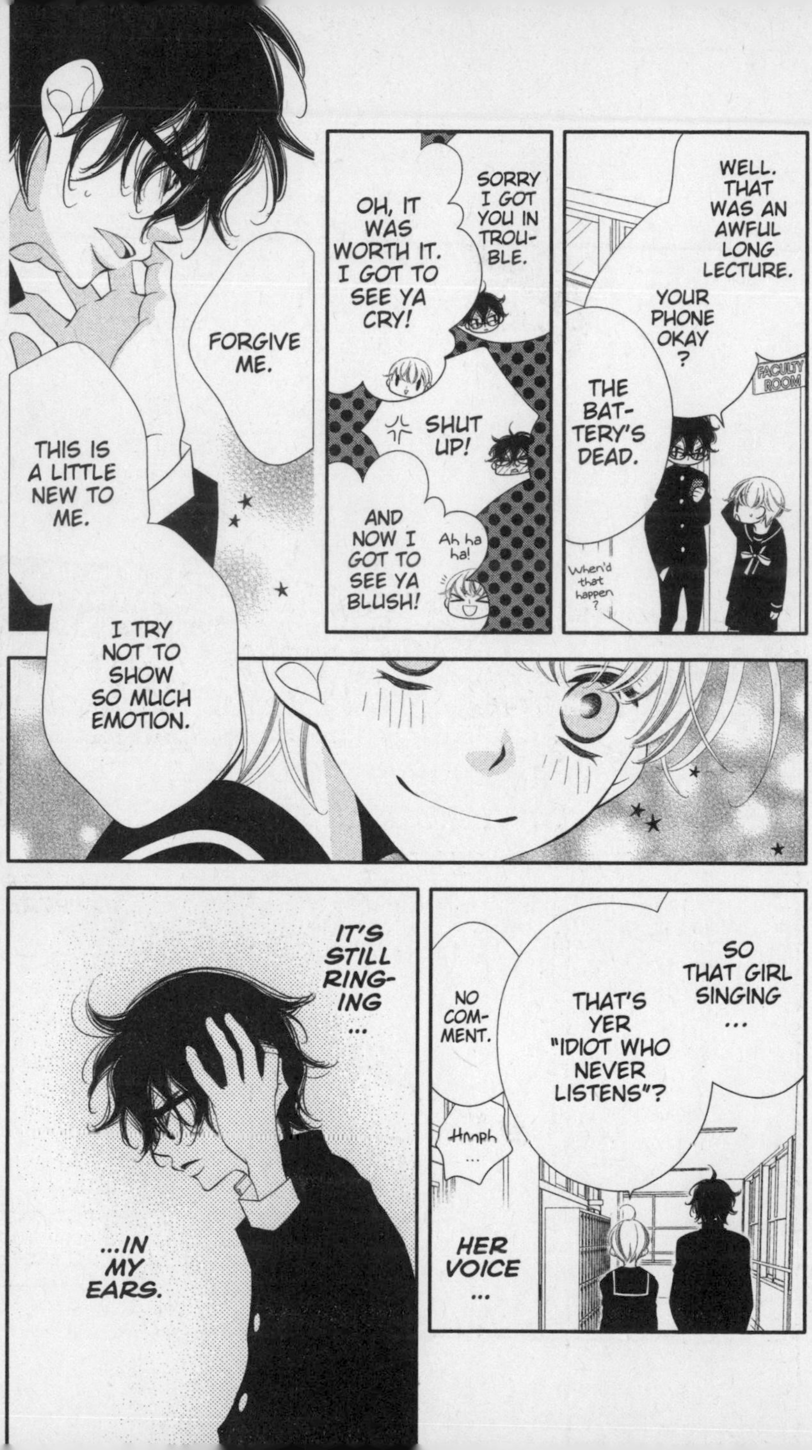
WELL. THAT WAS AN AWFUL LONG LECTURE.
YOUR PHONE OKAY?
FACULTY ROOM
THE BATTERY'S DEAD.
When'd that happen?
SORRY I GOT YOU IN TROUBLE.
OH, IT WAS WORTH IT. I GOT TO SEE YA CRY!
SHUT UP!
AND NOW I GOT TO SEE YA BLUSH!
Ah ha ha!
FORGIVE ME.
THIS IS A LITTLE NEW TO ME.
I TRY NOT TO SHOW SO MUCH EMOTION.
SO THAT GIRL SINGING...
THAT'S YER "IDIOT WHO NEVER LISTENS"?
NO COMMENT.
Hmph...
HER VOICE...
IT'S STILL RINGING...
...IN MY EARS.

NINO...

AT THIS POINT...

YOU'VE FOUND YOUR WINGS.

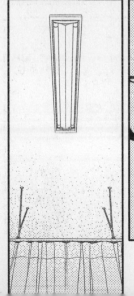

...THERE'S NOWHERE...

...YOU CAN'T FLY.

NURSE

113

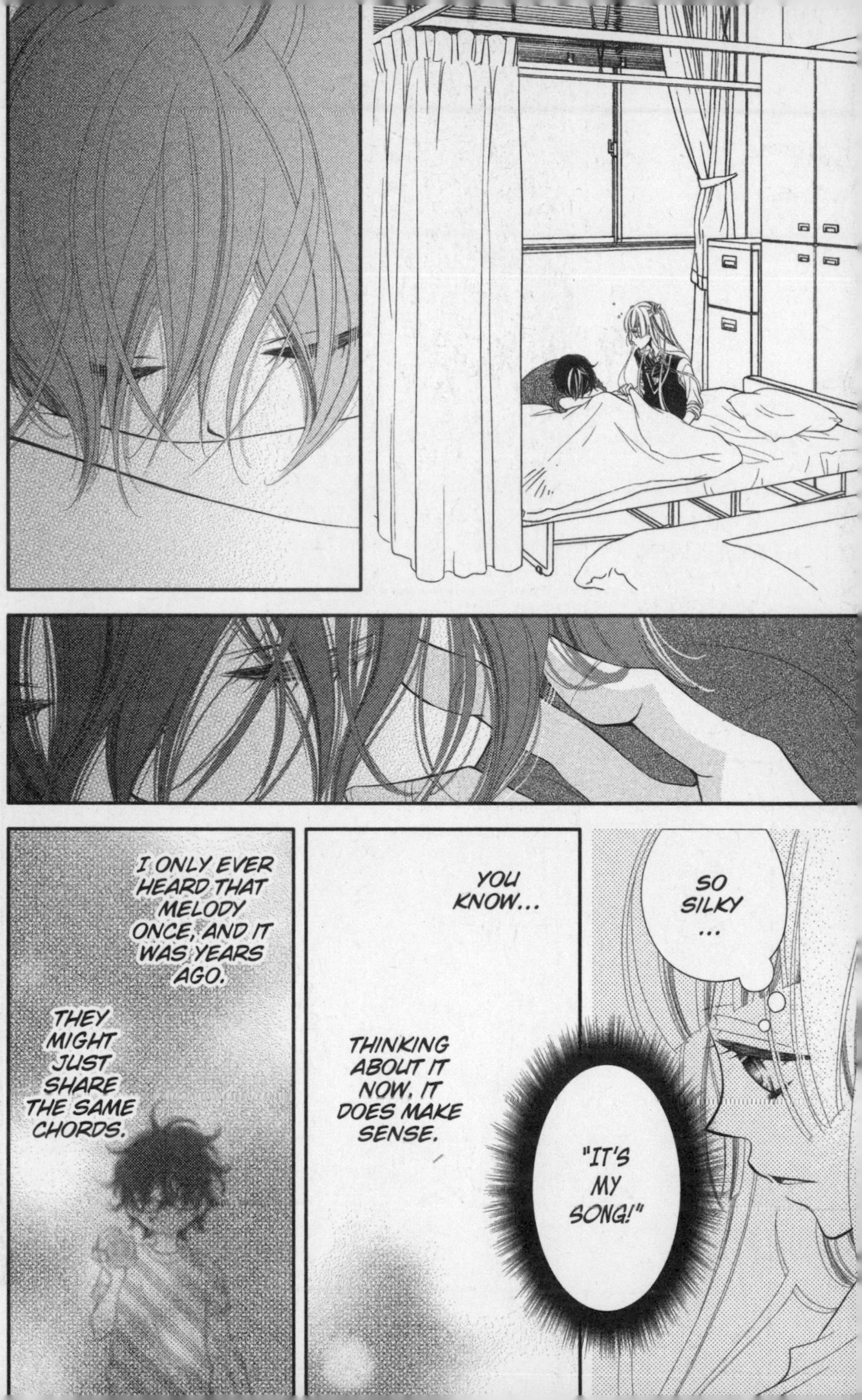
SO SILKY ...
"IT'S MY SONG!"
YOU KNOW...
THINKING ABOUT IT NOW, IT DOES MAKE SENSE.
I ONLY EVER HEARD THAT MELODY ONCE, AND IT WAS YEARS AGO.
THEY MIGHT JUST SHARE THE SAME CHORDS.

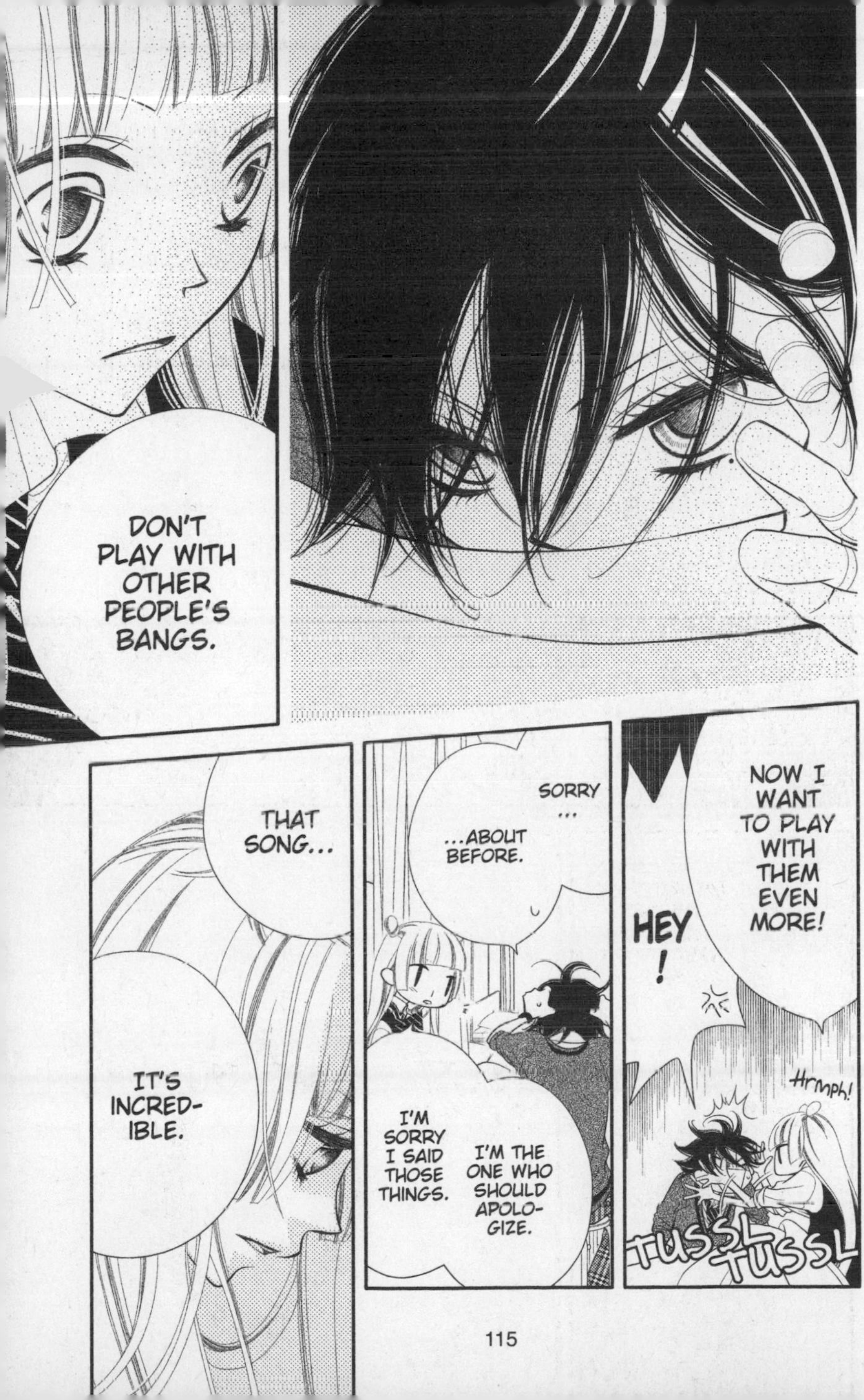
DON'T PLAY WITH OTHER PEOPLE'S BANGS.
NOW I WANT TO PLAY WITH THEM EVEN MORE!
HEY!
Hrmph!
TUSSL TUSSL
SORRY...
...ABOUT BEFORE.
I'M THE ONE WHO SHOULD APOLOGIZE.
I'M SORRY I SAID THOSE THINGS.
THAT SONG...
IT'S INCREDIBLE.

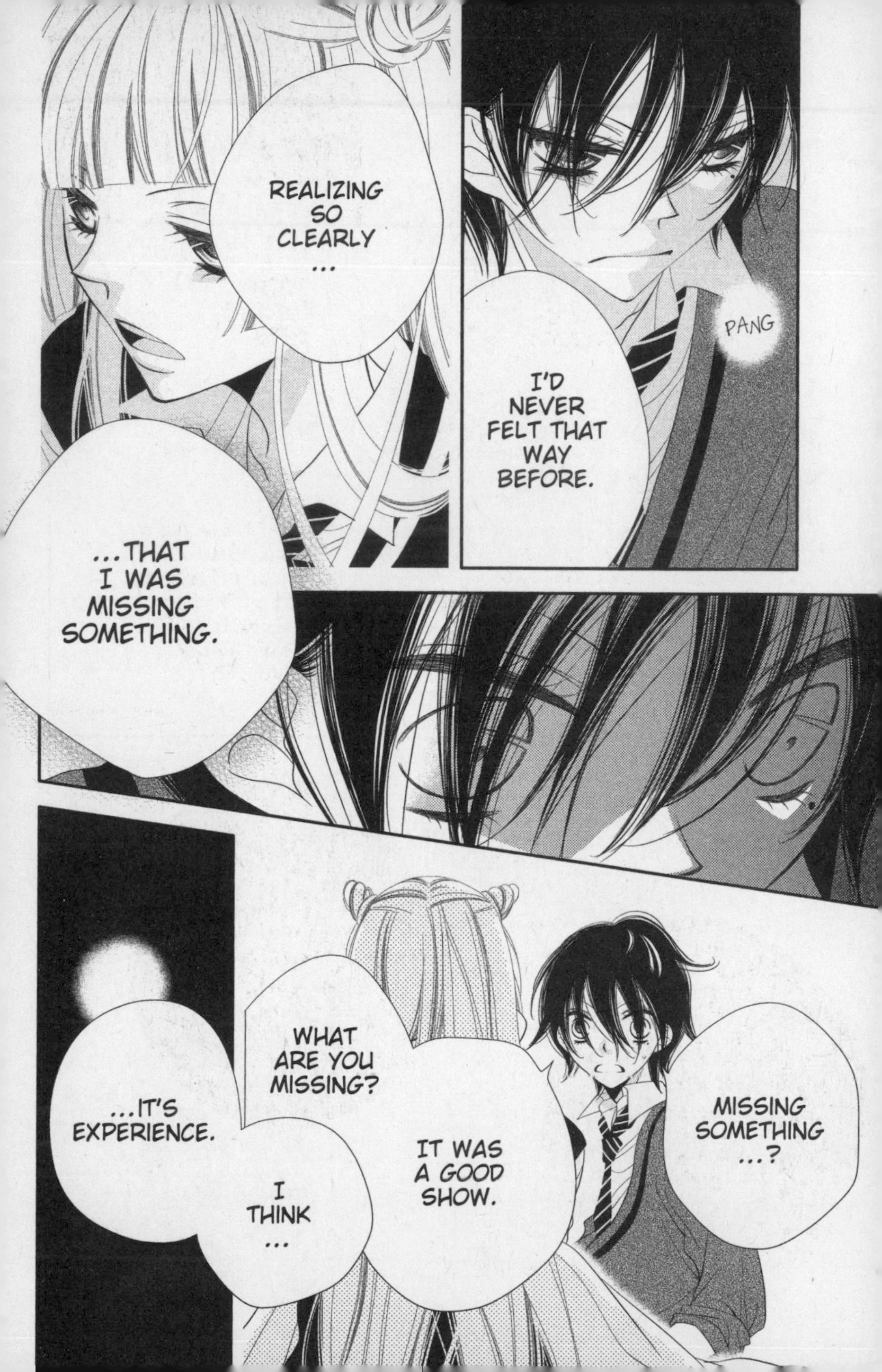
PANG
I'D NEVER FELT THAT WAY BEFORE.
REALIZING SO CLEARLY ...
...THAT I WAS MISSING SOMETHING.
MISSING SOMETHING ...?
WHAT ARE YOU MISSING?
IT WAS A GOOD SHOW.
I THINK ...
...IT'S EXPERIENCE.

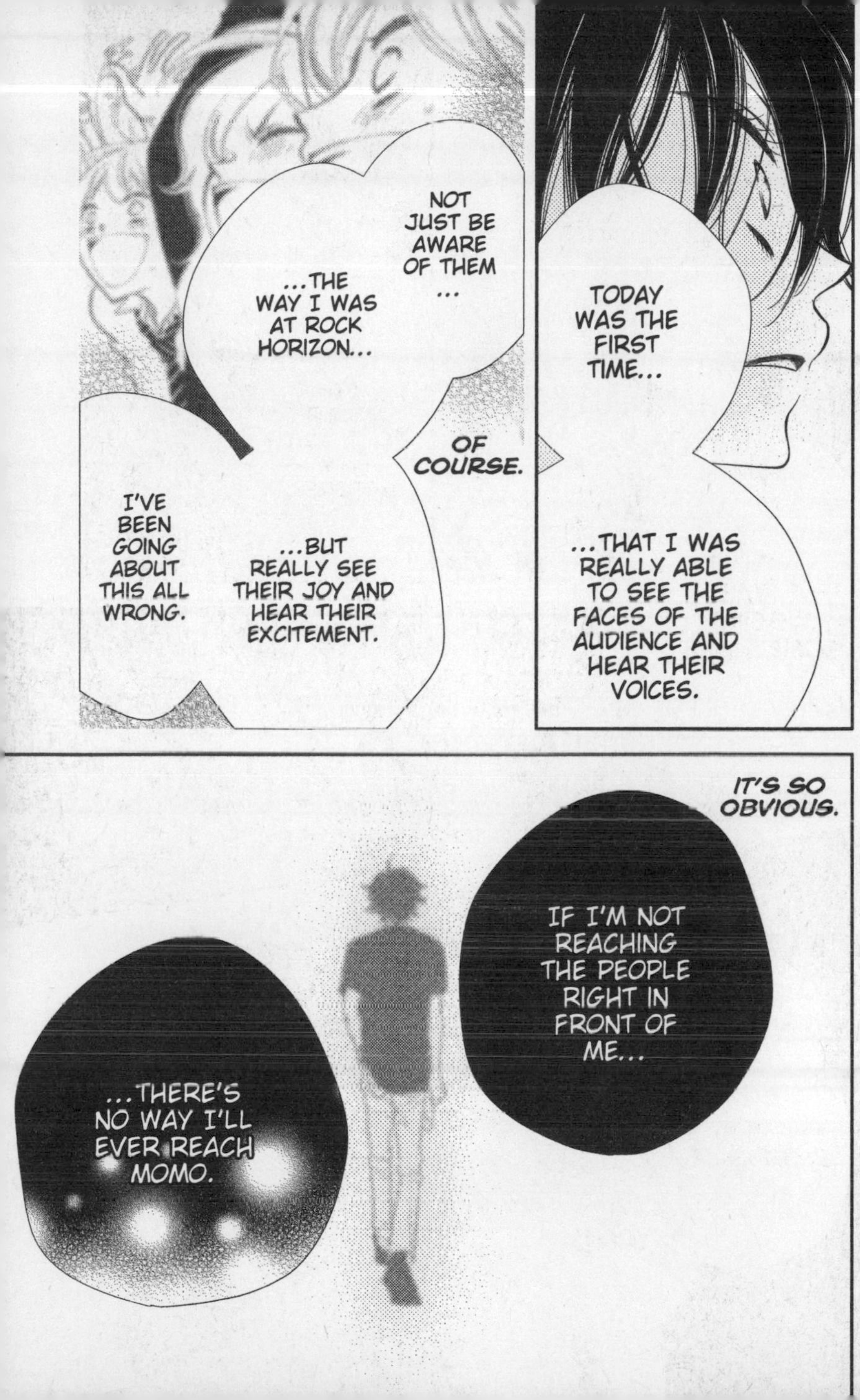
TODAY WAS THE FIRST TIME...
...THAT I WAS REALLY ABLE TO SEE THE FACES OF THE AUDIENCE AND HEAR THEIR VOICES.
OF COURSE.
NOT JUST BE AWARE OF THEM...
...THE WAY I WAS AT ROCK HORIZON...
...BUT REALLY SEE THEIR JOY AND HEAR THEIR EXCITEMENT.
I'VE BEEN GOING ABOUT THIS ALL WRONG.
IT'S SO OBVIOUS.
IF I'M NOT REACHING THE PEOPLE RIGHT IN FRONT OF ME...
...THERE'S NO WAY I'LL EVER REACH MOMO.

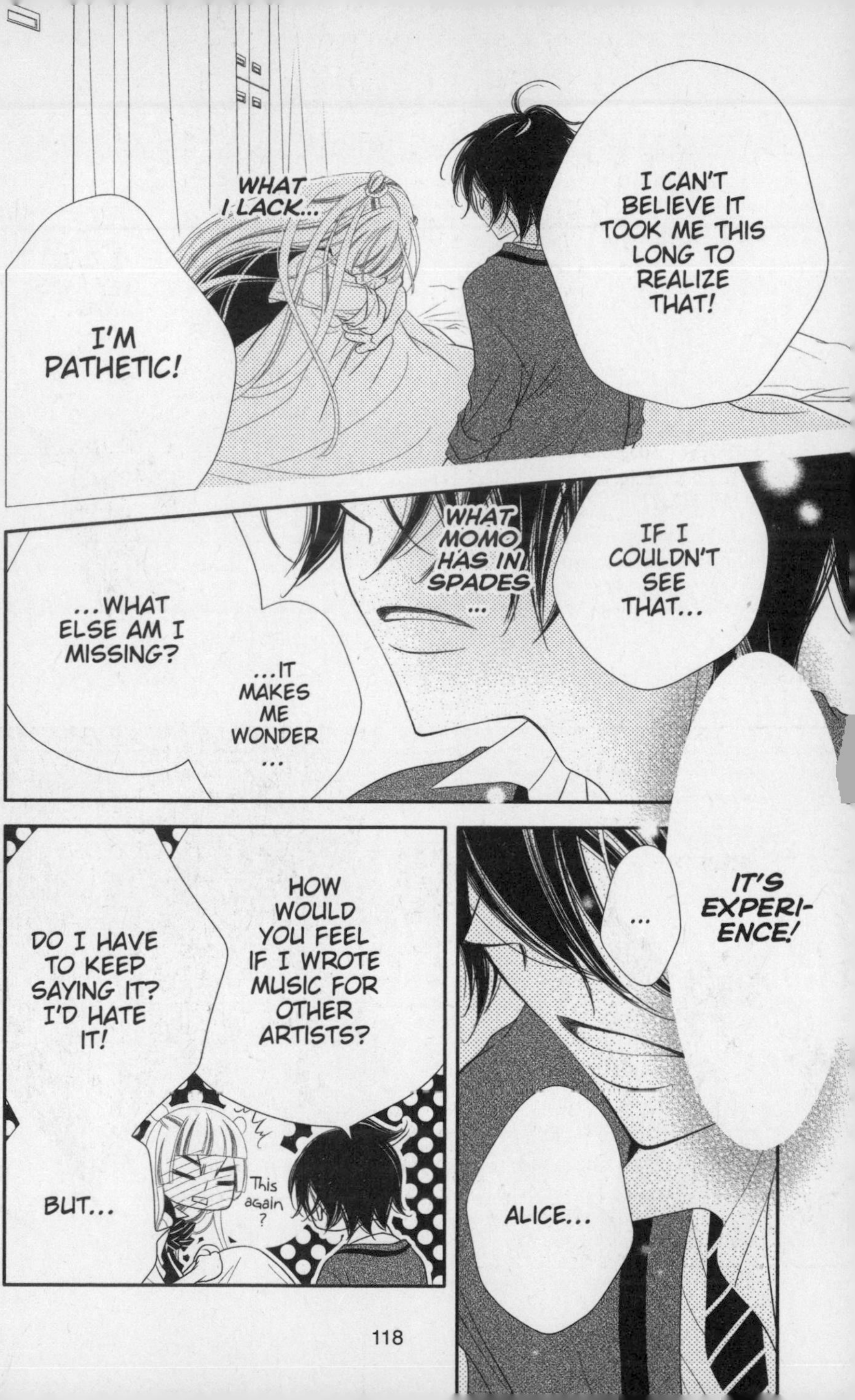
I CAN'T BELIEVE IT TOOK ME THIS LONG TO REALIZE THAT!
WHAT I LACK...
I'M PATHETIC!
IF I COULDN'T SEE THAT...
WHAT MOMO HAS IN SPADES...
...IT MAKES ME WONDER...
...WHAT ELSE AM I MISSING?
IT'S EXPERI-ENCE!
...
ALICE...
HOW WOULD YOU FEEL IF I WROTE MUSIC FOR OTHER ARTISTS?
DO I HAVE TO KEEP SAYING IT? I'D HATE IT!
This again?
BUT...

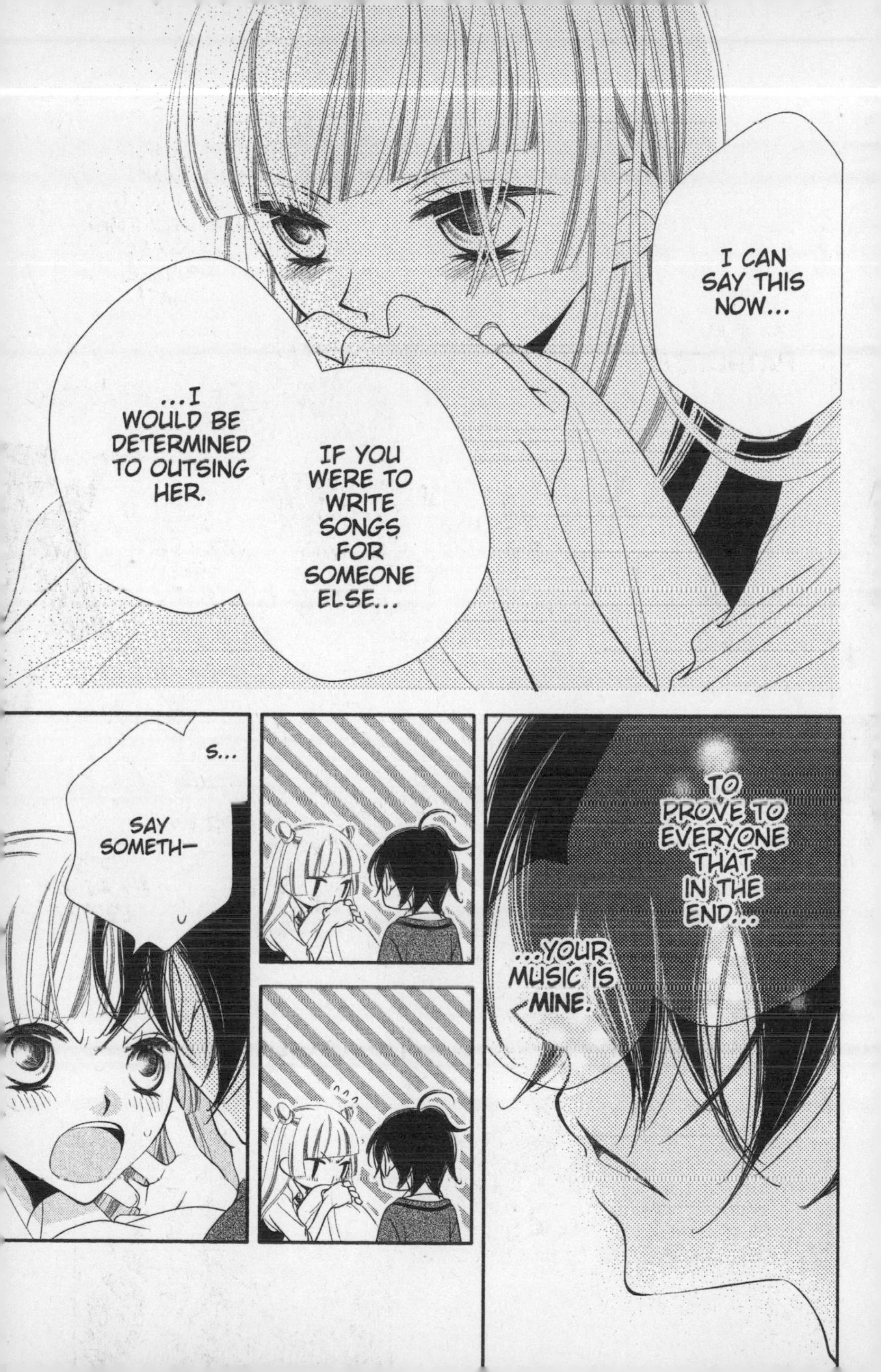
I CAN SAY THIS NOW...
IF YOU WERE TO WRITE SONGS FOR SOMEONE ELSE...
...I WOULD BE DETERMINED TO OUTSING HER.
TO PROVE TO EVERYONE THAT IN THE END...
...YOUR MUSIC IS MINE.
S...
SAY SOMETH—

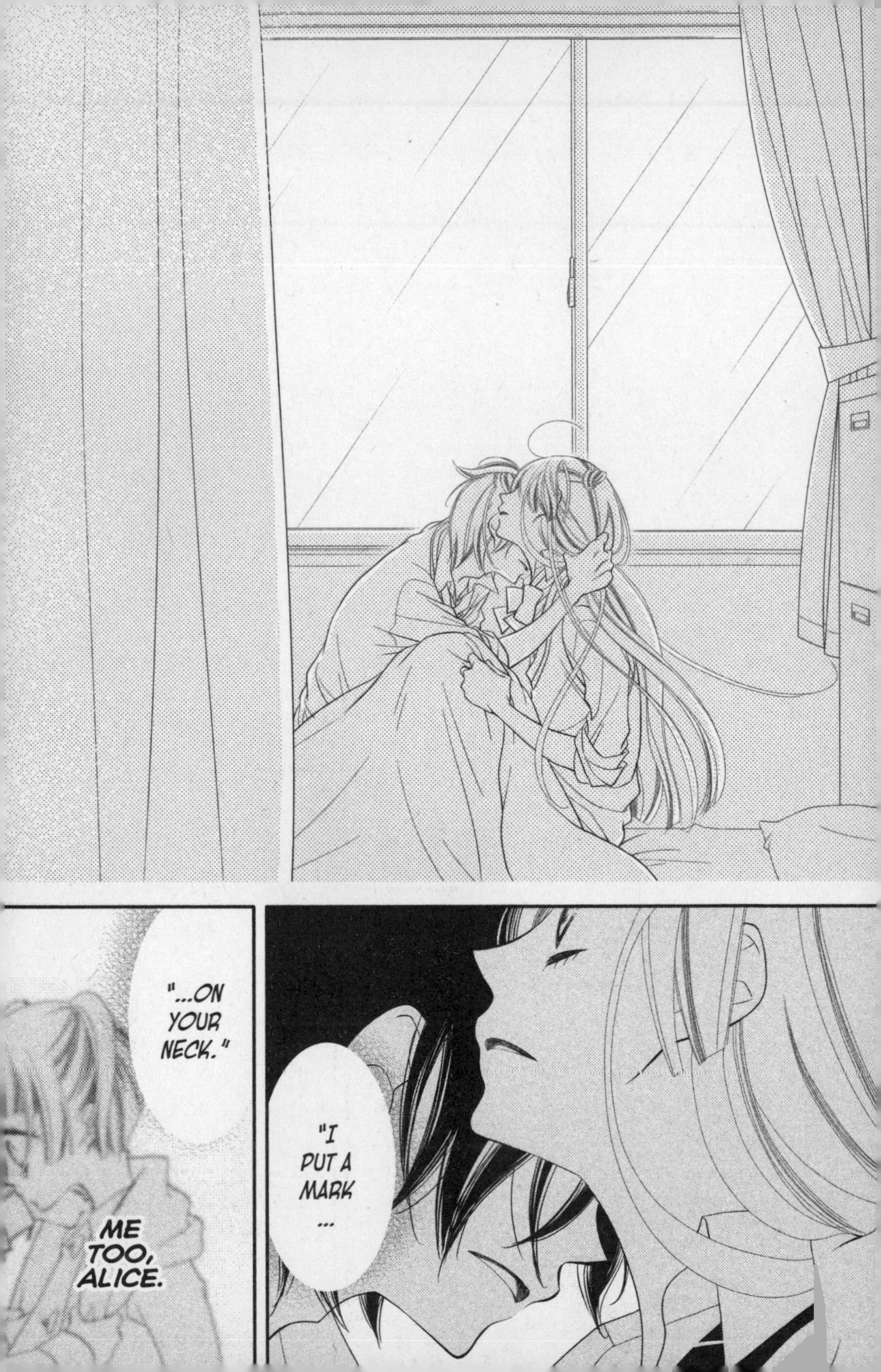
"I PUT A MARK ...
"...ON YOUR NECK."
ME TOO, ALICE.

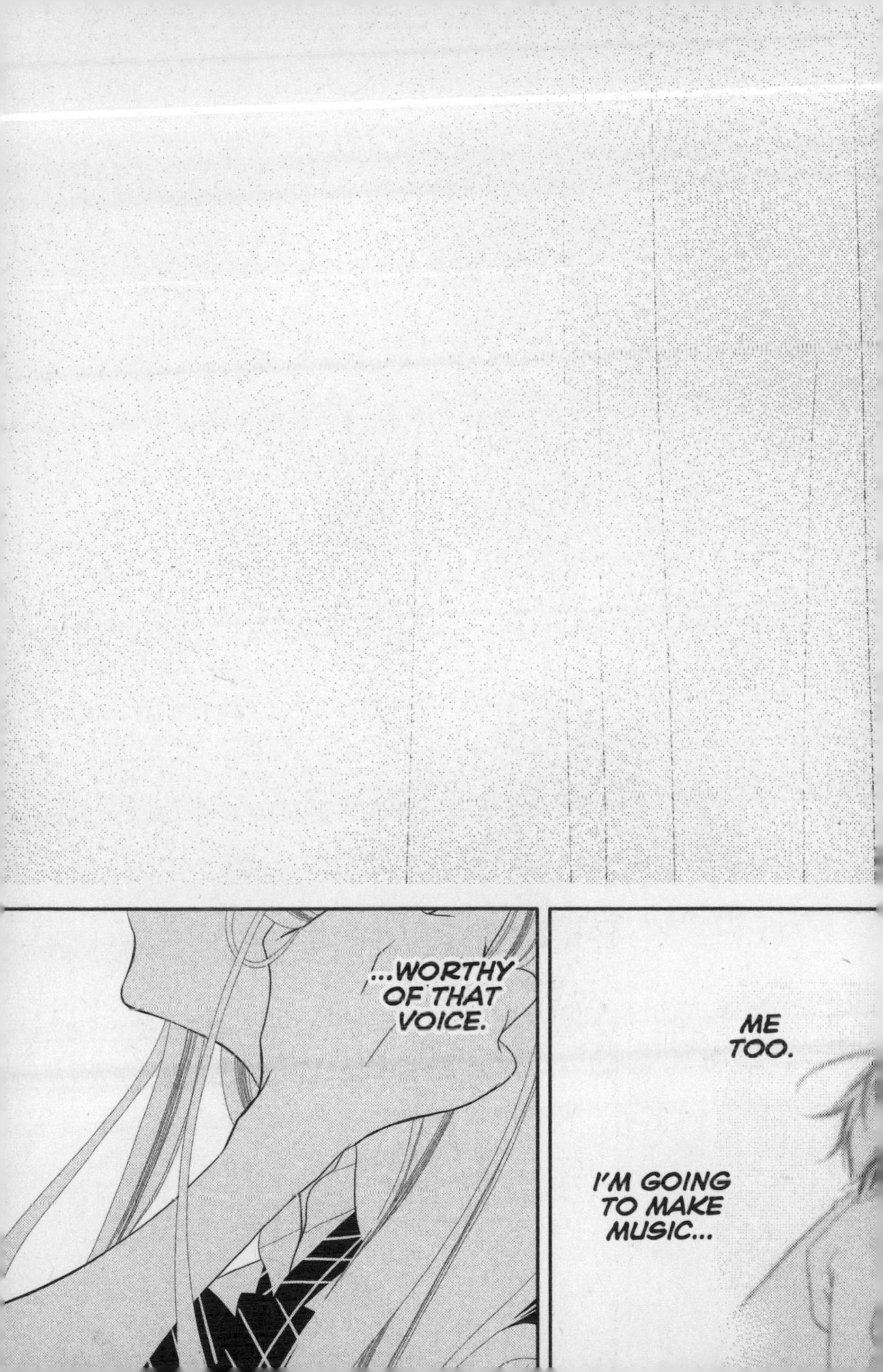
ME TOO.
I'M GOING TO MAKE MUSIC...
...WORTHY OF THAT VOICE.

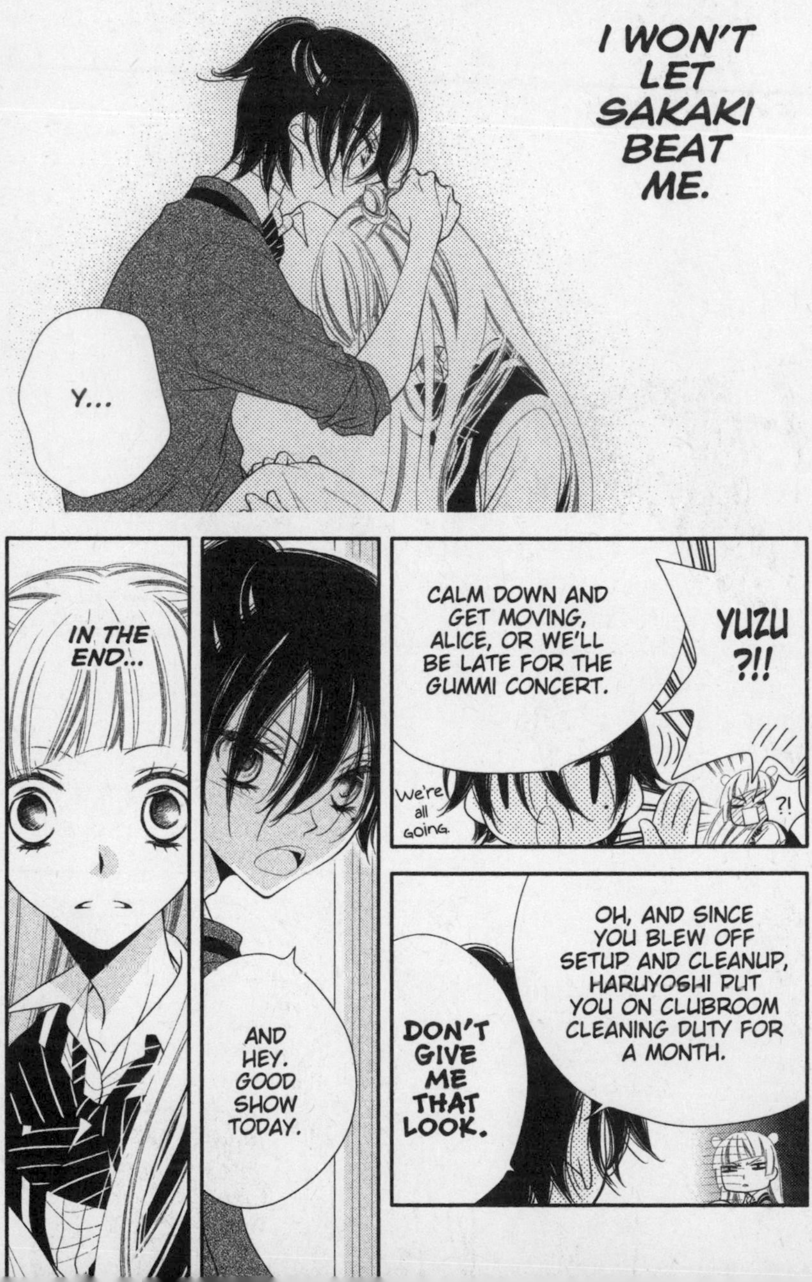
I WON'T LET SAKAKI BEAT ME.
Y...
YUZU ?!!
CALM DOWN AND GET MOVING, ALICE, OR WE'LL BE LATE FOR THE GUMMI CONCERT.
We're all going.
?!
OH, AND SINCE YOU BLEW OFF SETUP AND CLEANUP, HARUYOSHI PUT YOU ON CLUBROOM CLEANING DUTY FOR A MONTH.
DON'T GIVE ME THAT LOOK.
AND HEY. GOOD SHOW TODAY.
IN THE END...

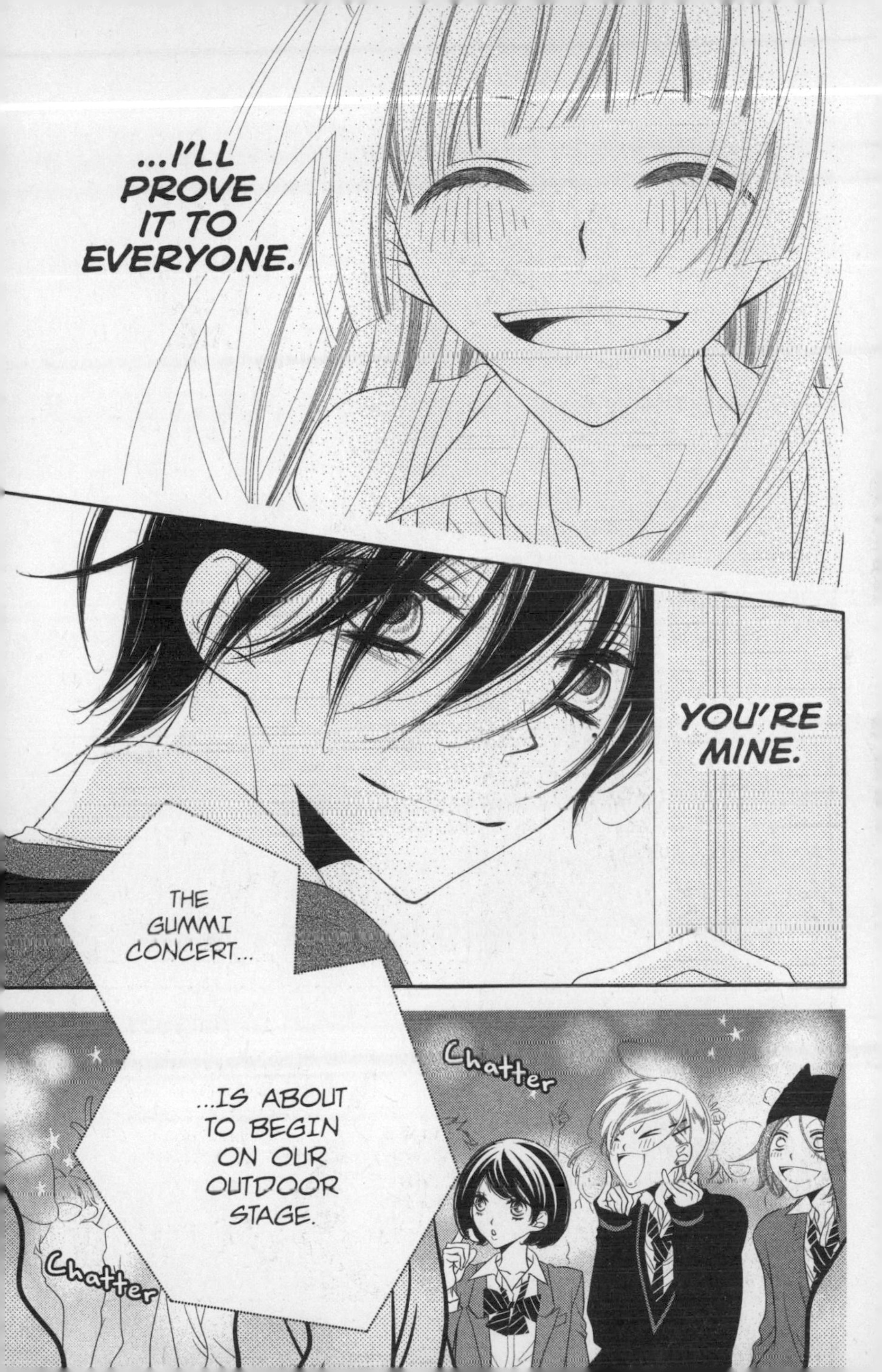
...I'LL PROVE IT TO EVERYONE.
YOU'RE MINE.
THE GUMMI CONCERT...
...IS ABOUT TO BEGIN ON OUR OUTDOOR STAGE.
Chatter
Chatter

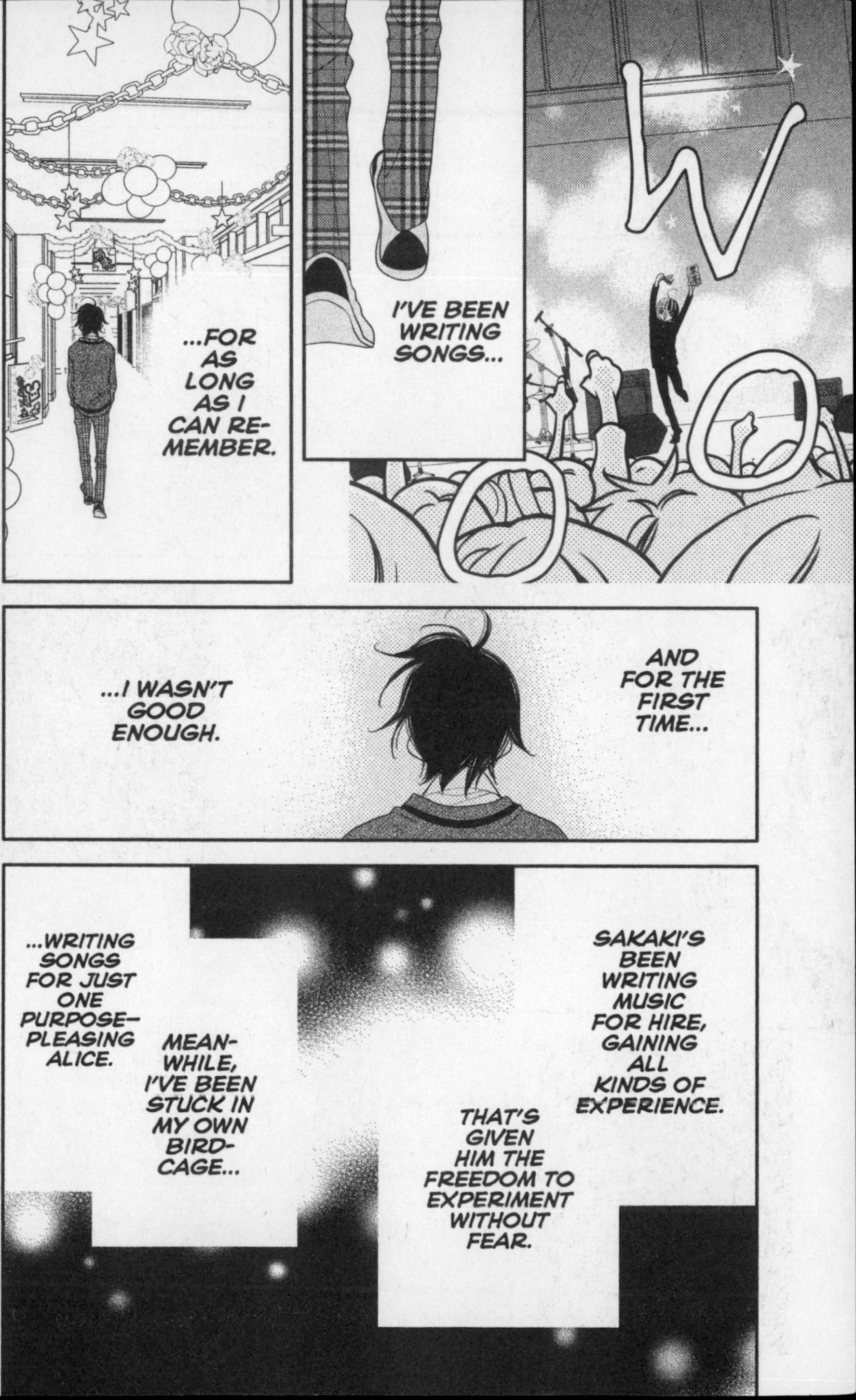
WOO
I'VE BEEN WRITING SONGS...
...FOR AS LONG AS I CAN REMEMBER.
AND FOR THE FIRST TIME...
...I WASN'T GOOD ENOUGH.
SAKAKI'S BEEN WRITING MUSIC FOR HIRE, GAINING ALL KINDS OF EXPERIENCE.
THAT'S GIVEN HIM THE FREEDOM TO EXPERIMENT WITHOUT FEAR.
MEANWHILE, I'VE BEEN STUCK IN MY OWN BIRDCAGE...
...WRITING SONGS FOR JUST ONE PURPOSE—PLEASING ALICE.

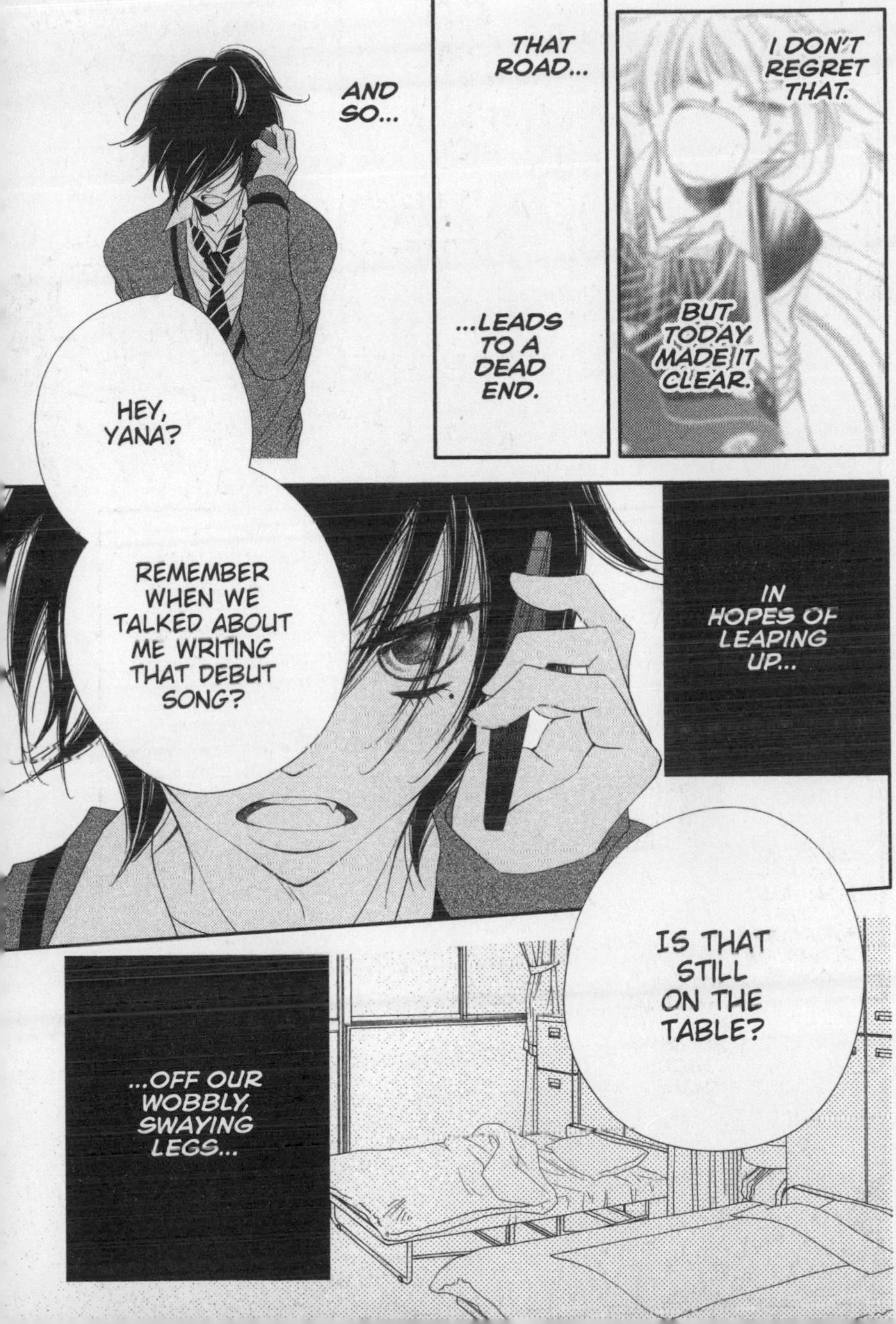
I DON'T REGRET THAT.
BUT TODAY MADE IT CLEAR.
THAT ROAD...
...LEADS TO A DEAD END.
AND SO...
HEY, YANA?
IN HOPES OF LEAPING UP...
REMEMBER WHEN WE TALKED ABOUT ME WRITING THAT DEBUT SONG?
IS THAT STILL ON THE TABLE?
...OFF OUR WOBBLY, SWAYING LEGS...

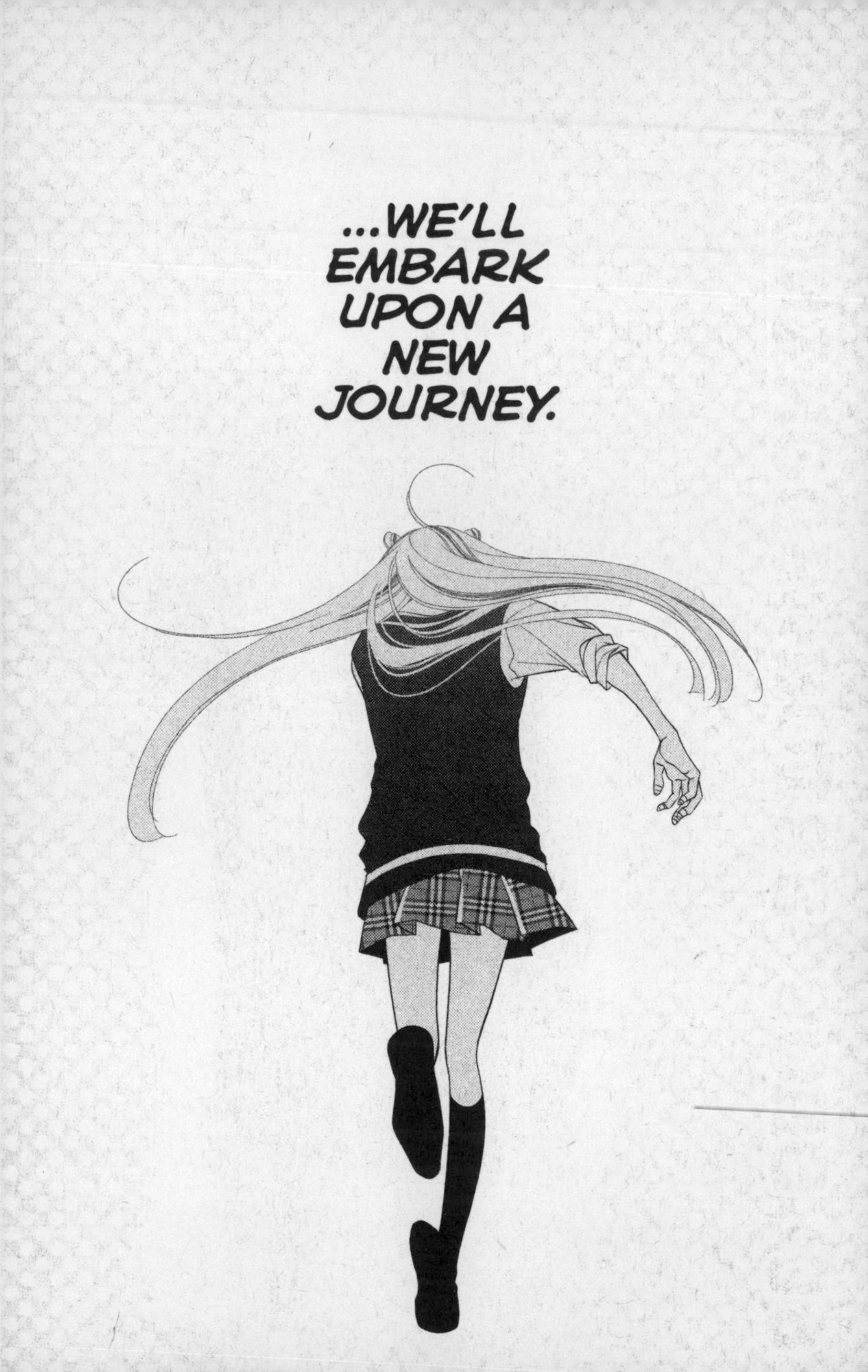
...WE'LL EMBARK UPON A NEW JOURNEY.

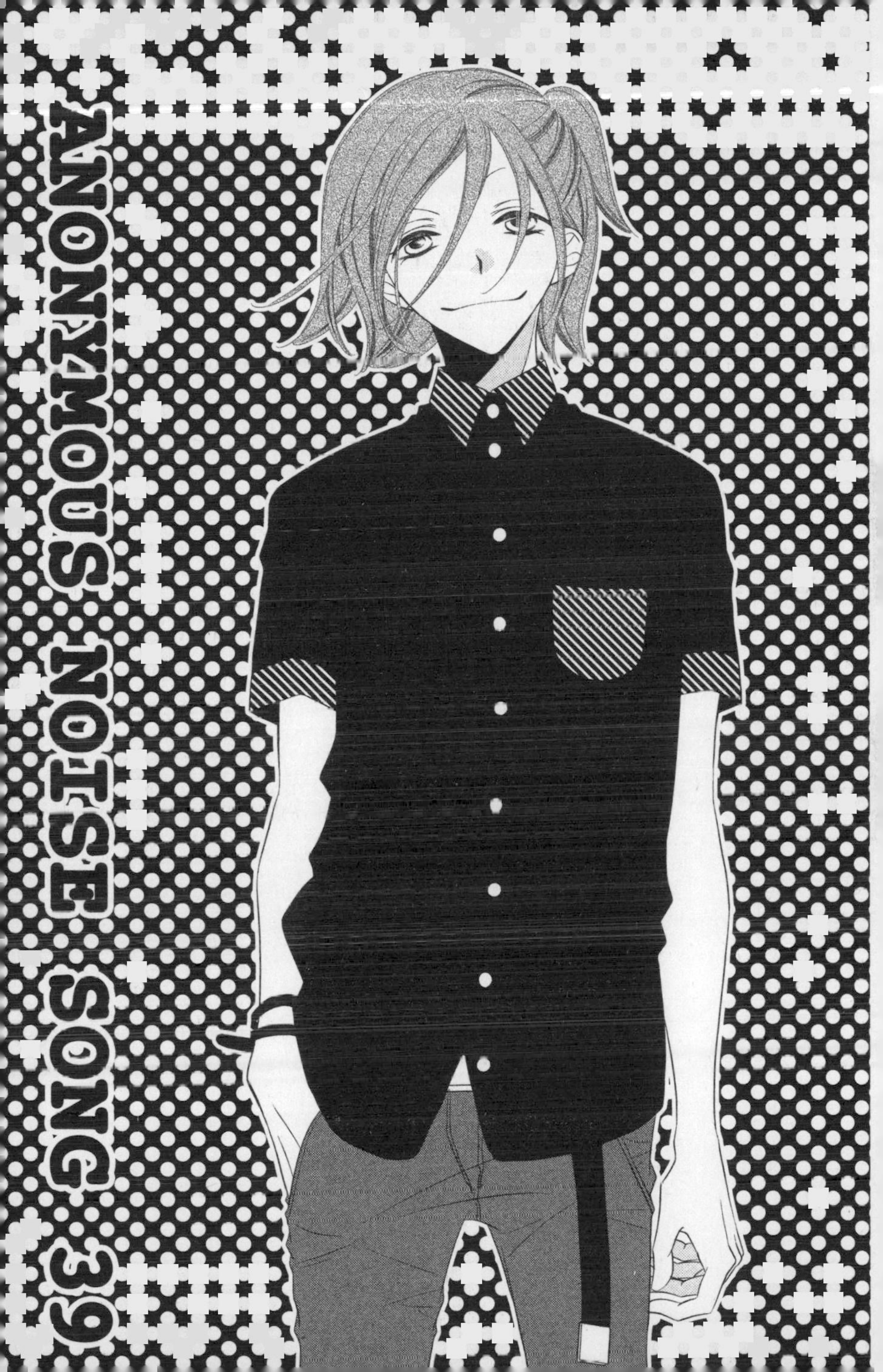
ANONYMOUS NOISE 39

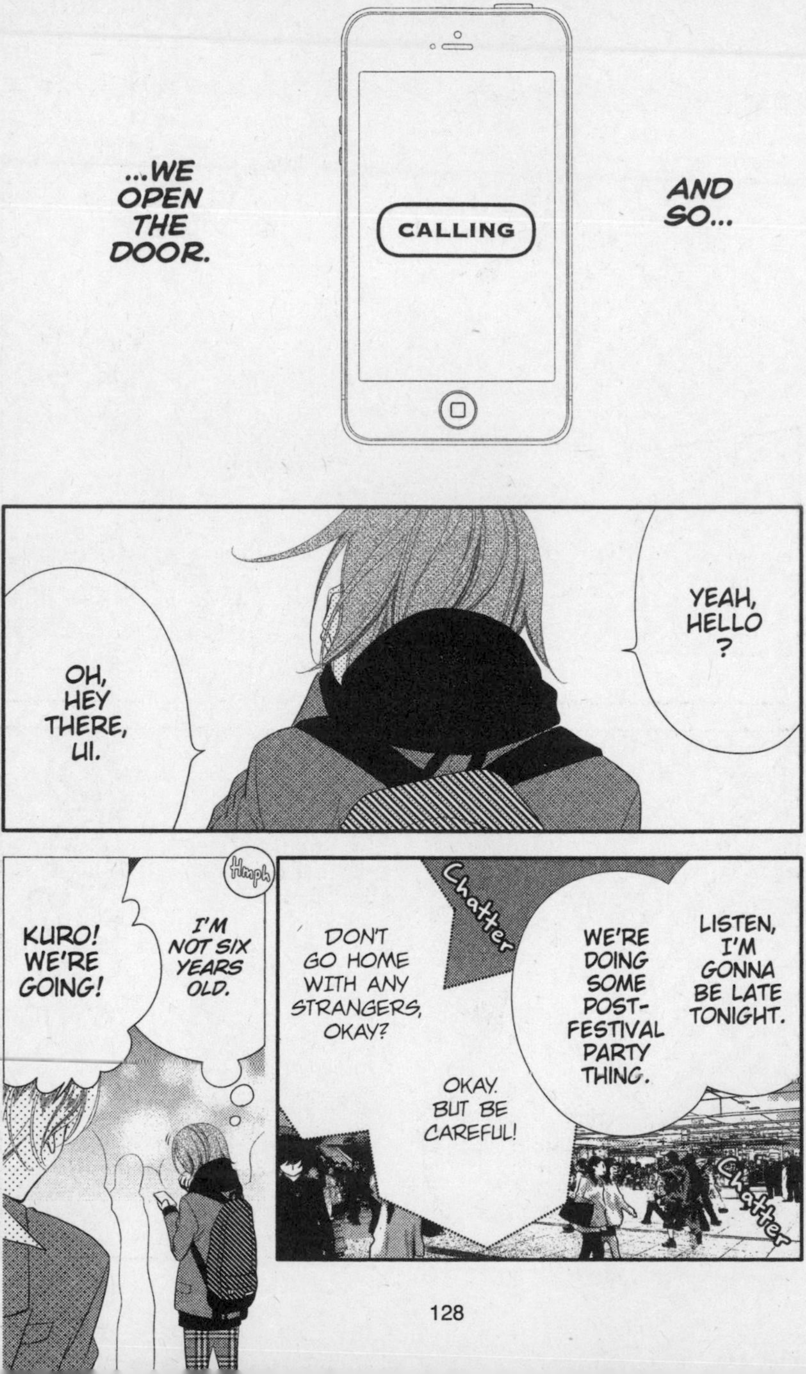
AND SO...
CALLING
...WE OPEN THE DOOR.
YEAH, HELLO?
OH, HEY THERE, UI.
LISTEN, I'M GONNA BE LATE TONIGHT.
WE'RE DOING SOME POST-FESTIVAL PARTY THING.
Chatter
DON'T GO HOME WITH ANY STRANGERS, OKAY?
OKAY. BUT BE CAREFUL!
Chatter
Hmph
I'M NOT SIX YEARS OLD.
KURO! WE'RE GOING!

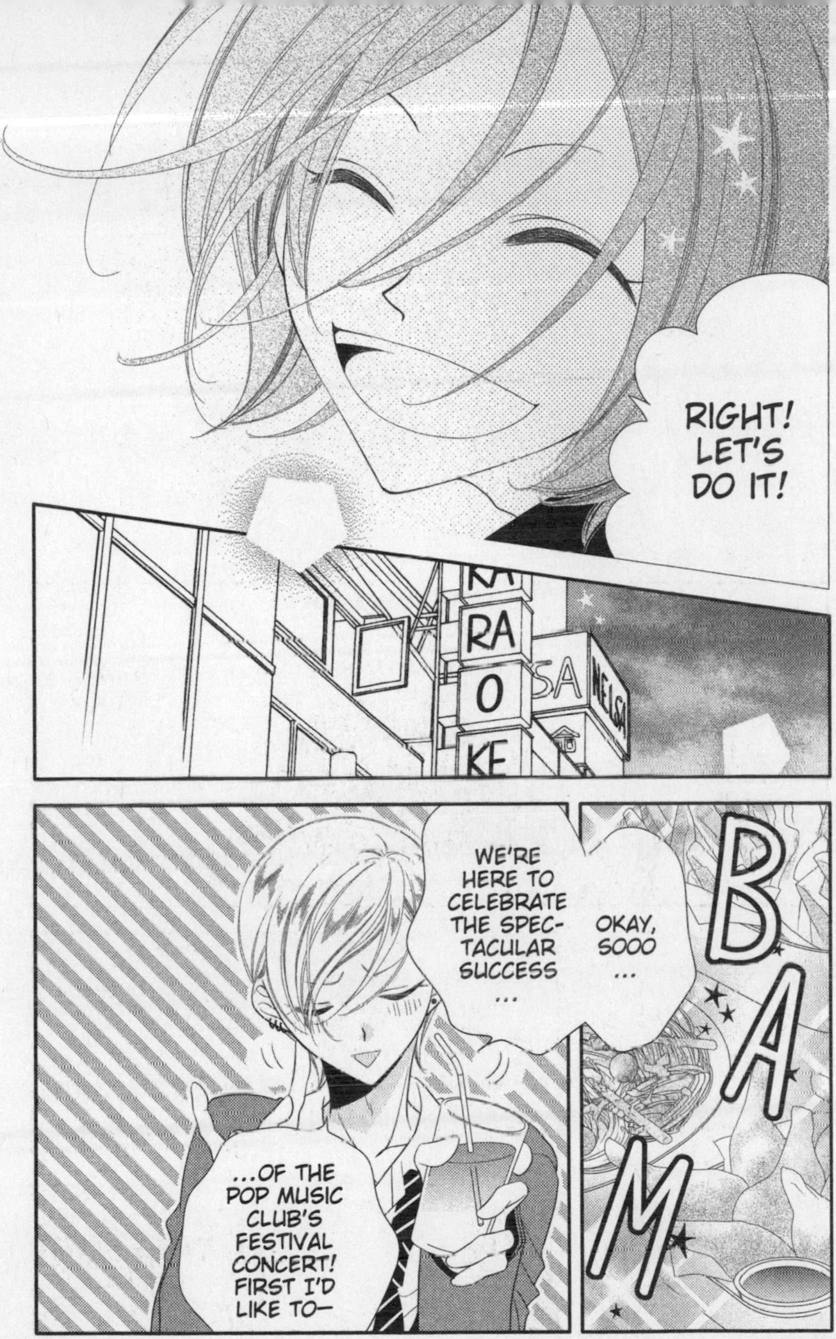
RIGHT! LET'S DO IT!
BAM
OKAY, SOOO ...
WE'RE HERE TO CELEBRATE THE SPEC- TACULAR SUCCESS ...
...OF THE POP MUSIC CLUB'S FESTIVAL CONCERT! FIRST I'D LIKE TO—

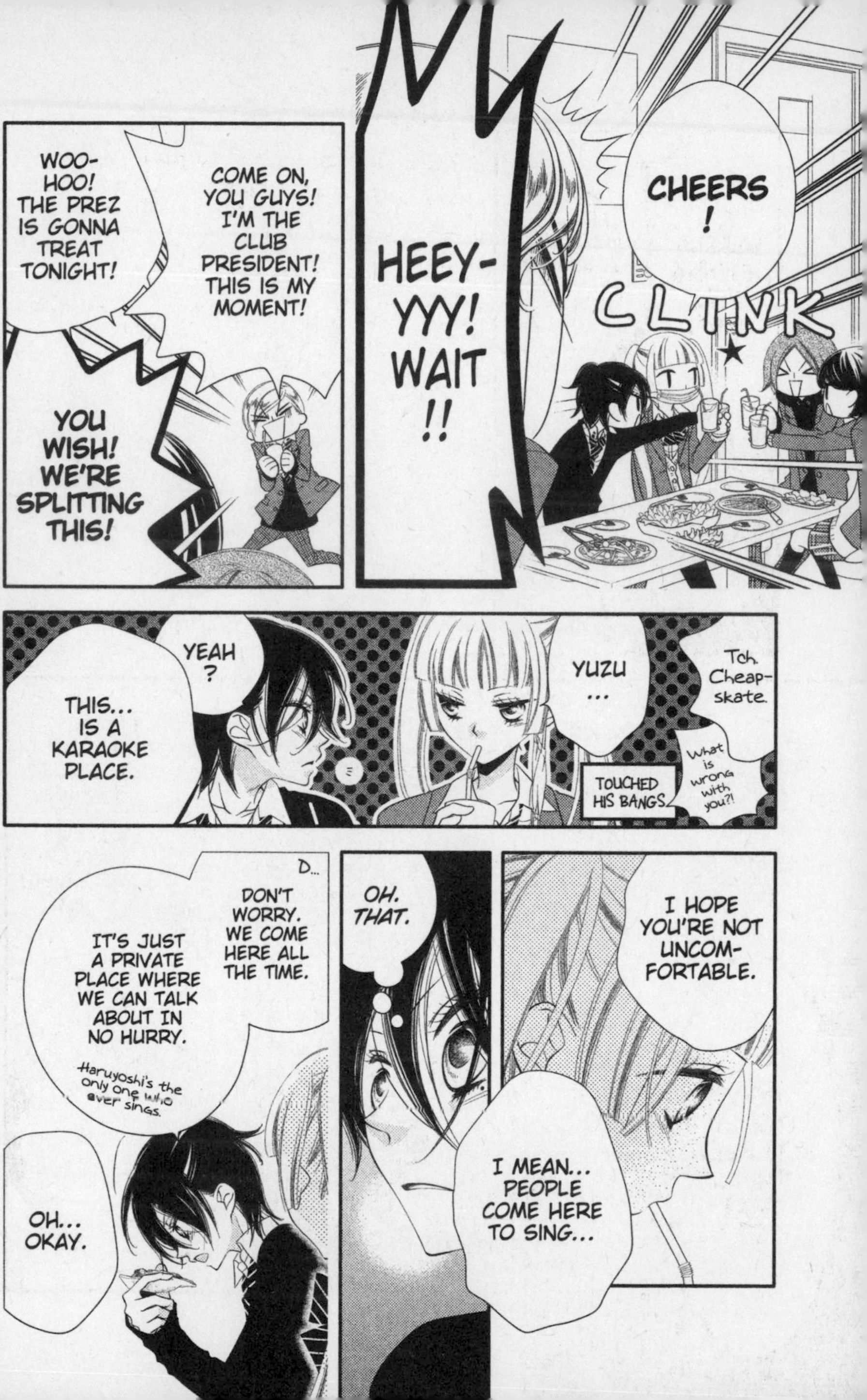
CHEERS!
CLINK★
HEEY-YYY! WAIT!!
COME ON, YOU GUYS! I'M THE CLUB PRESIDENT! THIS IS MY MOMENT!
WOO-HOO! THE PREZ IS GONNA TREAT TONIGHT!
YOU WISH! WE'RE SPLITTING THIS!
Tch. Cheap-skate.
What is wrong with you?!
YUZU...
TOUCHED HIS BANGS
YEAH?
THIS... IS A KARAOKE PLACE.
I HOPE YOU'RE NOT UNCOMFORTABLE.
I MEAN... PEOPLE COME HERE TO SING...
OH. THAT.
D...
DON'T WORRY. WE COME HERE ALL THE TIME.
IT'S JUST A PRIVATE PLACE WHERE WE CAN TALK ABOUT IN NO HURRY.
Haruyoshi's the only one who ever sings.
OH... OKAY.

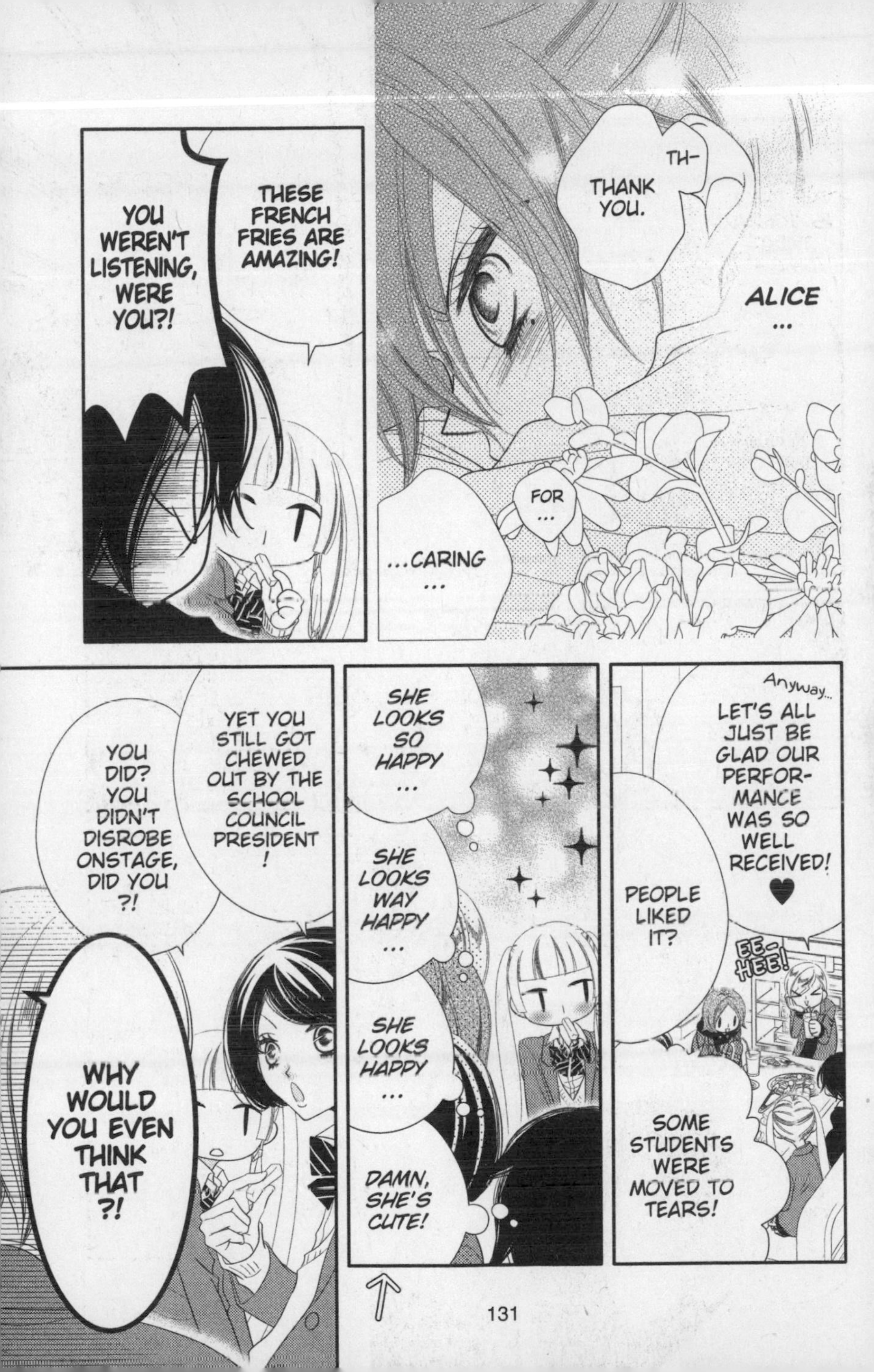
ALICE ...
TH- THANK YOU.
FOR ...
...CARING ...
THESE FRENCH FRIES ARE AMAZING!
YOU WEREN'T LISTENING, WERE YOU?!
Anyway...
LET'S ALL JUST BE GLAD OUR PERFORMANCE WAS SO WELL RECEIVED! ♥
PEOPLE LIKED IT?
EE-HEE!
SOME STUDENTS WERE MOVED TO TEARS!
SHE LOOKS SO HAPPY ...
SHE LOOKS WAY HAPPY ...
SHE LOOKS HAPPY ...
DAMN, SHE'S CUTE!
YET YOU STILL GOT CHEWED OUT BY THE SCHOOL COUNCIL PRESIDENT!
YOU DID? YOU DIDN'T DISROBE ONSTAGE, DID YOU?!
WHY WOULD YOU EVEN THINK THAT?!

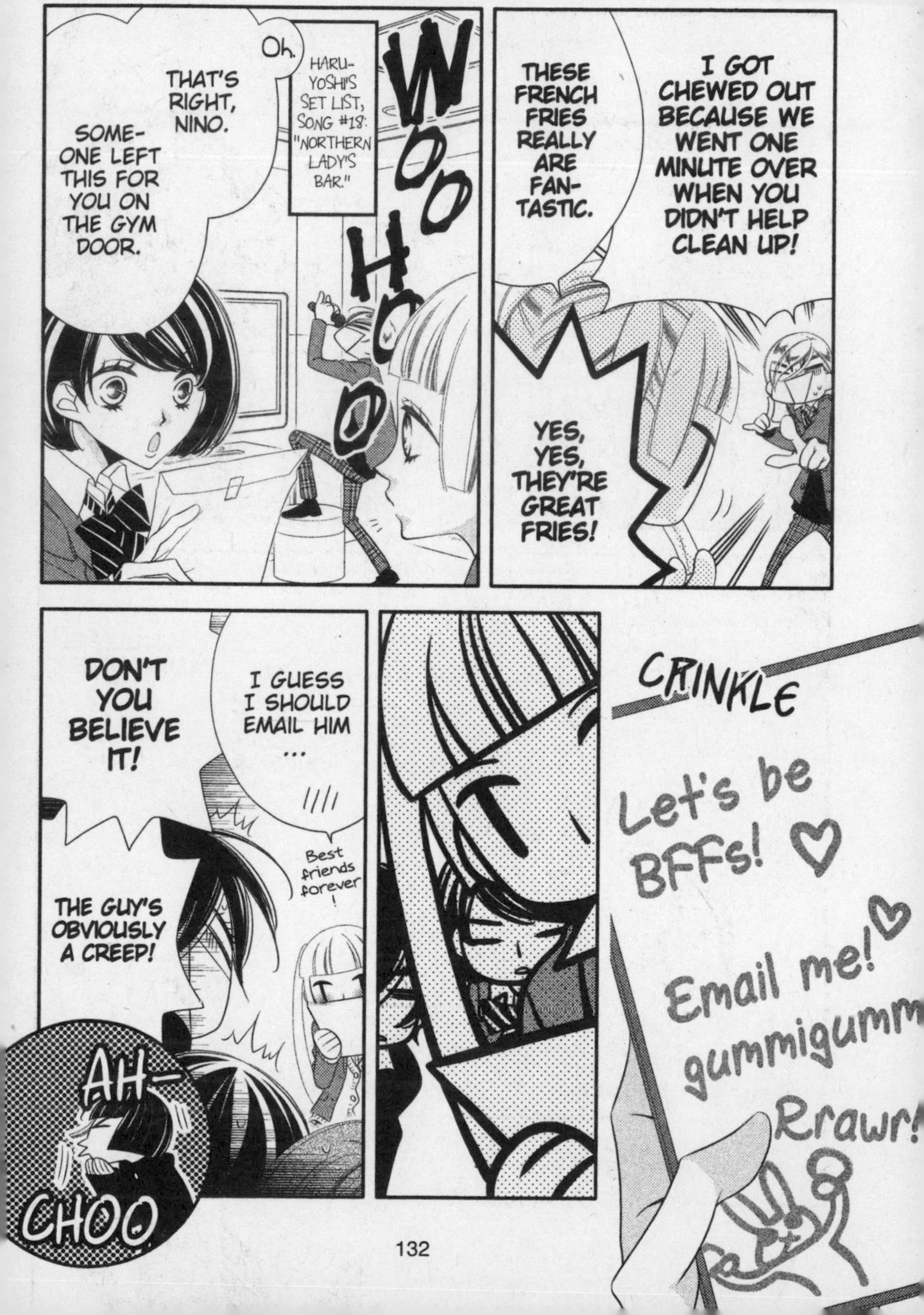
I GOT CHEWED OUT BECAUSE WE WENT ONE MINUTE OVER WHEN YOU DIDN'T HELP CLEAN UP!
THESE FRENCH FRIES REALLY ARE FAN-TASTIC.
YES, YES, THEY'RE GREAT FRIES!
WOOHOOHOO
HARU-YOSHI'S SET LIST, SONG #18: "NORTHERN LADY'S BAR."
Oh.
THAT'S RIGHT, NINO.
SOME-ONE LEFT THIS FOR YOU ON THE GYM DOOR.
CRINKLE
Let's be BFFs! ♡
Email me! ♡
gummigumm
Rrawr!
I GUESS I SHOULD EMAIL HIM ...
DON'T YOU BELIEVE IT!
Best friends forever!
THE GUY'S OBVIOUSLY A CREEP!
AH-CHOO

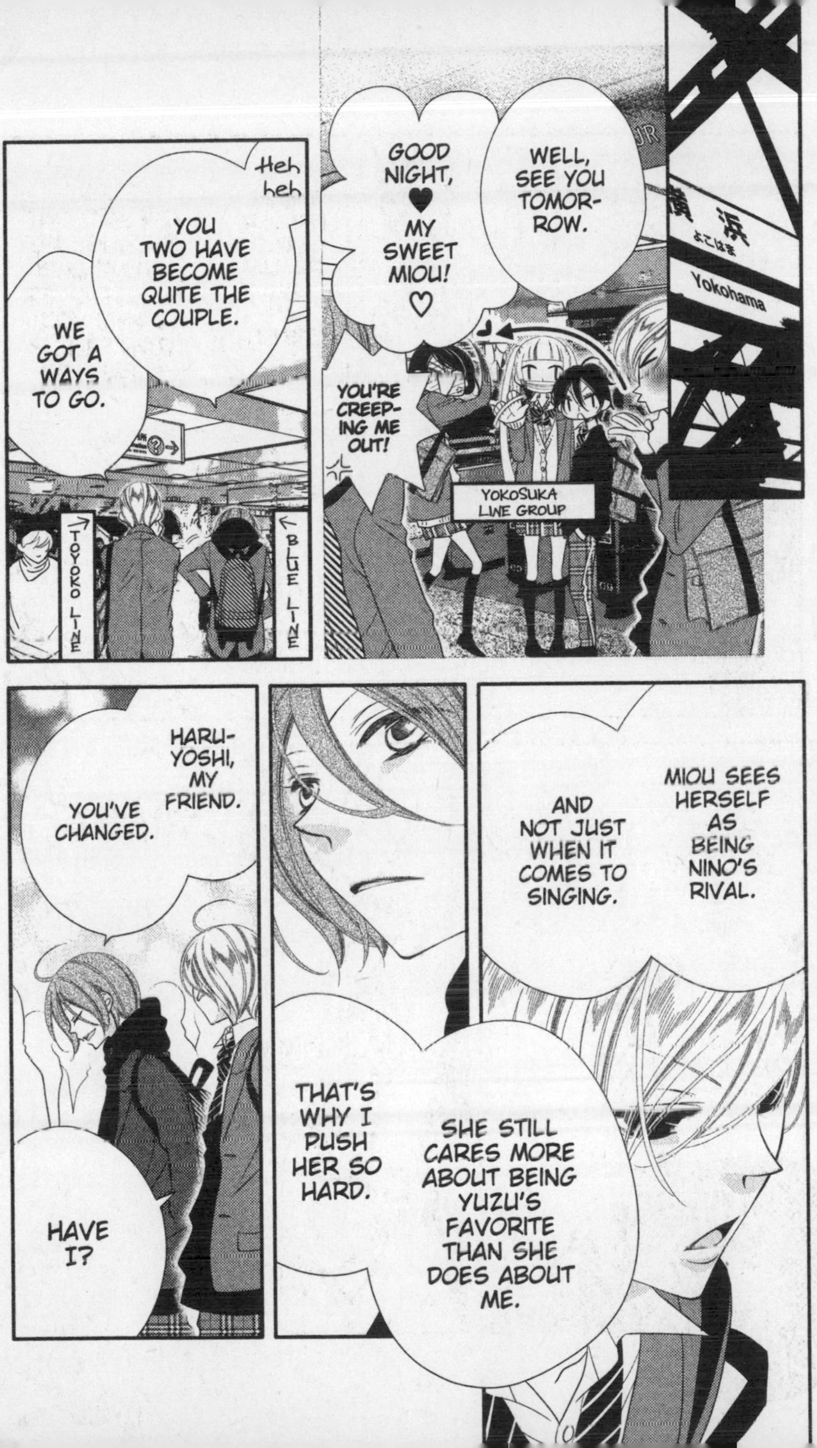
JR
横浜
よこはま
Yokohama
WELL, SEE YOU TOMORROW.
GOOD NIGHT, ♥ MY SWEET MIOU! ♡
YOU'RE CREEPING ME OUT!
YOKOSUKA LINE GROUP
Heh heh
YOU TWO HAVE BECOME QUITE THE COUPLE.
WE GOT A WAYS TO GO.
BLUE LINE
TOYOKO LINE
MIOU SEES HERSELF AS BEING NINO'S RIVAL.
AND NOT JUST WHEN IT COMES TO SINGING.
SHE STILL CARES MORE ABOUT BEING YUZU'S FAVORITE THAN SHE DOES ABOUT ME.
THAT'S WHY I PUSH HER SO HARD.
HARU-YOSHI, MY FRIEND.
YOU'VE CHANGED.
HAVE I?

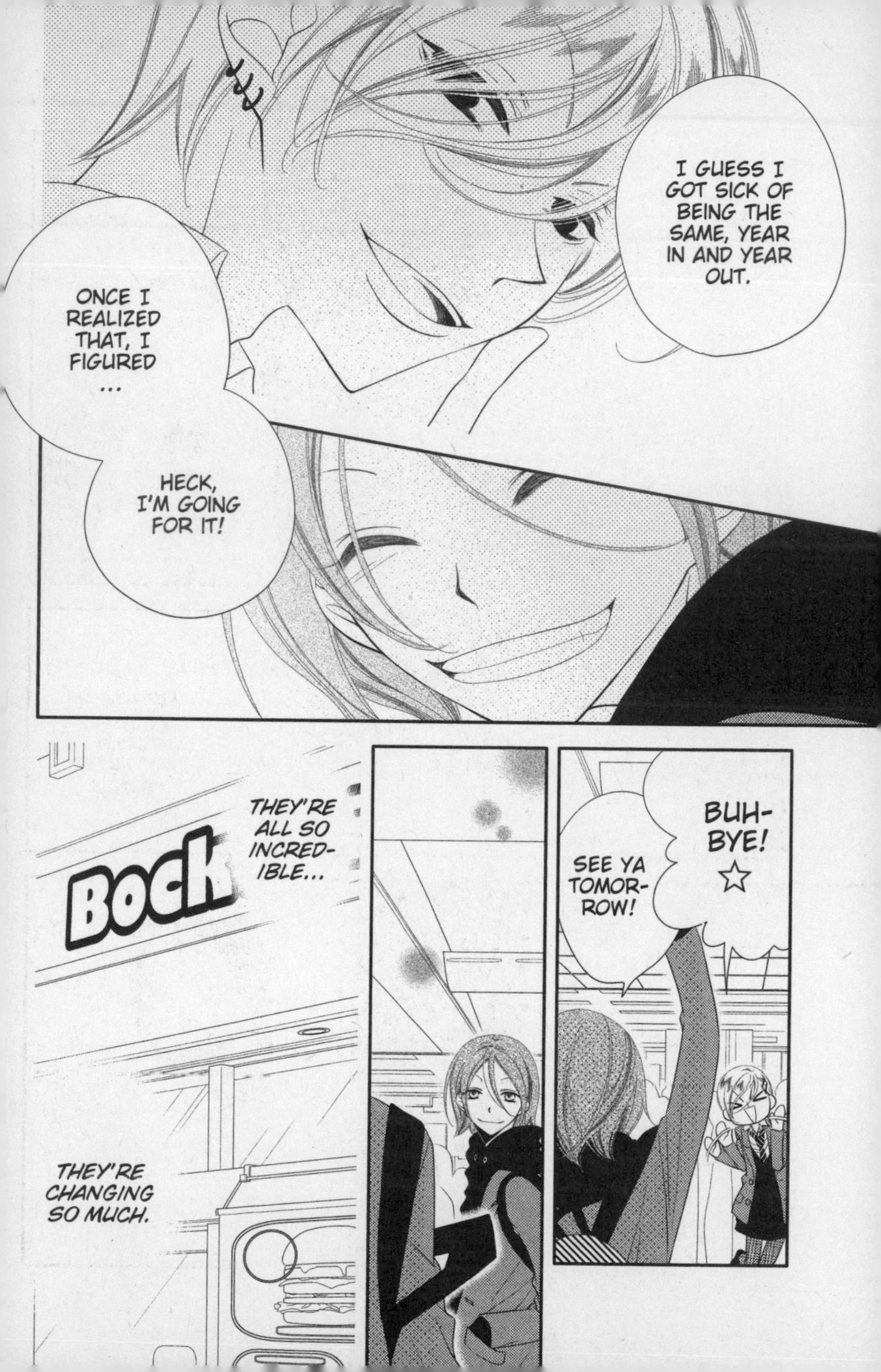
I GUESS I GOT SICK OF BEING THE SAME, YEAR IN AND YEAR OUT.
ONCE I REALIZED THAT, I FIGURED ...
HECK, I'M GOING FOR IT!
BUH-BYE! ☆
SEE YA TOMORROW!
THEY'RE ALL SO INCREDIBLE...
BOCK
THEY'RE CHANGING SO MUCH.

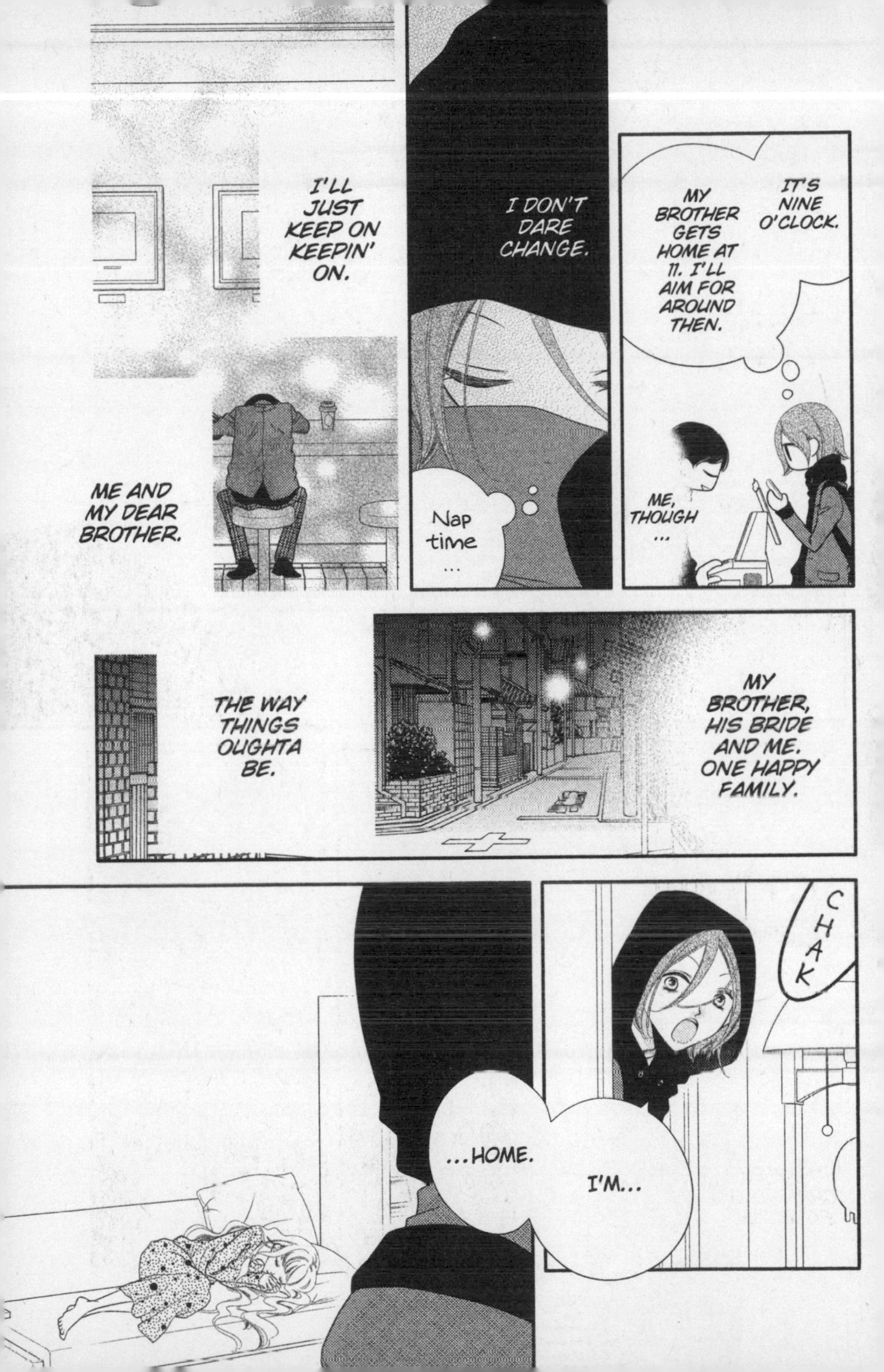
IT'S NINE O'CLOCK.
MY BROTHER GETS HOME AT 11. I'LL AIM FOR AROUND THEN.
ME, THOUGH ...
I DON'T DARE CHANGE.
Nap time ...
I'LL JUST KEEP ON KEEPIN' ON.
ME AND MY DEAR BROTHER.
MY BROTHER, HIS BRIDE AND ME. ONE HAPPY FAMILY.
THE WAY THINGS OUGHTA BE.
CHAK
I'M...
...HOME.

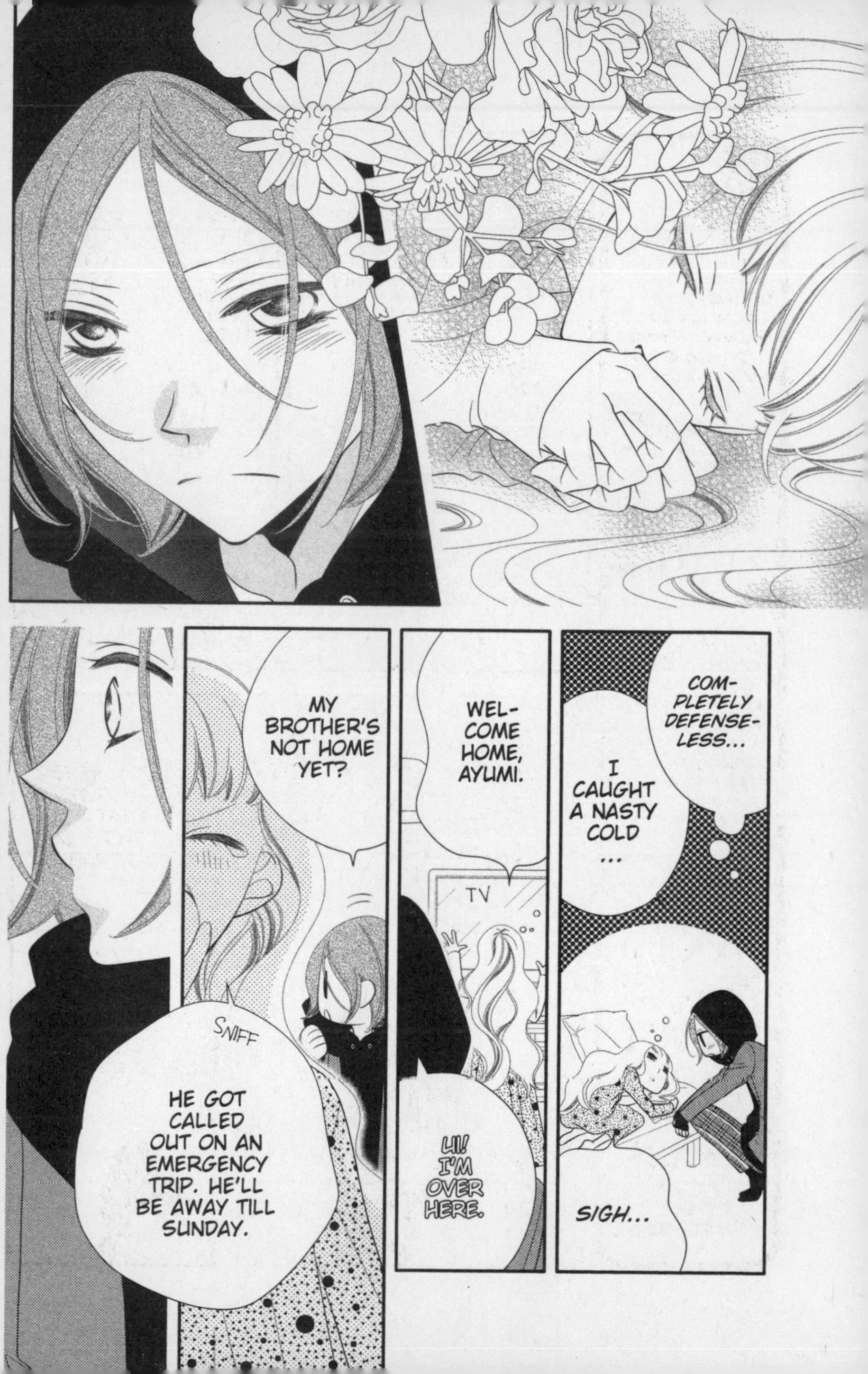
COMPLETELY DEFENSELESS...
I CAUGHT A NASTY COLD...
SIGH...
WELCOME HOME, AYUMI.
LI! I'M OVER HERE.
MY BROTHER'S NOT HOME YET?
SNIFF
HE GOT CALLED OUT ON AN EMERGENCY TRIP. HE'LL BE AWAY TILL SUNDAY.

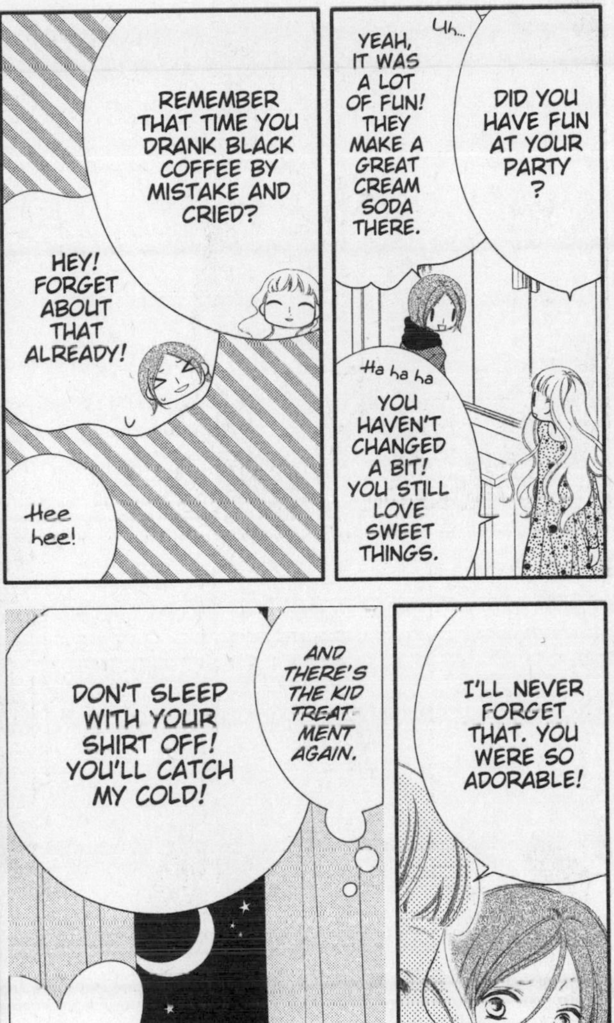
DID YOU HAVE FUN AT YOUR PARTY?
Uh...
YEAH, IT WAS A LOT OF FUN! THEY MAKE A GREAT CREAM SODA THERE.
Ha ha ha
YOU HAVEN'T CHANGED A BIT! YOU STILL LOVE SWEET THINGS.
REMEMBER THAT TIME YOU DRANK BLACK COFFEE BY MISTAKE AND CRIED?
HEY! FORGET ABOUT THAT ALREADY!
Hee hee!
I'LL NEVER FORGET THAT. YOU WERE SO ADORABLE!
AND THERE'S THE KID TREATMENT AGAIN.
DON'T SLEEP WITH YOUR SHIRT OFF! YOU'LL CATCH MY COLD!
GOOD NIGHT, UI.

5

I wrote that weird narration in the confused excitement of the early-morning hours, and when I read it on the day of the recording...

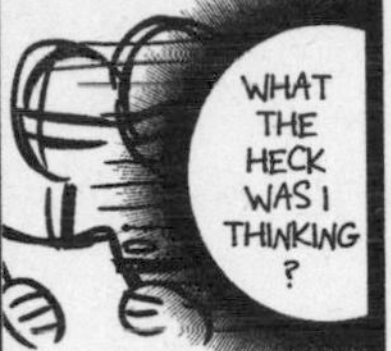
WHAT THE HECK WAS I THINKING?

...I was completely befuddled. Early mornings are scary. It's only going to be online for a limited time, so if you're able to check it out, please do so soon!

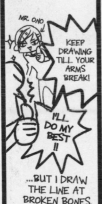

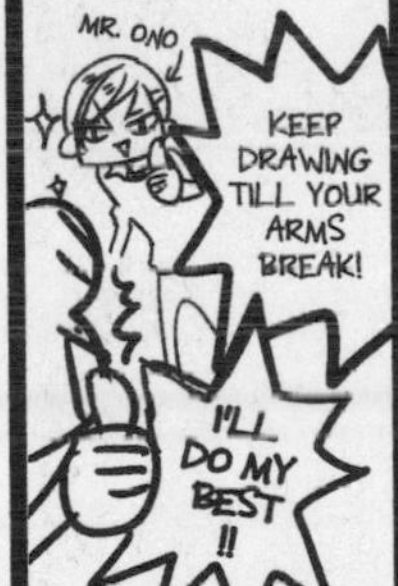
MR. ONO
KEEP DRAWING TILL YOUR ARMS BREAK!
I'LL DO MY BEST!!

...BUT I DRAW THE LINE AT BROKEN BONES.

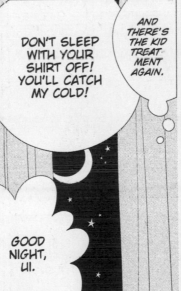

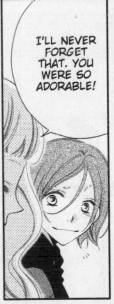

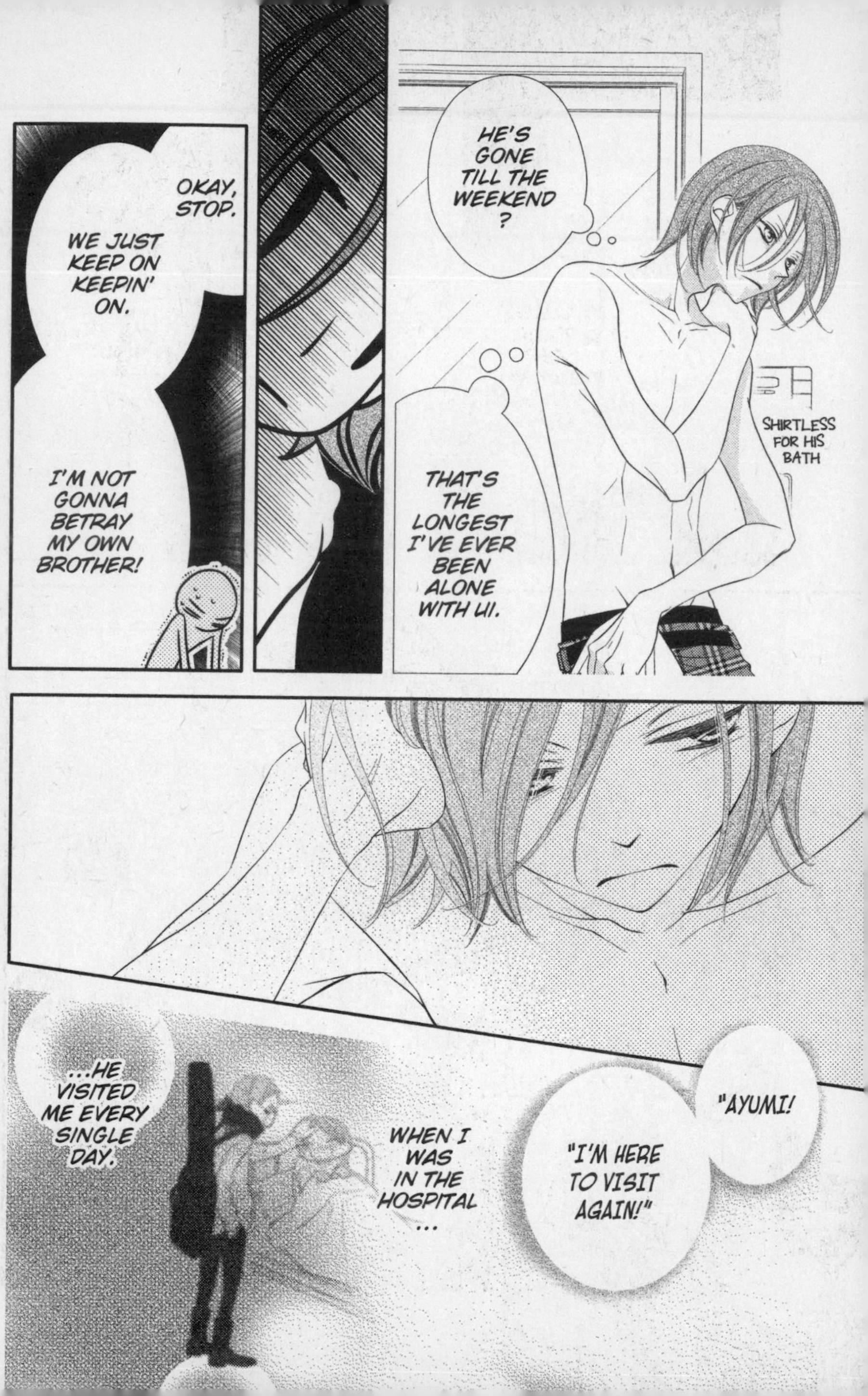
HE'S GONE TILL THE WEEKEND?
THAT'S THE LONGEST I'VE EVER BEEN ALONE WITH UI.
SHIRTLESS FOR HIS BATH
OKAY, STOP.
WE JUST KEEP ON KEEPIN' ON.
I'M NOT GONNA BETRAY MY OWN BROTHER!
"AYUMI!
"I'M HERE TO VISIT AGAIN!"
WHEN I WAS IN THE HOSPITAL...
...HE VISITED ME EVERY SINGLE DAY.

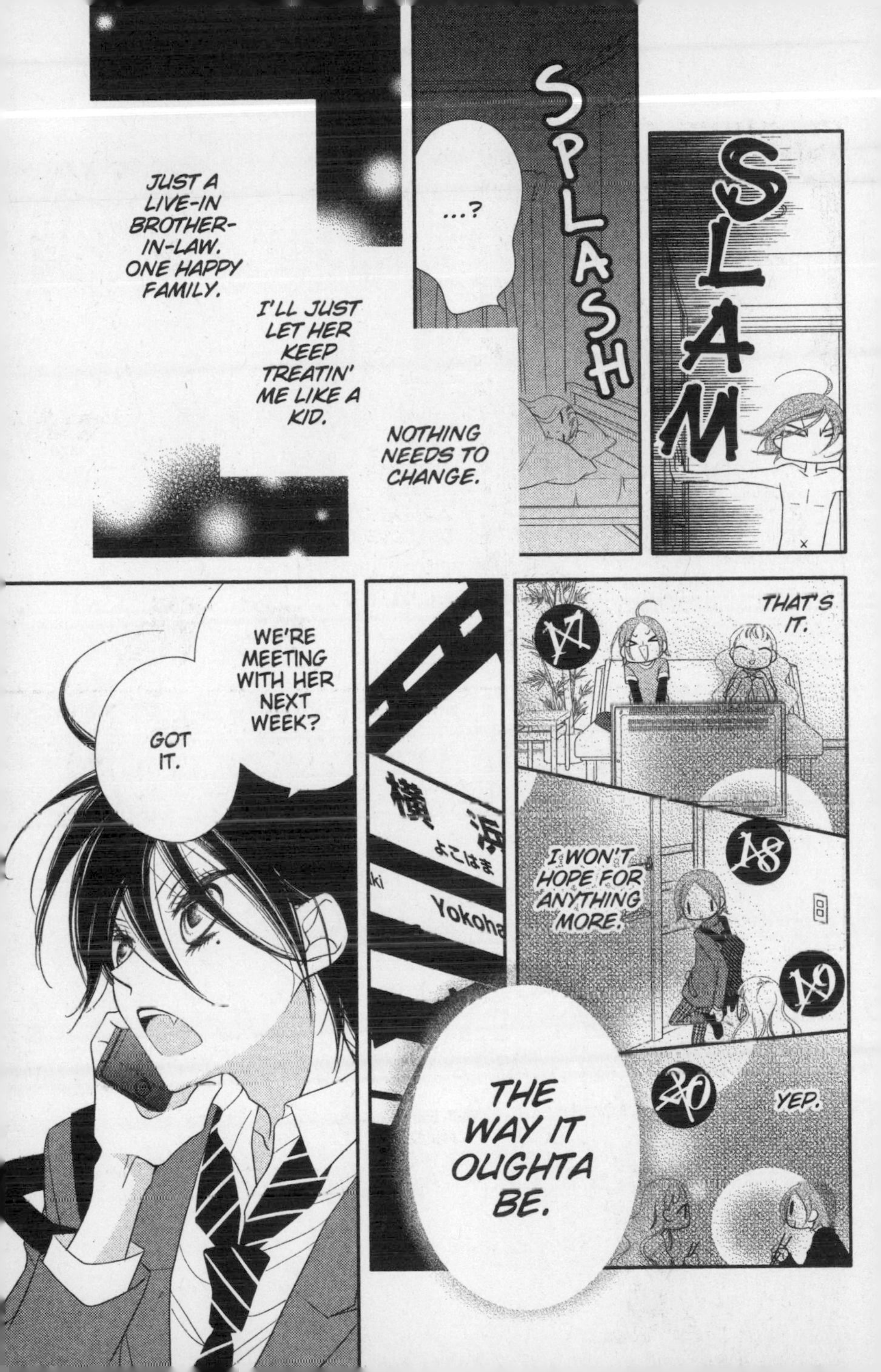
SLAM
SPLASH
...?
JUST A LIVE-IN BROTHER-IN-LAW. ONE HAPPY FAMILY.
I'LL JUST LET HER KEEP TREATIN' ME LIKE A KID.
NOTHING NEEDS TO CHANGE.
17
THAT'S IT.
18
I WON'T HOPE FOR ANYTHING MORE.
19
20
YEP.
THE WAY IT OUGHTA BE.
横浜
よこはま
Yokoha
WE'RE MEETING WITH HER NEXT WEEK?
GOT IT.

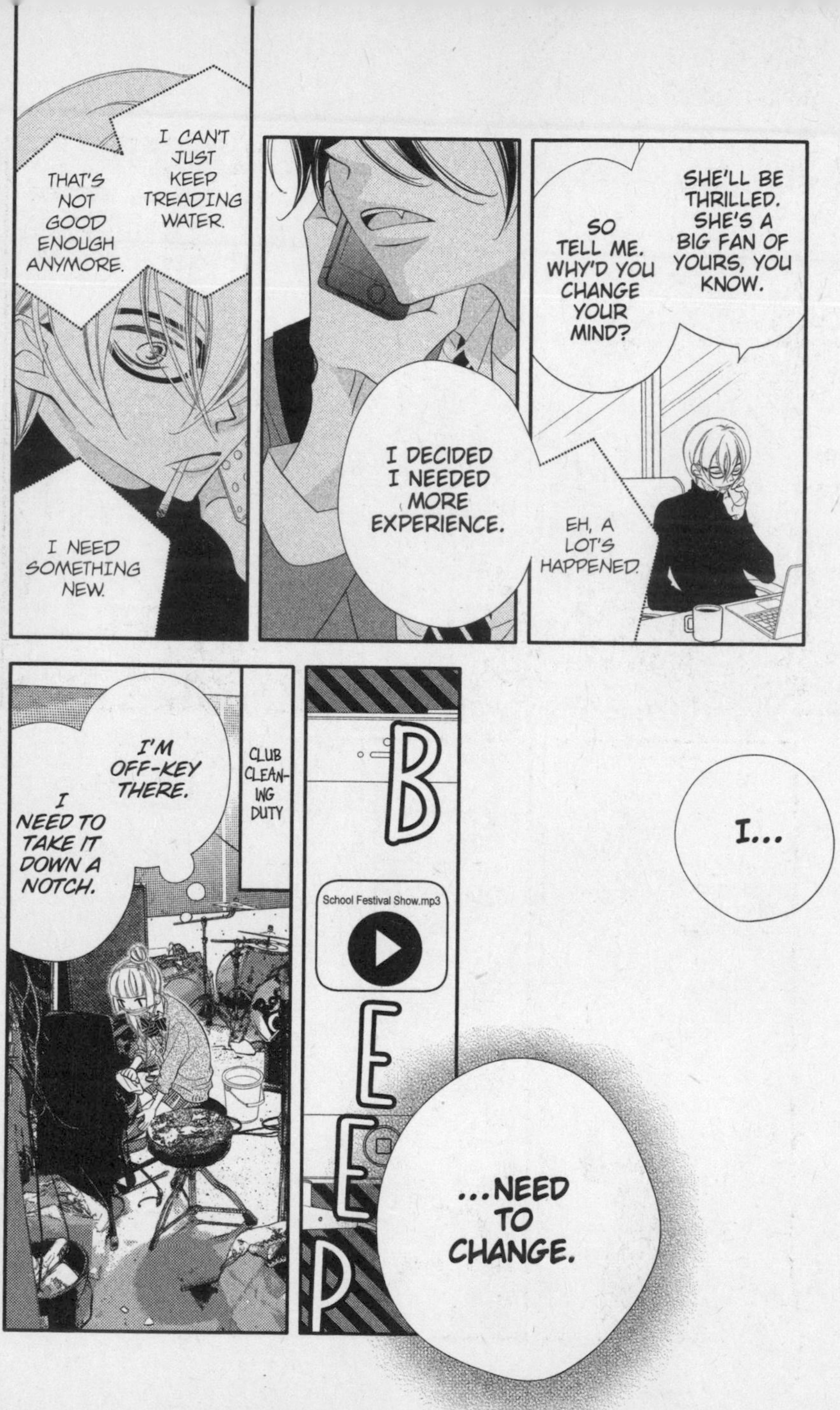
SHE'LL BE THRILLED. SHE'S A BIG FAN OF YOURS, YOU KNOW.
SO TELL ME. WHY'D YOU CHANGE YOUR MIND?
EH, A LOT'S HAPPENED.
I DECIDED I NEEDED MORE EXPERIENCE.
I CAN'T JUST KEEP TREADING WATER.
THAT'S NOT GOOD ENOUGH ANYMORE.
I NEED SOMETHING NEW.
I...
...NEED TO CHANGE.
BEEP
School Festival Show.mp3
CLUB CLEANING DUTY
I'M OFF-KEY THERE.
I NEED TO TAKE IT DOWN A NOTCH.

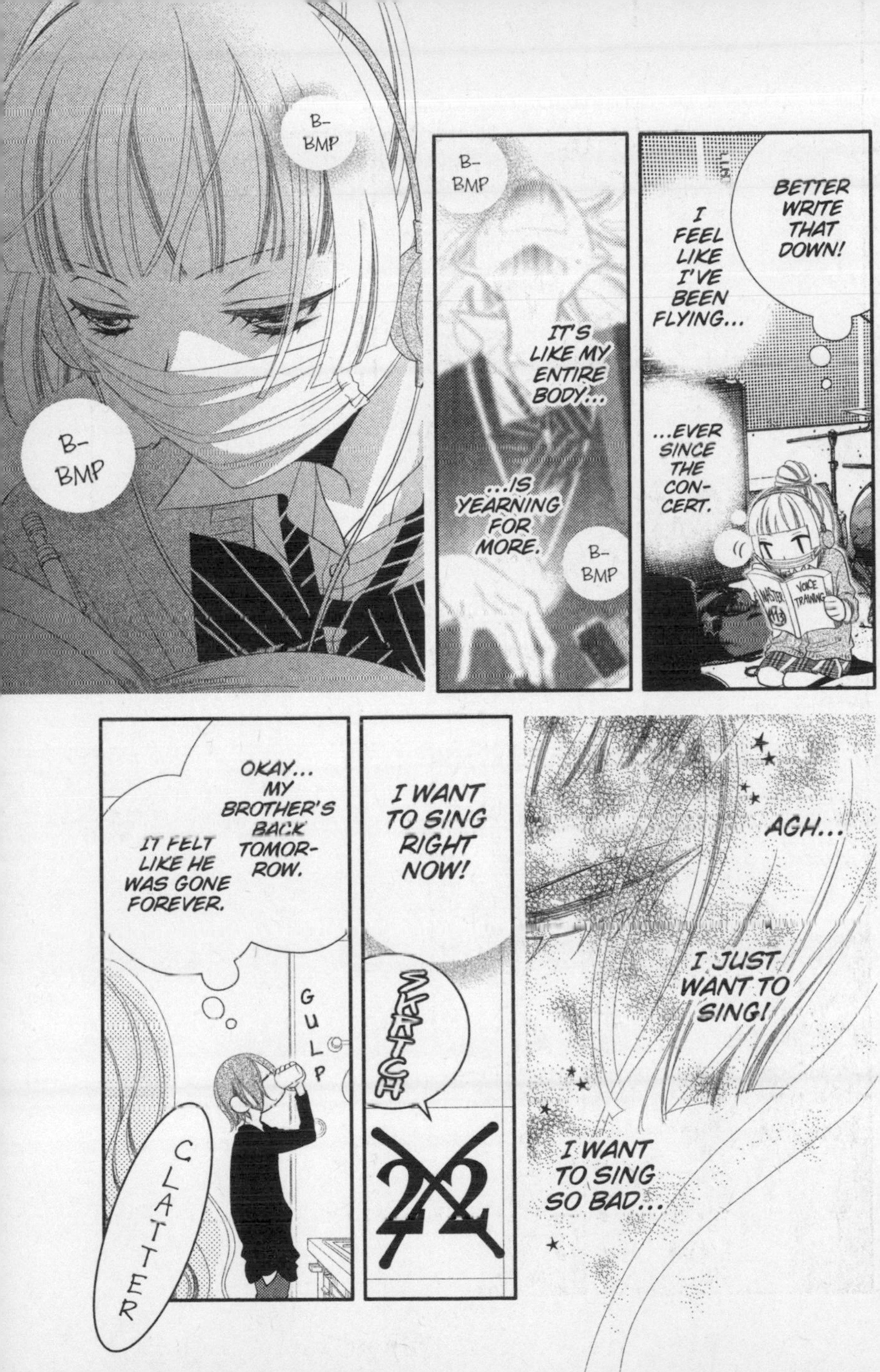
BETTER WRITE THAT DOWN!
I FEEL LIKE I'VE BEEN FLYING...
...EVER SINCE THE CON-CERT.
MASTER
VOICE TRAINING
B-BMP
IT'S LIKE MY ENTIRE BODY...
...IS YEARNING FOR MORE.
B-BMP
B-BMP
B-BMP
AGH...
I JUST WANT TO SING!
I WANT TO SING SO BAD...
I WANT TO SING RIGHT NOW!
SKRITCH
22
OKAY... MY BROTHER'S BACK TOMOR-ROW.
IT FELT LIKE HE WAS GONE FOREVER.
GULP
CLATTER

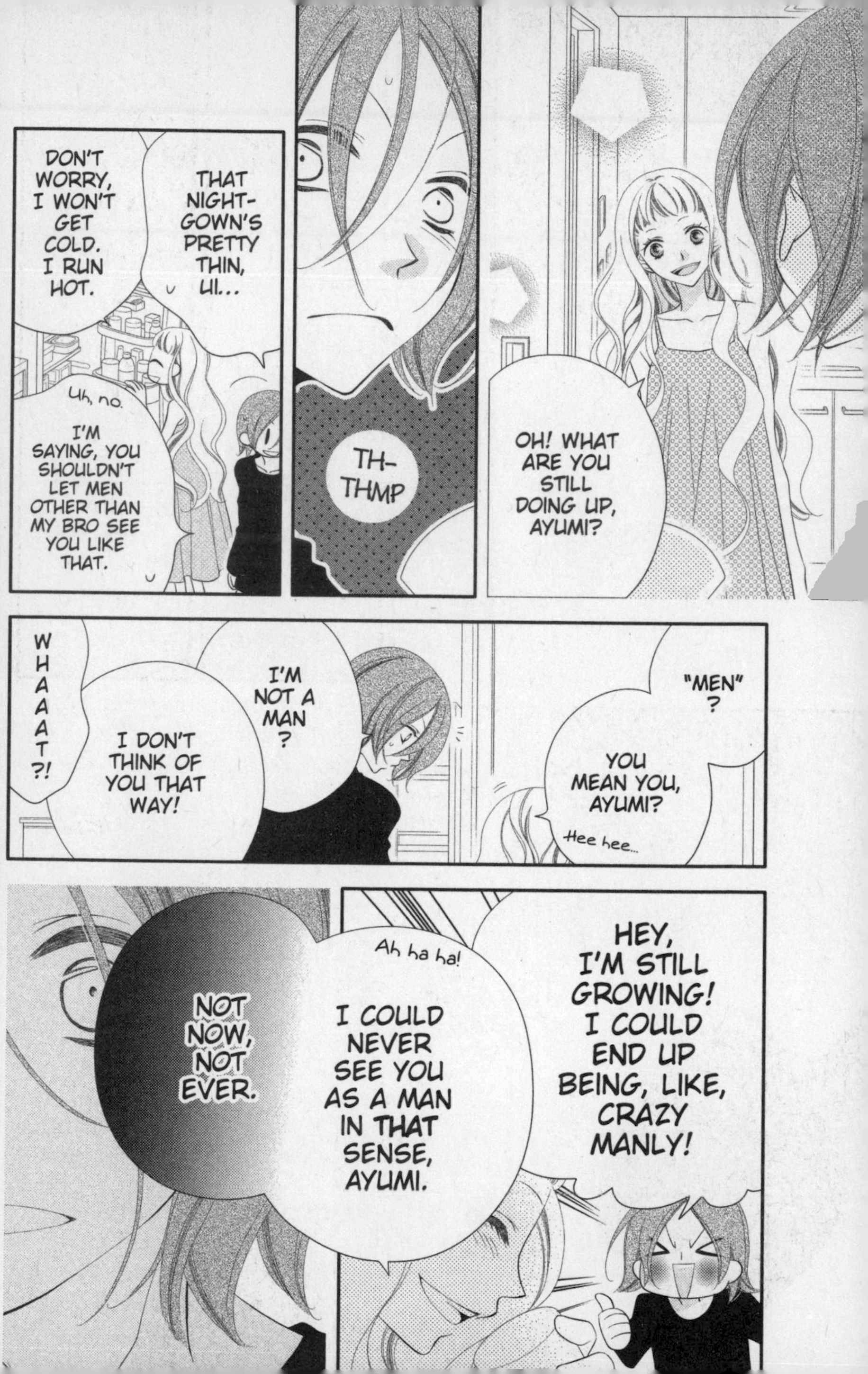
OH! WHAT ARE YOU STILL DOING UP, AYUMI?
TH-THMP
THAT NIGHT-GOWN'S PRETTY THIN, UI...
DON'T WORRY, I WON'T GET COLD. I RUN HOT.
Uh, no.
I'M SAYING, YOU SHOULDN'T LET MEN OTHER THAN MY BRO SEE YOU LIKE THAT.
"MEN"?
YOU MEAN YOU, AYUMI?
Hee hee...
I'M NOT A MAN?
I DON'T THINK OF YOU THAT WAY!
WHAAAAT?!
HEY, I'M STILL GROWING! I COULD END UP BEING, LIKE, CRAZY MANLY!
Ah ha ha!
I COULD NEVER SEE YOU AS A MAN IN THAT SENSE, AYUMI.
NOT NOW, NOT EVER.

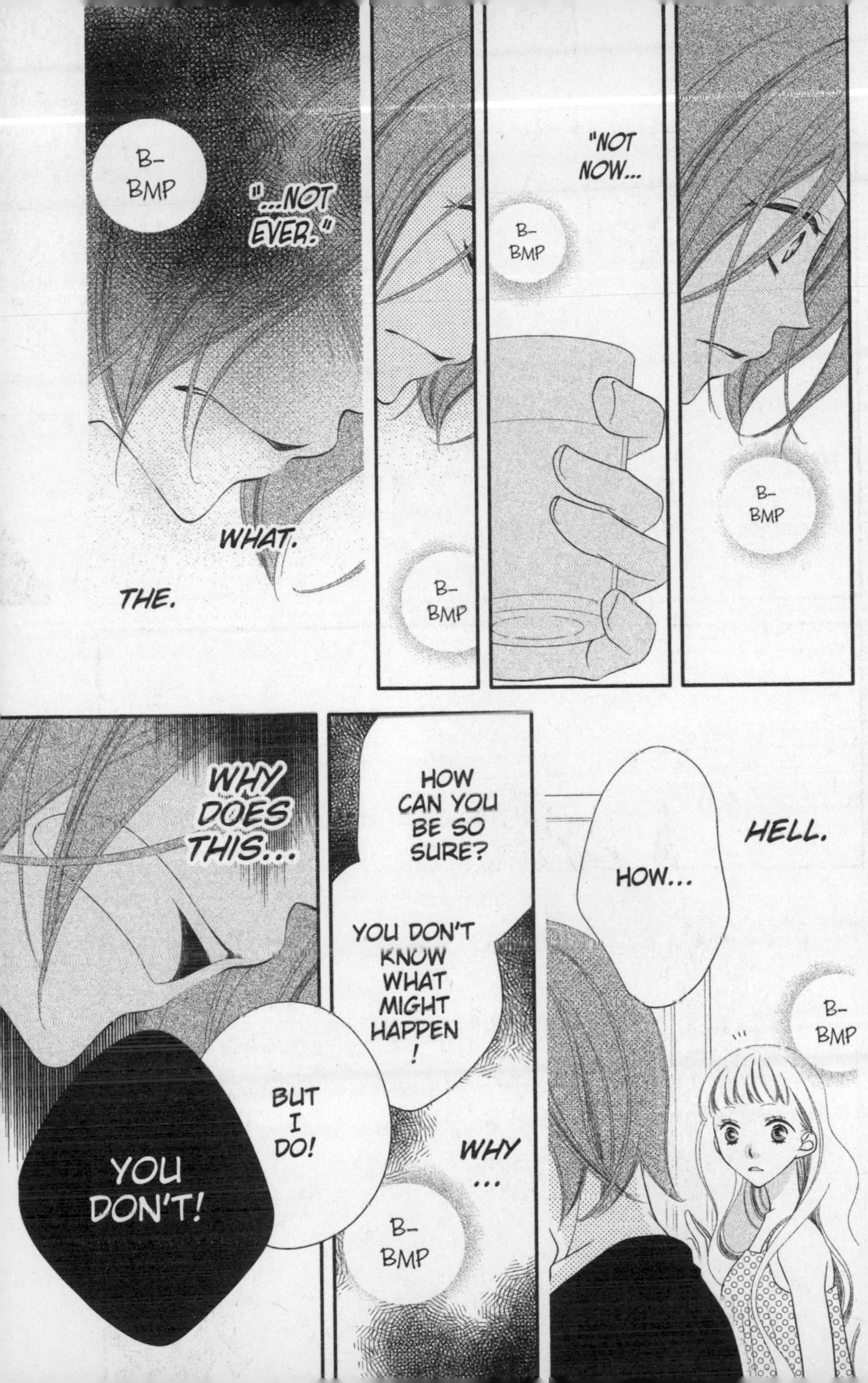
B-BMP
"NOT NOW...
B-BMP
B-BMP
B-BMP
"...NOT EVER."
WHAT.
THE.
HELL.
HOW...
B-BMP
HOW CAN YOU BE SO SURE?
YOU DON'T KNOW WHAT MIGHT HAPPEN!
WHY...
B-BMP
BUT I DO!
WHY DOES THIS...
YOU DON'T!

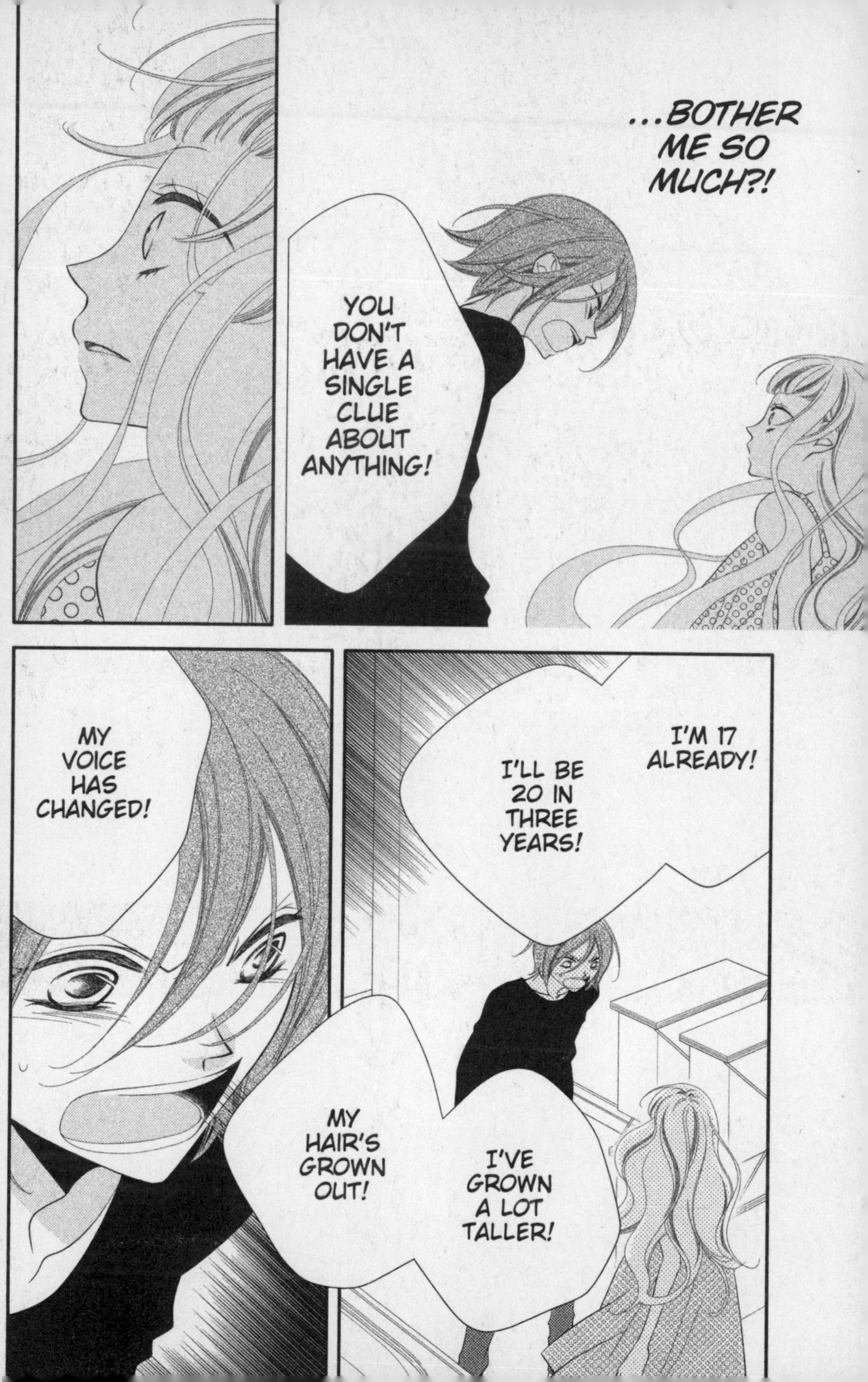
...BOTHER ME SO MUCH?!
YOU DON'T HAVE A SINGLE CLUE ABOUT ANYTHING!
I'M 17 ALREADY!
I'LL BE 20 IN THREE YEARS!
I'VE GROWN A LOT TALLER!
MY HAIR'S GROWN OUT!
MY VOICE HAS CHANGED!

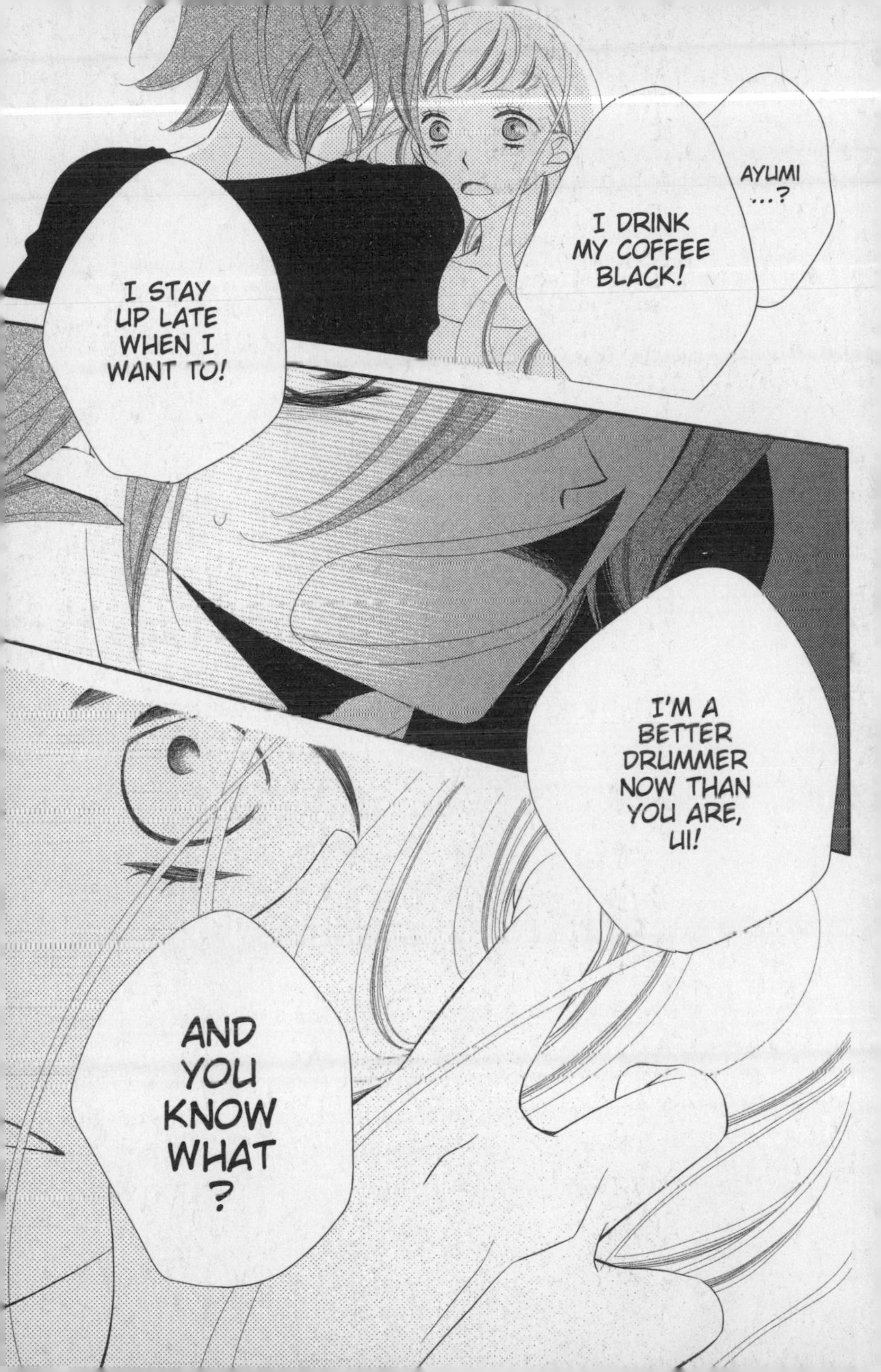
AYUMI ...?
I DRINK MY COFFEE BLACK!
I STAY UP LATE WHEN I WANT TO!
I'M A BETTER DRUMMER NOW THAN YOU ARE, UI!
AND YOU KNOW WHAT?

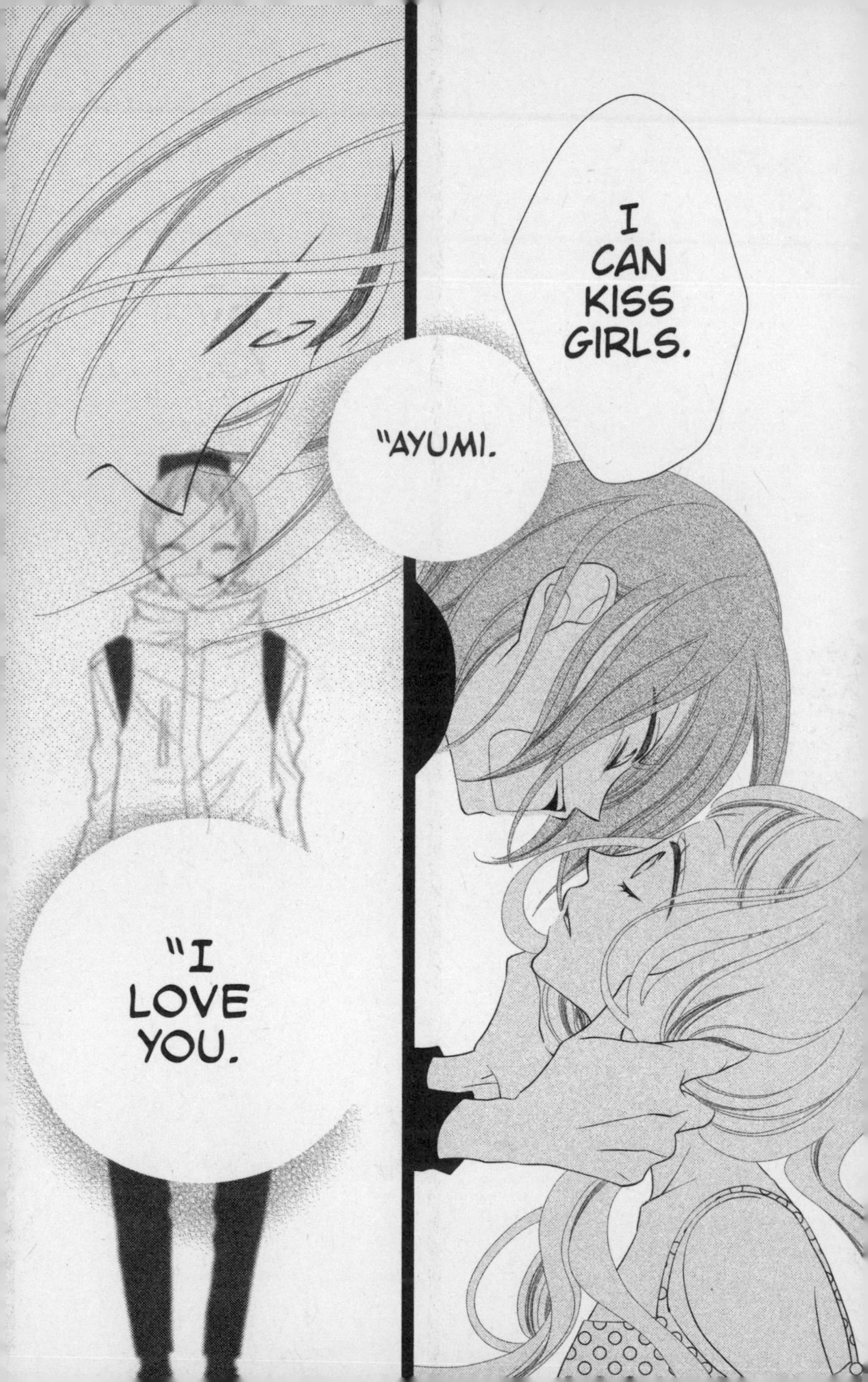
I CAN KISS GIRLS.
"AYUMI.
"I LOVE YOU.

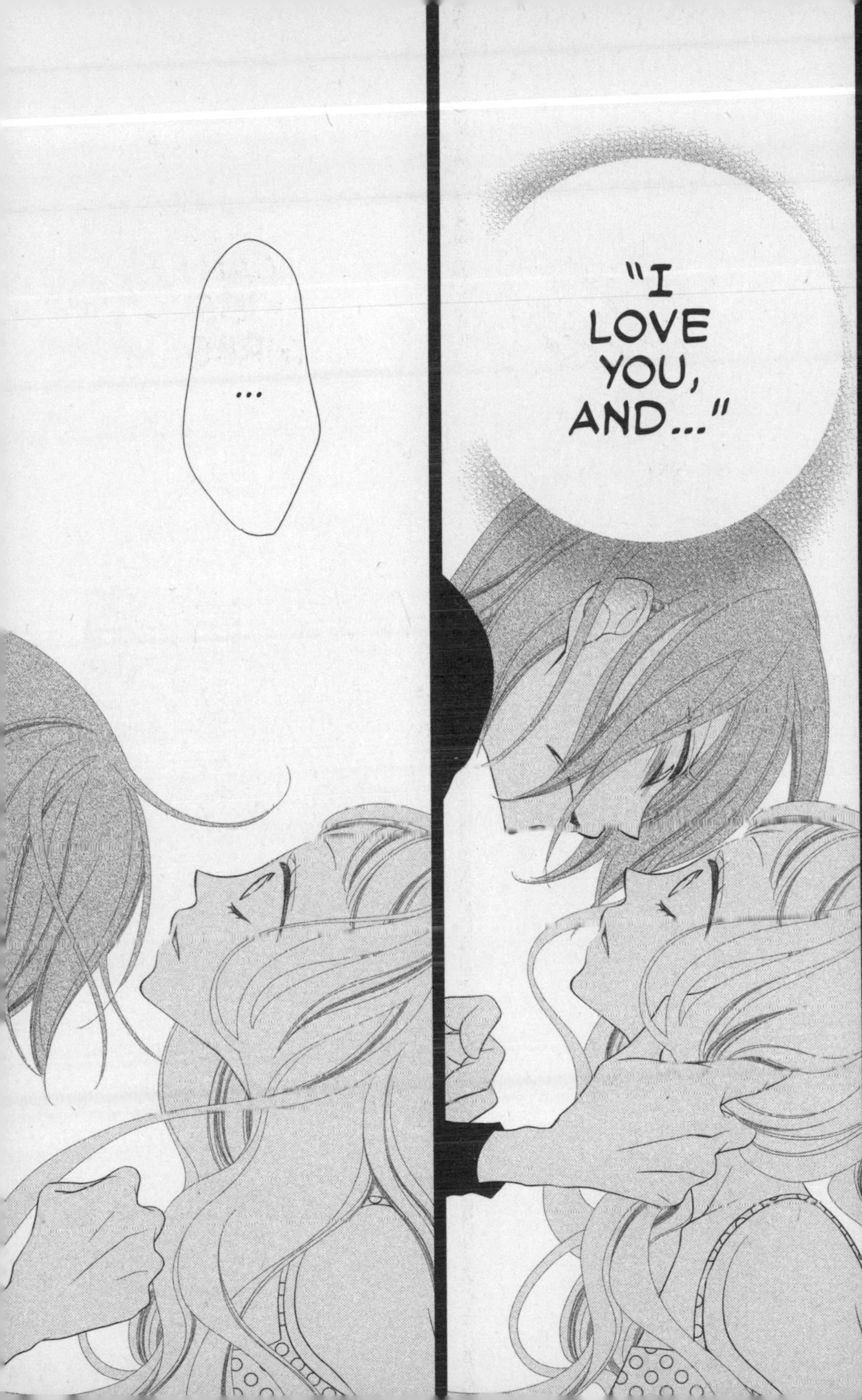
"I LOVE YOU, AND..."
...

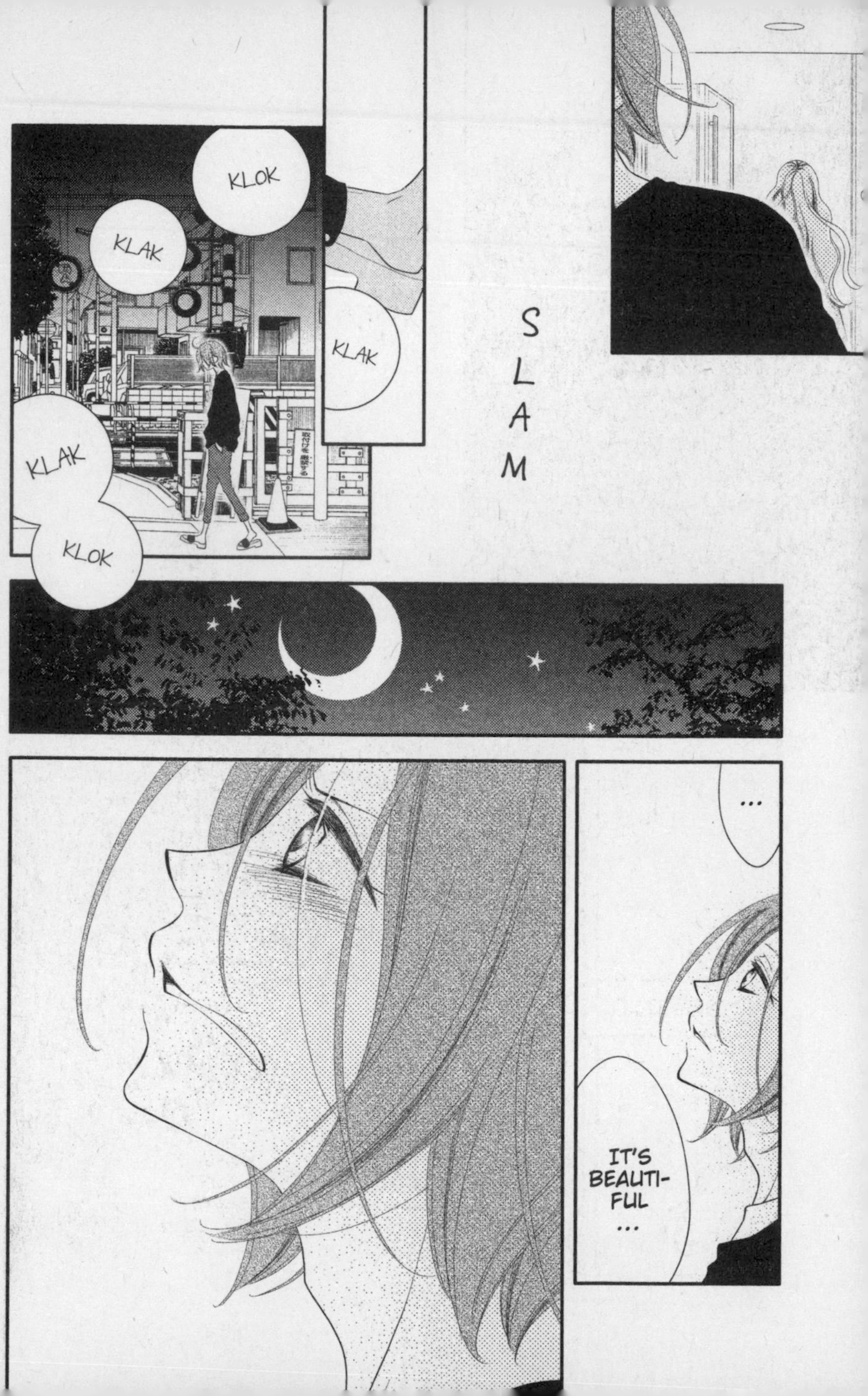
SLAM
KLAK
KLOK
KLAK
KLAK
KLOK
...
IT'S BEAUTI-FUL ...

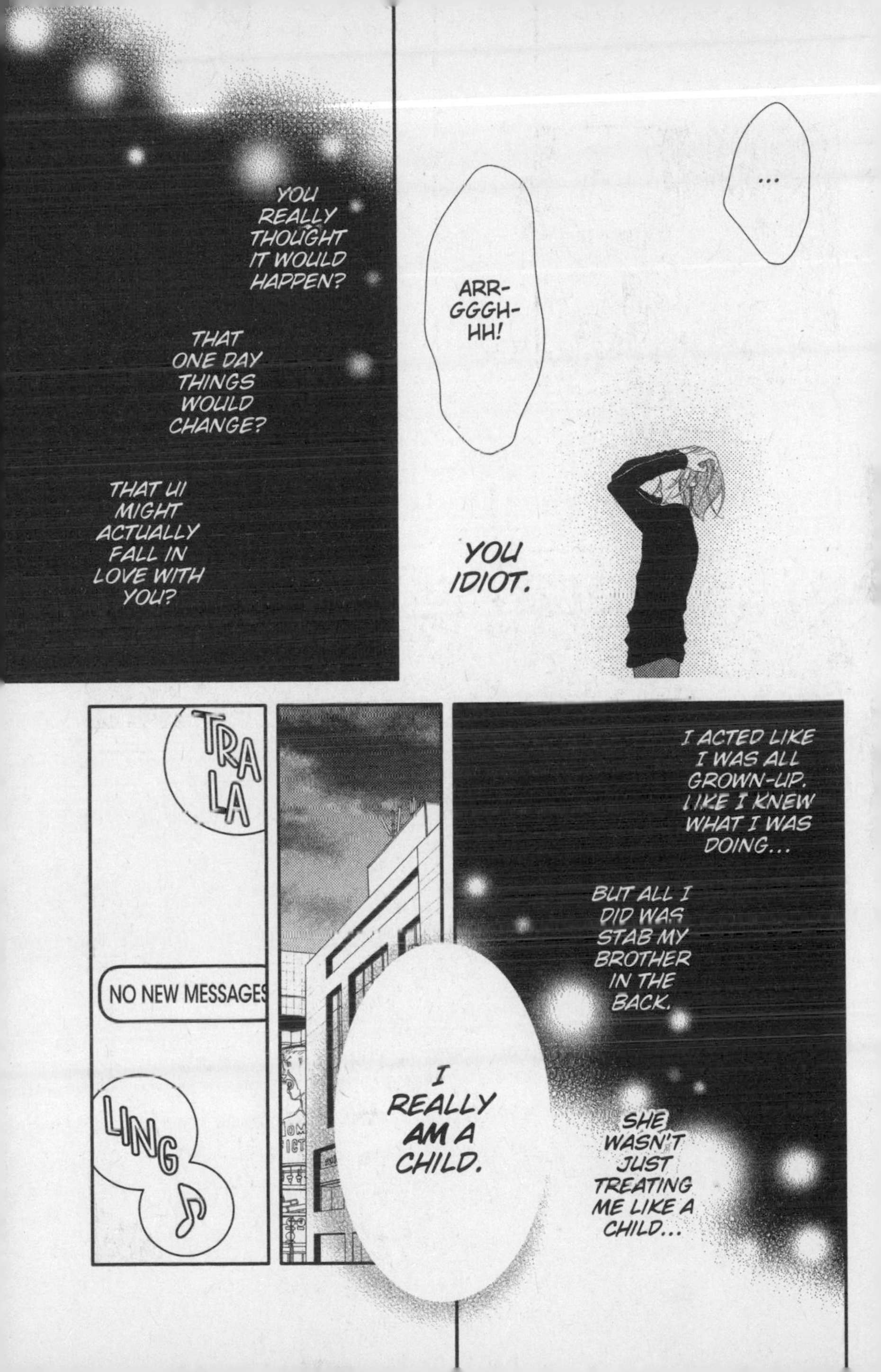
...
ARR-GGGH-HH!
YOU IDIOT.
YOU REALLY THOUGHT IT WOULD HAPPEN?
THAT ONE DAY THINGS WOULD CHANGE?
THAT UI MIGHT ACTUALLY FALL IN LOVE WITH YOU?
I ACTED LIKE I WAS ALL GROWN-UP. LIKE I KNEW WHAT I WAS DOING...
BUT ALL I DID WAS STAB MY BROTHER IN THE BACK.
SHE WASN'T JUST TREATING ME LIKE A CHILD...
I REALLY AM A CHILD.
TRA LA
NO NEW MESSAGES
LING ♪

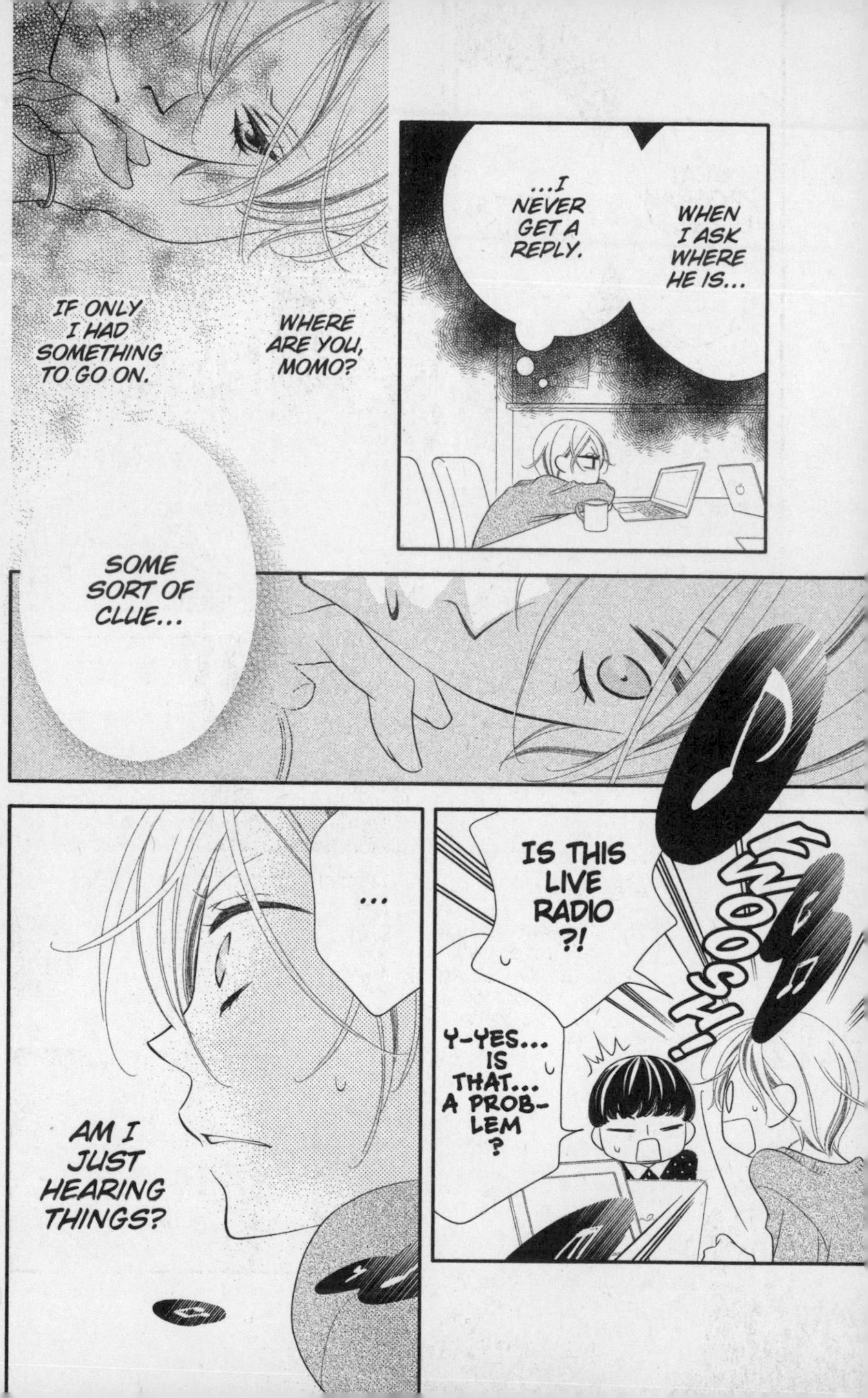
WHEN I ASK WHERE HE IS...
...I NEVER GET A REPLY.
WHERE ARE YOU, MOMO?
IF ONLY I HAD SOMETHING TO GO ON.
SOME SORT OF CLUE...
WHOOSH!
IS THIS LIVE RADIO?!
Y-YES... IS THAT... A PROBLEM?
...
AM I JUST HEARING THINGS?

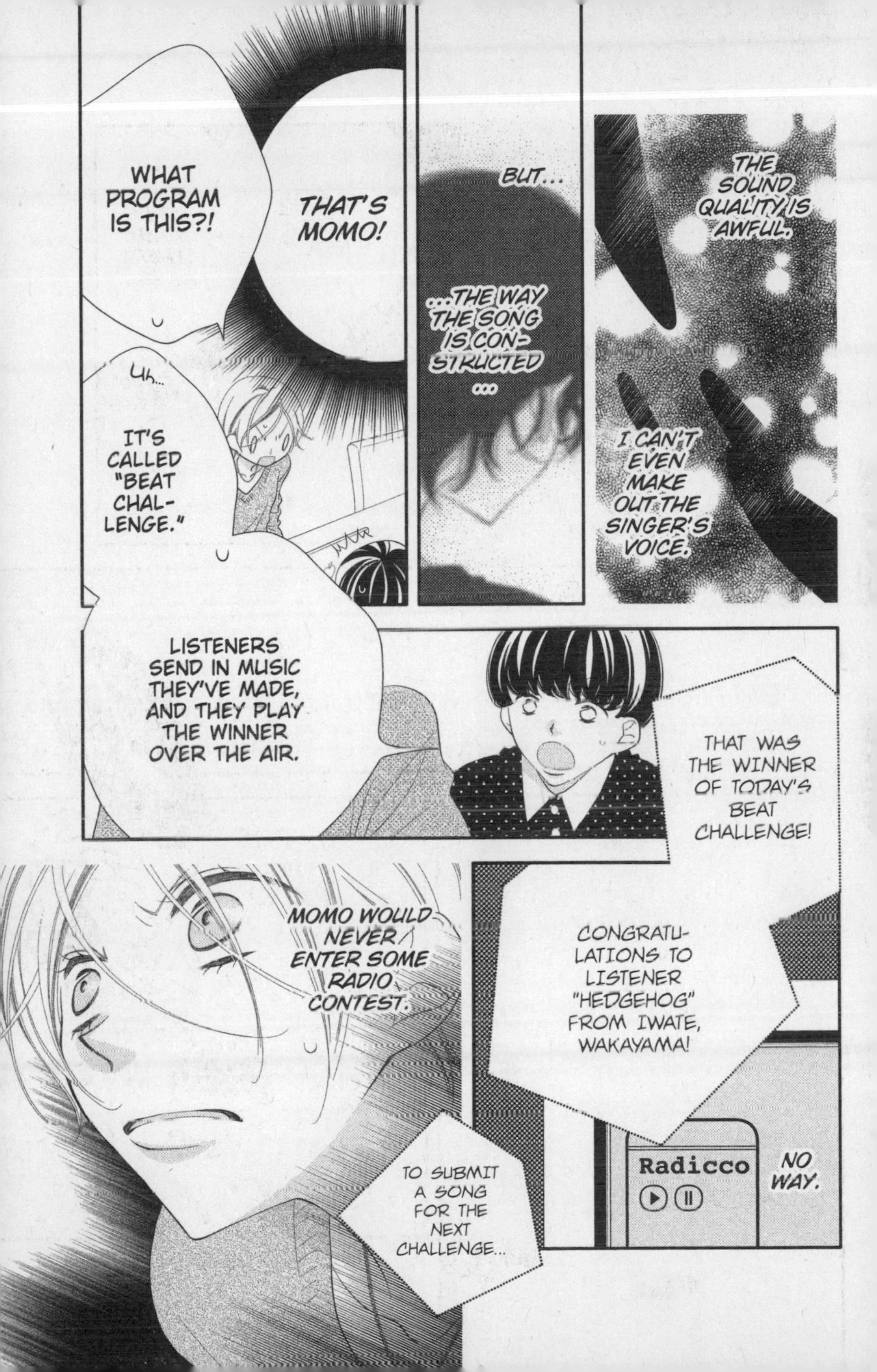
THE SOUND QUALITY IS AWFUL.
I CAN'T EVEN MAKE OUT THE SINGER'S VOICE.
BUT...
...THE WAY THE SONG IS CON-STRUCTED...
THAT'S MOMO!
WHAT PROGRAM IS THIS?!
Uh...
IT'S CALLED "BEAT CHAL-LENGE."
THAT WAS THE WINNER OF TODAY'S BEAT CHALLENGE!
LISTENERS SEND IN MUSIC THEY'VE MADE, AND THEY PLAY THE WINNER OVER THE AIR.
CONGRATU-LATIONS TO LISTENER "HEDGEHOG" FROM IWATE, WAKAYAMA!
NO WAY.
Radicco
TO SUBMIT A SONG FOR THE NEXT CHALLENGE...
MOMO WOULD NEVER ENTER SOME RADIO CONTEST.

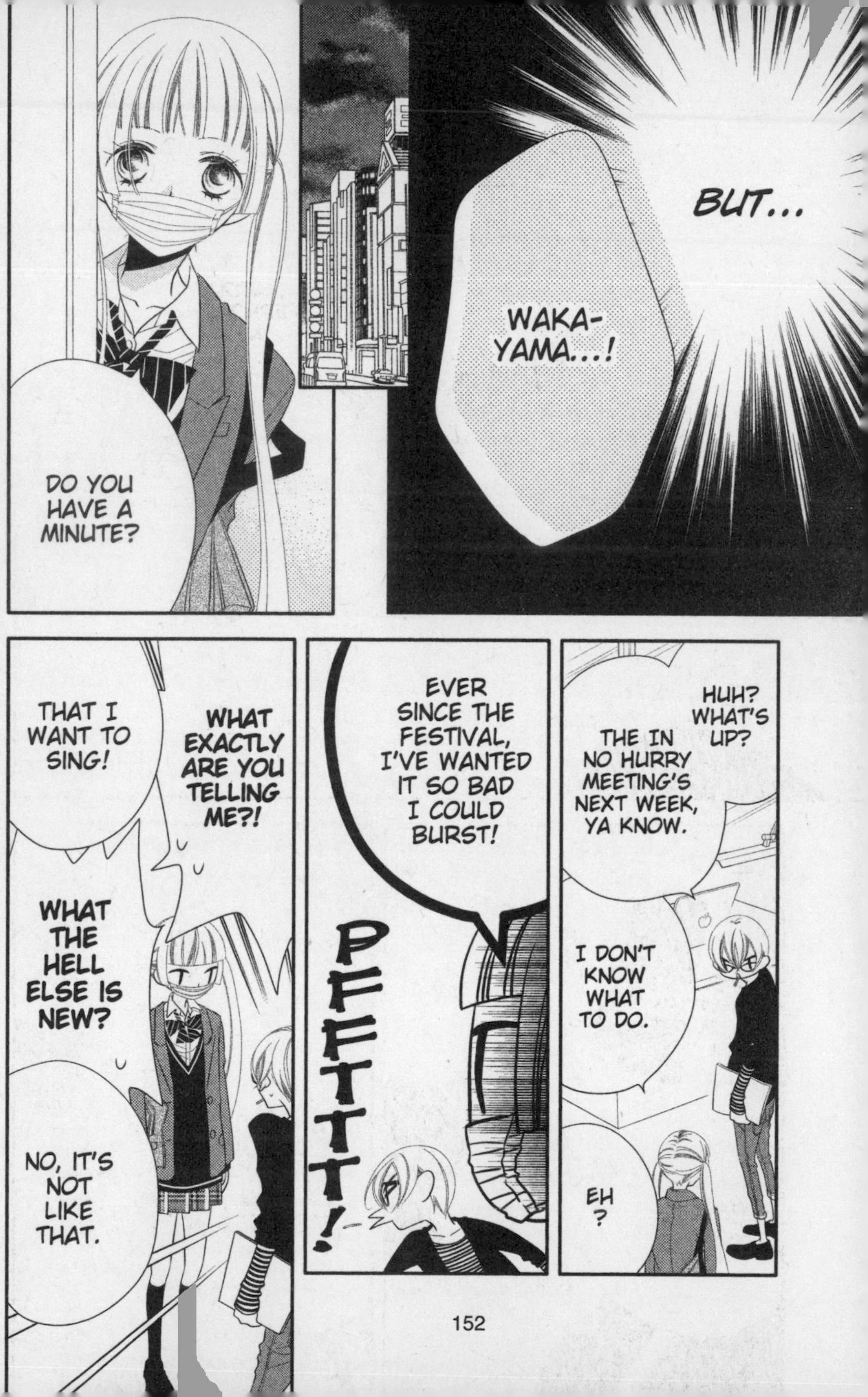
BUT...
WAKA-YAMA...!
DO YOU HAVE A MINUTE?
HUH? WHAT'S UP?
THE IN NO HURRY MEETING'S NEXT WEEK, YA KNOW.
I DON'T KNOW WHAT TO DO.
EH?
EVER SINCE THE FESTIVAL, I'VE WANTED IT SO BAD I COULD BURST!
PFFTTTT!
WHAT EXACTLY ARE YOU TELLING ME?!
THAT I WANT TO SING!
WHAT THE HELL ELSE IS NEW?
NO, IT'S NOT LIKE THAT.

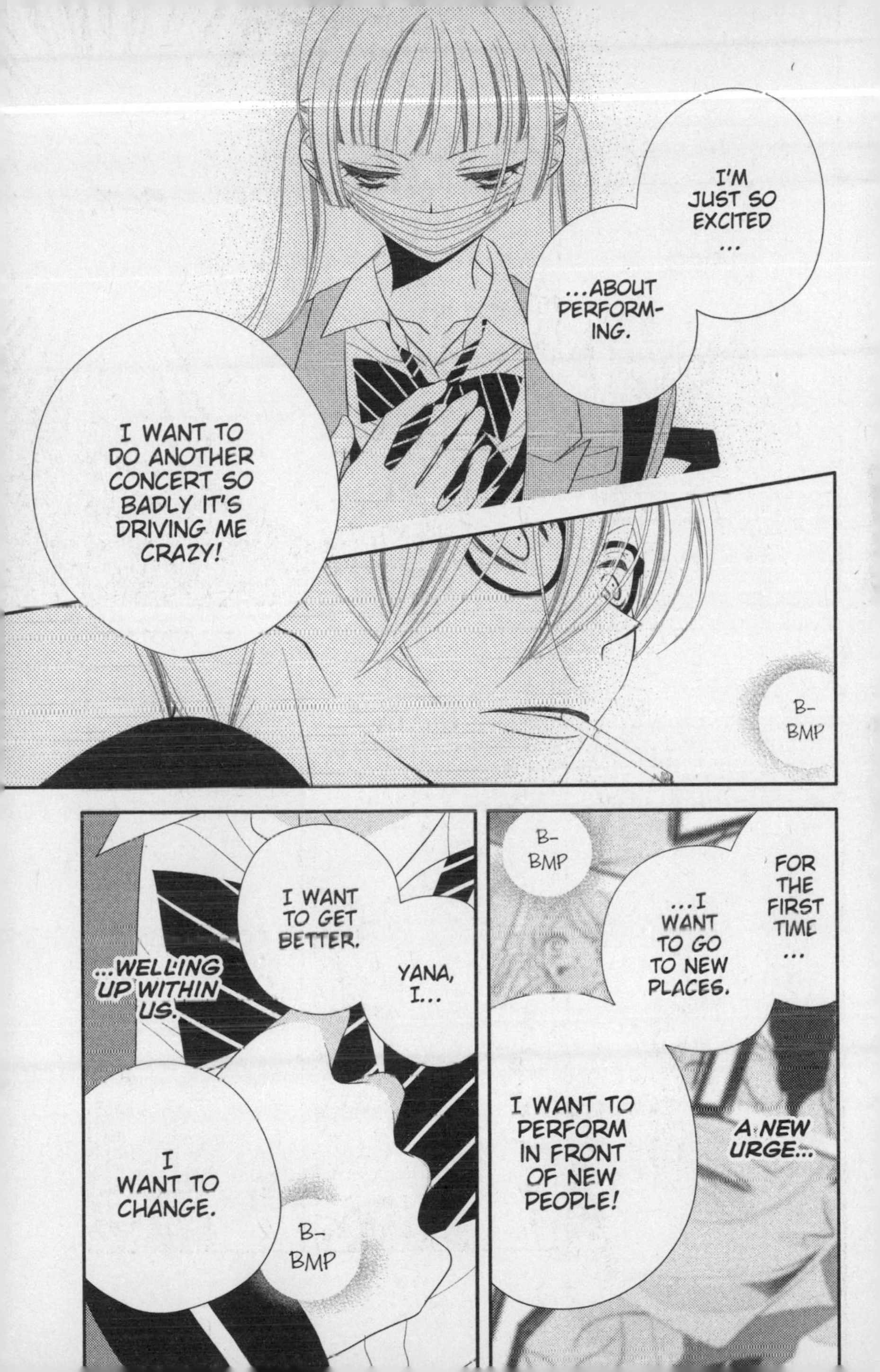
I'M JUST SO EXCITED ...
...ABOUT PERFORMING.
I WANT TO DO ANOTHER CONCERT SO BADLY IT'S DRIVING ME CRAZY!
B-BMP
FOR THE FIRST TIME ...
B-BMP
...I WANT TO GO TO NEW PLACES.
A NEW URGE...
I WANT TO PERFORM IN FRONT OF NEW PEOPLE!
YANA, I...
I WANT TO GET BETTER.
...WELLING UP WITHIN US.
I WANT TO CHANGE.
B-BMP

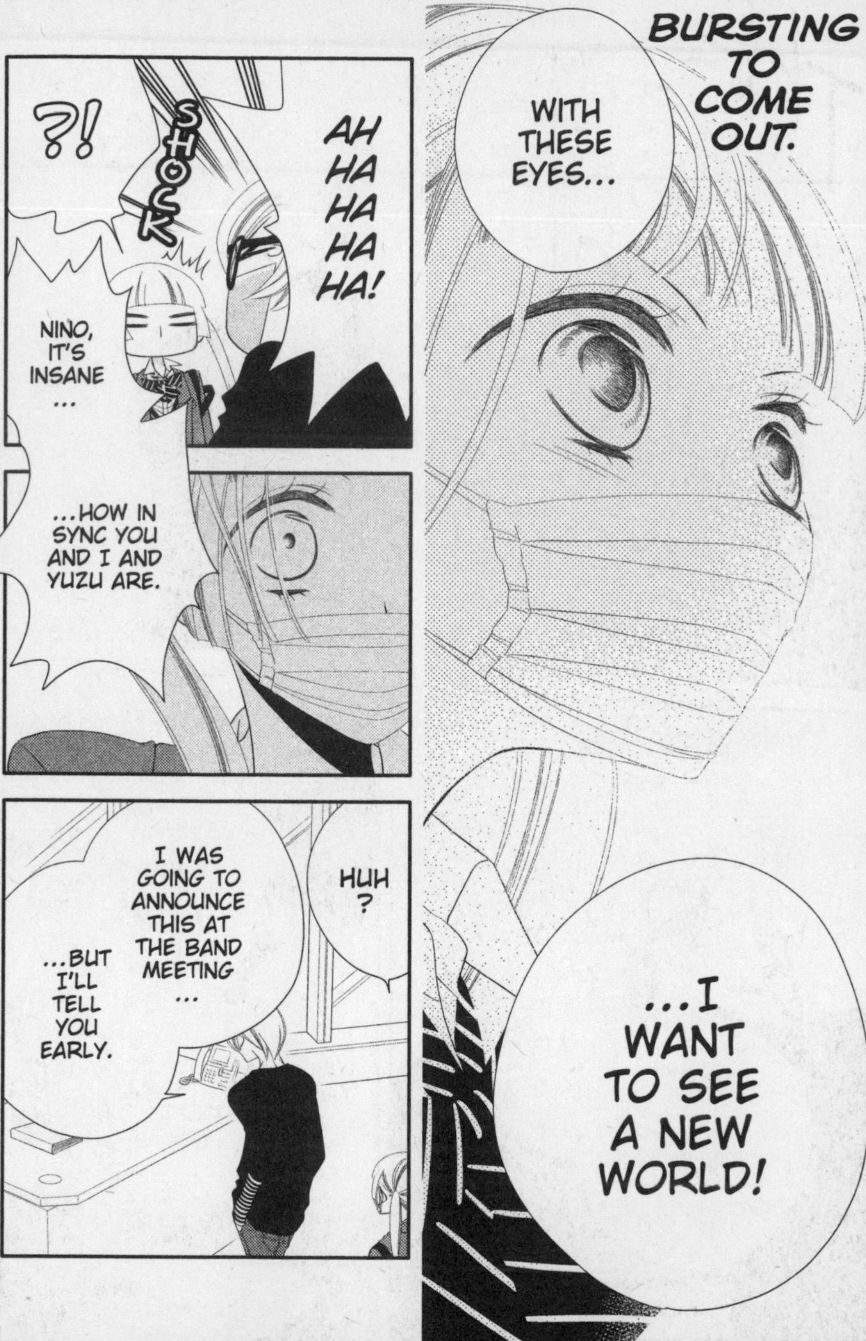
BURSTING TO COME OUT.
WITH THESE EYES...
...I WANT TO SEE A NEW WORLD!
AH HA HA HA HA!
SHOCK
?!
NINO, IT'S INSANE ...
...HOW IN SYNC YOU AND I AND YUZU ARE.
HUH ?
I WAS GOING TO ANNOUNCE THIS AT THE BAND MEETING ...
...BUT I'LL TELL YOU EARLY.

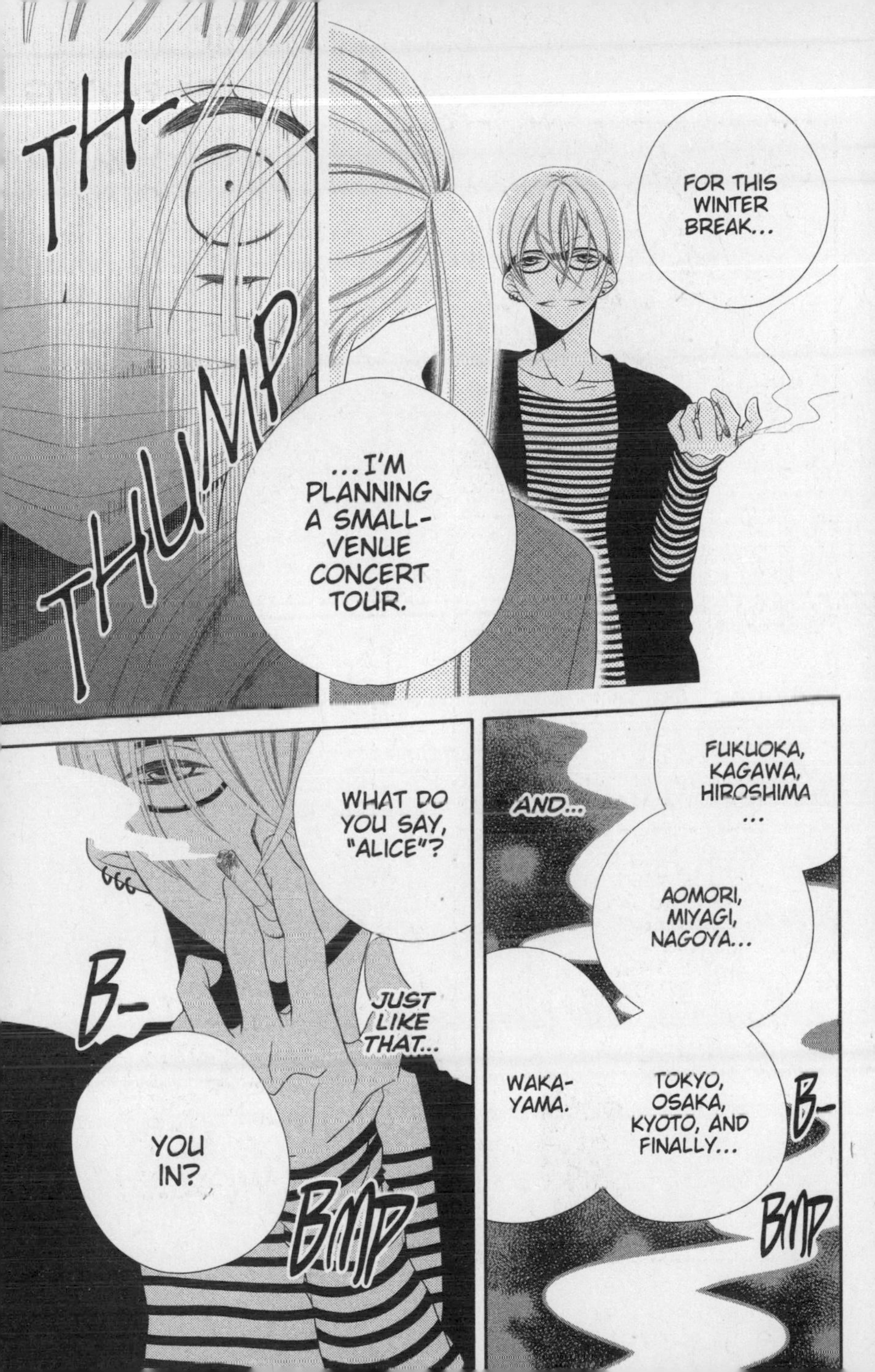
FOR THIS WINTER BREAK...
...I'M PLANNING A SMALL-VENUE CONCERT TOUR.
TH-
THUMP
FUKUOKA, KAGAWA, HIROSHIMA ...
AND...
AOMORI, MIYAGI, NAGOYA...
TOKYO, OSAKA, KYOTO, AND FINALLY...
WAKA-YAMA.
B-
BMP
WHAT DO YOU SAY, "ALICE"?
JUST LIKE THAT...
B-
YOU IN?
BMP

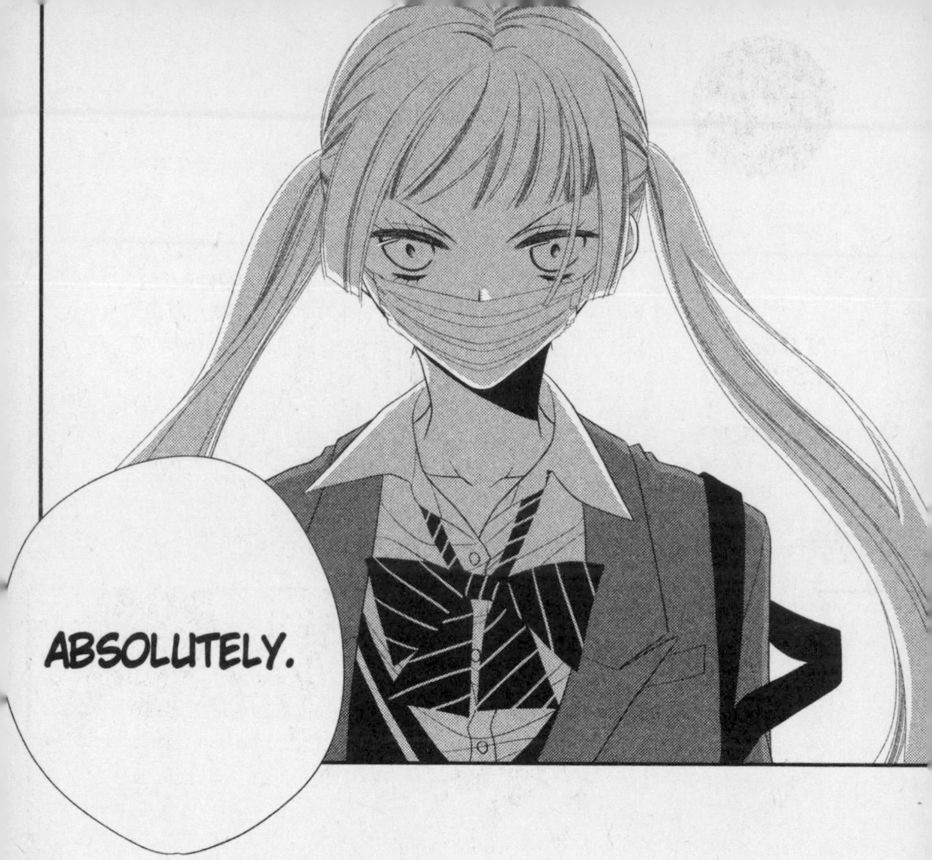
ABSOLUTELY.

...WE OPENED THE DOOR.

SONG 40

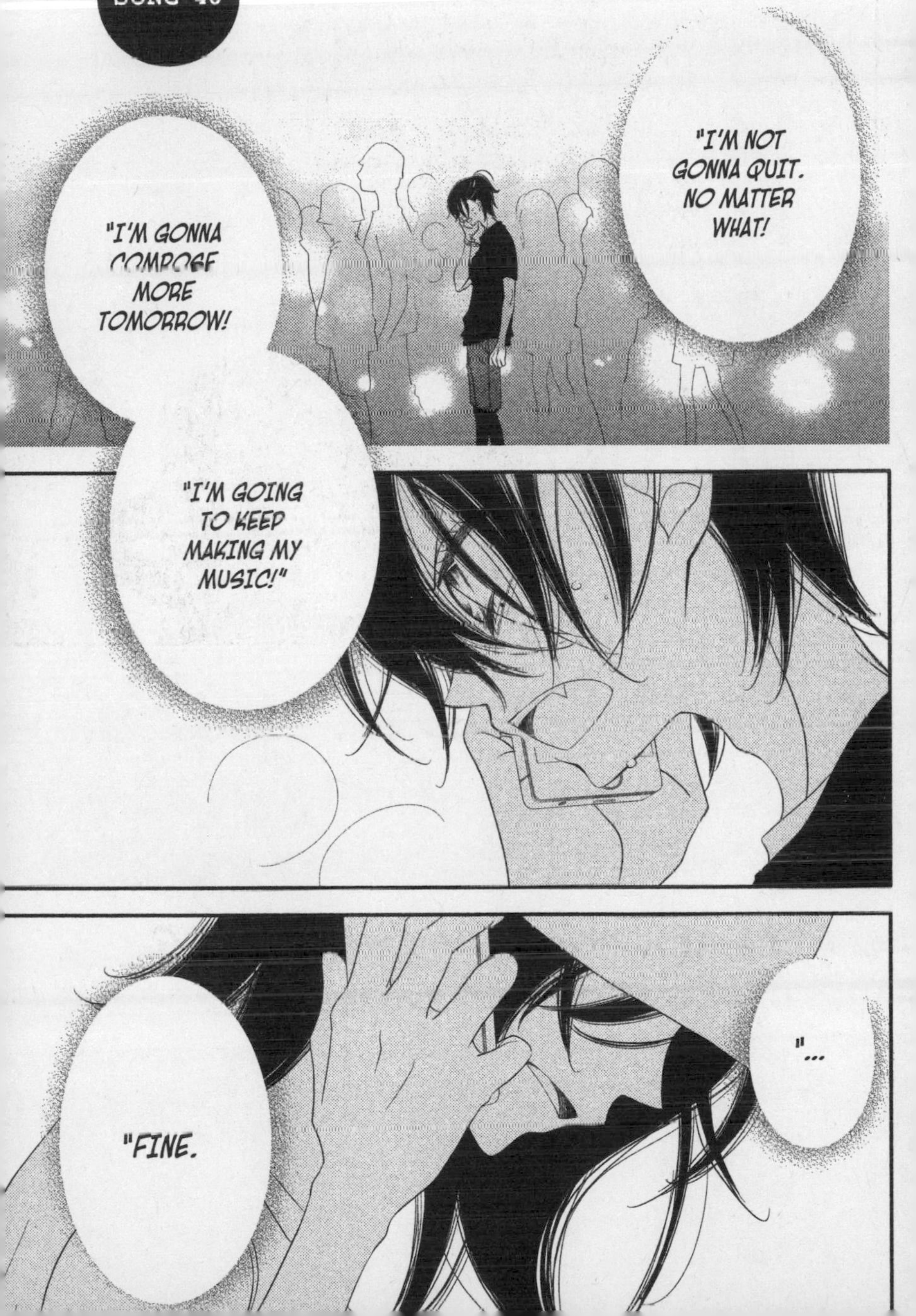
"I'M NOT GONNA QUIT. NO MATTER WHAT!
"I'M GONNA COMPOSE MORE TOMORROW!
"I'M GOING TO KEEP MAKING MY MUSIC!"
"...
"FINE.

ANONYMOUS NOISE SONG 40

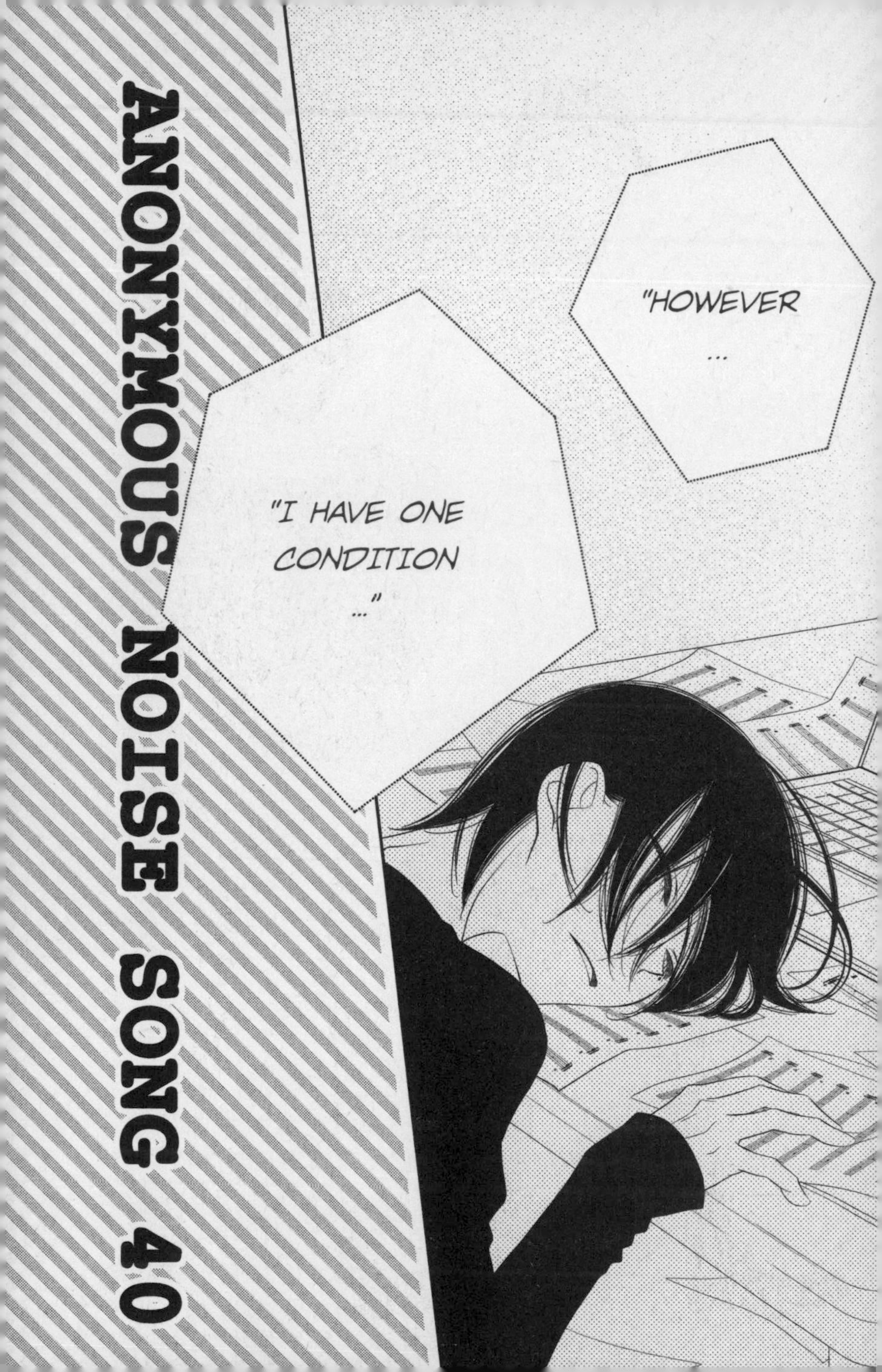
"HOWEVER ...
"I HAVE ONE CONDITION ..."

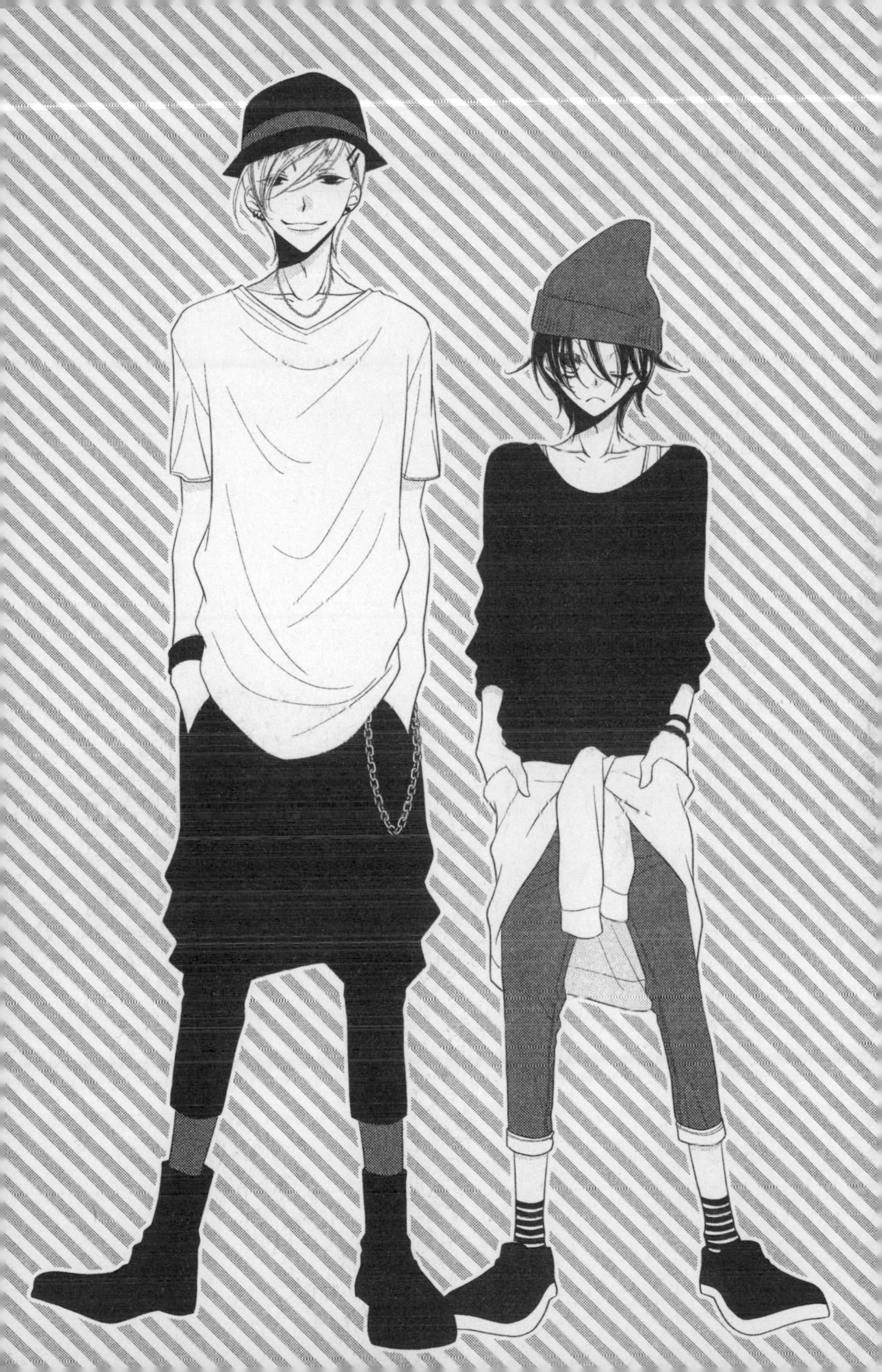

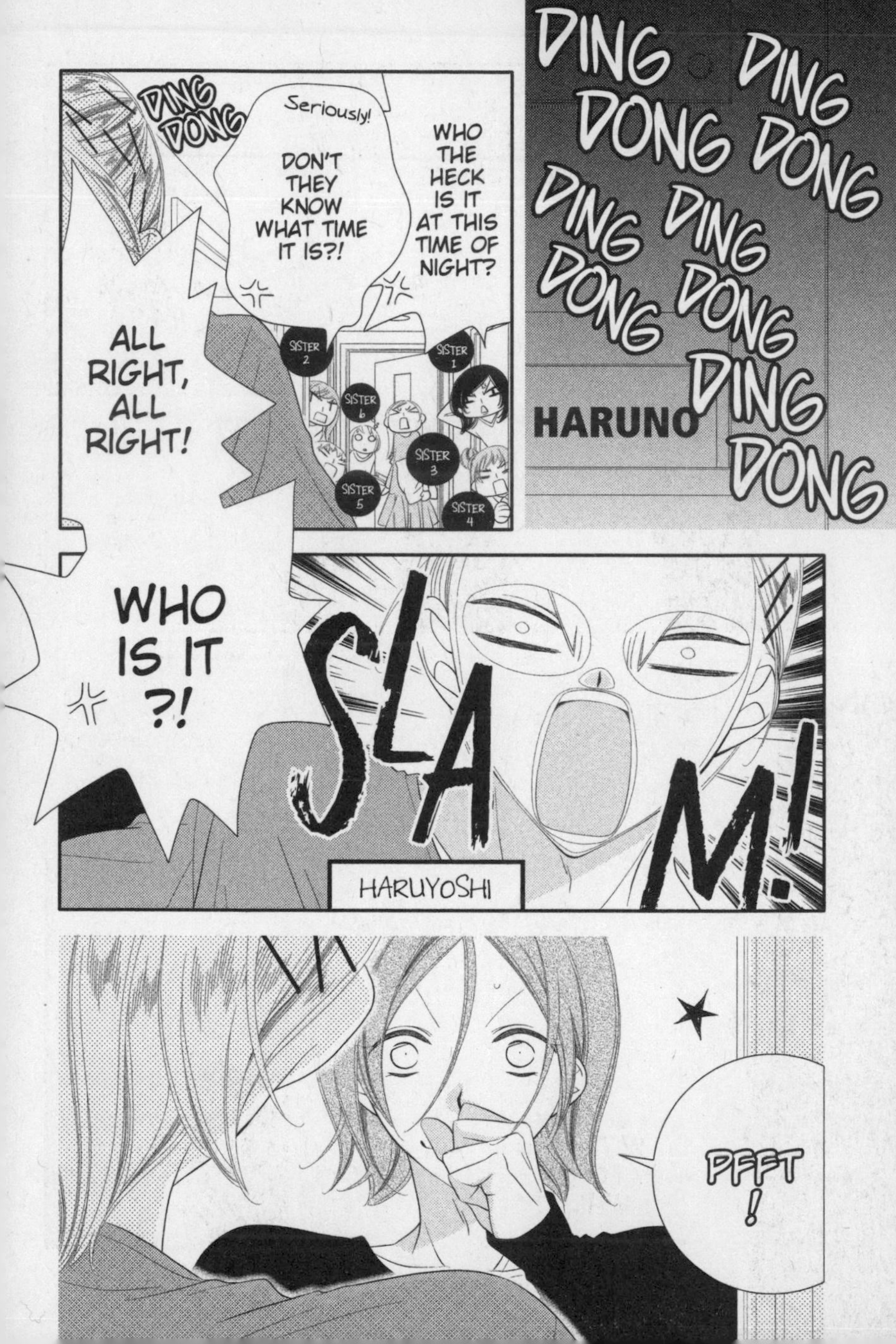
DING DONG DING DONG
DING DONG DING DONG
DING DONG
HARUNO
WHO THE HECK IS IT AT THIS TIME OF NIGHT?
Seriously!
DON'T THEY KNOW WHAT TIME IT IS?!
DING DONG
SISTER 1
SISTER 2
SISTER 6
SISTER 3
SISTER 4
SISTER 5
ALL RIGHT, ALL RIGHT!
SLAM!
WHO IS IT ?!
HARUYOSHI
PFFT !

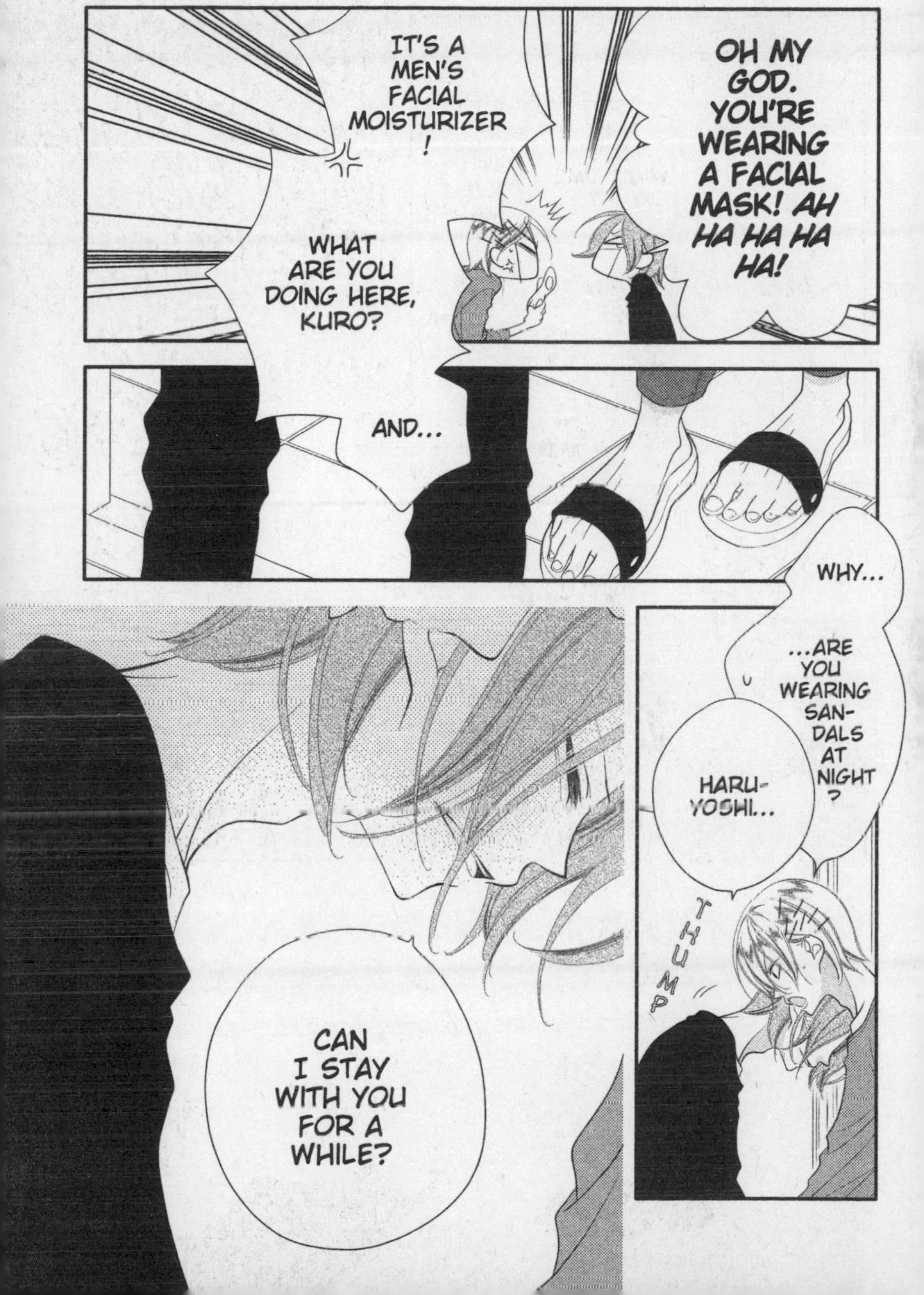
OH MY GOD. YOU'RE WEARING A FACIAL MASK! AH HA HA HA HA!
IT'S A MEN'S FACIAL MOISTURIZER!
WHAT ARE YOU DOING HERE, KURO?
AND...
WHY...
...ARE YOU WEARING SAN-DALS AT NIGHT?
HARU-YOSHI...
THUMP
CAN I STAY WITH YOU FOR A WHILE?

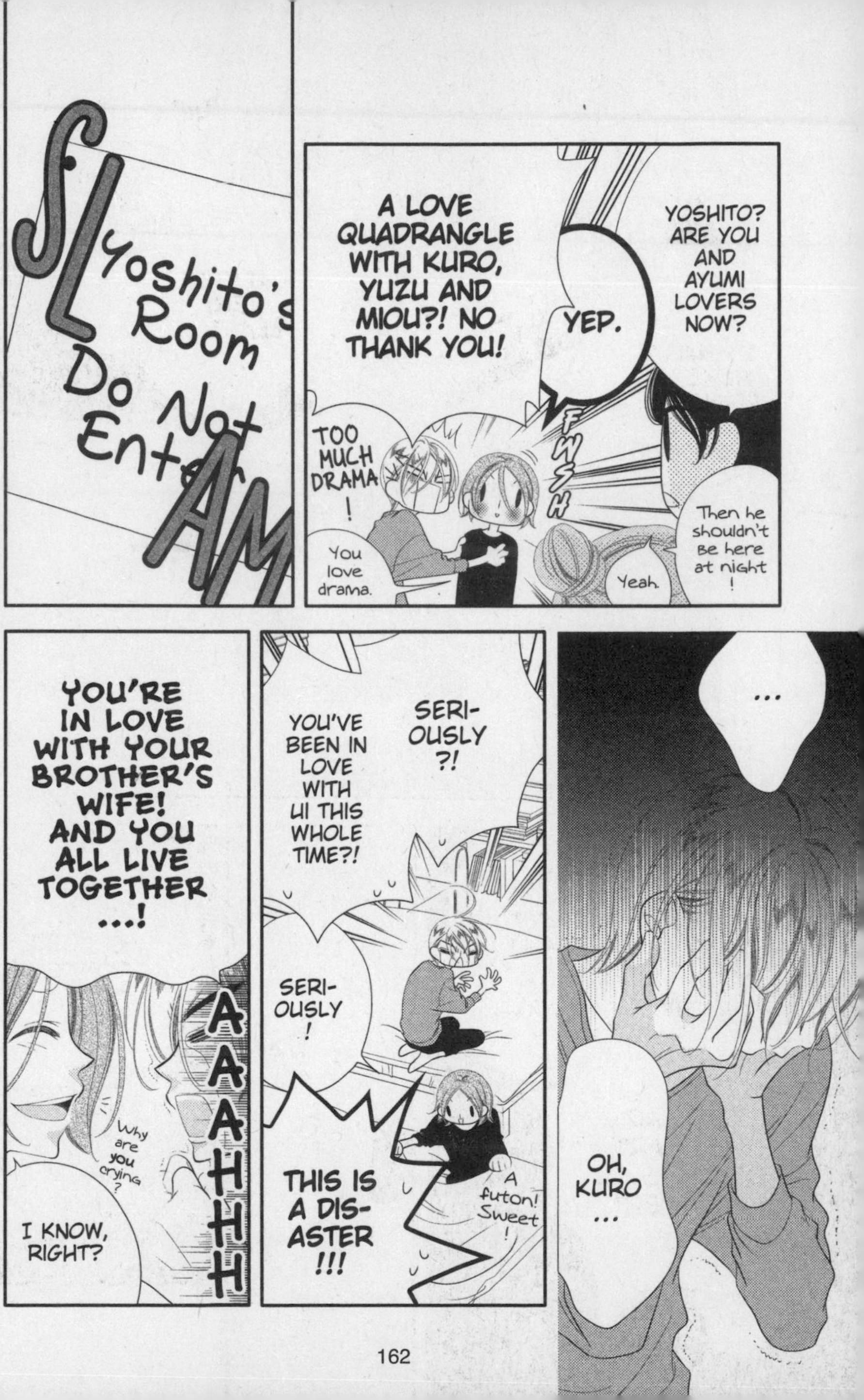
YOSHITO? ARE YOU AND AYUMI LOVERS NOW?
YEP.
A LOVE QUADRANGLE WITH KURO, YUZU AND MIOU?! NO THANK YOU!
FWSH
Then he shouldn't be here at night!
Yeah.
TOO MUCH DRAMA!
You love drama.
Yoshito's Room Do Not Enter
SLAM
...
OH, KURO...
SERI-OUSLY?!
YOU'VE BEEN IN LOVE WITH UI THIS WHOLE TIME?!
SERI-OUSLY!
THIS IS A DIS-ASTER!!!
A futon! Sweet!
YOU'RE IN LOVE WITH YOUR BROTHER'S WIFE! AND YOU ALL LIVE TOGETHER...!
AAAAHHH
Why are you crying?
I KNOW, RIGHT?

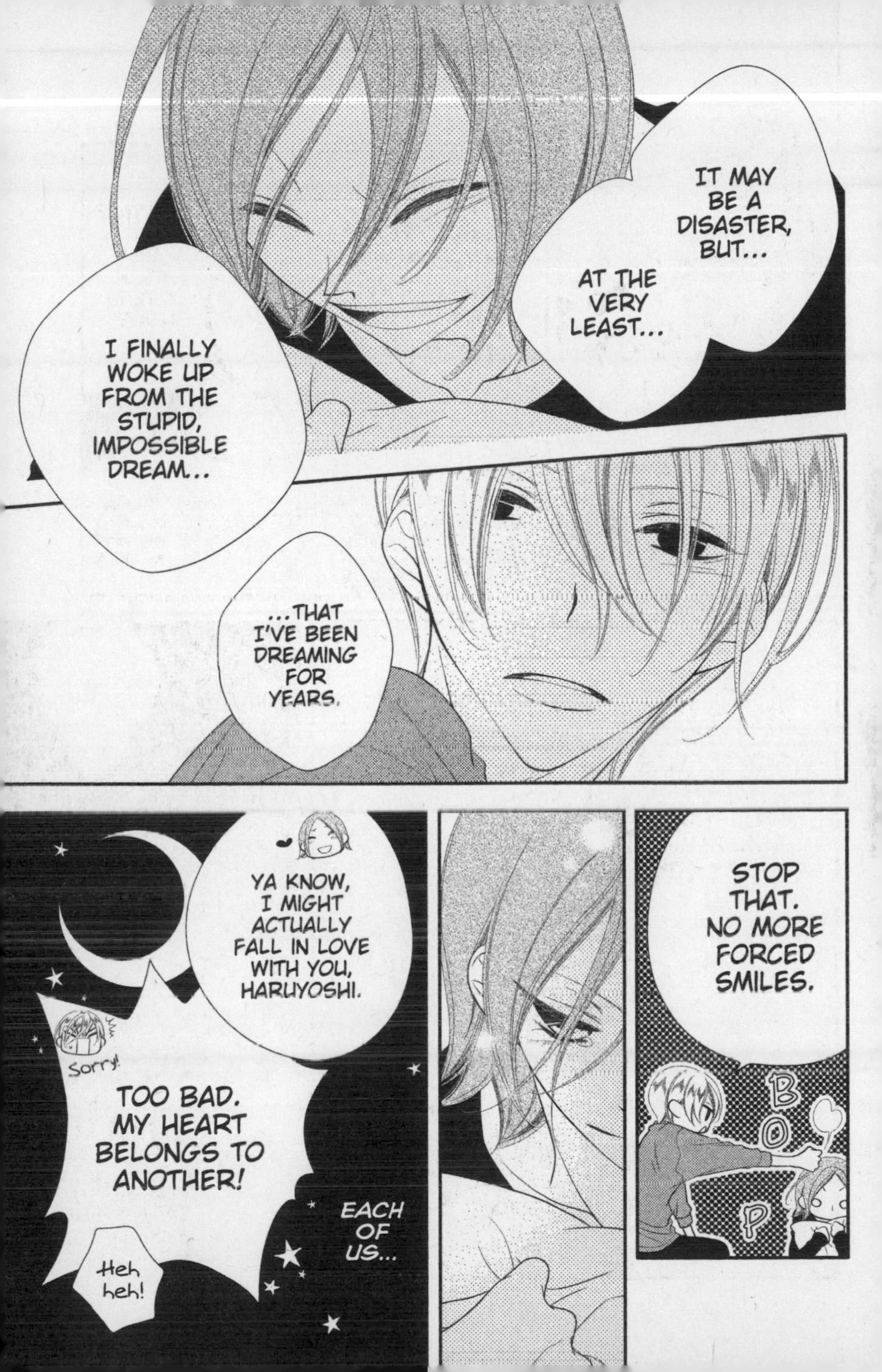
IT MAY BE A DISASTER, BUT...
AT THE VERY LEAST...
I FINALLY WOKE UP FROM THE STUPID, IMPOSSIBLE DREAM...
...THAT I'VE BEEN DREAMING FOR YEARS.
STOP THAT. NO MORE FORCED SMILES.
BOP
YA KNOW, I MIGHT ACTUALLY FALL IN LOVE WITH YOU, HARUYOSHI.
Sorry!
TOO BAD. MY HEART BELONGS TO ANOTHER!
EACH OF US...
Heh heh!

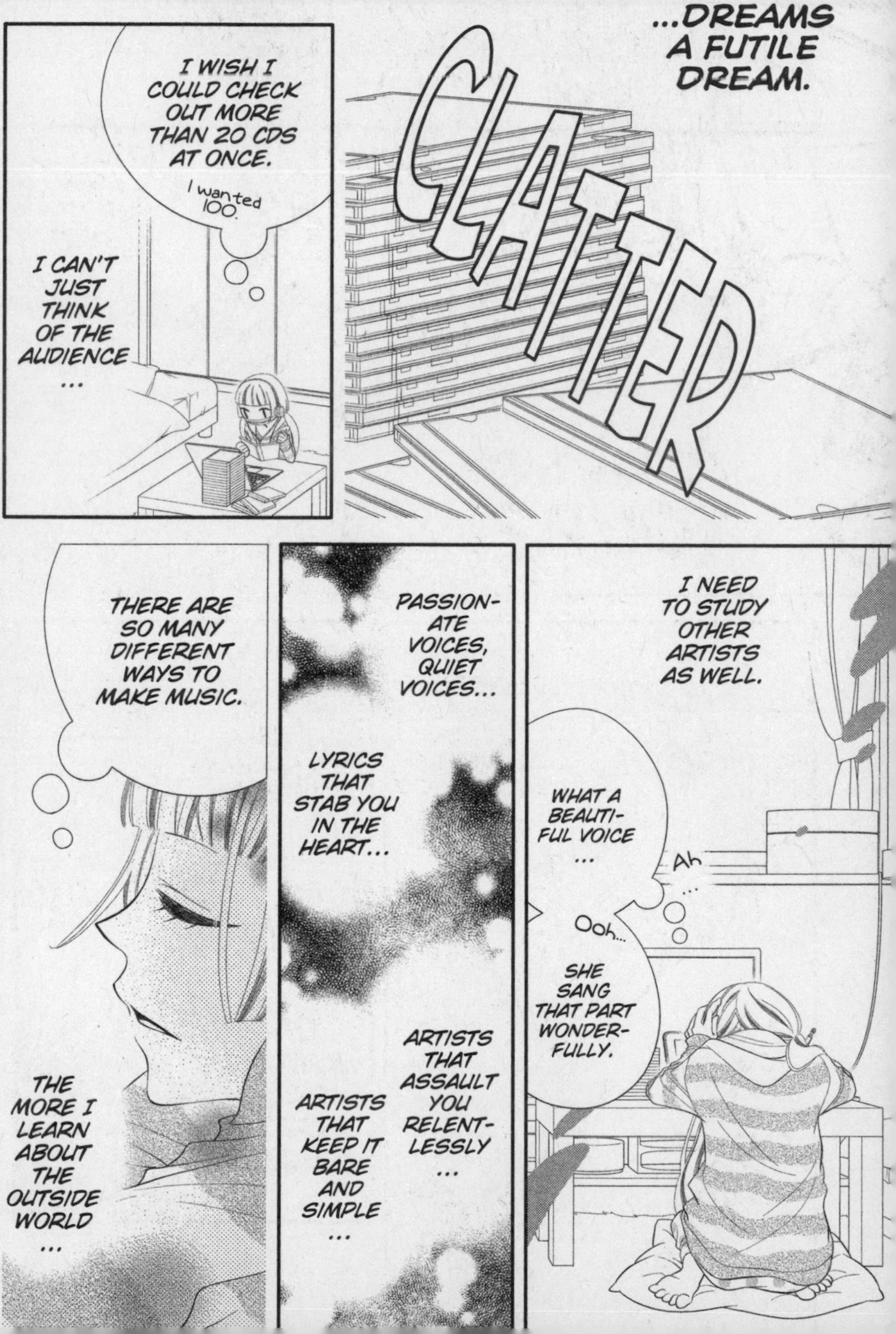
...DREAMS A FUTILE DREAM.
CLATTER
I WISH I COULD CHECK OUT MORE THAN 20 CDS AT ONCE.
I wanted 100.
I CAN'T JUST THINK OF THE AUDIENCE...
I NEED TO STUDY OTHER ARTISTS AS WELL.
WHAT A BEAUTIFUL VOICE...
Ah...
Ooh...
SHE SANG THAT PART WONDERFULLY.
PASSIONATE VOICES, QUIET VOICES...
LYRICS THAT STAB YOU IN THE HEART...
ARTISTS THAT ASSAULT YOU RELENTLESSLY...
ARTISTS THAT KEEP IT BARE AND SIMPLE...
THERE ARE SO MANY DIFFERENT WAYS TO MAKE MUSIC.
THE MORE I LEARN ABOUT THE OUTSIDE WORLD...

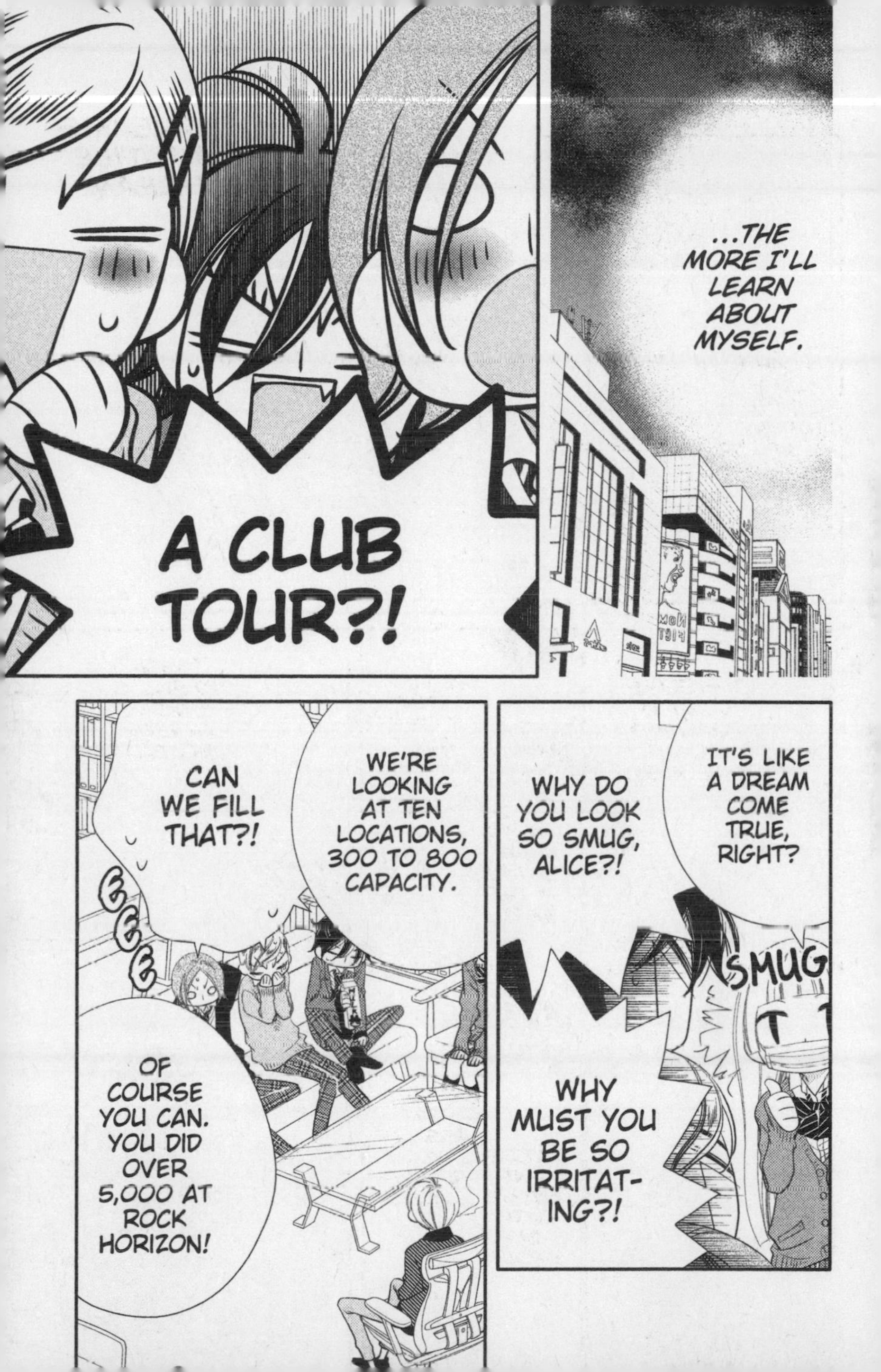
...THE MORE I'LL LEARN ABOUT MYSELF.
A CLUB TOUR?!
IT'S LIKE A DREAM COME TRUE, RIGHT?
SMUG
WHY DO YOU LOOK SO SMUG, ALICE?!
WHY MUST YOU BE SO IRRITAT-ING?!
WE'RE LOOKING AT TEN LOCATIONS, 300 TO 800 CAPACITY.
CAN WE FILL THAT?!
OF COURSE YOU CAN. YOU DID OVER 5,000 AT ROCK HORIZON!

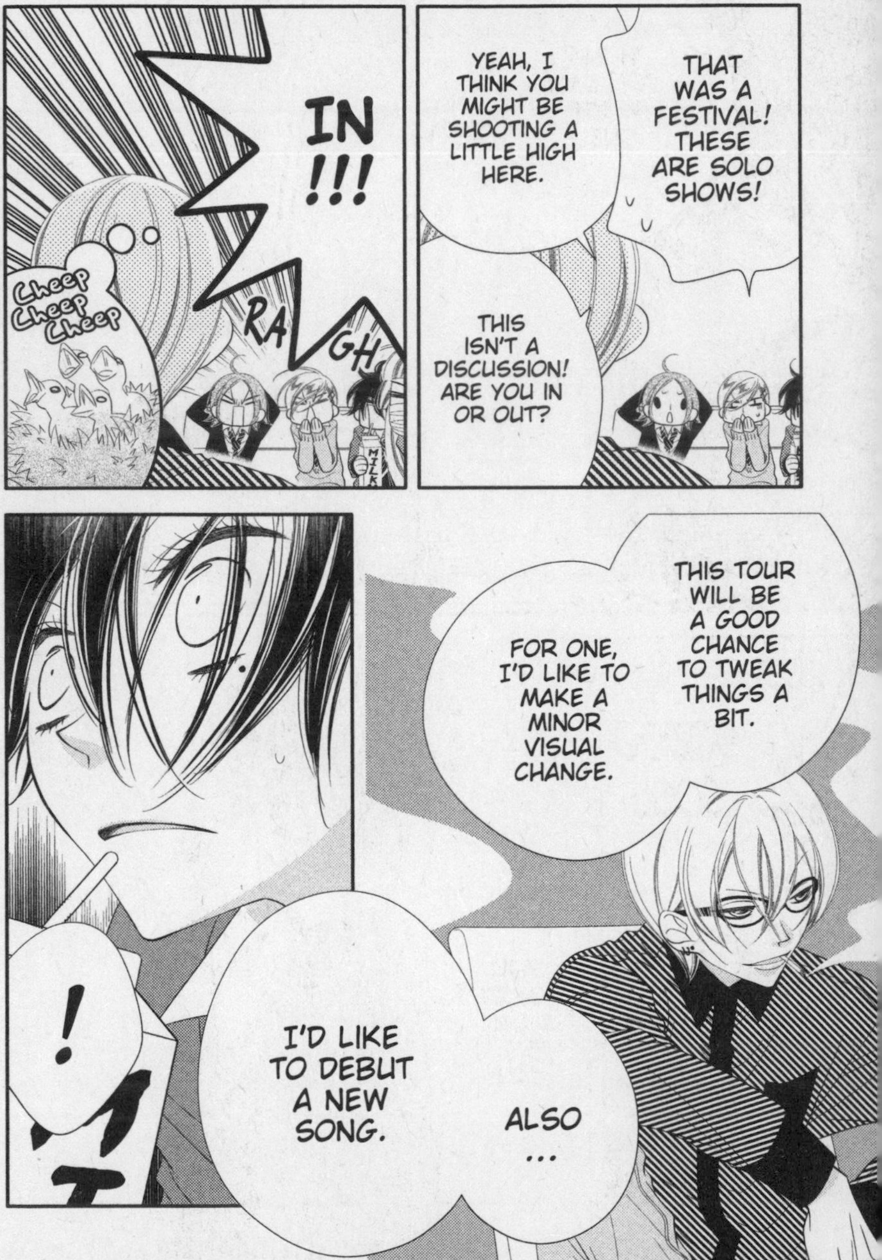
THAT WAS A FESTIVAL! THESE ARE SOLO SHOWS!
YEAH, I THINK YOU MIGHT BE SHOOTING A LITTLE HIGH HERE.
THIS ISN'T A DISCUSSION! ARE YOU IN OR OUT?
IN !!!
RAGH
Cheep Cheep Cheep
MILK
THIS TOUR WILL BE A GOOD CHANCE TO TWEAK THINGS A BIT.
FOR ONE, I'D LIKE TO MAKE A MINOR VISUAL CHANGE.
ALSO ...
I'D LIKE TO DEBUT A NEW SONG.
!

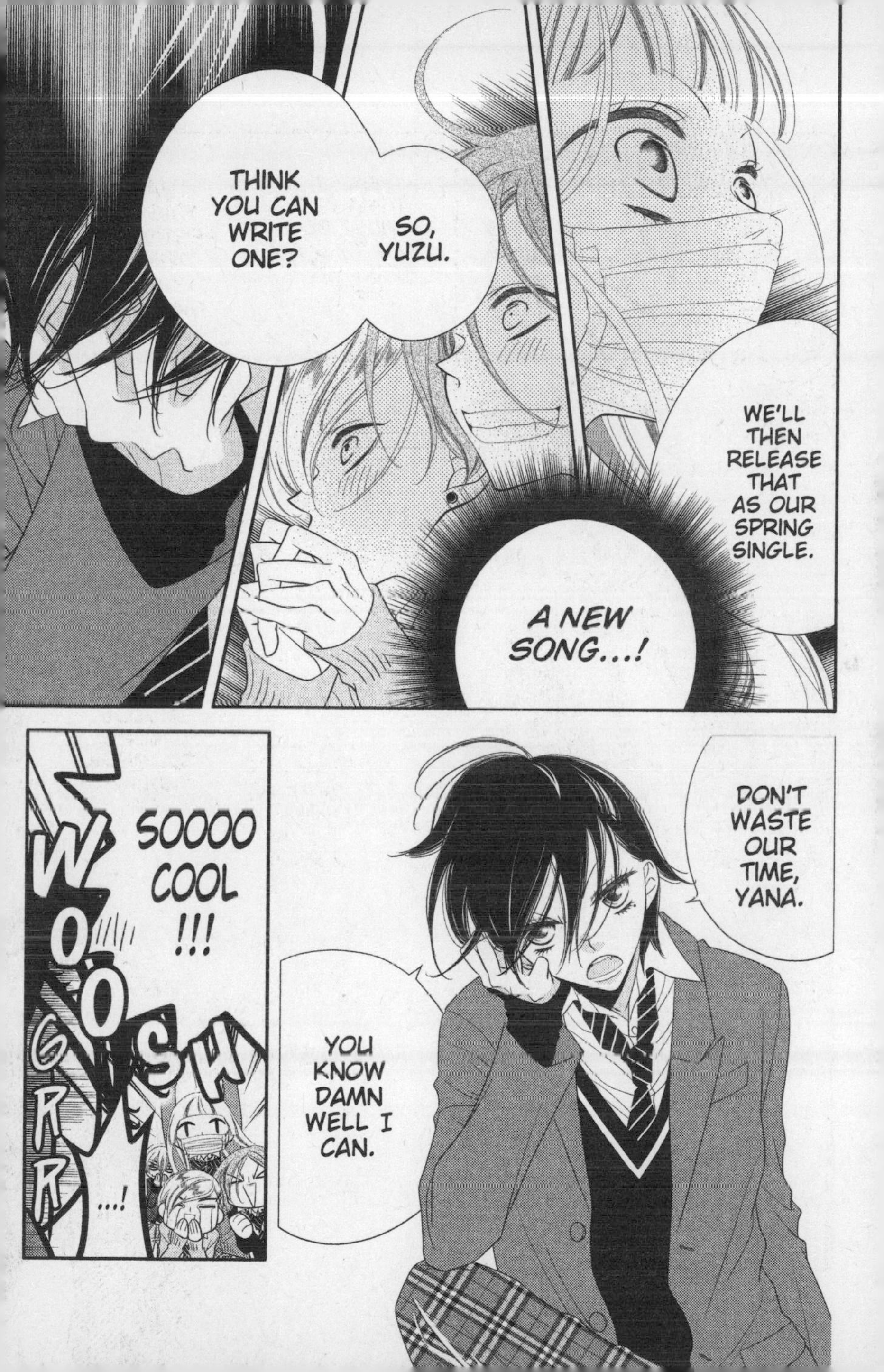
WE'LL THEN RELEASE THAT AS OUR SPRING SINGLE.
SO, YUZU.
THINK YOU CAN WRITE ONE?
A NEW SONG...!
DON'T WASTE OUR TIME, YANA.
YOU KNOW DAMN WELL I CAN.
SOOOOO COOL!!!
WOOOSH
GRRR
...!

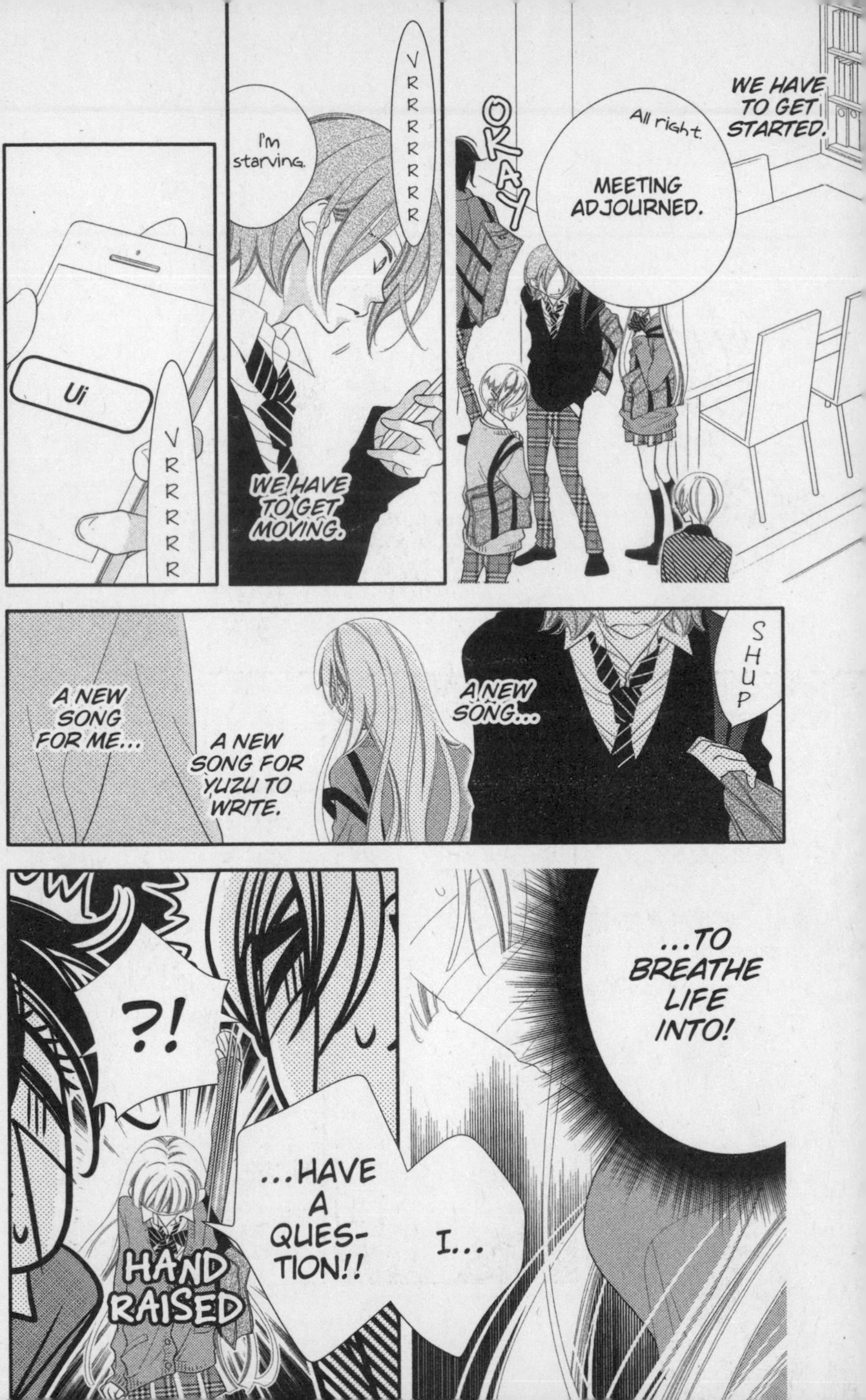
WE HAVE TO GET STARTED.
All right.
MEETING ADJOURNED.
OKAY
VRRRRRRR
I'm starving.
WE HAVE TO GET MOVING.
Ui
VRRRRR
SHUP
A NEW SONG...
A NEW SONG FOR YUZU TO WRITE.
A NEW SONG FOR ME...
...TO BREATHE LIFE INTO!
I...
...HAVE A QUESTION!!
?!
HAND RAISED

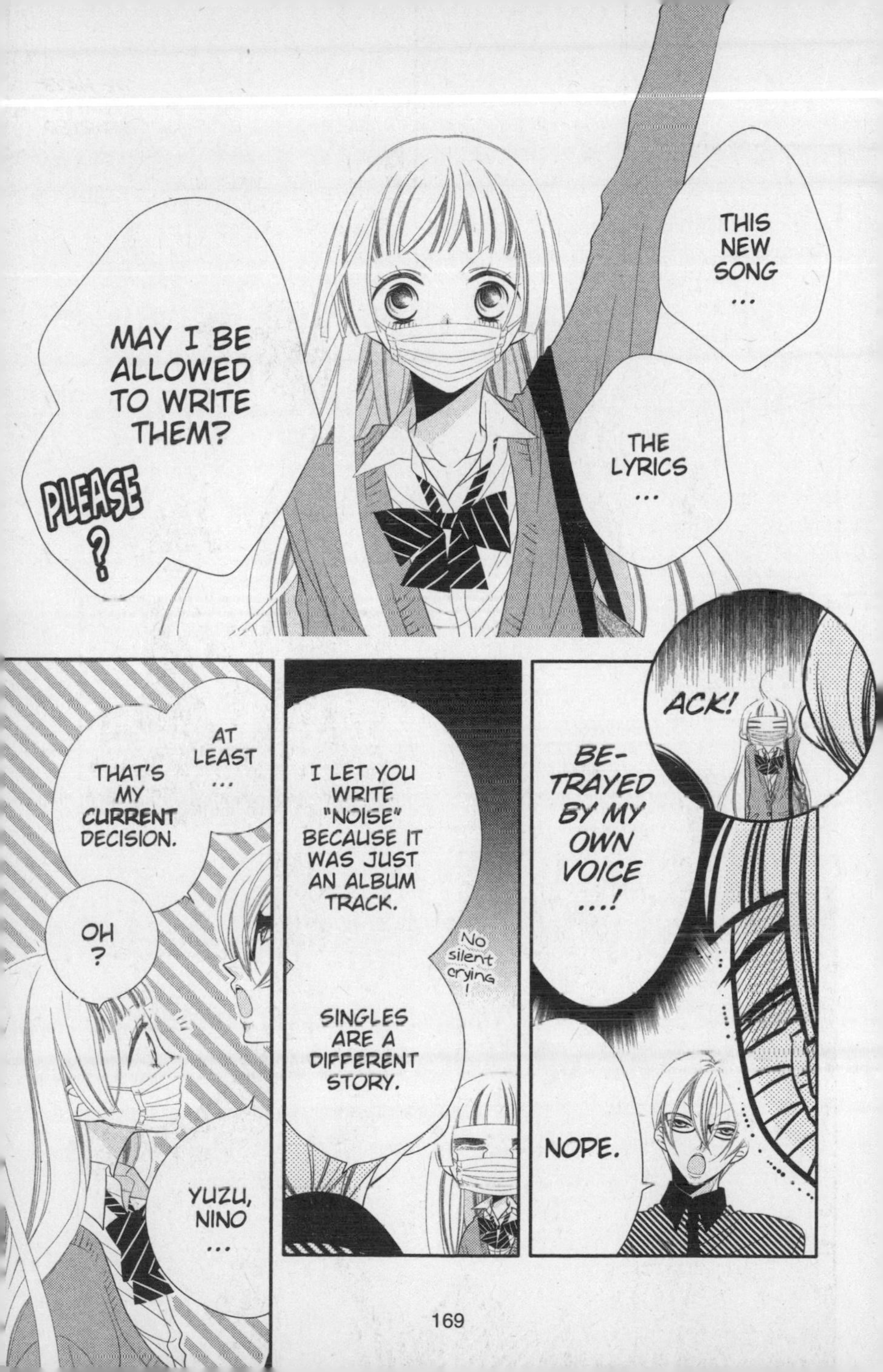
THIS NEW SONG...
THE LYRICS...
MAY I BE ALLOWED TO WRITE THEM?
PLEASE?
ACK!
BE-TRAYED BY MY OWN VOICE...!
NOPE.
I LET YOU WRITE "NOISE" BECAUSE IT WAS JUST AN ALBUM TRACK.
SINGLES ARE A DIFFERENT STORY.
No silent crying!
AT LEAST...
THAT'S MY CURRENT DECISION.
OH?
YUZU, NINO...

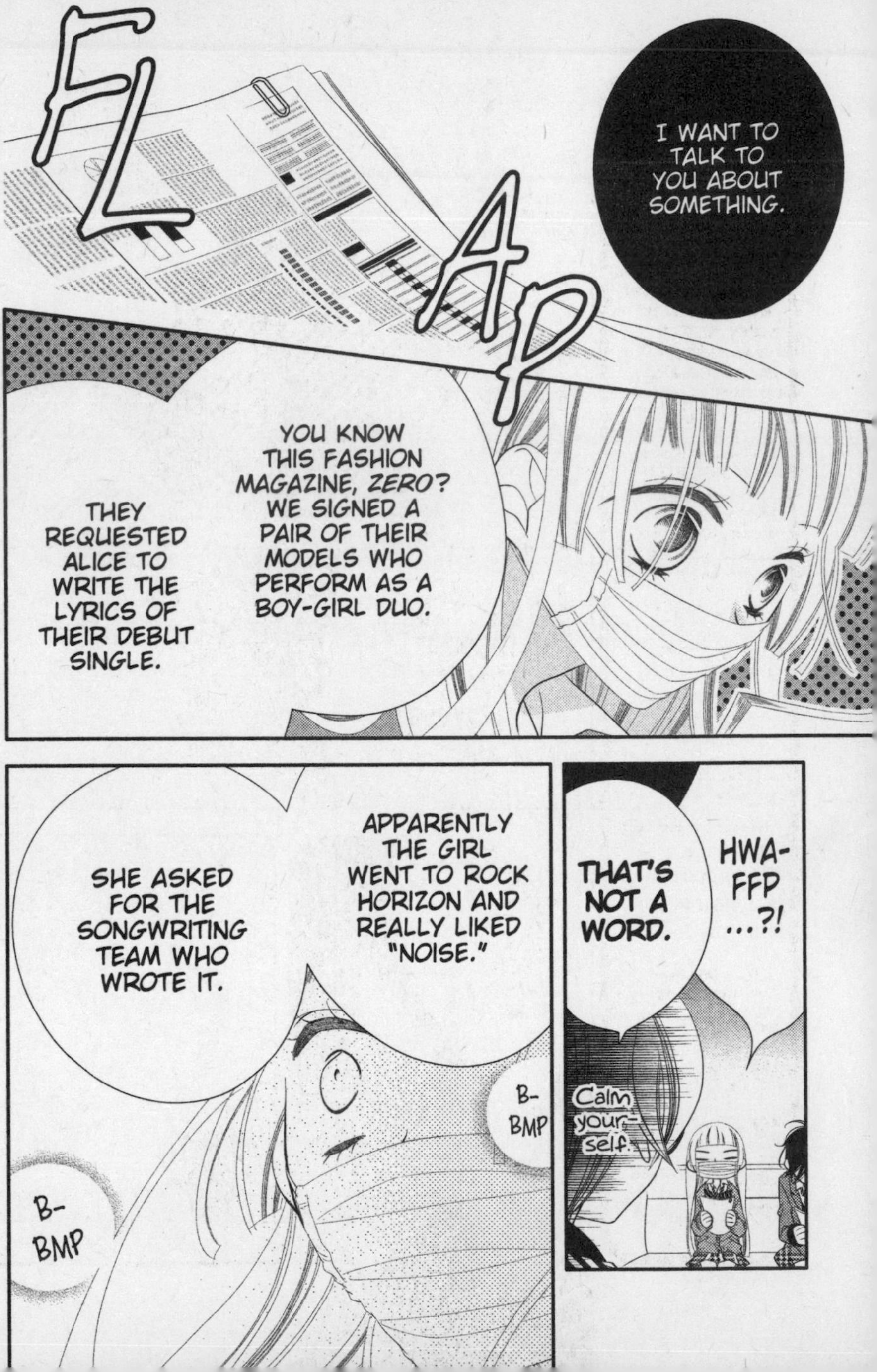
I WANT TO TALK TO YOU ABOUT SOMETHING.
FLAP
YOU KNOW THIS FASHION MAGAZINE, *ZERO*? WE SIGNED A PAIR OF THEIR MODELS WHO PERFORM AS A BOY-GIRL DUO.
THEY REQUESTED ALICE TO WRITE THE LYRICS OF THEIR DEBUT SINGLE.
HWA-FFP ...?!
THAT'S NOT A WORD.
Calm yourself.
APPARENTLY THE GIRL WENT TO ROCK HORIZON AND REALLY LIKED "NOISE."
SHE ASKED FOR THE SONGWRITING TEAM WHO WROTE IT.
B-BMP
B-BMP

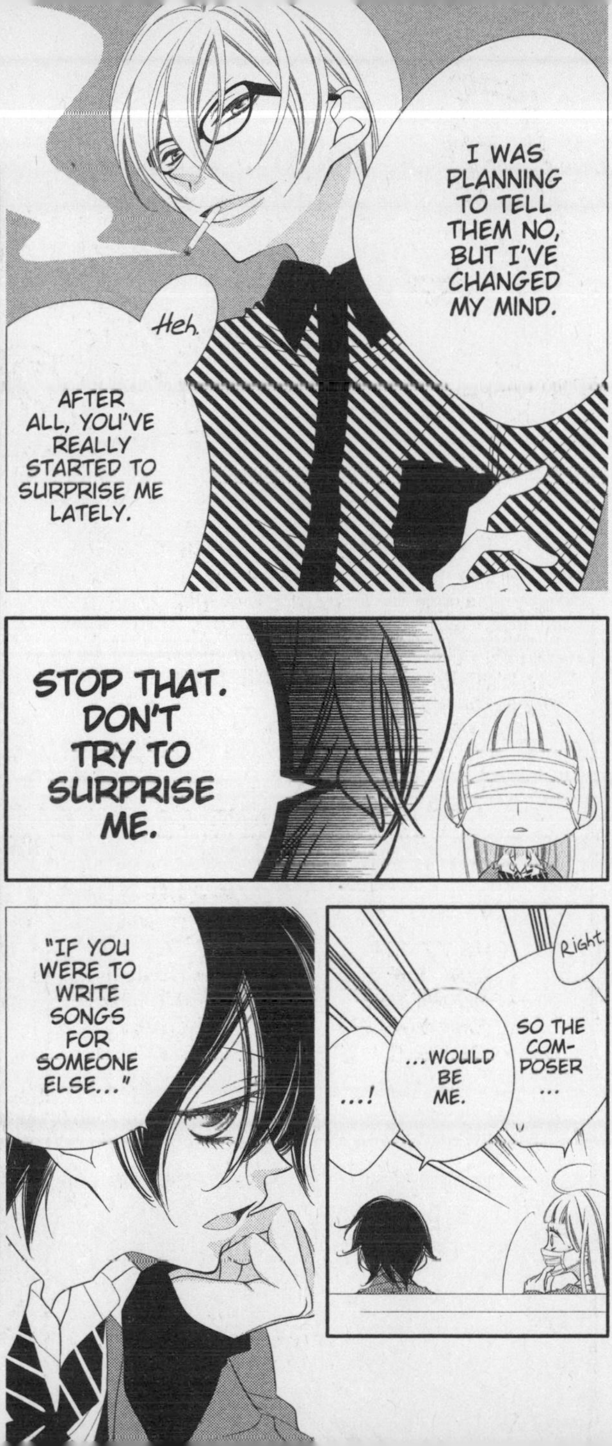
I WAS PLANNING TO TELL THEM NO, BUT I'VE CHANGED MY MIND.
Heh.
AFTER ALL, YOU'VE REALLY STARTED TO SURPRISE ME LATELY.
STOP THAT. DON'T TRY TO SURPRISE ME.
Right.
SO THE COMPOSER...
...WOULD BE ME.
...!
"IF YOU WERE TO WRITE SONGS FOR SOMEONE ELSE..."

6

And here we are, at my final column! I think my handwriting is even worse than usual in this volume, and even though I say it every time, I never stop being shocked by that.

So how did you like volume 7? I can't wait to hear what you thought! I hope to see you again in volume 8!

Until then!

10/20/2015
XXX
Ryoko Fukuyama

[SPECIAL THANKS]
MOSAGE
TAKAYUKI NAGASHIMA
KENJU NORO
MY FAMILY
MY FRIENDS
AND YOU!!

Ryoko Fukuyama
c/o Anonymous Noise Editor
VIZ Media
P.O. Box 77010
San Francisco, CA 94107

HP http://ryoconet/
@ryocoryocoryoco
http://facebook.com/ryocoryocoryoco/

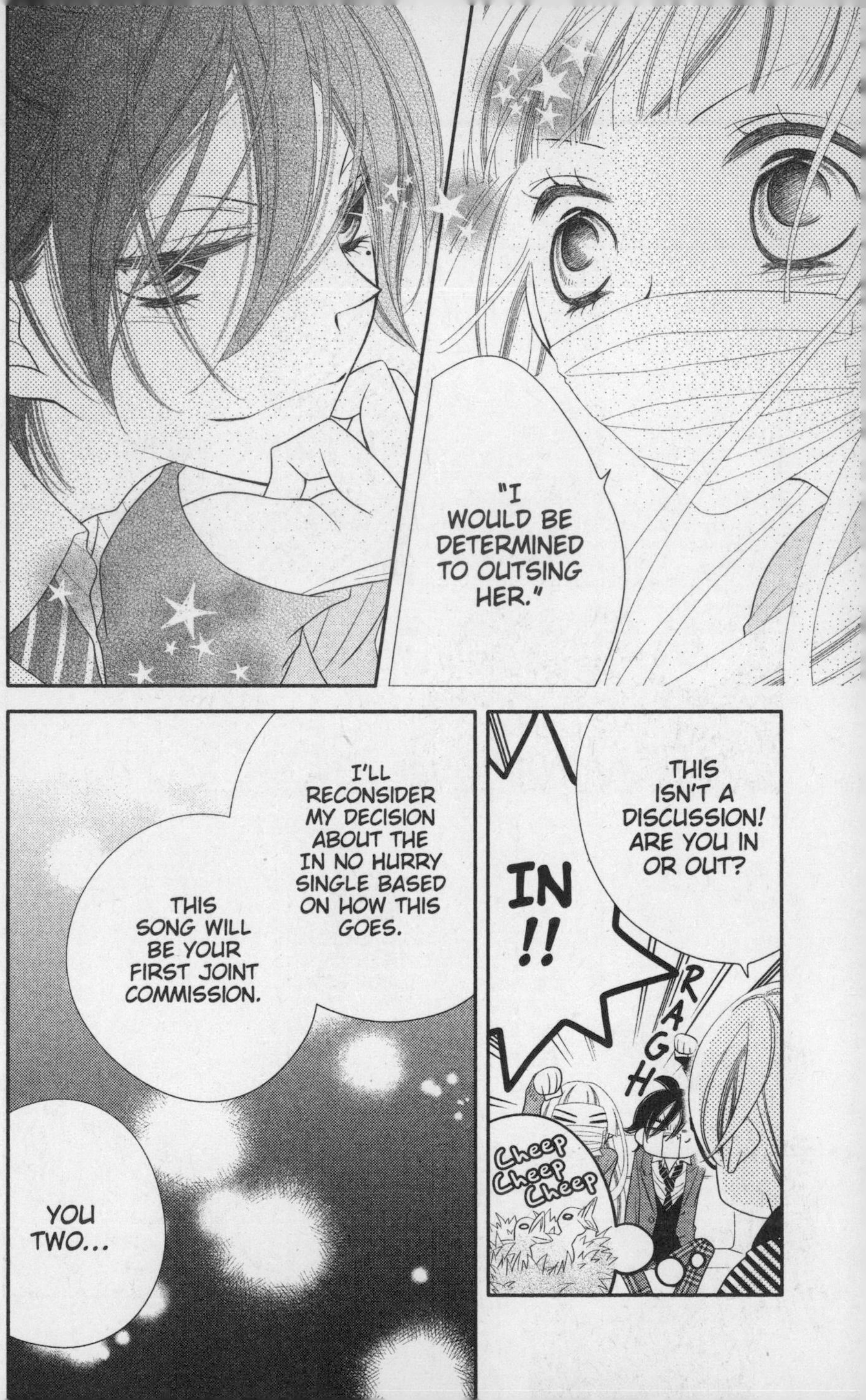
"I WOULD BE DETERMINED TO OUTSING HER."
THIS ISN'T A DISCUSSION! ARE YOU IN OR OUT?
IN !!
RAGH
Cheep Cheep Cheep
I'LL RECONSIDER MY DECISION ABOUT THE IN NO HURRY SINGLE BASED ON HOW THIS GOES.
THIS SONG WILL BE YOUR FIRST JOINT COMMISSION.
YOU TWO...

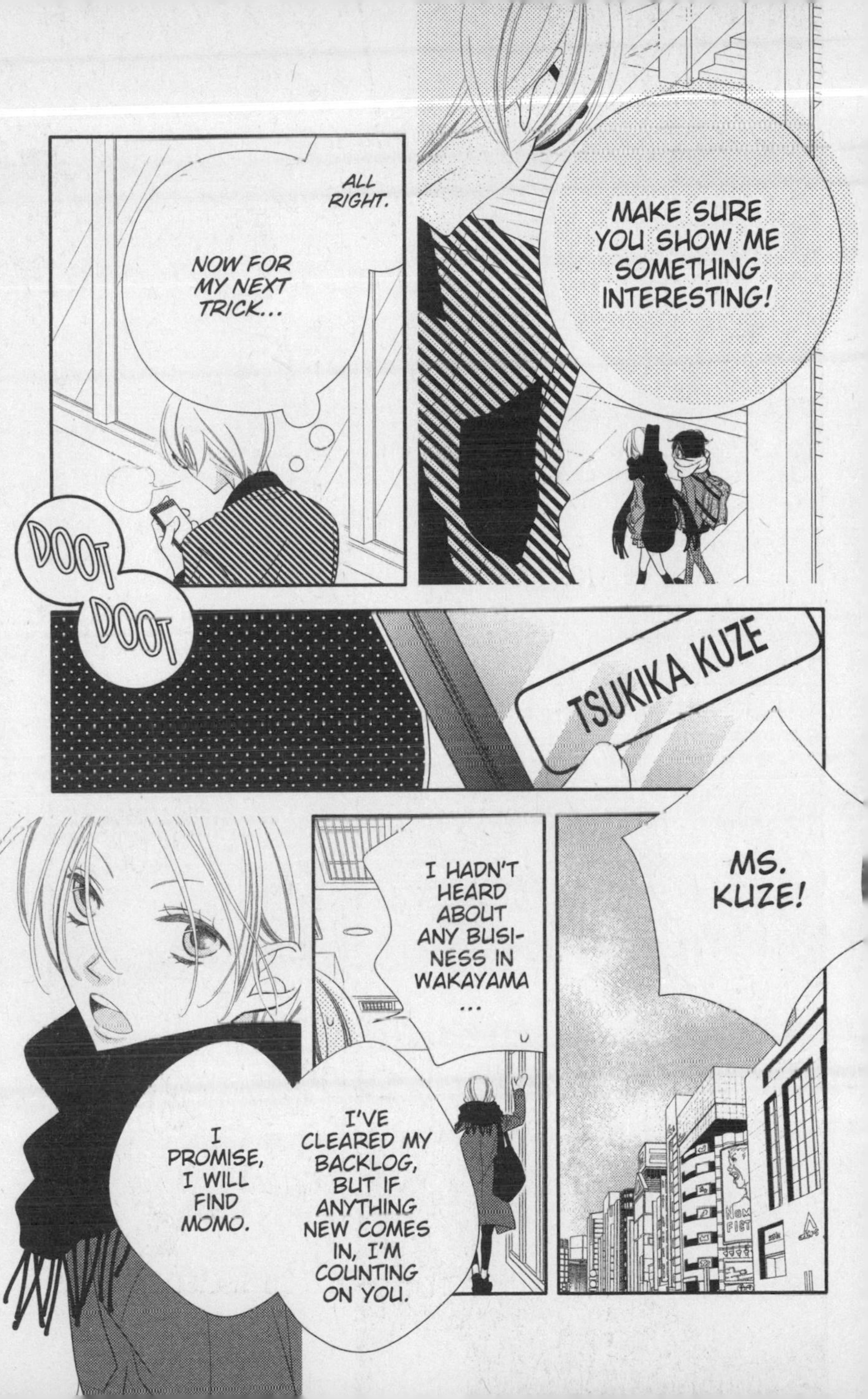
MAKE SURE YOU SHOW ME SOMETHING INTERESTING!
ALL RIGHT.
NOW FOR MY NEXT TRICK...
DOOT DOOT
TSUKIKA KUZE
MS. KUZE!
I HADN'T HEARD ABOUT ANY BUSINESS IN WAKAYAMA...
I'VE CLEARED MY BACKLOG, BUT IF ANYTHING NEW COMES IN, I'M COUNTING ON YOU.
I PROMISE, I WILL FIND MOMO.

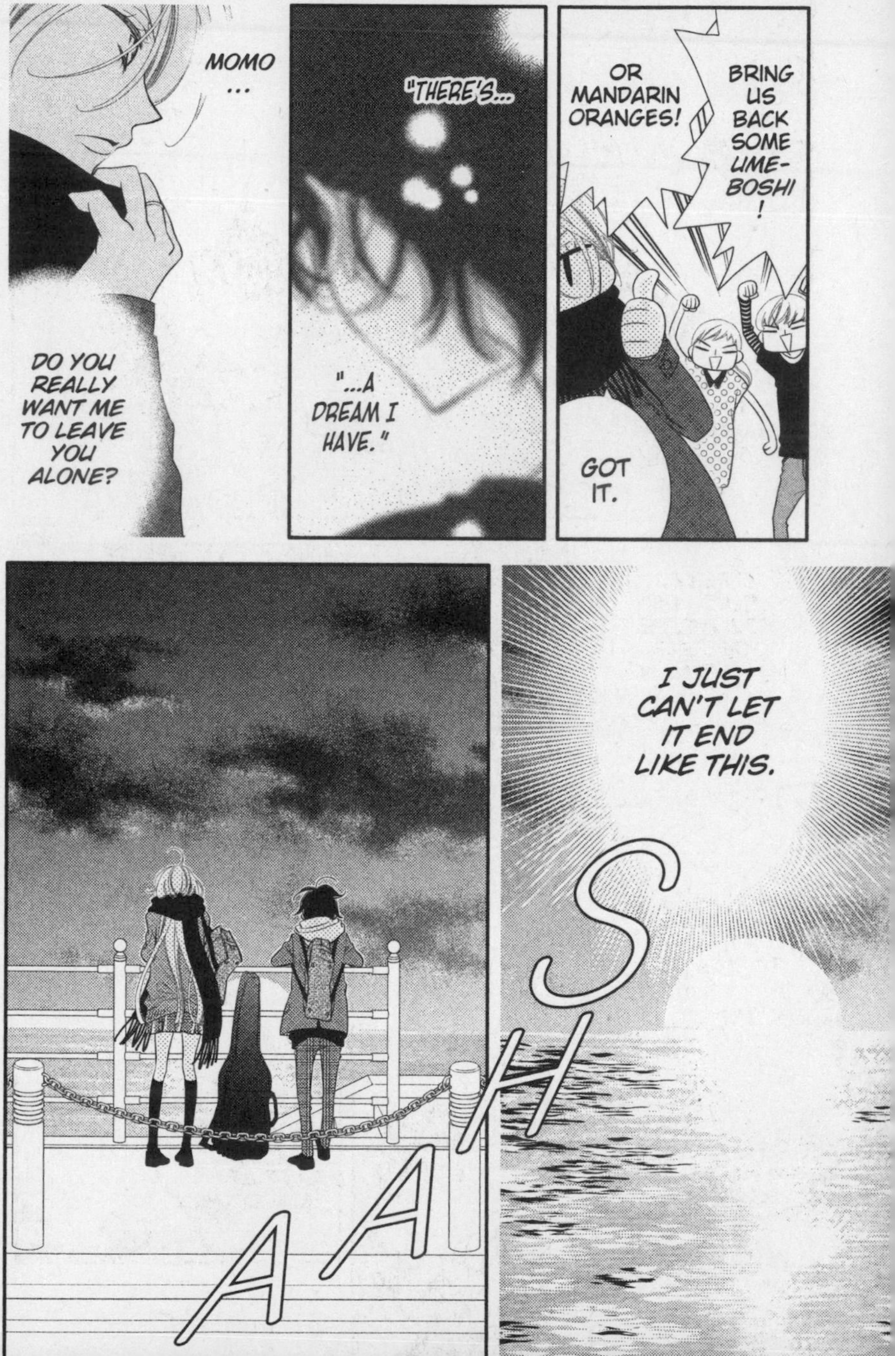
BRING US BACK SOME UME-BOSHI!
OR MANDARIN ORANGES!
GOT IT.
"THERE'S...
"...A DREAM I HAVE."
MOMO...
DO YOU REALLY WANT ME TO LEAVE YOU ALONE?
I JUST CAN'T LET IT END LIKE THIS.
SHAA

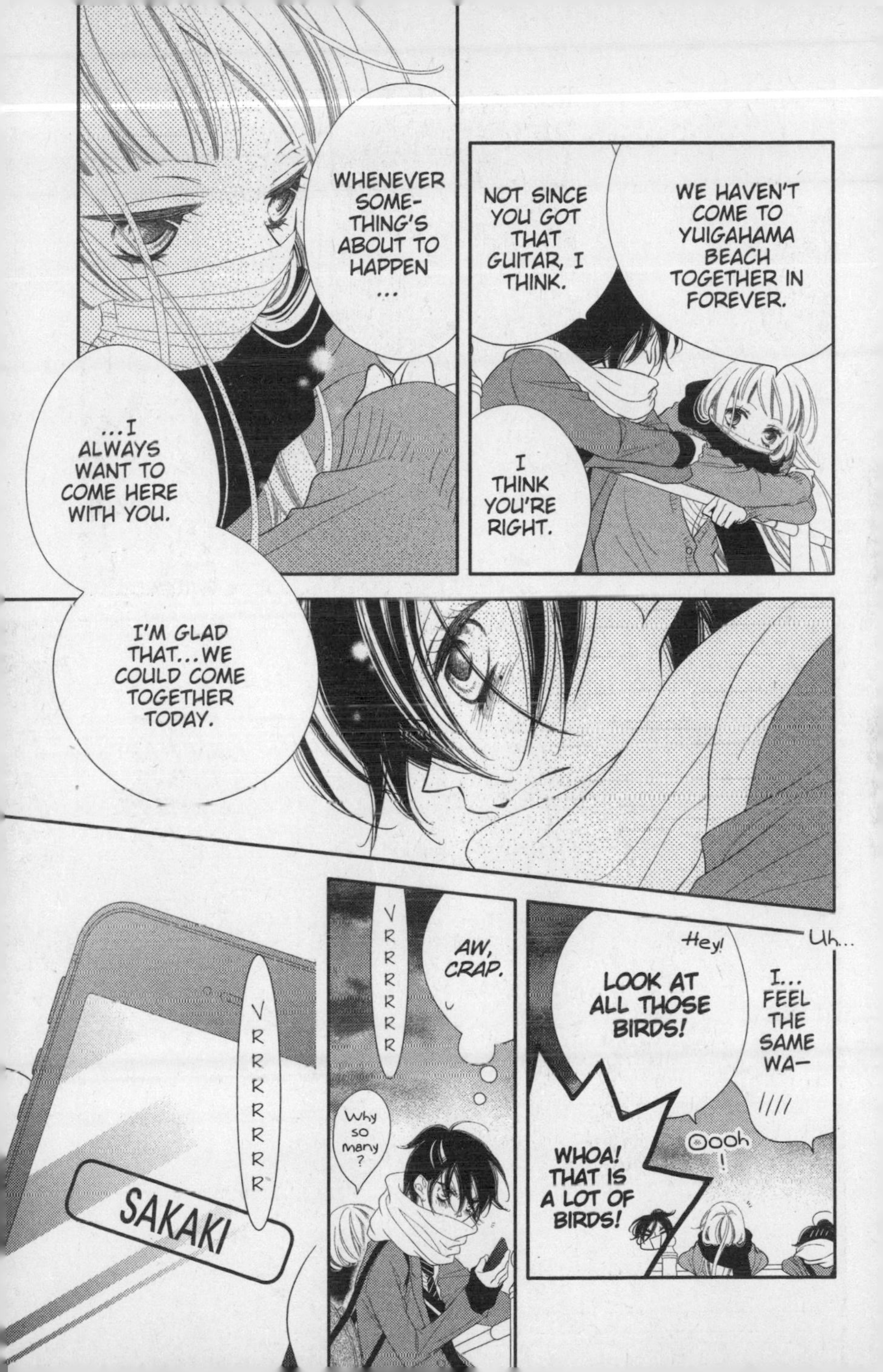
WE HAVEN'T COME TO YUIGAHAMA BEACH TOGETHER IN FOREVER.
NOT SINCE YOU GOT THAT GUITAR, I THINK.
I THINK YOU'RE RIGHT.
WHENEVER SOME-THING'S ABOUT TO HAPPEN ...
...I ALWAYS WANT TO COME HERE WITH YOU.
I'M GLAD THAT...WE COULD COME TOGETHER TODAY.
Uh...
I... FEEL THE SAME WA—
Hey!
LOOK AT ALL THOSE BIRDS!
Oooh!
WHOA! THAT IS A LOT OF BIRDS!
VRRRRRR
AW, CRAP.
Why so many?
VRRRRRRR
SAKAKI

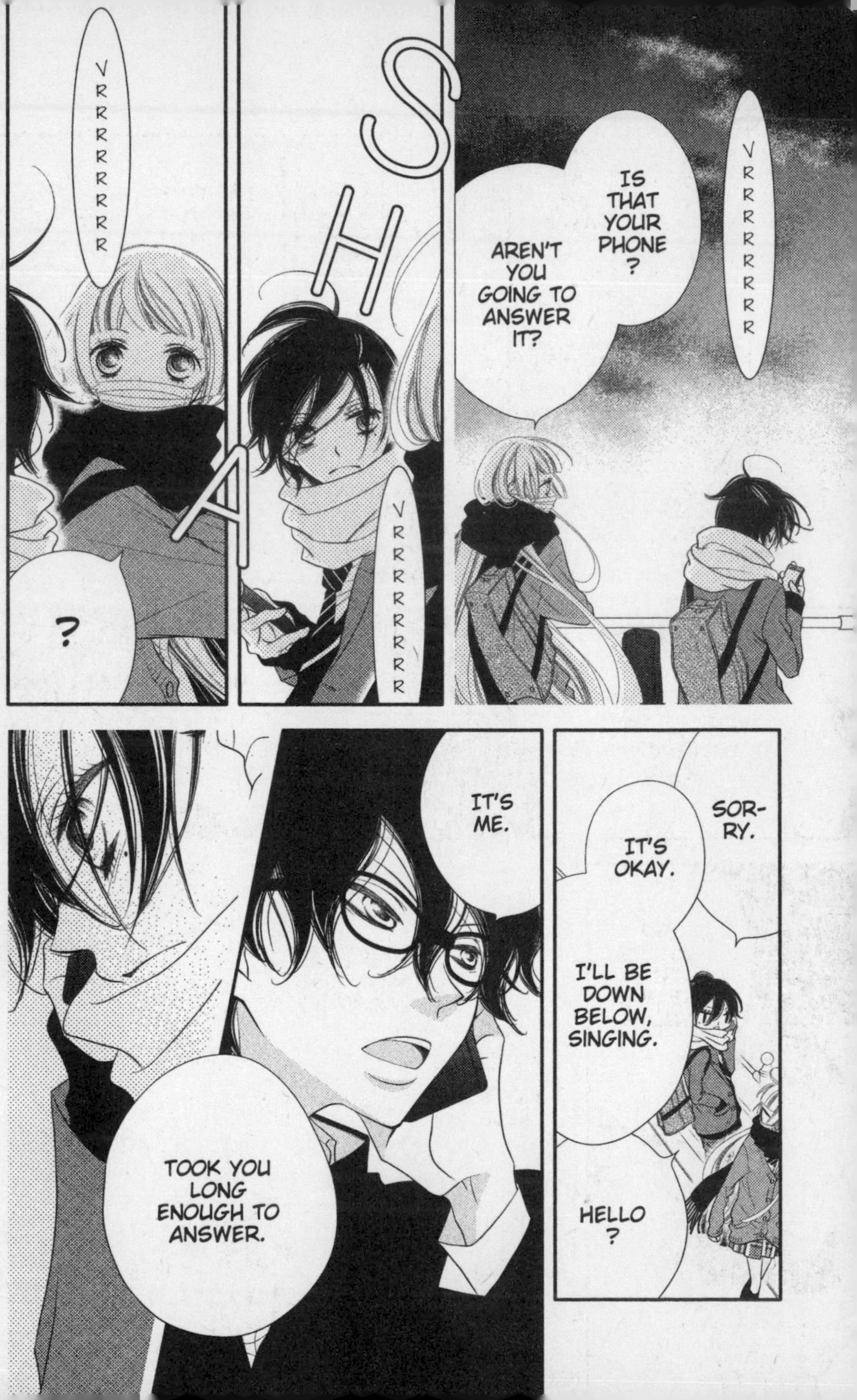
VRRRRRRRRR
IS THAT YOUR PHONE?
AREN'T YOU GOING TO ANSWER IT?
SHA
VRRRRRRRRR
VRRRRRRRRR
?
SORRY.
IT'S OKAY.
I'LL BE DOWN BELOW, SINGING.
HELLO?
IT'S ME.
TOOK YOU LONG ENOUGH TO ANSWER.

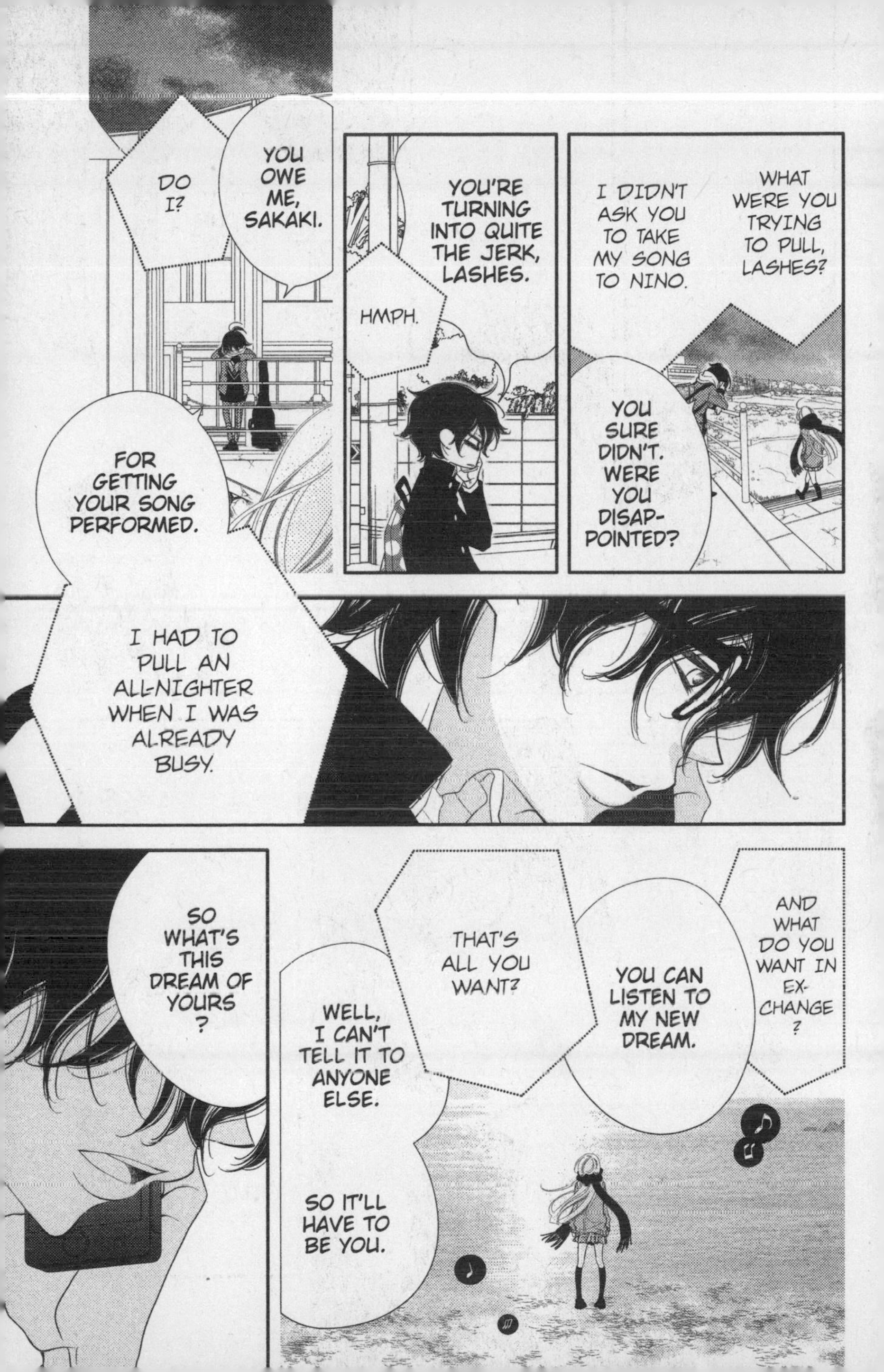
WHAT WERE YOU TRYING TO PULL, LASHES?
I DIDN'T ASK YOU TO TAKE MY SONG TO NINO.
YOU SURE DIDN'T. WERE YOU DISAPPOINTED?
YOU'RE TURNING INTO QUITE THE JERK, LASHES.
HMPH.
YOU OWE ME, SAKAKI.
DO I?
FOR GETTING YOUR SONG PERFORMED.
I HAD TO PULL AN ALL-NIGHTER WHEN I WAS ALREADY BUSY.
AND WHAT DO YOU WANT IN EXCHANGE?
YOU CAN LISTEN TO MY NEW DREAM.
THAT'S ALL YOU WANT?
WELL, I CAN'T TELL IT TO ANYONE ELSE.
SO IT'LL HAVE TO BE YOU.
SO WHAT'S THIS DREAM OF YOURS?

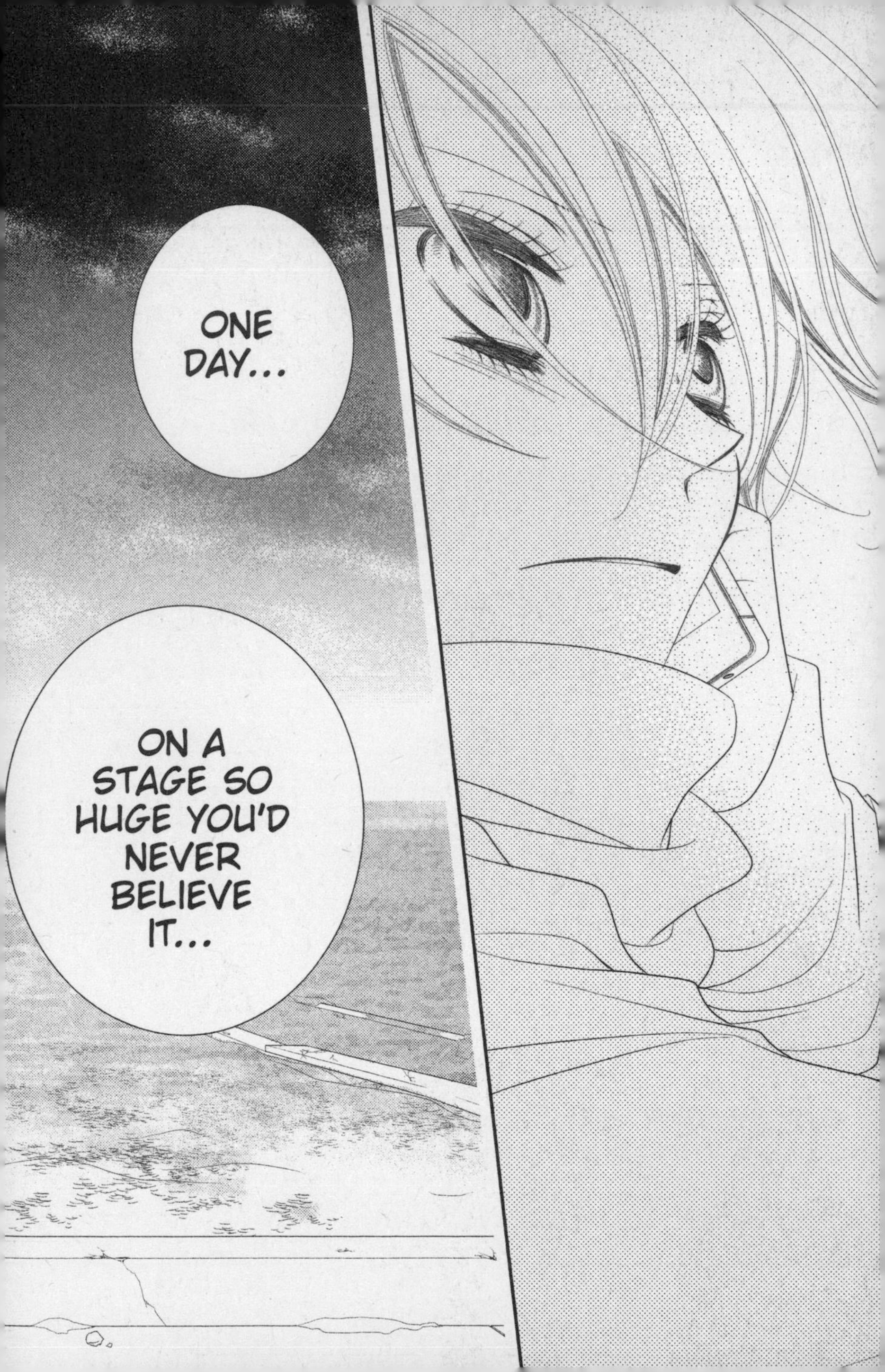
ONE DAY...
ON A STAGE SO HUGE YOU'D NEVER BELIEVE IT...

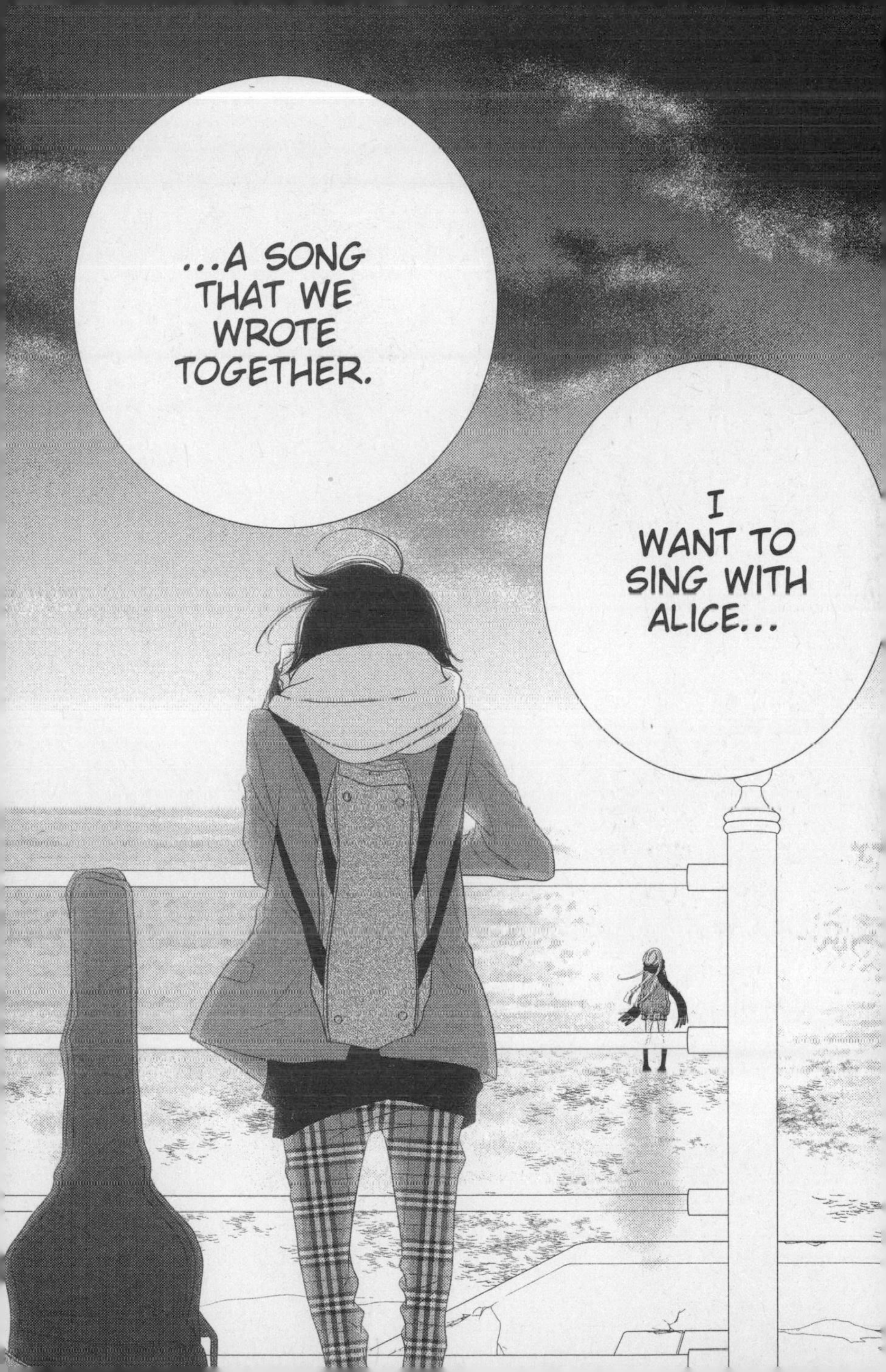
...A SONG THAT WE WROTE TOGETHER.
I WANT TO SING WITH ALICE...

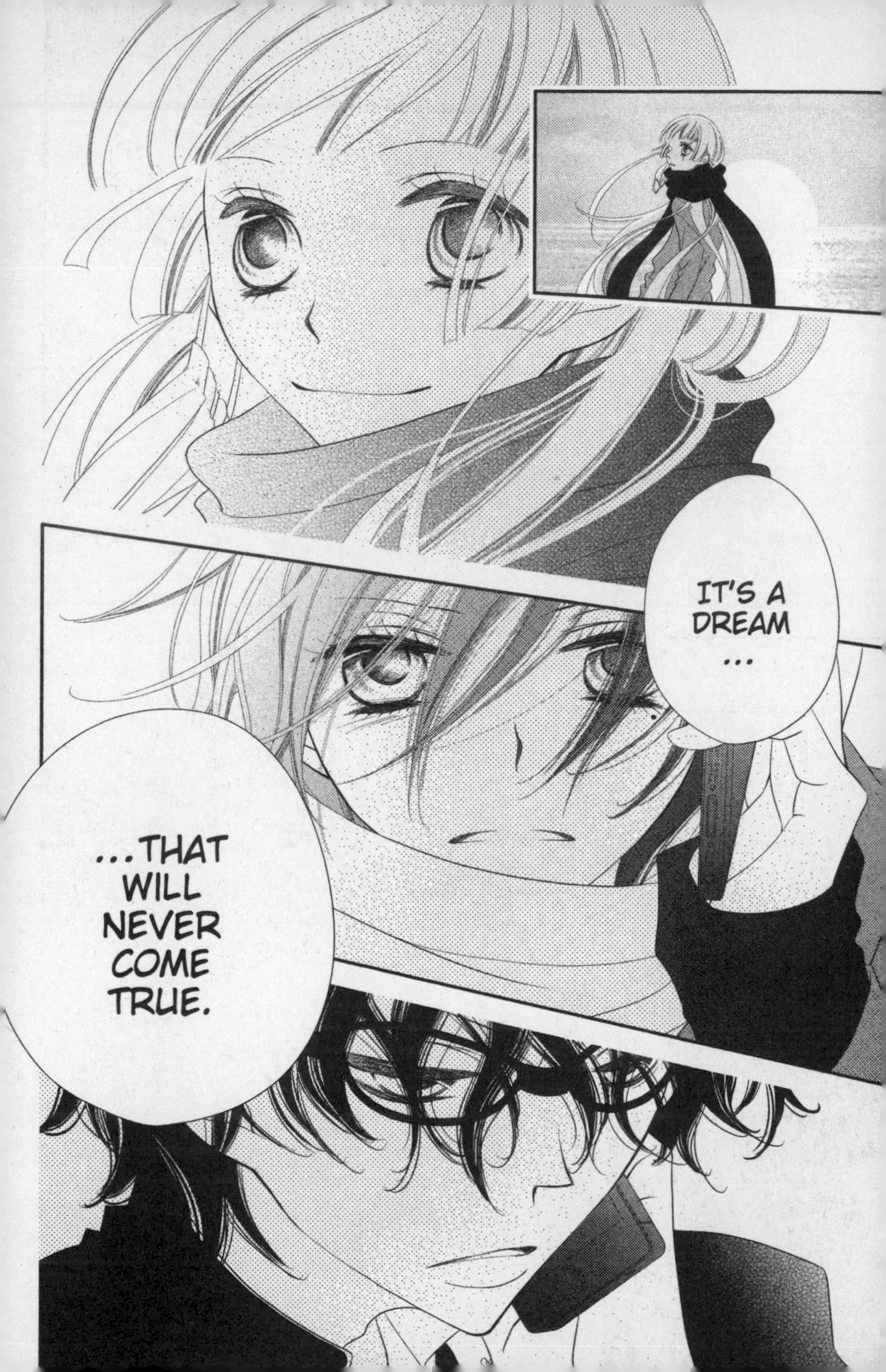
IT'S A DREAM ...
...THAT WILL NEVER COME TRUE.

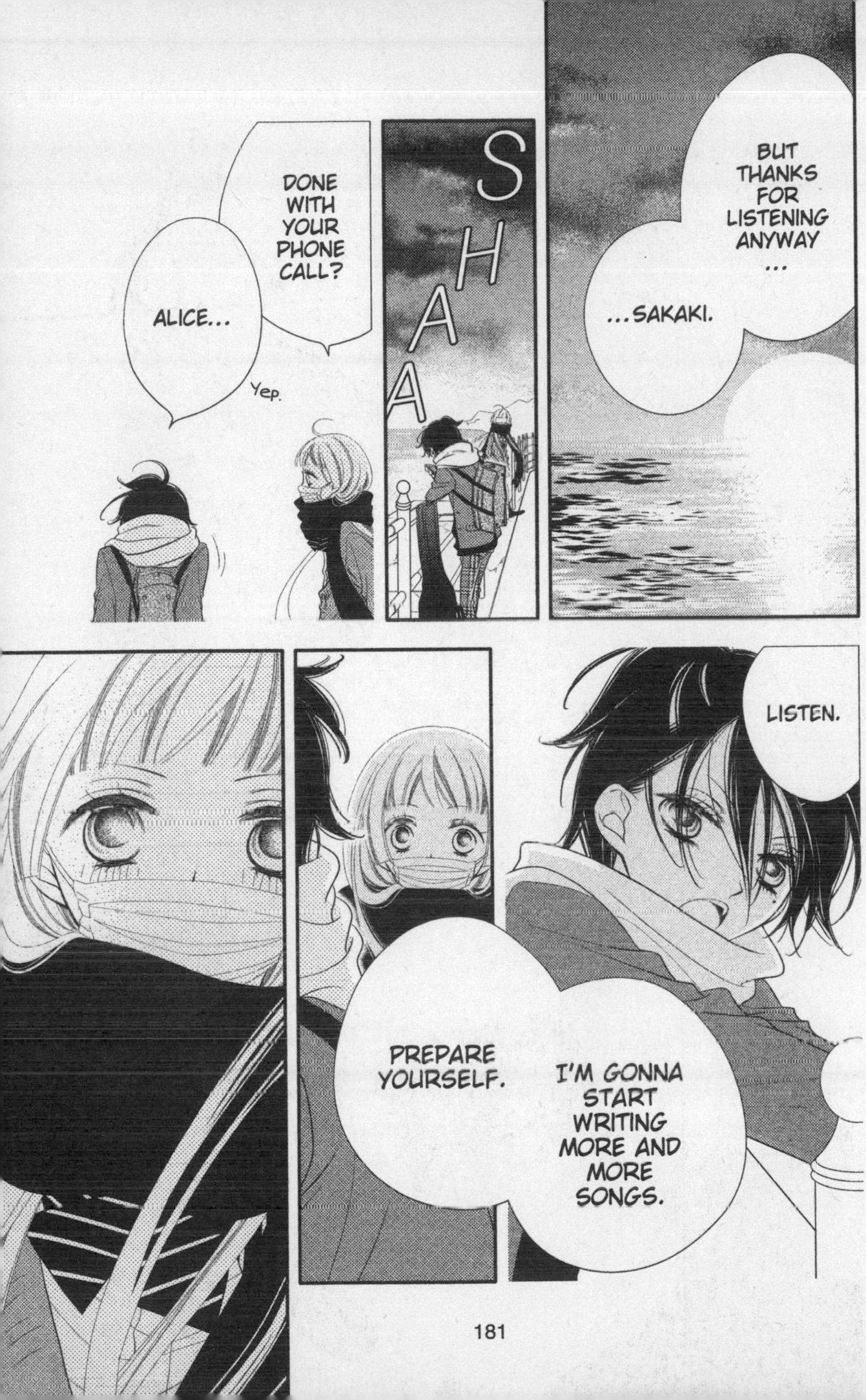
BUT THANKS FOR LISTENING ANYWAY ...
...SAKAKI.
SHAA
DONE WITH YOUR PHONE CALL?
ALICE...
Yep.
LISTEN.
I'M GONNA START WRITING MORE AND MORE SONGS.
PREPARE YOURSELF.

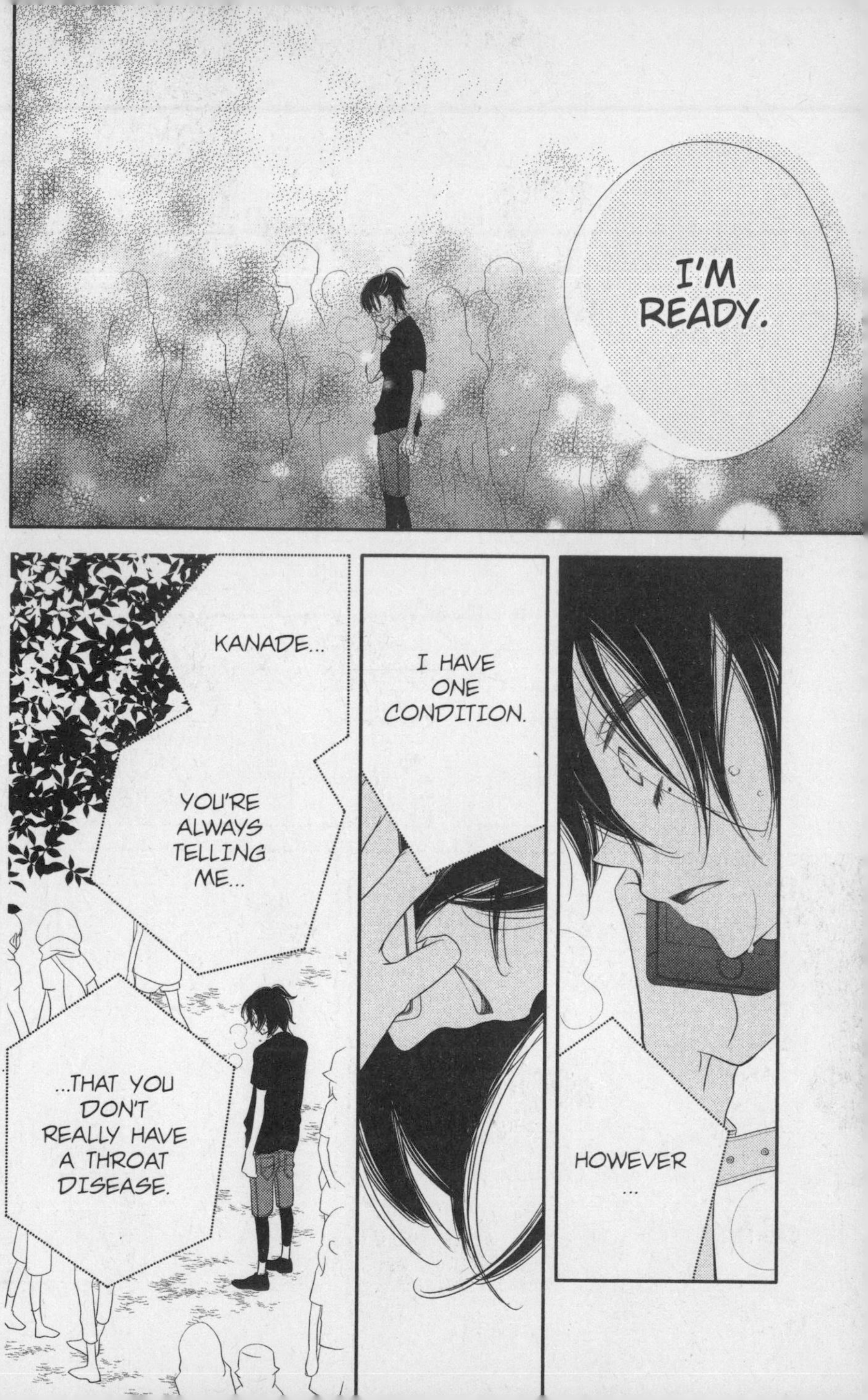
I'M READY.
HOWEVER ...
I HAVE ONE CONDITION.
KANADE...
YOU'RE ALWAYS TELLING ME...
...THAT YOU DON'T REALLY HAVE A THROAT DISEASE.

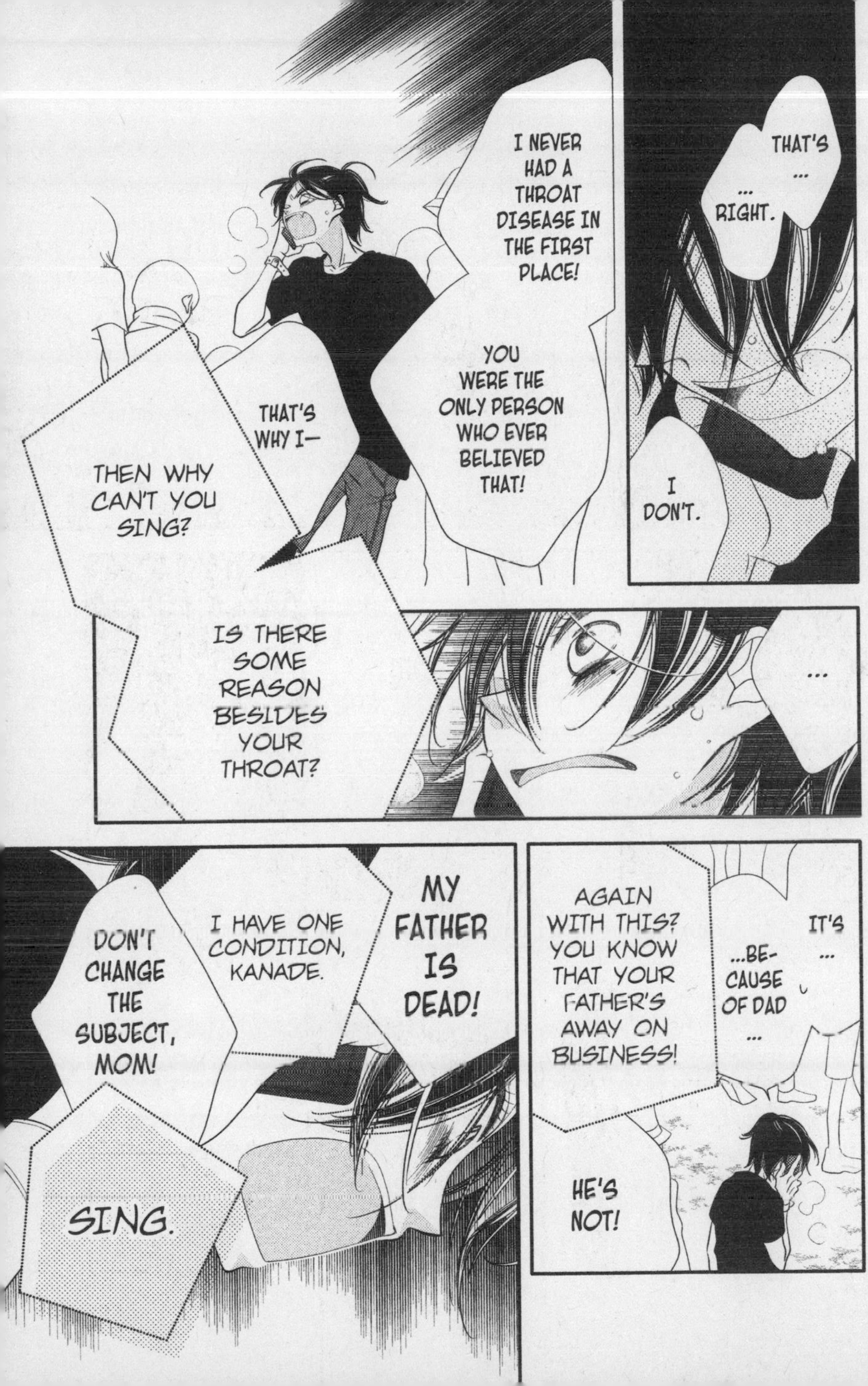
THAT'S ... ... RIGHT.
I DON'T.
I NEVER HAD A THROAT DISEASE IN THE FIRST PLACE!
YOU WERE THE ONLY PERSON WHO EVER BELIEVED THAT!
THAT'S WHY I—
THEN WHY CAN'T YOU SING?
...
IS THERE SOME REASON BESIDES YOUR THROAT?
IT'S ... ...BE-CAUSE OF DAD ...
AGAIN WITH THIS? YOU KNOW THAT YOUR FATHER'S AWAY ON BUSINESS!
HE'S NOT!
MY FATHER IS DEAD!
I HAVE ONE CONDITION, KANADE.
DON'T CHANGE THE SUBJECT, MOM!
SING.

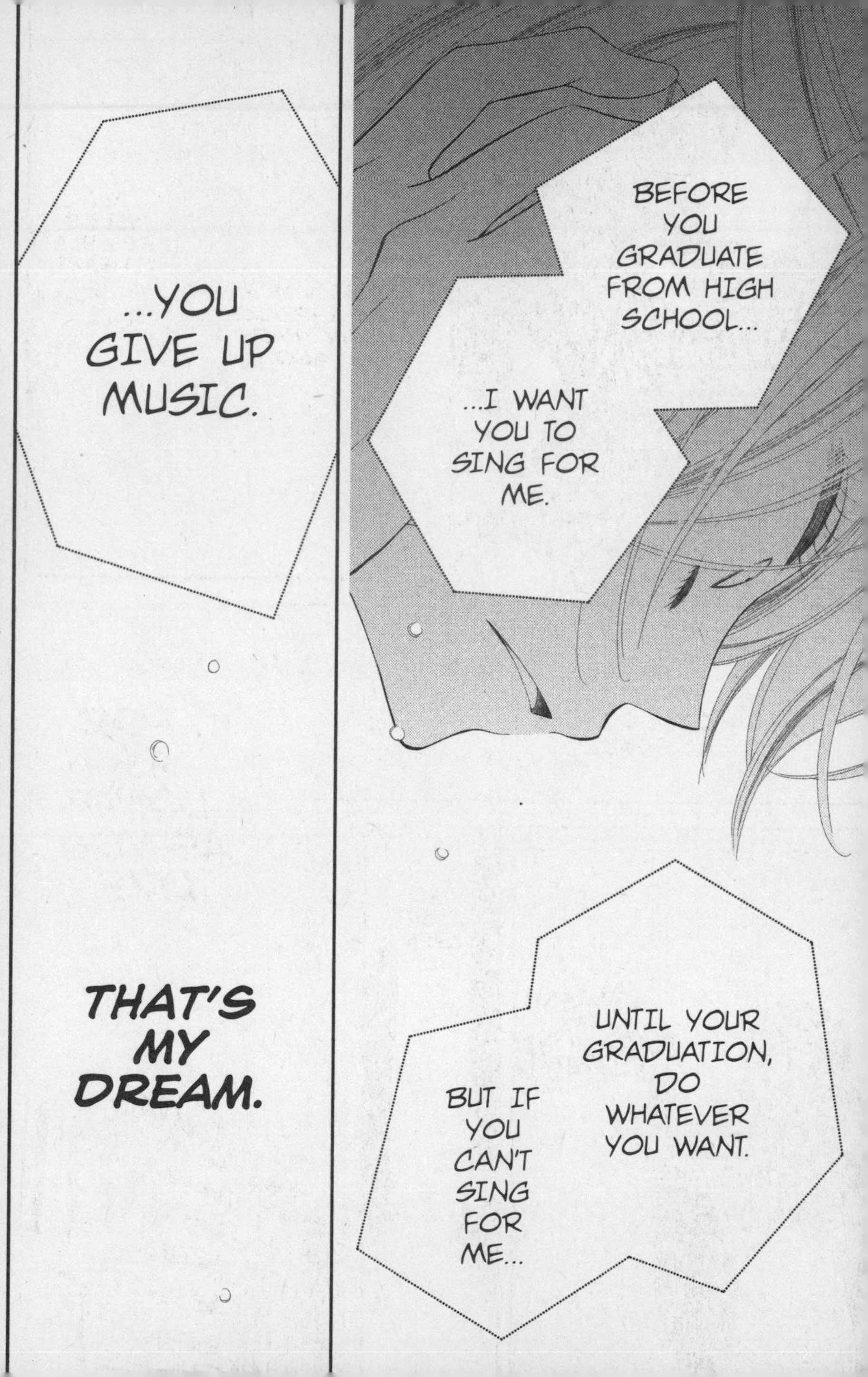
BEFORE YOU GRADUATE FROM HIGH SCHOOL...
...I WANT YOU TO SING FOR ME.
UNTIL YOUR GRADUATION, DO WHATEVER YOU WANT.
BUT IF YOU CAN'T SING FOR ME...
...YOU GIVE UP MUSIC.
THAT'S MY DREAM.

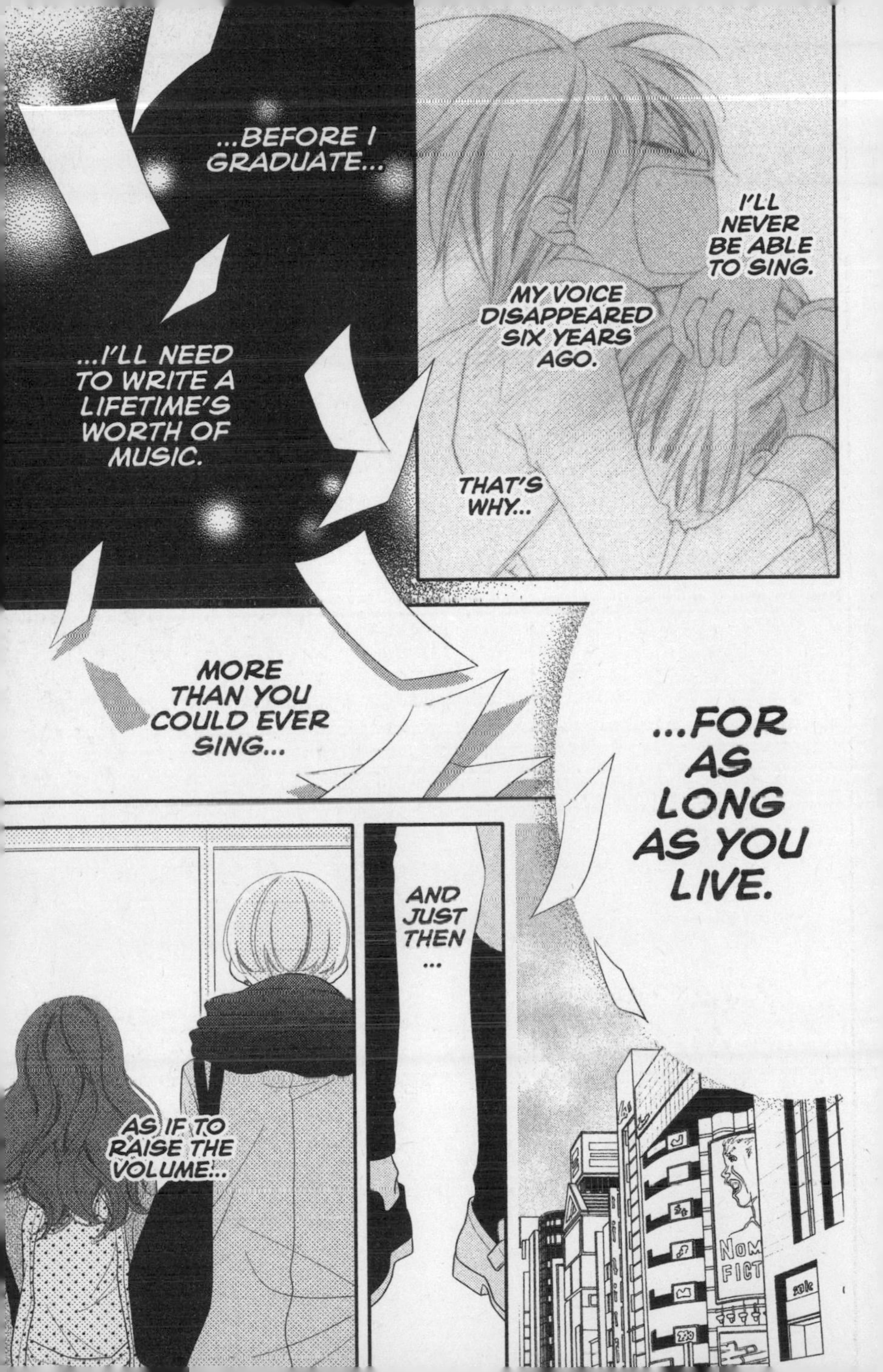
I'LL NEVER BE ABLE TO SING.
MY VOICE DISAPPEARED SIX YEARS AGO.
THAT'S WHY...
...BEFORE I GRADUATE...
...I'LL NEED TO WRITE A LIFETIME'S WORTH OF MUSIC.
MORE THAN YOU COULD EVER SING...
...FOR AS LONG AS YOU LIVE.
AND JUST THEN ...
AS IF TO RAISE THE VOLUME...

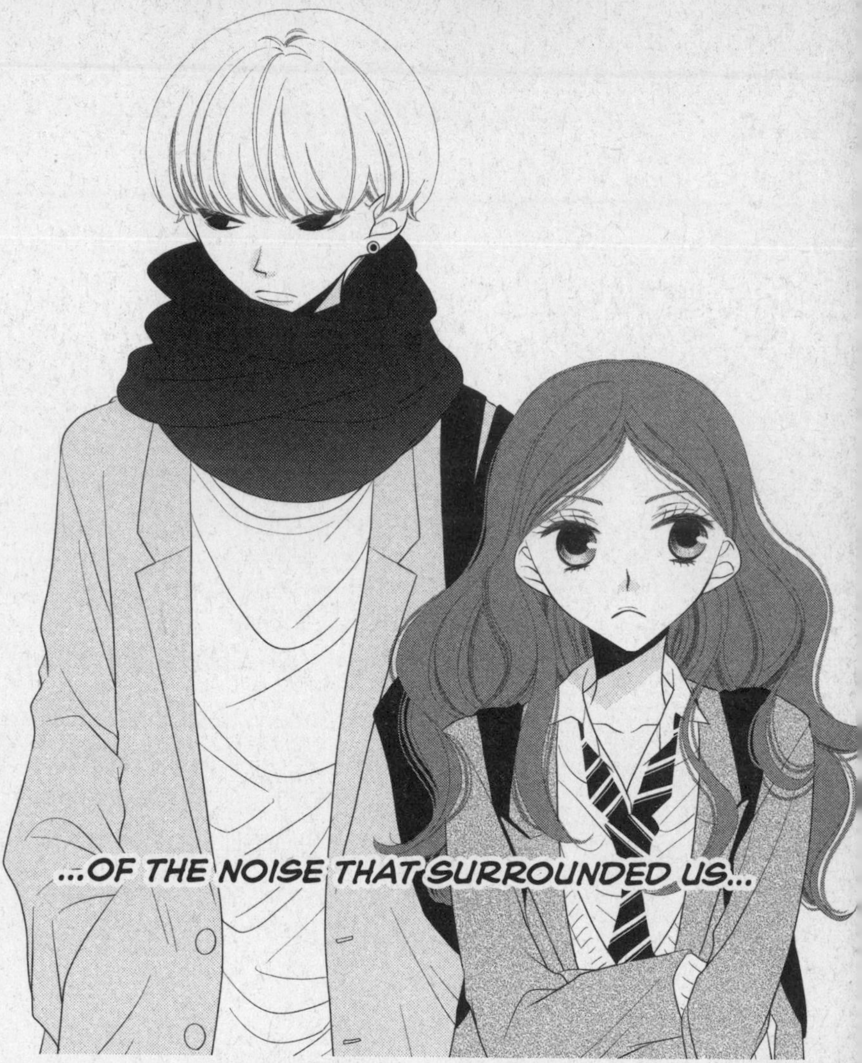
...OF THE NOISE THAT SURROUNDED US...

...THEY APPEARED.

ANONYMOUS NOISE ⑦ / THE END

TO BE CONTINUED IN ANONYMOUS NOISE 8

Even though I always find them extremely stressful for some reason, I always enjoy drawing the concert scenes. Going forward, I'd like to attempt some more diverse challenges. The next concert scene will be the band's long-awaited tour!

- Ryoko Fukuyama

Born on January 5 in Wakayama Prefecture in Japan, Ryoko Fukuyama debuted as a manga artist after winning the Hakusensha Athena Shinjin Taisho Prize from Hakusensha's *Hana to Yume* magazine. She is also the author of *Nosatsu Junkie*. *Anonymous Noise* was adapted into an anime in 2017.

ANONYMOUS NOISE
Vol. 7
Shojo Beat Edition

STORY AND ART BY
RYOKO FUKUYAMA

English Translation & Adaptation/Casey Loe
Touch-Up Art & Lettering/Joanna Estep
Design/Yukiko Whitley
Editor/Amy Yu

Fukumenkei Noise by Ryoko Fukuyama
© Ryoko Fukuyama 2015
All rights reserved.
First published in Japan in 2015 by HAKUSENSHA, Inc., Tokyo.
English language translation rights arranged with HAKUSENSHA, Inc., Tokyo.

Printed in Canada

Published by VIZ Media, LLC
P.O. Box 77010
San Francisco, CA 94107

10 9 8 7 6 5 4 3 2 1
First printing, March 2018

www.viz.com   www.shojobeat.com

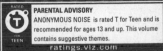

IDOL dreams

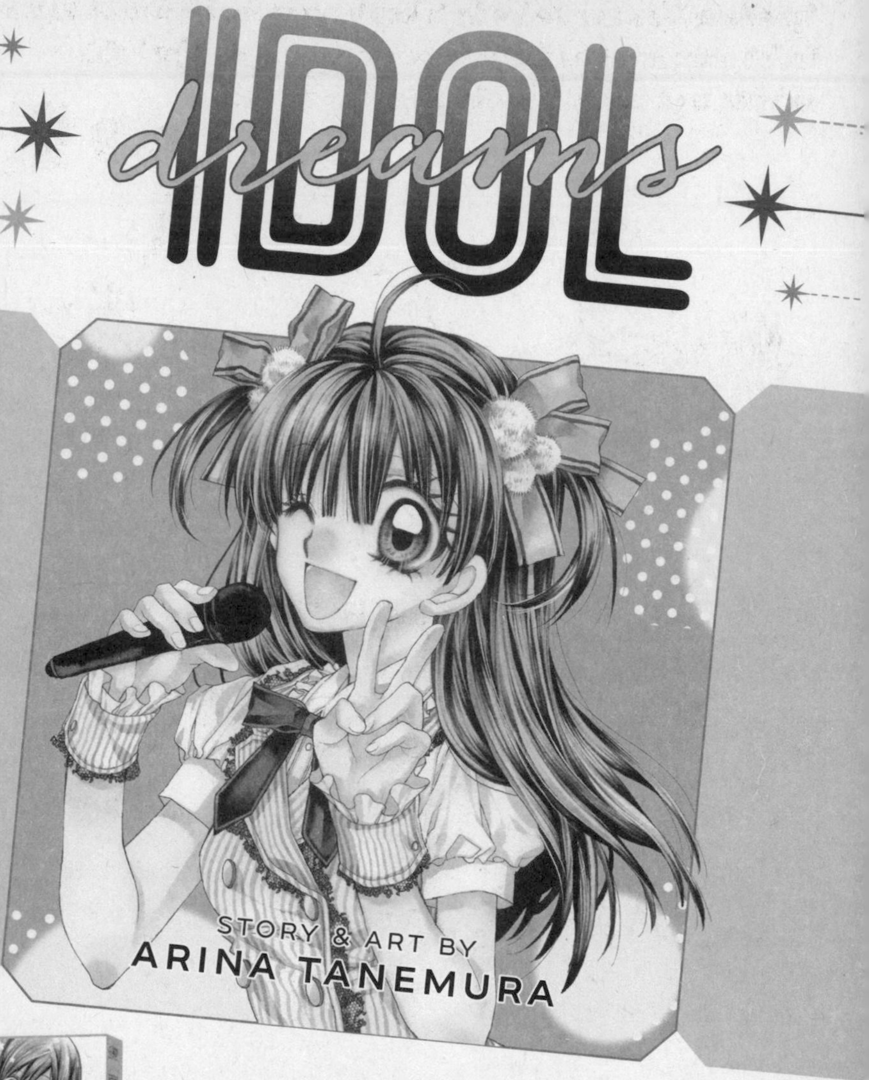

STORY & ART BY
ARINA TANEMURA

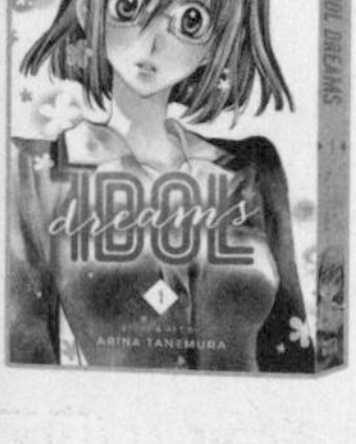
IDOL DREAMS
IDOL dreams
1
ARINA TANEMURA

At age 31, office worker Chikage Deguchi feels she missed her chances at love and success. When word gets out that she's a virgin, Chikage is humiliated and wishes she could turn back time to when she was still young and popular. She takes an experimental drug that changes her appearance back to when she was 15. Now Chikage is determined to pursue everything she missed out on all those years ago—including becoming a star!

Shojo Beat   VIZ media   www.viz.com   RATED T FOR TEEN ratings.viz.com